Untying the Afghan Knot

Untying
the Afghan Knot
Negotiating Soviet
Withdrawal

RIAZ M. KHAN

An Institute for the Study of Diplomacy Book

Duke University Press / Durham and London, 1991

Contents

Appendixes

Tables

Preface

As part of the Pakistan Ministry of Foreign Affairs, I had the opportunity to follow closely the protracted United Nations mediation effort and other diplomatic initiatives aimed at resolving the Afghan issue. I was a member of the Pakistan negotiating team to all Geneva rounds of indirect talks on Afghanistan from June 1982 to April 1988, was director general in the Pakistan Foreign Office dealing with Afghan affairs from July 1986 to June 1988, and participated in conferences and sessions relating to Afghanistan in the United Nations, the Non-Aligned Movement, and the Organization of the Islamic Conference from 1980 to 1988. The experience and insight gained during these years provided the initial impetus for the present study and the primary source for its contents.

The study also draws heavily upon the wealth of information available in UN documents, official reports and statements, press reports and commentaries, and scholarly works, which have been duly cited and acknowledged. It is my hope that the survey, analysis, and perspectives offered by the study will contribute to a better understanding of the Afghanistan negotiations and serve as a useful reference to all persons with a special interest in diplomacy and the conflict resolution role of international organizations, in particular the United Nations.

Structurally, the study has been divided to cover the three phases of the negotiations, interspersed with analysis of the domestic and international factors that constituted the backdrop. Broadly, these phases cover, first, the early initiatives, from 1980 to 1982, and the beginning of the UN role; second, the Geneva negotiating rounds to elaborate and finalize the Geneva Accords; and, third, the negotiations and political manoeuvring focused on the issues of a time frame for withdrawal and an acceptable political arrangement in Kabul. In chronological terms, the study is largely restricted to the period up to the signing of the Geneva Accords in April 1988, but briefly touches upon the subsequent diplomatic activity and prospects for the restoration of peace in Afghanistan. The study concentrates primarily on the history of the diplomatic process and in that context refers also to the internal developments and external environment of Afghanistan; it does not pretend to be a study of the Afghan conflict or of the sociopolitical conditions in the country.

My special thanks go to the Georgetown University Institute for the Study of Diplomacy (ISD) for offering me a position as Diplomat-in-Residence, which enabled me to pursue and complete this study. I am also grateful for the financial assistance provided by the J. Howard Pew Freedom Trust and the U.S. Institute of Peace. I am indebted to the director of the Institute for the Study of Diplomacy, Ambassador David D. Newsom, for his encouragement and valuable advice in organizing the study, and to Ambassador Harold E. Horan for the cooperation he readily extended to facilitate my stay at the Institute.

I am deeply obliged to Margery Boichel Thompson, the editor of ISD publications, for her painstaking efforts to edit the manuscript and her expert guidance in revision and presentation of the study; and to Charles Dolgas, Michael Snyder, Jeffry Robelen, Prakash Mehta, and Thomas Evans, and to my colleague from the Pakistan Foreign Office, Khalid Aziz Babar, for their valuable help and diligent processing of a succession of drafts. I also want to thank the many colleagues and friends who gave me the benefit of their experience and ideas and who persuaded me to undertake this study and made it possible. The findings and conclusions expressed in this book are those of the author and do not necessarily reflect the views of the U.S. Institute of Peace, the Institute for the Study of Diplomacy, or the Government of Pakistan.

RIAZ MOHAMMAD KHAN
Islamabad, 9 July 1990

Abbreviations

AIG	Afghan Interim Government
CPSU	Communist Party of the Soviet Union
DRA	Democratic Republic of Afghanistan
EC	European Community
INF	Intermediate-Range Nuclear Forces
ISI	Pakistan Inter-Services Intelligence
IUAM	Islamic Unity of Afghan Mujahideen
Khad	Khedamat-i Etelaát-i Dawlati (State Information Agency of Afghanistan)
NAM	Non-Aligned Movement
NFF	National Fatherland Front
NIFA	National Islamic Front of Afghanistan
NWFP	North West Frontier Province of Pakistan
OIC	Organization of the Islamic Conference
PDPA	People's Democratic Party of Afghanistan
SALT	Strategic Arms Limitation Talks
TASS	Soviet News Agency
UN	United Nations
UNGA	UN General Assembly
UNGOMAP	UN Good Offices Mission in Afghanistan and Pakistan
UNHCR	UN High Commissioner for Refugees

Maps

The Regional Context

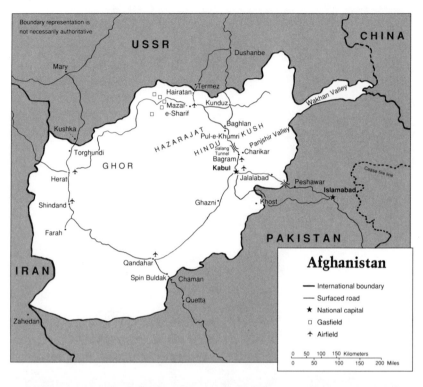

Boundary representation is
not necessarily authoritative

USSR

CHINA

Mary

Dushanbe

Hairatan
Termez
Mazar-
e-Sharif
Kunduz
Baghlan
Pul-e-Khumri KUSH

Kushka

HAZARAJAT
HINDU
Salang
Tunnel
Panjshir Valley
Charikar

Torghundi

GHOR

Bagram
Kabul

Herat

Jalalabad

Peshawar

Wakhan Valley

Cease-fire line

Islamabad

Shindand

Ghazni

Khost

Farah

PAKISTAN

IRAN

Qandahar

Spin Buldak
Chaman

Quetta

Zahedan

Afghanistan

— International boundary
— Surfaced road
★ National capital
□ Gasfield
✦ Airfield

0   50   100   150 Kilometers
0   50   100   150   200 Miles

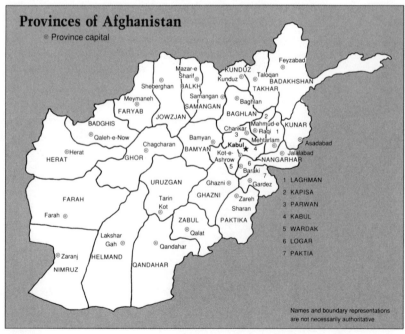

Provinces of Afghanistan

⊚ Province capital

Feyzabad

Mazar-e
Sharif
KUNDUZ
Kunduz
Taloqan
BADAKHSHAN

Sheberghan
BALKH
TAKHAR

Meymaneh
FARYAB
Samangan
SAMANGAN
Baghlan
BAGHLAN

BADGHIS

JOWZJAN

Charikar
3
Mahmud-e
Raqi 1
2
KUNAR

Qaleh-e-Now

Chagcharan

Bamyan
BAMYAN
Kabul
Mehtarlam
Asadabad

Herat
HERAT

GHOR

Kot-e-
Ashrow
5
4
NANGARHAR
Jalalabad

6
Baraki
7

URUZGAN

Ghazni
GHAZNI
Gardez

FARAH

Tarin
Kot
Zareh
Sharan
PAKTIKA

Farah

ZABUL
Qalat

1 LAGHMAN
2 KAPISA
3 PARWAN
4 KABUL
5 WARDAK
6 LOGAR
7 PAKTIA

Lakshar
Gah
HELMAND
Qandahar
QANDAHAR

Zaranj

NIMRUZ

Names and boundary representations
are not necessarily authoritative

1

Introduction

The spectacular political transformation of Eastern Europe in late 1989 almost eclipsed the momentous exit of the last Soviet soldier from Afghanistan earlier in the year. Behind that historic development lay the Soviet Union's longest military engagement beyond its borders, the resilient armed struggle by Afghans against the Soviet forces, and the protracted diplomatic search for a political settlement of the conflict.

The Geneva Accords, signed on 14 April 1988, were the culmination of a diplomatic process set in motion soon after the December 1979 Soviet military intervention and continuing through nearly seven years of United Nations mediation. For the new Soviet leader, Mikhail Gorbachev, the draft agreements negotiated at Geneva provided a convenient, face-saving vehicle to extricate the Soviet Union from the Afghan quagmire, and thereby free his far-reaching domestic and global initiatives from this debilitating inheritance from the Brezhnev era. By thus facilitating the Soviet decision to withdraw, the Geneva Accords enabled Moscow to claim that its forces were not defeated in Afghanistan, but withdrawn in compliance with the Accords.[1]

For the United Nations, the Accords represented the first major success in many years and held out hope for greater UN prominence and a more confident UN role on the world scene.[2] The Accords can therefore be counted among the watershed events that marked the emerging understanding and ease in East-West relations and a promising new phase of multilateralism.

A more circumspect view of the Geneva Accords originates in their failure to bring peace to Afghanistan. The Peshawar-based Afghan parties and resistance groups operating inside Afghanistan, who had been excluded from participation in the negotiations at Geneva, rejected the Accords as unacceptable.[3] (These groups are commonly referred to as the Afghan Resistance—a broad term applied to Afghan political forces opposed to the Soviet military intervention and the ruling People's Democratic Party of Afghanistan [PDPA].) Critics have viewed the Accords as flawed, and some have even dismissed them as a nonessential formality to lend respect to an inevitable development.

Admittedly, the Geneva Accords have been less than satisfactory in resolving the Afghan conflict. By 1988 when the Accords were signed, many changes had occurred that the framework for the UN-sponsored Geneva negotiations, devised six years earlier, had been unable to accommodate. Moscow's rejection of the legitimacy of the Afghan Resistance had restricted the scope of the Geneva negotiations, which proceeded, for the most part, by isolating or ignoring the internal dimension of the Afghan issue. The exclusion of the Afghan Resistance from the Geneva negotiating process thus produced an anomaly, accentuated over time, that could not be removed by a later diplomatic effort in 1987 to initiate parallel negotiations to address the internal aspects of the conflict. By then the political and military situation in Afghanistan had radically changed and the position of the Afghan Resistance as a principal party to the conflict had been established beyond doubt. The ramifications of the new situation were clearly visible in the final outcome of the negotiating process.

Pakistan and the United States were constrained to sign the Geneva Accords with a formal affirmation of their position of nonrecognition of one of the cosignatories of the Accords, namely the Kabul government. In addition, a quasi-legalistic qualification of "symmetry" was introduced to neutralize clear provisions of the Accords prohibiting transportation of arms to resistance groups from Pakistani territory. This measure had become necessary to accommodate the interests of the Afghan Resistance. Finally, the Geneva Accords failed in their intended purpose to restore peace to Afghanistan.

Undeniably, however, the Accords limited the external aspects of the conflict by creating the conditions for smooth and expeditious Soviet withdrawal. They also provided the basis for continuing UN efforts, under the secretary general's personal direction, to forge an internal political consensus.

The Case for a Detailed Survey

Despite their blemishes, the Geneva Accords and the negotiating process on Afghanistan constitute an important chapter in contemporary multilateral diplomacy and are significant in a number of ways.

First, the UN-sponsored negotiations and the broader diplomatic process interacted with the ongoing Afghan conflict. The process affected the attitudes, conduct, and positions of the major players, just as the process itself was conditioned by the constantly evolving circumstances of the conflict. The participants in the negotiations sought to preserve and promote their respective strategic goals through negotiations, and sometimes used the process to gain tactical advantage. Further, the diplomatic process affected the politics of the participants and even became an independent parameter in the constellation of factors influencing the thinking and decisions of policymakers. The existence of the UN negotiating process and a largely acceptable framework for a settlement, for example, helped Gorbachev put an end to an unpopular and "mistaken" military involvement in Afghanistan and thereby strengthen his political position vis-à-vis hard-liners in Moscow. Within Pakistan, another key participant country, the process produced intense political wrangles, especially when it came to a head in early 1988.

Second, the Accords gave a boost to the previously declining peacemaking role of the United Nations, thereby marking an important, albeit shaky, beginning for a revival of the multilateral approach to the settlement of regional and international issues. This UN success in clinching an accord on a major regional conflict improved atmospherics, possibly contributing to a succession of significant achievements in the shape of the cease-fire agreement in the Iran-Iraq War, the Tripartite Accords on Namibia under UN auspices, and significant movement in efforts to resolve the Kampuchean issue. Spurred by the transformed East-West relations, this trend had been foreshadowed in Gorbachev's statement of 8 February 1988, spelling out a definitive date for Soviet withdrawal and calling for the conclusion of the Geneva Accords.[4]

Third, because the negotiations had reached a mature stage early in the process, the Afghan issue was all along regarded as more amenable to a negotiated settlement than any other regional conflict.[5] This remarkable fact is a tribute to the UN mediation, given the complexity of the issues involved that combined many dimensions—international, regional, and domestic—intertwining an internecine political and ideological struggle with contending political and ideological interests of outside powers. In addressing a range of procedural and substantive issues over the years, the mediation effort often assumed a sui generis character; yet it has set important precedents for multilateral negotiations in the future.

Fourth, the Geneva negotiating process on Afghanistan has yielded a wealth of diplomatic experience which should enhance the effectiveness of the United Nations as an instrument for conflict resolution in the future. The negotiating and peacemaking role of the United Nations further evolved through the process, gaining new dimensions. The innovative format of indirect talks between Afghanistan and Pakistan; the proxy participation by at least one of the principal parties, the Soviet Union; and the later UN parallel negotiations for the formation of a transitional government in Kabul (the "second track" launched by Diego Cordovez in 1987)—all are precedent setting. UN dealings with political groupings outside a recognized government, such as the Afghan Resistance, have given the United Nations a new procedural flexibility and will enhance the organization's ability to overcome legal obstacles in the interest of addressing international issues on a more realistic basis. The UN negotiations on Afghanistan, in contrast with those on other major regional conflicts, did not owe their origin to a Security Council or General Assembly resolution. Instead, they were initiated by the UN secretary general and, in an institutional context, have strengthened his role.[6]

Fifth, the new Soviet policy orientation under Gorbachev also found an expression in the protracted Geneva negotiating process, altering long-standing Soviet misgivings and reservations about the peacemaking and peacekeeping roles of the United Nations. There was a gradual lessening and then disappearance of Soviet sensitivity to UN discussion of Soviet withdrawal or to UN monitoring of withdrawal. The scope and implications of the change in the Soviet attitude need to be examined in the light of this negotiating process.

Finally, the Geneva Accords include a set of identical guarantees of noninterference by Washington and Moscow. This is a unique arrangement given the sensitivity of the region, traditionally perceived as the backyard of the Soviet Union and commanding the strategically important oil lanes to the West and Japan. Interestingly, the guarantees are not a product of the post-Gorbachev détente; instead their origin lies in Soviet/Kabul allegations of U.S. interference in Afghanistan.[7] Negotiating these guarantees has been an unprecedented diplomatic undertaking on the part of the United Nations.

Beyond questions of the significance of the negotiating process and of the Geneva Accords and where and why they have fallen short in providing a peace settlement, there is a need to understand the history, procedure, and substance of the negotiations. Many questions remain: How did the negotiating process start? To what extent did it accommodate the often irreconcilable interests and agendas of the parties to the Afghan conflict? How did the process relate to the political and military situation in Afghanistan and to the external environment of the country, and to what extent did it influence the attitudes and positions of the parties? And were there or were there not possibilities for the negotiating process to reach fruition at an earlier stage?

Other questions arise from another perspective: How did Soviet thinking evolve on the negotiations, what factors and political changes influenced Soviet policymakers to decide on Soviet withdrawal, and how was this decision reached? How did U.S. positions and interests influence this negotiating process in which the United States was not a direct participant? What were the political considerations, pressures, and strategic interests that shaped Pakistan's positions and objectives over the long course of the negotiations? How did the positions of the Kabul government develop over the years and how did the Afghan Resistance view the negotiating process? And what light can be shed on the many facets of multilateral diplomacy surrounding a problem that engaged international attention for more than a decade?

The present study is an endeavour to answer these questions and provide insights into the thinking and workings of governments locked for years in a complex set of negotiations. It is a detailed chronicle and analysis that traces the evolution of the international diplomatic initiatives to resolve the Afghan issue, from early 1980 to the signing of the Geneva Accords in April 1988. Accordingly, the study examines the early diplomatic initiatives and circumstances leading to the Geneva negotiations on Afghanistan; the legal and political aspects of the UN mediation; the questions of participation, procedure, format, and substance addressed during the negotiations; the elaboration of the Geneva instruments; the later diplomatic focus on the internal dimension of the Afghan conflict; the changing political and military situation inside Afghanistan, in particular the character of the Afghan Resistance; the evolving interest and positions of the outside powers directly involved; and political developments and diverse trends and pressures at the regional and international levels that influenced the course of the negotiations.

The study appraises the long course of the diplomatic process in the light of Afghanistan's internal and external environments. At the same time, it relates the progress of the negotiations at various stages to the logic of the positions and underlying concerns of the principal parties—a critical factor affecting negotiations at any particular point that often escapes the scrutiny of outside observers. The absence of reliable information about the internal dynamics of the negotiations often leads analysts to look for extraneous factors to explain lack of progress or deadlocks that develop during the course of negotiations.

A detailed account of the negotiations will serve as more than a historical record. Much of the negotiations were shrouded in secrecy. The press statements intended to chronicle their progress were often made as a ritualistic requirement rather than to provide an insight into the real status of the process. Consequently, almost every round of the Geneva talks gave rise to exaggerated expectations and then to fresh speculation to explain lack of progress. Meanwhile, the public view of the negotiations was influenced by generalizations of a polemical character, as well as by partisan views disseminated through propaganda or calculated leaks to the press.

The Geneva negotiating process and the Accords have prompted diverse commentaries. Because of inadequate information, however, they share a tendency to oversimplify the motives and interests of the parties or an inclination to discern a single broad pattern determining the complex, protracted course of the negotiations in a dynamic regional and international environment. Some have shown susceptibility to posturings surrounding the negotiations. Often the result is a narrow, even unfairly dismissive, view of the process or an equally misleading "smoke and mirrors" image. The fog of misperceptions needs clearing up to develop a better understanding of the proceedings at the negotiating table and of the concerns and positions of the principal parties at various stages of the process.

2

Initial Reactions and
Search for a Settlement,
1980–82

Moscow's move to dispatch troops into Afghanistan in late December 1979 drew a swift and resounding worldwide censure. The Soviet action was generally perceived as part of an increasingly aggressive Soviet posture and a development that had seriously disrupted peace and political equilibrium in the region. A demand for unconditional withdrawal of Soviet troops was made at the specially convened Emergency Special Session of the UN General Assembly in early January 1980 and was repeated a few weeks later at the first-ever Extraordinary Ministerial Meeting of the Organization of the Islamic Conference (OIC). As the initial shock waves subsided and consequences of the Soviet action were weighed in capitals around the world, initiatives for negotiations began to emerge, motivated by varying political interests.

The first pressures for negotiations sprang from West European concern over the collapse of détente. The European Community (EC)—especially France and the Federal Republic of Germany—did not fully support the punitive U.S. sanctions or the U.S. decision to freeze arms control talks. Nonetheless, the EC shared the U.S. perception that the Soviet action posed a threat to their interests in the sensitive Persian Gulf region and sought to offer guaranteed neutrality for Afghanistan, provided Moscow withdrew its troops.

Surprised by the tenacity of the widespread Afghan Resistance and the continuing severity of international reaction, Moscow soon developed an interest in negotiations, provided these could serve as a means to secure legitimacy for the Kabul government and help to stabilize the latter's position. That was the crux of the Soviet-backed Afghan proposals made in May 1980 that envisaged direct talks between Kabul and neighbouring Pakistan and Iran as a prerequisite for negotiations.

With the Soviet advance into Afghanistan, Pakistan assumed a strategically critical role in the area. This position was further highlighted as Afghan refugees started pouring into the country and as the Afghan Resistance started taking root in the refugee population. Iran had remained largely insular, caught in revolutionary convulsions and the Iran-Iraq conflict. Pakistan had taken the lead in bringing the Afghan issue to the UN Security Council and throughout remained a key player in international fora in coordinating diplomatic pressure for Soviet withdrawal. Accordingly, no diplomatic initiative, evolved in whichever forum or capital, could conceivably ignore or bypass Pakistan. On its part, Pakistan had developed an interest in negotiations at an early stage in view of the need to contain Soviet hostility, coupled with the domestic compulsion that Pakistan should not be found remiss in efforts for a political settlement.

At Pakistan's behest, in May 1980, the OIC developed a diplomatic initiative to establish a dialogue with the Afghan parties and Moscow. The OIC initiative, therefore, attempted to promote an internal settlement while also seeking Soviet withdrawal. The internal and external dimensions of the Afghan issue were clearly interrelated, but Soviet rejection of the Afghan Resistance elements stymied initiatives that were intended to address both aspects.

The transition from the early initiatives, including those of the EC and the OIC, to the assumption of centre stage by the UN mediation marked an important evolution in the diplomatic process. The preceding diplomatic initiatives and activity had paved the way for this development, but Soviet acceptance of the UN channel was the critical factor. The UN modality suited the Soviet Union because, consistent with UN procedures, the UN framework treated the Kabul government as the sole Afghan interlocutor in the talks.

The UN mediation began tentatively, and it was not until early 1982 that the parties developed vague understandings on substantive agenda and procedure, which led to the holding of indirect talks at Geneva in June 1982. Movement in this direction became possible when Kabul softened its demand for direct talks and Islamabad dropped its proposal for the inclusion of self-determination as an item on the agenda. The indirect, albeit structured, negotiations began at Geneva amid low expectations against a backdrop of deteriorating East-West relations and an intensified military situation in Afghanistan.

The Soviet Military Intervention

The circumstances and underlying motivation of the Soviet decision to send troops into Afghanistan in late December 1979 have been widely discussed by scholars and political analysts and in capitals around the world.[1] A brief comment on the factors that apparently influenced Soviet thinking at the time suffices for the present study, which focuses primarily on the diplomatic process following the Soviet military intervention. Many observers now believe, in retrospect, that the top leadership of the Soviet Communist Party (CPSU) and the Soviet army were split over the decision. The present Moscow leadership under Mikhail Gorbachev blame Leonid Brezhnev for the fateful move.[2] In 1979, within the CPSU Politburo, the action was reportedly supported by Brezhnev and CPSU ideologue Mikhail Suslov, while Yuri Andropov, then head of the Soviet intelligence agency, the KGB, had expressed reservations. Within the top army echelon, Marshal Dimitry F. Ustinov, then defense minister, had overruled doubts over the advisability of the action said to have been expressed by Marshal Nikolai Ogarkov, former chief of the Soviet general staff, and by Marshal Sergei F. Akhromeyev, then first deputy chief of staff.[3]

Speculation over the motives underlying the Soviet action has varied. Right-wing conservative circles outside the Soviet Union perceived it as part of a Soviet push to the warm waters. The Soviet position is that the action was defensive in character and undertaken at the request of the Afghan government. Again, a clearer picture has emerged over the years as the circumstances of the intervention have been analyzed and information relating to the decision has been pieced together.

Two factors appear to have weighed most heavily in Soviet thinking leading to the decision to move into Afghanistan: First, was the need to protect Soviet interests and long-standing influence in Afghanistan, which the Soviets saw as linked to the political ascendancy and survival of the People's Democratic Party of Afghanistan (PDPA), a party with Marxist-Leninist orientation; second, was the need to contain the Islamic resurgence provoked by the radical reforms pushed by PDPA strongman Hafizullah Amin. Against the backdrop of the Islamic revolution in Iran, Moscow could not ignore such a potential threat to its Islamic Central Asian republics. Furthermore, in the 1970s, confident that it had equaled if not surpassed the United States in military strength, the Soviet Union showed an increasing propensity to take risks to protect its concept of political, military, and economic interests abroad by intervening while invoking "socialist internationalism."[4]

A credible explanation of why Moscow chose to send its troops into Afghanistan may be found in the murky power struggle between Hafizullah Amin and President Nur Mohammad Taraki, precipitated in September 1979.[5] The Soviet uneasiness with Hafizullah Amin and his unrelenting drive for reforms began with the large-scale rebellion in Herat against the Kabul government in March 1978, which resulted in the killing of many Soviet advisers stationed in the city.[6] Moscow now maintained a larger number of advisers in Afghanistan, who could see that the growing hostility toward the regime could not be contained as long as Hafizullah Amin kept his grip on the government and unless the regime broadened its political base.[7]

The Kremlin also desired a compliant leadership in Kabul. By midsummer 1979 the Soviets were reportedly looking for an alternative to Amin who could cooperate with Taraki to present a more benign face of the PDPA regime.[8] Within the PDPA setup, Taraki was regarded as a weak, elderly statesman with a mellow demeanour. Hafizullah Amin came to suspect Soviet intentions, especially when Taraki spent a few days in Moscow on his return from the September 1979 Non-Aligned Summit in Havana.

There are several versions of the Byzantine intrigue following Taraki's return to Kabul that ended in a shoot-out and the death of Taraki.[9] In the aftermath of this event, the disaffection between Moscow and Amin came into the open. Amin's foreign minister, Shah Wali, reportedly accused the Soviet embassy in Kabul of complicity in an abortive attempt to remove Hafizullah Amin.[10] He asked Moscow to replace its longtime ambassador, Aleksandr Puzanov,[11] who was finally recalled to Moscow in November 1979.

Moscow was thus faced with a serious crisis in Kabul. It could no longer trust Amin, who on his own could not have withstood the mounting revolt fed by Islamic and tribal reaction to his reforms. At the same time, Moscow could not allow the disintegration of the Saur Revolution of April 1978, which brought the PDPA to power. Moscow also feared the unlikely possibility that a desperate Amin might seek help from the United States and Pakistan.[12] Amin's control of the army made it difficult for Moscow to engineer an internal coup. Under the circumstances, a military intervention appeared to be the most viable recourse to get rid of Amin and install Babrak

Karmal, the remaining prominent leader of the Saur Revolution. Karmal had been exiled as Kabul's ambassador to Prague following an early intraparty struggle in July 1978.

Moscow did not anticipate a strong international reaction to its intervention. The West appeared to have already conceded Afghanistan to the Soviet sphere of influence. Within the region, the Americans had suffered a setback in Iran and their relations with Pakistan had reached a low point.

Contrary to Moscow's expectations, the Soviet action evoked the worst fears about Soviet motives and behaviour internationally—in particular in Pakistan, many other Islamic countries, and the West. Brezhnev's assurances a year later, in November 1980, that the Soviet action was not directed against any third country did little to assuage concerns.[13] By then the countries opposed to the Soviet action were far more preoccupied with the consequences of the Soviets' consolidating their military presence in Afghanistan than with the reasons for the Soviet action.

Pakistan's opposition to the Soviet military intervention in neighbouring Afghanistan stemmed from legitimate security concerns and was rooted in the country's Islamic ethos and the ideological orientation of President Mohammad Zia ul Haq, who felt morally bound to aid Islamic resurgence against an aggressive godless creed. Given the experience of czarist expansion into Central Asia during the nineteenth century, Zia was not alone in believing that the intervention had shifted the Soviet border from the Oxus River to the Khyber Pass.[14] Zia ul Haq and Pakistan's military also looked at the Soviet advance as a strategic development that opened up the possibility of obtaining Western—especially American—support for rebuilding Pakistan's flagging defense capability. In U.S. eyes the altered geopolitics had transformed the status of Pakistan to that of a "linchpin" and "frontline" state protecting one flank of the sensitive Persian Gulf region.[15] Thus, in a situation blending opportunity with risks, Pakistan embarked on a dual-faceted Afghan policy: one aspect military, to support and bolster the Afghan Resistance, the other diplomatic, to pursue a negotiated settlement.

Reaction to the Soviet Military Intervention

The overwhelming majority of nations in the Islamic and nonaligned worlds and in the West reacted strongly to the Soviet military intervention in Afghanistan, deploring the action as an invasion of a sovereign state and a serious breach of international norms. In an unprecedented move, Soviet troops had been committed in a non-Warsaw Pact country. The perceived disruption of the post-World War II balance of power raised security concerns about Soviet intentions in the region. Because of Afghanistan's credentials as an Islamic country and a founding member of the Non-Aligned Movement (NAM), shock and indignation over the Soviet move were deeply felt in most Islamic and nonaligned countries, with the exception of those closely linked to Moscow.

The Soviet ex post facto explanation that the military intervention was a defensive measure could justify neither the scale of the operation nor the surprise and speed with which it was undertaken. The glaring fact that the military action was focused on Kabul and had brought about the execution of Hafizullah Amin and the removal of his government belied the claim that Moscow had acted in fulfillment of a treaty obligation to defend the Kabul government from outside interference. The circumstances of the intervention left little doubt that, at a minimum, the Soviets were attempting to install and consolidate a client regime in Kabul that had no popular support in the country.

The depth and range of international opprobrium against the Soviet intervention was typically evident in the succession of deliberations undertaken by the United Nations and the Organization of the Islamic Conference during January 1980, in the immediate wake of the intervention. The following sections examine the early debates and the responses developed in the United Nations, the NAM, and the OIC. The resolutions and positions adopted in these major international fora not only set the tone for the sustained international demand for withdrawal of the Soviet troops, but also provided the early moorings for a diplomatic effort to promote negotiations through a multiplicity of channels. In addition, for nearly two years until the launching of the Geneva negotiating process in 1982, the UN General Assembly (UNGA) sessions and the OIC meetings provided important platforms for Afghanistan-related diplomatic activity.

The United Nations

The intense sentiment against the Soviet military intervention witnessed at the United Nations partly underscored the cumulative resentment of the ascendancy of radical states in the multinational fora. A high point in the radical dominance of international fora was reached at the Sixth Non-Aligned Summit at Havana in September 1979, where, despite strong challenges from a number of nonaligned states, Cuba succeeded in ousting the Sihanouk faction from the Kampuchean seat. This episode had deeply rankled the majority of the nonaligned membership and had left the NAM divided and polarized.[16]

The Soviet intervention in Afghanistan provided the antiradical forces the first credible issue around which to rally and assert themselves in international fora. Unlike the Kampuchean question, which raised contentious problems of ethics,[17] the Afghan issue involved no ambiguities. Moscow had clearly moved into Afghanistan to install a government of its choice. Hafizullah Amin, whom the Afghan representative portrayed as Afghanistan's Pol Pot at the Security Council meeting in January 1980,[18] was known to be the architect of the 1978 Saur Revolution and had enjoyed Soviet blessings until late 1979. The shock caused by the suddenness and massiveness of the Soviet action was such that an unprecedented fifty-two member states joined Pakistan in asking for the convening of the Security Council,[19] which met in the first week of 1980.

The weakness of the Soviet case was evident in the Soviet and Afghan statements made at the Security Council in defense of the Soviet action. Afghan Foreign Minister Shah Mohammad Dost dwelt at length on the ills of Amin's rule and on promises held out by the newly installed regime under Babrak Karmal. He made scant reference to outside interference and only en passant mention of the invitation to the limited Soviet military contingent. The Soviet representative at the United Nations, Oleg A. Troyanosky, on the other hand, had little comment on Amin and devoted his statement almost entirely to citations from the Western press to point out that insurgency in Afghanistan was foreign inspired. He referred extensively to the Soviet-Afghan treaty of 5 December 1978 and Article 51 of the UN Charter to justify the contention that the Soviet troops were in Afghanistan on invitation. In a subsequent statement, apparently prompted by the Soviet statement, Minister Dost tried to give Kabul's version of the events, arguing unconvincingly that, in addition to earlier invitations, the Karmal government had reiterated the request to the Soviets for assistance after having overthrown Amin.[20]

The first Pakistani comment, made on 29 December 1979 after two days of intensive deliberations, set the tone for Pakistan's position at the United Nations and influenced UN debate and resolutions adopted at this early stage.[21] The statement blandly described the introduction of foreign troops in Afghanistan as a "serious violation of the norms of peaceful coexistence and the [principles of the] Charter of the United Nations" and called for the immediate removal of these troops from Afghanistan. The draft resolution presented at the Security Council by its nonaligned members and the subsequent UNGA Emergency Special Session resolution adopted by 104 affirmative votes maintained a similarly restrained tone. At a time when, under pressure from the radical membership, UN resolutions increasingly resorted to harsh denunciations, this moderate approach served both to optimize support for the resolution, which further increased in succeeding years, and to neutralize an effort by the Soviet Union to impose an East-West construction on the Afghan issue. Pakistan also decided to keep the sponsorship of the UN resolutions on the Afghanistan situation restricted to Third World countries.[22]

The United States and the West European countries opted for a selective but critical role, as became evident immediately after the Soviet veto of the draft resolution on Afghanistan, presented in the Security Council by its nonaligned members. A procedural resolution from the council was needed to convene an Emergency Special Session of the UN General Assembly to discuss the issue. The alternative was to obtain the agreement of half of the UNGA membership to call for such a session,[23] which obviously involved a protracted signature campaign that would have detracted from the urgency of the issue. It was also desirable to have sponsorship of the procedural resolution from a nonaligned, Third World member. Accordingly, Pakistan had approached the Philippines. But it was U.S. intercession in Manila and in Mexico City that secured the agreement of the two capitals in time to move the procedural resolution in the council.[24]

The Sixth Emergency Special Session of the UN General Assembly, 11–14 January 1980—an extraordinary measure invoked after over twelve years[25]—had a touch of drama even though its proceedings followed predictable lines. A notable exception was the Indian statement, which departed from the mainstream, nonaligned sentiment in its charitable treatment of the Soviet action, linking it to "other foreign activities" in the region.[26] The statement set out the parameters for the future Indian position and conditioned the Indian role, which will be discussed at a later stage.

Adopted against the backdrop of fast-moving events and initial shock reaction to the Soviet action, the first UNGA resolution from the Sixth Emergency Special Session addressed the issue of the intervention but did not call for negotiations or a settlement. The resolution deplored "the recent armed intervention in Afghanistan" without naming the Soviet Union and called for "the immediate, unconditional and total withdrawal of the foreign troops from Afghanistan in order to enable its people to [freely] determine their own government." A humanitarian appeal was also included for relief assistance for the Afghan refugees.[27]

The need to explore openings for negotiations and the possibility of an eventual settlement was, nonetheless, not far from the minds of the participants, especially the chief Pakistan delegate, Agha Shahi, then foreign minister and a veteran UN personality. Indeed, this concern had partly influenced Pakistan's thinking on one vital issue, namely, that of challenging the credentials of the Karmal government to continue occupying the seat of Afghanistan in the United Nations—an issue repeatedly raised by the Afghan Resistance and their sympathizers at later stages. Pakistan had doubts about such a challenge. It felt that when the dust had settled, Islamabad would have to deal with Kabul and Moscow. Another reason for lack of attention given to the credentials issue was the fast pace of developments, especially during the short interval between the Security Council meeting and the convening of the UNGA Emergency Special Session. The details of organizing that debate completely absorbed Pakistan, the principal mover.

The issue of credentials received some attention at subsequent regular sessions of the UN General Assembly. By then, the prospects of success of any move to challenge the credentials of the Kabul government had greatly narrowed. The initial shock had subsided, and there was growing reluctance within the UN system to suspend membership of states and thereby damage the system's universality. In fact, by 1980 Vietnam had abandoned its attempt to dislodge Democratic Kampuchea from representing Cambodia in the General Assembly. In 1982 the defeat of the ill-prepared attempt by Iran to oust Israel from the General Assembly, with the backing of certain radical member states, foreclosed similar initiatives in the United Nations for the future.[28]

The Organization of the Islamic Conference (OIC)

Following the Sixth UNGA Emergency Special Session, the centre of diplomatic activity on Afghanistan shifted to the OIC, where it stayed for most of 1980. Since the issue involved the violation of the independence and sovereignty of a member Islamic state, it was only logical for the OIC to make an appropriate response.

There were several important converging interests that spurred the OIC to play an active role. The OIC was a preferred forum for Pakistan, given the Islamist disposition of Zia ul Haq's government and the fact that positions and initiatives taken collectively by Islamic states enjoyed greater domestic acceptability.[29] For conservative Islamic states, Afghanistan provided an opportunity to reinvigorate the OIC, which was suffering from political inactivity and eclipse, mainly because international focus on the Palestine question, the raison d'être of the OIC, stayed with the United Nations and the Non-Aligned Movement. For the United States, the OIC engagement with Afghanistan was welcome because it underlined the much desired identity with an Islamic cause. The OIC also proved to be advantageous in facilitating active Iranian participation, especially when the OIC launched its initiative for a negotiated settlement. Above all, Pakistan found the OIC an attractive forum in which it could hope to keep the initiative in its hands—an important consideration that preoccupied Pakistan throughout the diplomatic process.

The first-ever extraordinary session of the Islamic Foreign Ministers, convened in Islamabad on 25–27 January 1980 to discuss the Soviet intervention in Afghanistan, was essentially meant to be a part of the campaign to mobilize and agitate international opinion. In retrospect, however, it represented a high point in conservative backlash against the Soviet action. Held at the request of Bangladesh, the session was dominated by the Saudi delegation, who determined the tone and tenor of its outcome.[30] Pakistani officials had prepared a draft resolution along the lines of the preceding UNGA resolution, with minor changes to lend it greater specificity. They also prepared two supplementary drafts, to suspend Afghanistan's membership in OIC and to boycott the Moscow Olympics as already decided upon by the United States. Separation of these subjects from the main draft resolution underscored differences within the Pakistani side over the desirability of the proposed measures. However, following a meeting between Foreign Minister Prince Saud al Faisal of Saudi Arabia and President Zia ul Haq, it was decided that the Saudis would draft a resolution to be cosponsored by Pakistan.

The Saudi draft resolution carried a strong indictment of the Soviet intervention and recommended specific measures, notably, suspension of membership of Afghanistan in the organization; asking member states to withhold recognition of the Karmal regime and sever diplomatic relations with Afghanistan; boycott of the Moscow Olympics; and a call to stop all forms of assistance to the Kabul regime, support the Afghan people, and show solidarity with their struggle to safeguard "their faith, national independence and territorial integrity."[31] A paragraph calling for the suspension of trade was dropped at the insistence of Pakistani officials, who argued that landlocked Afghanistan depended on transit through Pakistan for its commerce. The reservations by Democratic Yemen, Syria, Libya, and the Palestine Liberation Organization (PLO), and the discomfiture of a few others who advocated a less strident approach could not block the adoption of the resolution.[32]

Thus, within one month Pakistan had moved from espousal of a moderate stance to the endorsement of a hard-line position. Considerable speculation surrounds this development. Conjectures vary from the possibility of the Americans influencing the conference through the Saudis to a more likely explanation that the shift was a calculated signal from Zia ul Haq to the Americans, indicating his willingness to pursue a tough line on Afghanistan. By late January, Pakistan and the United States were already engaged in a discussion on an assistance programme. Washington had already communicated a preliminary offer of $400 million—somewhat disappointing from Pakistan's point of view. Pakistan's apparent change to a hardline position proved short-lived and was reversed by the time the OIC foreign ministers met again in Islamabad in May 1980.[33]

Like the first UNGA response, the first OIC resolution had restricted itself to a straightforward demand for "immediate and unconditional" withdrawal of the Soviet troops and lacked any reference to negotiations or consultations to achieve this objective. The concept of a negotiated settlement had not yet emerged. The OIC response, however, had imparted an Islamic identity to the issue and established strong Islamic interest in its solution.[34] A lasting legacy of the first OIC resolution was its call for nonrecognition of the Karmal government, which furnished Pakistan with a convenient argument to refuse direct talks with Kabul.

The OIC resolution intensified an internal debate within the Pakistan government on the implications of the Afghan situation and what policy Pakistan should pursue. A whole range of issues was involved, especially if Pakistan wanted to support the Afghan Resistance. The military felt that Pakistan could not take the heat on its northern border with Afghanistan without rebuilding its relations with the United States, for which an opportunity seemed to exist. The military thinking was partly influenced by its desperate need for modern equipment. On the other hand, there were questions of whether the United States and the West could be trusted to stand by Pakistan, whether it would be prudent to risk the ire of the superpower next door, and whether the Afghans would be able to take on the military might of a superpower. Within the Foreign Office, Agha Shahi entertained strong reservations over any course of action that could lead to confrontation with the Soviet Union. The debate simmered while Zia ul Haq, in his characteristic style, allowed diverse policy options to develop.

The Non-Aligned Movement

Contrary to the United Nations and the OIC, the Non-Aligned Movement was slow to react to the Soviet intervention, mainly because, under Cuban chairmanship, the leadership of the movement had passed into the hands of a vocal minority of radical, pro-Moscow members. The Afghan issue had isolated this minority in the United Nations, but NAM procedures enabled them effectively to block a decision reflecting majority sentiment in the NAM. This anomaly was evident from the composition of the NAM Coordinating Bureau: fifty-six of the ninety-two UN members belonging to the NAM had voted in favour of the UNGA resolution, and the proportion kept increasing with time, whereas sixteen out of a thirty-four-member NAM Coordinating Bureau endorsed outright, or sympathized with, the Soviet position.[35]

As a recent entrant to an unfamiliar and ostensibly unfavourable domain, Pakistan by itself had little incentive to mobilize the NAM, especially when its diplomatic resources were committed to the United Nations and the OIC. Subsequently, Pakistan kept its objectives at the NAM at a minimum level, strictly limited to securing a position that barely satisfied its essential concerns.

Discussion on the Afghan issue was forced at the NAM Coordinating Bureau by Ambassador Jorges Enric Illueca of Panama at the bureau's routine meeting on 31 January 1980 to consider "implementation of the decisions of the Sixth Non-Aligned Summit at Havana." A bitter debate ensued under this item when the radical membership successfully thwarted attempts to introduce the Afghan issue as a separate subject. After several weeks, an open-ended drafting group—with a nucleus comprising the Democratic Republic of

Afghanistan (DRA), Algeria, Bangladesh, Cuba, Guyana, India, Iran, Malta, Pakistan, Tunisia, and Yugoslavia—was set up to prepare a joint communiqué. Kuwait joined the effort later and even presented a tentative draft. The group remained stalled, mainly because Cuba and the DRA insisted on mentioning "outside interference in the internal affairs of Afghanistan" alongside the reference to the Soviet military intervention. Pakistan and its allies in the group refused to accept such an equation.

The idea of a NAM communiqué on the Afghan issue was finally abandoned in June 1980, when it was decided that the issue would be discussed at the next meeting of NAM foreign ministers, to be held in New Delhi, and the date of the meeting was advanced to February 1981. This was a pyrrhic triumph for the radicals and impaired the credibility of the NAM, because by now every other major international forum had adopted a position on the issue. Within the movement, the high-handed tactics used to block the majority view bred disillusionment. This was underscored by another decision, also taken in June 1980, which required the NAM not to pronounce itself on any new international political developments until it had taken a position on Afghanistan. The deadlock virtually stifled the NAM's ability to launch a credible initiative for the resolution of the Afghan issue. India and Cuba made short-lived individual soundings at early stages, which were overtaken by more potent initiatives with substantial international support.

The Afghan issue dominated the February 1981 NAM foreign ministers meeting in New Delhi. Sensitive to pressures for evolving an acceptable nonaligned position, India played a lead role negotiating with the Pakistan and DRA delegations to develop a consensus. The effort had a déjà vu quality, except that it was compressed into two days, during which India suggested several drafts. The Pakistani position diverged from that of India in three areas: first, India wanted to weave in the issues of noninterference and withdrawal as the basis for a settlement; second, India desired to treat the Afghan issue in the broad context of the Southwest Asian region, while Pakistan insisted on specific reference to the situation in Afghanistan; and third, India strove for a compromise text acceptable to all, including the DRA representative. The last point was relevant because a text agreeable to both Kabul and Islamabad would have diminished the value of the OIC and UN resolutions, thereby attenuating moral pressure on the Soviets.

On substance, Pakistan's position ruled out any inference of a linkage between the twin issues of noninterference and withdrawal. Nonetheless, Pakistan accepted that guarantees reaffirming the principle of noninterference in mutual relations could be part of a settlement. After considerable testing of nerves—not unusual in such conferences—India relented and accepted a precariously balanced formulation, over the objections of the DRA representative, in the interest of securing the much delayed NAM decision on the Afghan issue. The key phrase of the decision urged a "political settlement *on the basis of* withdrawal of foreign troops, full respect for the independence, sovereignty, territorial integrity and non-aligned status of Afghanistan and strict observance of the principle of non-intervention and non-interference" (emphasis added).[36]

Firmness in the Pakistani stand was attributable in large measure to the solidarity on the issue reaffirmed at the Taif Islamic summit a few weeks before the New Delhi NAM meeting. This helped Pakistan to mobilize Islamic countries to block a surprise move made at the final NAM plenary session by the DRA delegation, with encouragement from India and Cuba, calling on technical grounds for changing references to "Afghanistan" in the text to read "Democratic Republic of Afghanistan." Besides alluding subtly to DRA legitimacy, the substitution, if carried, would have allowed the DRA delegation to soften its objection to the text.

The 1981 NAM decision was maintained in all subsequent meetings of the Non-Aligned Movement. The New Delhi meeting also represented the high watermark of India's involvement with the Afghan issue in an international forum. Despite its status as a major regional power, India remained on the sidelines of the diplomatic process on Afghanistan, which was dominated by the OIC and UN-oriented initiatives.

The West

The Soviet military intervention in Afghanistan came at a time when the Carter administration was beleaguered by the Iran hostage crisis and the Soviet Union was generally seen to have made strategic advances around the globe during the course of the late 1970s.[37] The swift and sharp reaction to the surprise Soviet move reflected an element of shock and personal outrage on the part of President Jimmy Carter. His harshly worded statements condemning the Soviet action and describing it as "the greatest threat to peace since the Second World War,"[38] stood in contrast with the largely quiescent attitude maintained by the United States toward the coup against Sardar Mohammad Daoud Khan in April 1978 and later toward the killing of the U.S. envoy in Kabul.[39]

Apart from the impression that the Soviet action in Afghanistan was preceded by a series of perceived Soviet advances, this was the first time since World War II that Moscow had sent its forces to a non-Warsaw Pact country.[40] The Soviet motives underlying the intervention were unclear, but strategically the direction of the move evoked old fears of a Soviet drive to warm waters. President Carter declared that U.S. security "was directly threatened. There is no doubt that the Soviets' move into Afghanistan, if done without adverse consequence, would have resulted in the temptation to move again . . . until they reached warm water ports or until they acquired control over a major portion of the world's oil supplies."[41]

The American response soon took shape in two directions: one, a strategic doctrine delineating vital U.S. interest in the region, and two, a series of punitive sanctions and symbolic decisions to demonstrate U.S. indignation over the Soviet action. The president's State of the Union address to the Congress in January 1980 spelt out "the Carter Doctrine": that "an attempt by any outside force to gain control of the Persian Gulf region will be regarded as an assault on the vital interests of the United States of America, and such an assault will be repelled by any means necessary, including military force."[42] Simultaneously, Carter indicated U.S. intent "to help Pakistan defend its independence and its national security against the seriously increased threat it now faces from the north."[43]

These and similar pronouncements were minutely examined in Islamabad. Among several punitive sanctions such as curtailment of grain shipments, cutoff of high technology sales, and boycott of the Moscow Olympics, a more significant step was the freezing of arms control negotiations and a request to the U.S. Senate to postpone consideration of the pending Strategic Arms Limitation Treaty (SALT II).[44] It took a couple years before arms control efforts were delinked from the issue of Afghanistan and regained a dynamics thought to be independent of the vagaries of Soviet-U.S. relations.[45] The punitive sanctions, which attracted some controversy among West European and nonaligned nations and drew a sharp retort from Moscow, could hardly have been designed to force Soviet withdrawal. The purpose appeared to be to preempt domestic criticism of the Carter administration, which was already on the defensive as a result of the conservative backlash that culminated in a landslide victory for Republican candidate Ronald Reagan in 1980.[46]

The reaction of the West European governments was tempered by varying degrees of concern over the fate of détente and the consequences of the Soviet action for a whole range of allied issues, especially arms control. There were even complaints over inadequate U.S. consultation with other NATO members prior to imposing sanctions and divergence over the value of U.S. actions, especially the boycott of the Olympics.[47] The position adopted by Bonn and Paris betrayed differences with the strong U.S. reaction. While denouncing the Soviet move, both underlined their desire to avoid tension with Moscow. West German Chancellor Helmut Schmidt was reportedly concerned over "exaggerated responses" to the Soviet action, and Bonn was not expected to follow the United States in retaliating against Moscow.[48] At successive meetings in Brussels and Rome during February 1980, the EC foreign ministers could not agree to President Carter's call to boycott the Moscow Olympics.

The Soviet intervention had, nonetheless, drastically undermined détente, weakening political forces wanting to sustain détente and continue arms control talks, in particular the peace movements in Western Europe. Even the communist parties in several of the West European countries were compelled to criticize the Soviet Union.[49] The Soviet efforts to use European concern for détente to drive a wedge between the United States and its NATO allies made little headway, especially after the European leaders were disappointed in their early efforts to secure negotiated withdrawal of the Soviet troops.

Revitalization of U.S.-Pakistani Relations

During the late 1970s, U.S.-Pakistani relations were at a low ebb until the Soviet military intervention drastically changed the coordinates of the regional situation, which had already been transformed by the Islamic Revolution in Iran. For years, Pakistan had suffered a U.S. arms embargo, considered particularly damaging to its military capability because, unlike India, it depended for the bulk of its supplies on the United States.[50] U.S. concern over nuclear proliferation had resulted in the virtual discontinuation of U.S. economic assistance to Pakistan, and under U.S. pressure France reneged on its agreement with Pakistan for a reprocessing plant and a nuclear power plant near Chashma.

Strategically, Pakistan had lost its significance as an ally, and the emerging U.S. policy under Carter was predicated on promoting India and Iran as the two "regional influentials" to protect its interests in the area. The cumulative effect in Pakistan was a growing sense of resentment and a popular view of the United States as an unreliable ally. The relations between the two countries touched their nadir in November 1979, when the U.S. embassy in Islamabad was set on fire by an angry crowd incited by an inflammatory foreign broadcast reporting U.S. complicity in the takeover by fanatics of the Holy Mosque in Mecca.

The Soviet intervention catapulted Pakistan and the isolated military government of Zia ul Haq into sudden prominence. The United States could do little without Pakistani cooperation to help the Afghan Resistance against the Soviet military intervention. Pakistan, on the other hand, found itself in a precarious security environment. Seen in historical perspective, especially regarding the post-Saur Revolution developments in Afghan-Soviet relations, it was generally believed that Pakistan would have to reconcile to the Soviet presence along its northern border. This sentiment, widely shared in Pakistan, was clearly expressed by Zia ul Haq. In an interview reported in the *New York Times* he said, "Pakistan must adjust itself to the Soviet presence in the area as a political fact of life. You cannot live in the sea and create enemies with whales."[51]

On Pakistan's eastern border, the short reprieve in relations between Pakistan and India during the period of the Janata government had disappeared with the return to power of Prime Minister Indira Gandhi.[52] Being a military person, Zia ul Haq's priority was to build Pakistan's defense capability, which at that time was dismally lacking in modern equipment. He and the military establishment in Pakistan saw a unique opportunity in the strong U.S. reaction to the Soviet advance into Afghanistan.

In the context of its relations with the United States, one of Pakistan's preoccupations was the status of the 1959 U.S.-Pakistan Bilateral Security Agreement, which committed the United States to defend Pakistan against a communist threat. Until the Soviet intervention, it was regarded as a dead letter. The changed circumstances and U.S. pronouncements renewed hopes within Pakistani military circles of a revival of the U.S. security guarantee.[53] Nonetheless, these expectations had an illusory quality, since no realistic threat scenario except India was ever envisaged in Pakistan. The much-debated Carter Doctrine was ambiguous; it hedged on the issue of Pakistan's security and begged the question whether Pakistan was covered by the definition of "the Persian Gulf."[54] Notwithstanding the issue of interpreting the 1959 agreement in the new circumstances, Pakistan desired a substantial U.S. commitment if it were to risk confrontation with the Soviet Union.

President Carter's offer of $400 million in sales credits and economic assistance, made during Agha Shahi's meeting with Secretary of State Cyrus R. Vance in Washington during mid-January 1980, came as a disappointment. It was far short of Pakistan's expectations. The inadequacy of the offer was compounded by restrictions on the items to be purchased under the military sales credit. President Zia declined the offer as "peanuts" and stated that Pakistan expected greater "moral" support from the West, implying strengthening of the 1959 agreement.[55] Without resources, however, any measure of moral support or the lifting of the ban on military sales to Pakistan could do little to assuage Pakistani concerns.[56]

The visit by President Carter's national security adviser, Zbigniew Brzezinski, and Deputy Secretary of State Warren M. Christopher in the first week of February 1980, the first high-level U.S. visit since Zia ul Haq's takeover, produced a change in atmospherics of the hitherto low-intensity U.S.-Pakistani relations, but kept the question of credits or assistance subject to further consultation. Nevertheless, Brzezinski accorded an enthusiastic U.S. endorsement of Pakistani perception of a Soviet threat developing from the direction of Afghanistan—a view advocated without success by Pakistan since the Saur Revolution.

It was well after the change of administration in Washington that Pakistan received a sufficiently attractive offer of U.S. support. Meanwhile, nonacceptance of the $400 million offer proved to be an astute move on the part of the Zia government, not only because it improved Pakistan's bargaining position with the succeeding U.S. administration, but also because this decision helped its image at home, preempted political adversaries who had started accusing the regime of playing the U.S. game, and enhanced Pakistan's credibility as an independent actor on the scene. The dampening of the initial euphoria brought about balance and pragmatism in Pakistan's overall approach, inducing it actively to pursue efforts to develop diplomatic options.

Pakistan's initiatives involving the OIC and the UN secretary general had taken firm root by the time the new U.S. administration reactivated and completed negotiations on the six-year, $3.2 billion military sales credits and economic assistance package and cleared sale of forty F-16 jet fighters to Pakistan.[57] The U.S. administration's decision to allow sale of F-16s provoked strong Indian protests, but Pakistan had made this decision into a test of U.S. seriousness to help strengthen Pakistan in the changed circumstances.

Early Soundings for a Negotiated Settlement

The first impulses for a negotiated settlement of the Afghan issue did not result from Pakistan's apprehensions regarding the Soviet threat or its doubts over the adequacy of U.S. response to its security needs; these sprang from European concern over the collapse of détente. Yet another consideration prompting West European leaders to take early initiatives was their apprehension that with the passage of time, international pressure on the Soviets would diminish and permit them to consolidate their advance. On 19 February 1980 the EC foreign ministers met in Rome and adopted for the first time a proposal, initiated by British Secretary for Foreign and Commonwealth Affairs Lord Peter Carrington, for guaranteed neutrality of Afghanistan, provided Moscow withdrew its troops.[58] The proposal was later endorsed by President Carter in a letter addressed to President Josip Broz Tito of Yugoslavia, who had earlier made a fervent plea to Carter and Brezhnev calling for the "widest" effort for salvaging détente.[59] In presenting his proposal to the Soviets, Lord Carrington described it as a major diplomatic initiative, suggesting that the "neutralization" idea could be discussed either at a reconvened session of the UN General Assembly or at a special conference on Afghanistan.[60] U.K. special envoy Curtis Keeble discussed the proposal in Moscow in early March, but within a few days the Soviets rejected it, publicly accusing "the authors of neutralization proposals" of attempting to decide "the fate of the Afghan people."[61]

A later elaboration of the proposal by Lord Carrington suggested a two-stage conference. The first stage envisaged working out international arrangements to bring about the cessation of external intervention and the establishment of safeguards to prevent such intervention in future. It called for the participation of the Permanent Members of the UN Security Council and of Pakistan, Iran, India, the UN secretary general, and the OIC secretary general. The second stage aimed at an agreement on the implementation of the international arrangements worked out at the first stage and on all "other matters designed to assure future Afghanistan as an independent and non-aligned state." The second stage visualized the additional participation of the representatives of the Afghan people.[62] Accordingly, these proposals reflected an implicit recognition that a political settlement would entail an internal settlement in Afghanistan. The EC plan was abandoned after Lord Carrington's visit to Moscow in July 1981, when Soviet Foreign Minister Andrei Gromyko rejected it as "unrealistic."[63] Variants on the ideas of "neutralization" and an international conference on Afghanistan kept surfacing, even though somewhat tentatively, throughout the protracted diplomatic activity built around the Afghan issue.

Individual efforts by Yugoslavia, India, and Cuba made at the early stages, deserve mention. These were influential members of the NAM, but they chose to act outside the movement, which was deadlocked over the issue. In addition to President Tito's letters to Carter and Brezhnev, Yugoslavia tried to explore the idea of an international conference.

For its part, India tried to develop a regional consensus.[64] Indian Foreign Secretary Ram Sathe took a trip to Islamabad in early February 1980 to promote a common approach envisioning regional guarantees and cooperative action. President Zia ul Haq apparently encouraged Sathe and expressed the hope that India, because of its special relationship with the Soviet Union, would be able to persuade Moscow to withdraw from Afghanistan.[65] Zia ul Haq made similar suggestions to Indira Gandhi when the two leaders met in Harare on 18 April 1980. Pakistan was less responsive to subsequent Indian approaches in view of the $1.6 billion Indo-Soviet deal for purchase of arms, confirmed in late May 1980.[66] However, what put brakes on the Indian initiative was its failure to elicit a promising response from Andrei Gromyko, who had visited New Delhi on 12–14 February.[67]

Confident of their success against the ill-equipped and ill-organized Afghan Resistance, the Soviets did not encourage the Indian effort. During a subsequent visit to Moscow by Indian Foreign Minister Narasima Rao in early June, the Soviets felt convinced that the main opposition to Babrak Karmal had already been crushed and that the Soviet troops could afford to stay in Afghanistan "as long as necessary." By this time, however, the Indians regarded any initiative by them as inopportune because Moscow now fully backed Kabul's 14 May proposals (discussed later in this chapter).[68]

Cuban Foreign Minister Isidoro Malmierca Peoli visited Kabul, Islamabad, and Tehran in early May 1980 to explore the possibility of a nonaligned initiative. It was more of a familiarization trip except in Tehran, where Iranian President Abolhassan Bani-Sadr made a proposal based on a Soviet pullout simultaneous with the establishment of a five-member, nonaligned committee (three Muslim and two non-Muslim members) to address other aspects of the Afghan problem.[69]

The Soviet reservation against ideas based on an international conference on Afghanistan stemmed from the fear that such a conference could internationalize the Afghan issue. The closest Moscow came to the idea was Brezhnev's offer made in December 1980 in New Delhi to discuss the security of the Gulf with Western nations to assuage their concerns over the safety of oil lanes.[70] The offer was revised in February 1981 to include "the international aspects of the Afghan problem."[71] But it remained silent over withdrawal of Soviet forces and excluded internal dimensions of the issue. Moscow, however, consistently opposed an international conference on Afghanistan. Following its rejection of the revised EC proposal in July 1980, Soviet Deputy Foreign Minister Nikolai Firyubin explained the Soviet objection during an August 1980 visit to Islamabad, saying that an international conference could go on indefinitely without positive results and could only further complicate the issue.

The Soviet view on withdrawal was first expressed with greater specificity and authority by Brezhnev when he stated, in his election speech of 22 February 1980, that the Soviets would "be ready to begin withdrawing troops as soon as there is a complete cessation of all forms of outside interference directed against the government and people of Afghanistan. Let the United States, together with Afghanistan's neighbours, guarantee that, and then the need for Soviet military aid will cease to apply."[72] The guarantee of noninterference from the United States and Afghanistan's neighbours—specifically Pakistan—subsequently became the centrepiece of the comprehensive proposals offered by Kabul on 14 May 1980.

Moscow-Kabul Position Delineated:
The 14 May Proposals

The growing diplomatic activity for a negotiated settlement generated pressure on Moscow and Kabul to make a response. Also, by
mid-1980 the increasing Soviet difficulties in pacifying the inflamed
Afghan situation and the negative international implications of the
Soviet action had become evident. Kabul and other major cities were
scenes of continuing violent demonstrations and riots.[73] Military
action produced flows of refugees, causing Moscow increasing embarrassment internationally. The Third World countries remained
agitated over the Soviet intervention while protagonists of tension-
free relations with Moscow came under conservative criticism in
Western Europe. The pro-Moscow nations saw in the Soviet intervention an emerging threat to their ascendancy and political activism in the international arena.

The immediate expediency for the well-publicized 14 May 1980
proposals by Kabul[74] appeared to be created by the approaching OIC
Foreign Ministers Conference. In this context, it is worth recalling
that close to the Venice Economic Summit of 22 June 1980, Moscow
had announced its intention to withdraw some units of Soviet
troops. This was generally viewed as a tactic designed to influence
the proceedings of the summit.[75] Nonetheless, the 14 May proposals
represented a significant Kabul-Moscow initiative, and their content
and structure provided crucial clues to Soviet-Afghan thinking during negotiations at later stages.

The crux of the 14 May proposals was direct bilateral dialogue
between the DRA and Pakistan and between the DRA and Iran. The
DRA-Pakistani dialogue was supposed to work out "bilateral agreements on the normalization of relations" on the basis of principles
of good neighbourliness and noninterference and "concrete obligations on non-admissibility of any armed or hostile activity from
one's territory against the other." The proposal envisaged "appropriate political guarantees" specifically on behalf of the Soviet Union
and the United States, in addition to any other states agreed upon by
the parties to the proposed bilateral accord, to become part of the
political settlement. The guarantee on behalf of the United States
aimed for a clearly expressed obligation not to wage any subversive
activities against Afghanistan. The cessation and "guaranteed non-
recurrence" of military invasions and other forms of interference in

the internal affairs of Afghanistan were seen as prerequisite for the resolution of "the question of withdrawal of the Soviet limited contingents from Afghanistan."

The carrot offered by the proposal was DRA readiness to accept voluntary return of refugees and reaffirmation of its offer of "general amnesty." More important, the DRA promised to negotiate Afghanistan's long-standing differences with its neighbours, an allusion to the Durand Line boundary dispute vis-à-vis Pakistan and the Helmand Waters problem in the case of Iran.[76] The proposal also referred to "military political activity" in the region of the Indian Ocean and the Persian Gulf by "states not belonging to the area" and underlined its support of efforts to transform the area into a "Zone of Peace." This idea appeared to have been injected to attract Iran and to gather support for the proposal within nonaligned circles.

In their substance, the Kabul proposals were predicated on the well-known Soviet justification for the military intervention, which they sought to validate. The procedure of direct bilateral dialogue betrayed the dominant concern on the part of Kabul to gain the legitimacy denied to it by international reaction to the Soviet military intervention. As to worth, the proposals served more as a comprehensive delineation of Kabul-Soviet demands than as a basis for negotiations. Mention of the security of the Persian Gulf and the Indian Ocean region, read in the context of frequent Soviet references to the U.S. military presence in the area and the implied threat to Soviet security, also raised questions about long-term Soviet intentions. The Kremlin appeared to be conveying the message that a solution of the Afghan problem was not simply a matter of ending outside support to the Afghan insurgency, but also of guaranteeing Soviet interests "around Afghanistan," including the wider region of the Indian Ocean.

Pakistan's Initiative through the OIC

The search for a negotiated settlement created an anticipation that the OIC, with its Islamic credentials, should develop an independent diplomatic approach. The nonbloc and quasi-regional character of the Organization of the Islamic Conference encouraged the notion that Moscow would be better disposed to an OIC initiative than it had been to the proposal from the West Europeans who had taken the lead. Meanwhile, Pakistan was groping for policy options. In Pa-

kistan there existed a broad sentiment inclined to help the Afghan
Resistance, but at the same time the Zia ul Haq government could
not be oblivious to Soviet reaction. Gromyko's visit to New Delhi
in mid-February 1980 and the implicit warning in harshly worded
Pravda comments on Brzezinski's visit to Pakistan conjured up images of an emerging "Indo-Soviet collusion" against Pakistan.[77] The
U.S. policy was yet to evolve in regard to its commitment to Pakistan
and little could be expected before the American elections. Thus,
support to the Afghan Resistance had to be constantly weighed
against the direct risk to Pakistan's own security. In order to diminish the threat, it was imperative to engage in active diplomacy and
to initiate a negotiating process.

Reliance on a military option alone also did not make good sense
because the Afghan Resistance could hardly be counted upon to reverse the Soviet military advance. In order to be credible domestically and internationally, the Afghan policy had to have a strong
diplomatic component. Domestic considerations also demanded that
the diplomatic initiative be perceived to be with Pakistan. The opportunity was provided by the Eleventh Regular Session of the Islamic Foreign Ministers Conference, held in Islamabad on 17–22
May 1980.

The proceedings of the Eleventh OIC Foreign Ministers Conference regarding the Afghan issue were noteworthy in two respects:
first, the OIC resolution, which provided for a modality to pursue a
political settlement of the issue; and second, the active participation
of Iran. The Iranian participation at the First Extraordinary Session
in January had been low-key, because the Iranians had expected that
they might come under pressure on the issue of the American hos-
tages. The muted OIC resolution adopted on the subject in January
removed possible Iranian reservation to sending Foreign Minister
Sadegh Qutbzadeh to attend the OIC conference in May.

The OIC approach at the May session shifted from a censure of the
Soviet action to the need for negotiations. The resolution adopted at
this session established a standing committee, comprising the foreign ministers of Iran and Pakistan and the secretary general of the
OIC, with the mandate "to seek ways and means, including appropriate consultations as well as the convening of an international conference under the auspices of the United Nations or otherwise," for
a comprehensive solution of the Afghan crisis, "provided it is not
inconsistent with the resolution."[78] While this mandate was flexible
enough and allowed a number of options, including informal con-

tacts with the Karmal regime, there were constraints on the OIC Standing Committee in terms of the objectives identified by the resolution. These were similar to those set out in the earlier UNGA resolution, namely, (a) the immediate, total, and unconditional withdrawal of the Soviet troops; (b) respect for the right of the Afghan people to determine their own form of government, and to choose their own economic, political, and social system free from outside pressure or interference; (c) respect for the independence, sovereignty, territorial integrity, and nonaligned status of Afghanistan (in the case of the OIC resolution an additional reference was made to the Islamic identity of Afghanistan); and (d) creation of conditions that would permit the early return of the Afghan refugees to their homeland in safety and honour.

While the EC proposals had touched on the internal dimension of the Afghan issue indirectly, the question of future government in Kabul figured prominently in the OIC approach, especially because the January OIC resolution had explicitly withdrawn recognition from the Karmal government. Several leaders of the Afghan Resistance, also known as the mujahideen, had participated in both OIC sessions as observers, and their spokesmen had made statements in the plenary meetings claiming to be the legitimate representatives of the Afghan people.[79]

The question of future government in Kabul, which evoked strong Soviet sensitivities, also followed logically from the belief that the Soviets had intervened to save a Marxist regime from inevitable collapse at the hands of the Afghan Resistance. The sustained conflict inside Afghanistan further strengthened the view that the issue was germane to any political settlement of the Afghan crisis aimed at achieving normality. Nonetheless, with the exception of the OIC initiative, discussions on this issue remained confined to informal exchanges. The UN-sponsored negotiations, which later supplanted virtually all other initiatives, came to grips with it only at the final stages.

Proceedings of the OIC Standing Committee

The OIC Standing Committee had an impossible mandate, yet it had its moments of expectation. It convened two meetings in June 1980: in Tehran in early June and at Mont Pélerin, near Geneva, toward the end of June. At the Tehran meeting, OIC Secretary General Habib Chatti briefed other members of the committee on his contacts with the Soviet ambassador in Paris to explain the committee's mandate and desire for a visit to Moscow in pursuit of a political settlement. Moscow's response, received through the ambassador, strongly endorsed the 14 May proposals, linking them with the security of the Indian Ocean and the Persian Gulf, and described the Saur Revolution as "irreversible." Nonetheless, the Soviets advised Habib Chatti to contact the Afghan government, which, they said, would enable them to consider the question of the committee's visit to Moscow.

In response Habib Chatti conveyed the committee's readiness to meet Kabul representatives, making it clear that the committee maintained its right to hear the Afghan mujahideen representatives. At Tehran the committee decided to invite the Kabul regime and the mujahideen representatives, separately, to meet with the committee in Paris (the venue was subsequently changed to Mont Pélerin). If the Kabul regime were to refuse, it was left to Habib Chatti to establish contacts with it in a manner he deemed appropriate.

During its second meeting (20–22 June 1980), the committee at first received an ambiguous signal through the Kabul chargé d'affaires in Jeddah, conveying the willingness of Foreign Minister Shah Mohammad Dost to meet the committee in secret as a representative of the PDPA and not as a representative of the government. However, before the end of the meeting, a second message was received to make it clear that Shah Mohammad Dost would be prepared to meet the foreign ministers of Pakistan and Iran separately on a strictly bilateral basis, provided the Standing Committee would not go ahead with the hearing of the delegation of Afghan mujahideen. Clearly, Moscow-Kabul preoccupation with the issue of legitimacy and recognition had prevailed. On the other hand, the committee's mandate was firmly tied to the OIC resolution, which deferred in favour of the Afghan mujahideen position.

The committee proceeded to hear the Afghan mujahideen delegation led by Abdul Rab Rasul Sayyaf, who put forth a hard-line position and staked a demand for recognition of the mujahideen as legitimate representatives of the Afghan people. Betraying a radical Islamist bias, Sayyaf advocated the convening of an Islamic summit and severance of relations with the Soviet Union by Islamic countries and expressed concern over the increase of superpower presence, both military and naval, in the region. Another noteworthy aspect of the meeting was the introduction by Agha Shahi of the concept of a "Provisional Government of National Reconciliation," headed by an Afghan personality acceptable to the mujahideen.

The OIC initiative, like the diplomatic activity built around the idea of an international conference, had peaked by the time eyes started focusing on the Thirty-Fifth Session of the UN General Assembly convened in September 1980. The question of handling the Afghan issue at the United Nations and the role the organization could play now became pertinent. The decline of Iranian Foreign Minister Qutbzadeh and the uncertainties of Iran's domestic situation had impaired the effectiveness of the OIC Standing Committee. Its expansion through the inclusion of Tunisia and Guinea in January 1981 did little to activate the committee. Nonetheless, the OIC initiative did not completely fade out; it remained on the table and eventually served as a bridge to overcome an important procedural hurdle for the commencement of the UN-sponsored negotiations at Geneva.

For Moscow and Kabul, the OIC Standing Committee, seen in the context of its mandate, was inherently partisan and its initiative an attempt to accord political status to the resistance and to negotiate on its behalf. At a time when the Soviets were confident of pacifying the Afghan Resistance and expected, for good reason, an early diminution of international concern over the Afghan issue, they spurned the OIC approach. On its part the OIC Standing Committee had not expected a quick breakthrough, but desired a beginning of contacts with Kabul.

For Pakistan, such diplomatic activity was important in deterring the threat of a punitive Soviet strike, which appeared real at a time when Pakistan's defenses were highly vulnerable. Additionally, the flexible and broadly defined nature of the OIC proposal allowed Pakistan to keep the initiative in its hand at a critical period. This was evident in the range of diplomatic contact sought by Pakistan between the Eleventh OIC Session held in May 1980 and the Thirty-Fifth UNGA Session convened that September. Beginning in 1981, however, the OIC played a pro forma, albeit visible, role in endorsing and rallying support for the Afghanistan resolution at the UN General Assembly. The Organization of the Islamic Conference also remained an important international forum for providing an international profile to the Afghan Resistance leadership.

Bilateral Contacts

The OIC initiative in May 1980 provided Pakistan with a basis and a position to engage in active diplomacy. Foreign Minister Agha Shahi undertook an extensive tour in June, visiting several West and East European capitals to explore prospects for negotiating a settlement. Since the OIC initiative had provided the context, talks with his counterparts in London, Paris, Bonn, Belgrade, Warsaw, Budapest, and Bucharest helped clarify and delineate positions, especially on the question of Afghanistan's future government and the idea of an international conference referred to in the May 1980 OIC resolution.

Leaders in London, Paris, and Bonn saw little willingness on the part of the Soviets to consider an early withdrawal. In their view, Moscow would push for wider recognition of Babrak Karmal and was unlikely to accept any suggestion for a change in Kabul. Similarly, they were concerned over the possibility of the world losing interest in Afghanistan, especially the softening in Arab attitudes.[80] Concern for détente was palpable in these capitals, as well as in Belgrade. The Yugoslav assessment of Soviet support for Karmal carried an important nuance, namely, that the Soviets could be expected to drop him in favour of a more acceptable leader in the interest of a settlement that could restore Afghanistan to its position prior to the Soviet intervention.

Exchanges between Agha Shahi and President Nicolae Ceauşescu in June 1980 in Bucharest, followed by the visit of the latter's special envoy to Islamabad in August, were of special significance. With the benefit of consultations in other capitals and in the belief that Romania possessed the credentials of an effective intermediary, Agha Shahi developed in Bucharest a comprehensive theme for a settlement. This included: (a) withdrawal of Soviet troops; (b) cessation of hostilities in Afghanistan; (c) establishment of a government of national reconciliation under a figure acceptable to the Afghans, including the PDPA factions; (d) restoration of the right of the Afghans to choose their own form of government in accordance with their traditions, such as the convening of a Loya Jirga; (e) recognition by Pakistan of any government in power in Kabul upon withdrawal of the Soviet troops; (f) reciprocal guarantees between Afghanistan, Iran, and Pakistan; and (g) stationing of international observers to monitor implementation of guarantees. Agha Shahi explained the rationale for a broad-based government essentially in terms of the unacceptability of Babrak Karmal to the Afghan people and the need for tranquility in Afghanistan. In this context, he pointed to the OIC Standing Committee's intention to seek contacts with the various Afghan parties.

The elements identified by Agha Shahi marked a substantial

evolution in Pakistan's diplomatic initiative and provided a well-structured framework for its negotiating position. The Romanian president promised help in the search for a political settlement, but cautioned against a preoccupation with the issue of future government in Afghanistan. While conceding the possibility that the Kabul government could broaden its political base to include representatives of the "social and religious forces," he emphasized Soviet sensitivity to any suggestion that would dilute, much less negate, the gains of the Saur Revolution. Similarly he felt that the OIC Standing Committee's intended contacts with the "anti-government elements" would be unacceptable to the Soviet Union. In his view, the questions of primary importance were the Soviet troop withdrawal; securing Afghanistan's independence; mutual guarantees between Afghanistan and its neighbours, including guarantee of recognized frontiers; and guarantees of noninterference in the affairs of Afghanistan, Pakistan, and Iran.

In late August 1980 Ceauşescu dispatched a special envoy, V. Pungan, who arrived in Islamabad after a visit to Kabul. The special envoy conveyed the familiar Moscow-Kabul demand for separate direct dialogues with Pakistan and Iran and asserted that withdrawal was possible only when Moscow and Kabul were convinced that no outside interference against Afghanistan was taking place. The same attitude was revealed in Agha Shahi's discussions in Warsaw and Prague. It was hinted that, with the passage of time, international acceptance would come to the Karmal regime, as it had to the János Kádár government.

The extensive diplomatic contacts within and outside the context of the OIC Standing Committee helped Pakistan to develop a clear picture of the Soviet concerns and positions. It seemed beyond doubt that Moscow was determined not to give up the gains of the Saur Revolution and unwilling to risk them by agreeing to any diplomatic process aimed at seeking changes in Kabul. It sought recognition for the Karmal regime and insisted on direct dialogue between Afghanistan and its neighbours.

The Soviet bait for Pakistan was an assurance of the security of Pakistani borders—an implicit offer to recognize the Durand Line. Characteristically blending veiled threats with this offer, Gromyko told Agha Shahi in September 1981 that he did not see "why Pakistan could not understand its interest, [that] its borders will be tranquil as never before." The future of the Karmal/PDPA regime was not negotiable, and its stability was the precondition for Soviet withdrawal.

Given the narrow base of that regime, its stability required not merely a guarantee of noninterference, but collaboration on the part of Pakistan to stifle the Afghan Resistance, as well as an active Soviet military presence in Afghanistan for the foreseeable future.

Pakistan had no incentive to oblige. In pursuing diplomatic options, Pakistan had an interest in containing Soviet hostility and countering domestic criticism against a perceived high-risk Afghan policy. Nonetheless, there was little reason for Pakistan to make a desperate bid for a settlement on Soviet terms.

Turning to the United Nations

At the Thirty-Fifth Session of the UN General Assembly beginning in September 1980, the central question relevant to its proceedings under the agenda item on Afghanistan[81] was the formulation of a new resolution that would address the need for a negotiated settlement. The Soviet Union and Afghanistan firmly opposed a UN General Assembly debate or a resolution on Afghanistan, repeating that the debate constituted an interference in the internal affairs of that country.

For Pakistan and its many nonaligned and Western supporters, the resolution was to be the barometer of international concern over the Afghan issue and thus an instrument of pressure against the Soviet Union. At the same time, Pakistan was keen to invoke a UN role in aid of negotiations because, by September 1980, there was clear need for an alternative to the OIC initiative, which had reached a dead end. Pakistan's desire to keep the initiative in hand, coupled with its disposition to look up to the United Nations in times of crisis, added to the incentive.[82] Pakistan had supported the EC initiatives for an international conference and neutralization, yet it could not feel entirely comfortable with the idea of major powers making decisions in an international conference that conjured up images of a new Yalta. Such fears were, indeed, reinforced when Brezhnev proposed his Persian Gulf plan in December 1980.[83]

Crafting of the Resolution on Afghanistan

The resolution on Afghanistan adopted by the Thirty-Fifth UNGA Session in 1980 and maintained until the Forty-Second UNGA Session in 1987 was evolved in an informal group of interested member states from Asian, African, and Latin American regional groups, with Ambassador Abdullah Bishara of Kuwait as its coordinator. For Pakistan and its supporters, the objective was to have a resolution that attracted the widest possible support, pronounced clearly on principles, provided elements for a UN role, and at the same time served as a censure of the Soviet action.

The problem was not the adoption of a resolution critical of the Soviet Union. This was not difficult to accomplish, given the majority sentiment in the UN General Assembly. The effort was to gain the support of several nonaligned nations that suspected the United States and the West of using the Afghan issue to embarrass and undercut the Soviet position in multilateral fora, and who thus advocated a resolution that would help resolve the problem rather than complicating it. The final resolution was evolved after a series of revisions. Because its authorship was attributed to Kuwait, the resolution was immunized against attacks describing it as a U.S.-sponsored resolution.

The Soviet sympathizers, especially Cuba, tried to push for a consensus resolution playing upon sentiment favouring progress toward a settlement, instead of adopting a less than unanimous resolution for the sake of affirming a position, however principled. The Cuban delegation tentatively sounded out the Yugoslavs regarding a package of three elements, namely, normalization of relations among the regional states, withdrawal of troops, and conditions for return of refugees. The Cubans did not pursue the idea, apparently for lack of encouragement from the Soviets, who wanted their intervention to be clearly linked to "outside interference" in the internal affairs of Afghanistan. The Cubans had failed to deliver on such a formulation, even in the nonaligned forum where they enjoyed considerable clout.

Another move seen by Pakistan and its supporters as tactics to neutralize their resolution was a suggestion for two resolutions: one so-called propagandist resolution that Pakistan and its supporters could table, and another to be adopted by consensus. The idea was to formulate the second resolution in neutral terms, urging all concerned to intensify efforts for a political settlement and containing points common to the 14 May proposals, the May 1980 resolution of the OIC, and the earlier resolution of the UNGA Emergency Special Session. No specific proposals were put forward for the suggested consensus resolution.

The question of a specific modality to be recommended by the UN General Assembly to pursue a political settlement posed difficulties to the drafters of the resolution. The Soviets appeared to be firmly opposed to the internationalization of the issue. Moscow had already rejected proposals for an international conference in both the EC and OIC contexts. The prospects for such a conference had become slim, even though it was regarded as a useful card to be played at an opportune time.

Furthermore, in conveying their opposition to the consideration of the Afghan issue by the General Assembly, the Soviets had informed UN Secretary General Kurt Waldheim that any initiative, even his good offices, would not be acceptable to the Soviet Union if these were offered in the context of a General Assembly resolution. Accordingly, the secretary general expressed reservations concerning any direct reference that could curtail his freedom to pursue a desired course.

Some of the Western bloc countries had suggested either appointing a special committee of the General Assembly or asking the secretary general to designate a special representative on Afghanistan. During discussions in the informal drafting group, the idea of a special committee was dropped. It would have been deadlocked right from inception as a result of Soviet opposition, and many of the nonaligned states were reluctant to agree to the setting up of a special committee similar to those already operating on the issues of Palestine and Southern Africa.[84] It was agreed to recommend the appointment of a special representative in the text of the resolution, leaving the timing of the appointment to be decided by the UN secretary general.

Unlike the preceding resolution of the Emergency Special Session, the resolution adopted at the Thirty-Fifth Session—Resolution 35/37, 20 November 1980—did not explicitly deplore the Soviet intervention.[85] Instead, it focused on the requirement of withdrawal and outlined the following elements for a political solution:

1. "preservation of the sovereignty, territorial integrity, political independence and nonaligned character of Afghanistan";
2. "the right of the Afghan people to determine their own form of government and to choose their economic, political and social system free from outside intervention, subversion, coercion or constraint of any kind whatsoever";
3. "immediate withdrawal of the foreign troops from Afghanistan" (the phrase "unconditional" was omitted this time to underscore that withdrawal would be part of a settlement);
4. "creation of the necessary conditions which would enable the Afghan refugees to return voluntarily to their homes in safety and honour."

An effort to accommodate Soviet concerns was visible in the text of the sixth operative paragraph, which requested the secretary general to undertake efforts

with a view to promoting a political solution, in accordance with the [above] provisions of the present resolution, and the exploration of securing appropriate guarantees for the non-use of force, or threat of use of force, against the political independence, sovereignty, territorial integrity and security of all neighbouring States [Afghanistan, Iran, and Pakistan], on the basis of mutual guarantees and strict non-interference in each other's internal affairs and with full regard for the principles of the Charter of the United Nations.

Interpreting, Agha Shahi stated to the General Assembly that "this provision should meet a major component of the 14 May proposals which call for mutual guarantees of security and non-interference."[86]

The moderate and, by UN standards, nonrhetorical resolution served well the purpose of maintaining international pressure on the Soviet Union. At the United Nations, the resolution helped to isolate support for the Soviet position literally to the hard core of pro-Moscow membership. Privately, delegates from some of these countries made no secret of their discomfiture with the position they were obliged to take. Internationally, the resolution was successfully projected as an emphatic censure of the Soviet Union and evidence of undiminished international concern.

The experience of handling the Afghan issue at the Thirty-Fifth Session set the framework and precedent for a remarkable campaign in subsequent years to maintain and enhance membership support for the General Assembly resolution on Afganistan. The campaign technique and coordination improved and developed with time. Every year prior to the General Assembly debate, Pakistan engaged in well-timed, elaborate contacts with member states at UN headquarters, as well as through dispatch of special envoys to selected capitals. This meticulous planning paid off. The UNGA vote on the Afghanistan resolution showed a marginal increase every session with the exception of 1982 (see table 1). Then, under the Hungarian UNGA President Imre Hollai, the debate was timed to coincide with the Thanksgiving holiday, resulting in its fragmentation and confusion about the timing of the vote.

It would be wrong to say that in opting for nonrhetorical resolution, Pakistan was motivated by propagandistic considerations alone. The desire to keep the door open for diplomacy was manifest in Agha Shahi's statement to the General Assembly. He advocated a political

Table 1: Record of Votes on
the Afghanistan Resolution, 1980–1987

Year	For	Against	Abstentions
1980[1]	104	18	18
1980[2]	111	22	12
1981	116	23	12
1982[3]	114	21	13
1983	116	20	17
1984	119	20	14
1985	122	19	12
1986	122	20	11
1987	123	19	11

Notes:
[1] Emergency Special Session.
[2] Regular Session.
[3] Belize and Vanuatu could not participate in the vote, but later conveyed that they would have cast a positive vote.

solution which wove in some elements of Kabul's 14 May 1980 proposals with the principles outlined in the OIC and UN resolutions. In Agha Shahi's view, such a solution could best be pursued by the appointment of a special representative of the UN secretary general.

Pakistani-Soviet Parleys Converge on the UN Role

During December 1980 and January 1981, several weeks before the Non-Aligned Meeting in New Delhi, a significant dialogue had developed between Islamabad and Moscow which eventually paved the way for the involvement of the UN secretary general. Why did the Soviets encourage this dialogue?

Several factors could have influenced the Soviet thinking. The landslide victory of Republican candidate Ronald Reagan, heightened in its impact by the defeat of an incumbent president, pointed to a stiffening of the American position on the whole range of East-West issues. The sustained international pressure and the Soviet failure to pacify the Afghan Resistance may have impelled the Soviets to explore diplomatic options. At the same time, Pakistan's pronouncements betrayed an eagerness to start a diplomatic process, and its position was temptingly close to the Soviet-Kabul demand for a direct dialogue.

The Pakistani-Soviet parleys through the Soviet ambassador in Islamabad, Vitaly S. Smirnov, concentrated on promoting an understanding to enable the UN secretary general to take the initiative. Many of the discussions were held directly with President Zia ul Haq. A tentative understanding developed first on having the secretary general appoint a "personal representative." (Note the difference in nomenclature: the UNGA resolution had used the term "special representative.") Tacitly, Pakistan was to refrain from linking the appointment to the UN resolution, while Kabul and Moscow were to reciprocate by not denying explicitly the relevance of the UN resolution as a framework for the talks.

Pakistan had envisaged a trilateral format, similar to the one proposed under the OIC Standing Committee, namely Pakistan, Iran, and PDPA representatives would meet under the auspices of the United Nations—a term vaguely defined but intended to mean "in the presence and with active participation" of the UN secretary general or his personal representative. Pakistan insisted that publicly it would maintain that it was engaging in talks with the representative of the PDPA and not the Afghan government. Moscow at first agreed. There were corroborating signals from Kabul.[87] But within days, Moscow modified its position, conveying Kabul's objection to the procedure, and once again demanded separate bilateral talks.

Apart from the Kabul objection, which Pakistan expected the Soviets to help in removing, an additional difficulty arose as a result of increased disinterest on the part of Iran and its position that any negotiating process on the Afghan issue must involve the Afghan mujahideen.[88] Pakistan's insistence on the participation of Iran was therefore seen by the Soviets as a pretext to refuse recourse to negotiations.

Flexibility on this point was first reflected in a controversial but significant proposal made by Pakistan known as "the empty chair formula," conveyed to Ambassador Smirnov by Sardar Shahnawaz, the secretary general of the Pakistan Foreign Office. While the new Pakistani proposal maintained the principle of trilateral talks—invoking the OIC mandate—it opened the possibility of Pakistan's engaging in talks with PDPA representatives in the presence of the UN secretary general's representative in the event that Iran would refuse the secretary general's invitation to participate in the talks.[89]

An additional point of interest was a suggestion that, following his appointment, the UN secretary general's representative should hold consultations in the capitals of all the countries concerned, including Moscow, to show that Moscow was among the interlocutors. At the time this formula was being conveyed to the Soviet ambassador, Zia ul Haq was in the Gulf region on a state visit prior to the Taif Islamic summit of 25–28 January 1981. His statements were visibly conciliatory, ruling out confrontation with Moscow and stressing the need to find alternatives within the UN framework and to keep options open to solve the problem.

The empty chair formula attracted reservations and misgivings on the part of some of the Islamic countries, notably Saudi Arabia, as it would have compromised the OIC stand. Additionally, Pakistan, on further consideration, became concerned that a political dialogue with Kabul, while keeping an empty seat for Iran, might draw a sharp reaction from Iran. OIC Secretary General Habib Chatti entertained reservations against Pakistan's moves to involve the United Nations, which appeared to undercut the OIC role. However, on the question of UN involvement, Pakistan stood firm, and Agha Shahi succeeded in eliciting Saudi support for a recommendation from the Taif summit that the expanded OIC Standing Committee should "cooperate with the Secretary General of the United Nations and his special representative in their endeavour to resolve the situation in Afghanistan."[90] Henceforth, the OIC initiative for a political settlement was effectively subordinated to UN mediation.

The mixed signals exchanged between Moscow and Islamabad had thus yielded a tacit understanding on the appointment of a representative of the UN secretary general. Differences persisted on the format of the talks, whether trilateral or bilateral, and the role of the secretary general's representative, but the ground for active involvement of the United Nations had been prepared. On 2 January 1981 Agha Shahi addressed a message to UN Secretary General Kurt Waldheim, inviting him to designate his "special representative."[91] On 11 February 1981, at the conclusion of the New Delhi meeting of the Non-Aligned Foreign Ministers, Waldheim nominated Javier Pérez de Cuéllar, a senior Peruvian diplomat who was then UN under secretary general for special political affairs, as his "personal representative" to promote "peace talks between the Parties concerned."[92]

Antecedents of the Geneva Negotiations
on Afghanistan

The first exploratory visit to the region by Pérez de Cuéllar in April 1981 elicited little more than reiterations of the respective positions in Kabul and Islamabad. Kabul was preoccupied with procedural issues and wanted first to settle the modalities—for bilateral talks or trilateral talks with an empty chair for Iran. With its position hardened on the procedural questions, Pakistan wanted the personal representative to take up substantive issues through the medium of shuttle diplomacy. On the procedural questions, the Pakistani side had already conveyed to the Soviets that it considered the trilateral nature of the talks as a fundamental aspect, that these talks should be held under the auspices of the United Nations, and that the UN secretary general or his personal representative must play the role of an organizer and active participant. Additionally, the participation of the DRA was acceptable only as a representative of the PDPA.

The outcome of Pérez de Cuéllar's first contacts in the region was, nonetheless, an explicit acceptance of "UN good offices" and "active participation" in the diplomatic process by the personal representative. The same understanding was secured by Secretary General Waldheim during his visit to Moscow in May 1981. Soviet Foreign Minister Gromyko supported the continuation of the UN initiative, but made it clear that the Soviets regarded Pakistan as the "key country" that the UN representative must lead to "the negotiating table" (that is, direct talks) with the DRA. Moscow had obviously decided in favour of the UN role. This was further borne out by its continued indifference to the West European initiative for an international conference. From the Soviet viewpoint, a basic advantage of the UN-sponsored talks lay in the fact that, despite Pakistani reservations, the United Nations, in deference to its rules of procedure, treated the DRA government as the sole Afghan interlocutor.

Agenda for Shuttle Diplomacy

The second visit of Pérez de Cuéllar to the area in early August 1981 was significant from Pakistan's point of view. Pérez de Cuéllar was inclined to bypass procedure and negotiate substantive issues, adopting a form of shuttle diplomacy. He identified a four-point agenda, comprising the format of the negotiations, international guarantees against intervention, the question of refugees, and withdrawal of Soviet troops, and proposed to use the issue of refugees to engage Kabul in negotiations. Agha Shahi agreed to this approach but suggested the inclusion in the agenda of the question of the right of Afghans to freely choose their own economic, political, and social system. Pérez de Cuéllar parried the issue, arguing that this point was not mentioned by the February 1981 NAM decision adopted at New Delhi and that it could be raised only after the Afghans had been securely drawn into the negotiations.

The choice of the refugee issue as a wedge to break the impasse was an astute suggestion, inspired by a keen perception of Kabul's changing position on the issue. Kabul no longer dismissed the refugees as nomads.[93] Their growing numbers provided Pakistan a powerful instrument of propaganda; more seriously, the refugee population was becoming a reservoir of potential recruits for the Afghan Resistance. International assistance appeared to lessen the burden on Pakistan, which showed no sign of relenting under the pressure. Kabul had therefore begun issuing appeals to the refugees to return to their homeland and accusing Pakistan of obstructing their return.[94] For its part, Pakistan had opened the refugee camps to international relief and humanitarian agencies and blamed the incoming refugee flows on the Soviet military campaigns inside Afghanistan.

Pérez de Cuéllar's approach received support from Zia ul Haq, but Zia made two points. First, he underlined the "linkages" between the various aspects of the Afghanistan crisis: the return of refugees required the right conditions, which depended on the nature of the government in Kabul and the withdrawal of the Soviet troops, whose presence in the first place had created the refugee situation. These linkages and interrelationships became germane to discussions held later at Geneva for the evolution of the structure of the Geneva documents. Zia's second point noted the "intermingling" of the political and military aspects of the refugees. Since there could be no representative purely of the refugees, conditions for return should be acceptable to both the refugees and the mujahideen. Accordingly, the mujahideen interests could not be ignored. The issue of "representation of the refugees" and the need to consult them were later used by Pakistan to seek the association of the mujahideen with the Geneva negotiations on Afghanistan.

Precondition for Direct Talks Softens

In Kabul, Pérez de Cuéllar raised his four-point agenda with the Afghan leadership and the Soviet chargé d'affaires, omitting reference to the fifth point suggested by Agha Shahi on the Afghan right to self-determination. The four points did not attract objection, but the Afghans insisted that these could be discussed only in direct talks and continued to press for an understanding on the format of the negotiations. Pakistan refused direct talks with the DRA without Iranian participation, but was ready to discuss substantive issues in indirect talks through the intermediary of the UN secretary general. Before agreeing to such indirect talks, Kabul made one more well-publicized effort to secure direct talks.

On the eve of the Thirty-Sixth UNGA Session convened in September 1981, Kabul announced a revised version of the 14 May 1980 proposals, which came to be known as the 24 August 1981 proposals.[95] Procedurally, the new proposals accepted trilateral negotiations between the DRA, Iran, and Pakistan, and also endorsed the empty chair formula—should any country decide not to join the negotiations in the beginning, such country would be free to join the dialogue at a subsequent stage. Kabul further affirmed its acceptance of having the UN secretary general attend the talks, as well as its readiness to participate in an international guarantee "simultaneously and parallel" with bilateral and trilateral talks. As to substance, the 24 August 1981 proposals had gone little beyond their precursor, the 14 May 1980 proposals. This time, however, the refugee issue had received greater attention and conditions for their return had been spelt out in detail.

The revised proposals succeeded neither in putting pressure on Pakistan to accept direct talks, trilateral or otherwise, nor in making a favourable impact on the membership of the UN General Assembly, which debated the Afghan situation the following November. The apparent concessions on procedure were negated by the inflexible demands on substance, reflective of the Soviet position on the issue. If direct talks were the goal, a purely procedural proposal with a statement of flexibility on the contents of talks could have better served the Soviet-Kabul interest.

In September 1981 the Soviet foreign minister made yet another bid for direct dialogue between Pakistan and Afghanistan. Gromyko offered to Agha Shahi long-term economic cooperation and a Soviet promise to ensure that Pakistan had a secure border with Afghanistan, provided Pakistan would modulate its policies to Soviet liking and come to an acceptable arrangement with Babrak Karmal.

The Soviet position on direct talks had, nonetheless, started showing flexibility. Moscow clearly desired a diplomatic process to start in the hope of shoring up Karmal's position and lessening international pressure. The absence of negotiations did not serve the need of the Karmal regime for international recognition.

Overall, the situation had deteriorated from the Soviet perspective. Reagan had embarked on a determined opposition to perceived Soviet advances. Pakistan and the United States were able to sign a long-term package for economic assistance and military sale credits. Within Afghanistan, a major summer offensive by Soviet forces in Paktia and Kunar had been fruitless. Economic costs imposed on Moscow by the war had started rising. Further, there appeared to be no finality in Pakistan's rejection of direct talks. The empty chair formula, despite the manner in which it was made and then withdrawn, suggested that at an opportune time, under pressure, Pakistan could be expected to acquiesce in direct talks.

In the course of the Thirty-Sixth UNGA Session in 1981, Agha Shahi and Shah Mohammad Dost held a number of separate meetings with Secretary General Waldheim and Pérez de Cuéllar during which Kabul agreed to set aside the question of direct talks for the time being and to discuss substantive issues. Pérez de Cuéllar had already suggested the question of refugees as the starting point, and Pakistan had formally asked that conditions be offered by the Kabul regime to the returnees so that the refugees could be consulted concerning these conditions. As an incentive, Pakistan also agreed to a suggestion from Pérez de Cuéllar for shifting the activities of the Office of the UN High Commissioner for Refugees (UNHCR) to Afghanistan as and when the refugees started returning. Shah Mohammad Dost promised to convey to the secretary general the conditions set out by Kabul for the return of refugees.

Toward the end of 1981, in a cavalier manner, Kabul transmitted these conditions to the secretary general in the shape of six general policy documents issued since 1979, including the 14 May 1980 and 24 August 1981 proposals, with the portions relating to refugees underlined in yellow marker. These were familiar statements and proposals, circulated routinely by the Afghan representative at the time of their issuance as documents of the Security Council and the General Assembly. Pakistan was expected to place them before the Afghan refugees in order to ascertain their reaction.

Pakistan had little interest in circulating the six long statements of the DRA among the refugees. Nevertheless, instead of dismissing the Kabul response as frivolous, Pakistan suggested that for the sake of credibility the refugee response be elicited by an impartial agency such as the UNHCR, which had access to the refugees through its relief assistance activities. In a formal communication to the UN secretary general, Pakistan also promised to extend to the UNHCR the necessary logistical support and facilities for carrying out the exercise.

UNHCR chief Poul Hartling, however, after raising several issues of procedure, realized the political nature of the exercise and declined to undertake it, asserting that a political role was inconsistent with the UNHCR mandate. Arguments that such a role would be sanctioned by the secretary general did not convince him. Similarly, the alternative of using the International Committee of the Red Cross (ICRC) did not appear to be feasible, especially after the ouster of the organization from Kabul in June 1980.[96] While the idea of having UNHCR ascertain the views of the refugees survived, the approach that a start be made by tackling the refugee issue first became irrelevant as the Kabul objection to indirect talks on substantive issues faded out and the four-point agenda prepared by Pérez de Cuéllar for such talks moved to centre stage in the UN discussions with Pakistani and Afghan representatives.

Discussions at the 1981 UNGA session had helped to clarify and refine the substantive agenda and the timing and format of the talks through the personal representative. On the format of talks, two possible options were explored, namely, active shuttle diplomacy, or having the two delegations stay in separate hotels in a city outside the region, with the UN mediator shuttling between them. The Pakistani side regarded both alternatives as variations of indirect talks but preferred shuttle diplomacy, thinking that a shuttle could facilitate close consultations with the refugees.

On substance, besides the question of the return of refugees, preliminary discussion was held on the issue of withdrawal and guarantees of noninterference. Pakistan's position on "interference" had evolved as a result of the inescapable logic of its public assertions of noninvolvement in Afghanistan and the indigenous character of the "insurgency" inside Afghanistan. This prepared Pakistan to agree to give guarantees of noninterference as part of a package settlement. Pakistan's demand for inclusion of the "right to self-determination" got diluted in the face of the argument that withdrawal of foreign forces would automatically ensure conditions for the Afghans to freely choose their government. Pakistan had already conceded publicly that its nonrecognition of the Karmal regime was due to the fact that the regime was sustained by Soviet forces in Afghanistan and not because of the commonly perceived Marxist orientation of the regime.[97] Notwithstanding this declaratory position, the issue of replacement of the government in Kabul constantly preoccupied Pakistan's policymakers and figured prominently at informal discussions, despite its exclusion from the Geneva format. Kabul's po-

sitions on the two issues, however, remained embedded in the 14
May 1980 and 24 August 1981 proposals.

Diego Cordovez as Mediator

Toward the end of 1981 Pérez de Cuéllar was elected as the new secretary general of the United Nations. His mantle was passed to Diego
Cordovez, an outstanding UN official from Ecuador, who was promoted to the post of under secretary general for political affairs when
Pérez de Cuéllar vacated that portfolio. Diego Cordovez, endowed
with irrepressible ambition and vitality, brought with him a new
style. He displayed the vibrant disposition of a master practitioner
of pressure tactics such as those often witnessed in the UN corridors.
He would not flinch from making a fantastic suggestion or conjuring
up an equally implausible scenario to apply pressure or test the
ground. He could be counted upon to make any number of proposals,
and to withdraw them if they did not work. His fertile imagination,
his varied skills, even his controversial style of diplomacy imparted
vigour to the UN-sponsored diplomatic process and helped to sustain
it until such time as the combination of circumstances took a propitious turn for a political settlement.

Immediately upon his appointment as the personal representative
of the secretary general, Diego Cordovez undertook a shuttle to the
area in mid-April 1982. The major task before him was to clinch an
agreement on the commencement of substantive talks and on the
agenda. Cordovez started his visit from Islamabad, where he proposed the holding of indirect talks in Geneva. He also wanted an
indication from Pakistan that it would accept direct talks at some
stage down the road. Cordovez thought that such an indication
would enable him to engage Kabul in serious negotiations on substantive issues. Secondly, he identified withdrawal, noninterference,
international guarantees, and the return of refugees as subjects for
articulating a four-part annotated agenda. He suggested that there
should be no set order for the items, especially in view of the negotiations already afoot in respect of the refugee question. In a meeting
with Zia ul Haq during the April 1982 shuttle, Cordovez received
Pakistan's concurrence in the four-point agenda and agreement to
the holding of "indirect talks" at Geneva.

The nomenclature, more than the form, of the indirect talks was
important to avoid the impression that Pakistan had withdrawn
from the OIC decision. President Zia called the indirect talks at Ge-

neva a practical option, while reaffirming Pakistan's public position on direct talks. He also underlined the importance of persuading Iran to participate in the talks.

On his return from Kabul, Cordovez conveyed Kabul's agreement to the package agenda and to discussing substantive issues at the indirect talks. Yet, at the same time, he also hinted at some caveats. On procedure, he appeared to have held out to the Afghan regime a promise of direct talks at an appropriate stage. He insisted, however, that he would safeguard Pakistan's position on recognition. On substance, he spoke in general terms about Kabul's position on withdrawal, that this was a matter exclusively between Moscow and Kabul. Cordovez carefully kept it ambiguous as to whether Kabul had stated this position to qualify the agenda or had done so merely to place it on record. Later on, the interlocutors got used to Cordovez's studied lack of clarity, which he deployed to advance the negotiations. Yet, as the future course of the diplomatic process would reveal, fundamental problems of perception could not simply be wished away or resolved through constructive ambiguity. They had to be faced and addressed fully.

Foremost among Pakistan's concerns conveyed to Cordovez during the April 1982 shuttle was the requirement that the settlement spell out the timing and modalities of withdrawal. In addition, questions were raised about the elements and scope of guarantees, emphasizing that they should be reciprocal and include guarantees of international borders. The need to ascertain the wishes of the refugees about the conditions for their voluntary return was reaffirmed. On his part, Cordovez pressed hard for some movement in Pakistan's position on direct talks, arguing that this was essential for progress in substantive negotiation. Nonetheless, chastised by its experience on the empty chair formula, Pakistan maintained its insistence on Iran's participation as a sine qua non for direct talks.

Immediately on his return from the area, Cordovez addressed letters to the foreign ministers of Pakistan and Afghanistan, summing up his conclusions and providing a broad framework for discussion on the four agenda items. The letters introduced innovative annotation for the agenda items, which later spawned the first outline of the text for a comprehensive settlement, and addressed the procedural question deftly, squeezing in a highly qualified reference to direct talks.

The annotation on withdrawal loosely interfused the positions of the two interlocutors. It restricted discussion on withdrawal to the interrelationships governing implementation of the measures to be identified under the other three items. Furthermore, the formulation of these interrelationships had to consider the circumstances, modalities, and timing of withdrawal. This blend of Afghan and Pakistani positions on withdrawal thus referred to "interrelationships" that were conceded by the two sides, albeit along divergent lines. It spoke of circumstances of withdrawal that showed clear deference to the Afghan position predicated on the conditions that would convince Kabul to agree to the departure of the troops, and it mentioned the timing and modality of withdrawal reflecting Pakistan's concerns. On "non-interference in internal affairs," the suggested annotation showed a tilt in favour of the Afghan position. The discussion under the item was supposed to define "measures" that would ensure the implementation of the principles of nonintervention and noninterference in the internal affairs of the states concerned. Under "international guarantees" and "return of refugees," the purpose of discussion was stated in general and neutral terms. The annotation on refugees referred to the conditions, modalities, and time frame for their return, and the role of the relevant international agencies.

On the issue of procedure, Cordovez's annotation combined several elements, namely, the agreement on indirect talks at Geneva; the need to keep Iran informed; Cordovez's readiness to receive Iranian views; his intention to undertake shuttles to Islamabad, Kabul, and Tehran in the future; and a provision envisaging consultations to be held, depending on the progress achieved through the existing format, to determine "the most appropriate manner" to pursue further negotiations. The consultations, if and when held, could consider the secretary general's organizing "trilateral meetings for the purpose of direct discussions" in which he or his personal representative would participate. Such meetings were to be organized without prejudice to the positions of the participants on questions of representation and recognition. This formulation was sufficiently conditional not to attract objections from Pakistan. At the same time, it introduced an allusion to direct talks to assuage Afghan concerns.

Cordovez suggested that the order in which the agenda issues were listed was without prejudice to the priorities attributed to them by the interlocutors, thus implying that these could be taken up for discussion flexibly in the interest of advancing the talks. Finally, Cordovez affirmed in his letters that because the issues were interlinked, agreement on any of them would be implemented only within the context of a comprehensive settlement.

By recommending a structure for discussion and by identifying and skillfully juxtaposing the issues of concern to his interlocutors, Cordovez had devised in his letter a launching pad for the Geneva negotiations. This was a laudable contribution from an intermediary, notwithstanding the felicitous circumstances that had enabled the UN secretary general to assume an active role in initiating the Geneva negotiating process. The stage was thus set for the first Geneva round of indirect talks.

A Change of Guard at the Pakistan Foreign Office

During 1981 Pakistan was engaged in developing three Afghanistan-related policy directions: first, diplomatic pressure through preserving international demand for withdrawal and pursuing a negotiated settlement; second, long-term commitment from the United States for meeting Pakistan's defense needs and for providing economic assistance; and third, material support to bolster the Afghan Resistance. The Pakistan Foreign Office handled the first two areas, whereas the third aspect was coordinated by President Zia almost exclusively with the Inter-Services Intelligence (ISI) chief, Lieutenant General Akhtar Abdur Rahman.

In negotiating the package of U.S. economic assistance and military sales credit, the Pakistan Foreign Office was wary lest the U.S. confrontationalist mood and ideological stridency create obstacles in progress toward agreement on indirect talks. Furthermore, there was a general concern that the new relationship being sought with the United States should not be at the cost of Pakistan's nonaligned status and policies. This was expressly stated when the $3.2 billion package was agreed and announced in September 1981.[98] Agha Shahi took pains to explain that no political quid pro quo was involved and that the U.S. government was left in no doubt that Pakistan would neither dilute its nonalignment nor alter its position on the nuclear issue, nor would it acquiesce in "the strategic consensus" being promoted by the United States in the Middle East.[99]

Agha Shahi's concern for Pakistan's nonalignment went further. He opted for market-related rates of interest on U.S. loans to purchase military equipment instead of concessionary rates, which the

United States was willing to offer. According to Agha Shahi, "The rationale behind this decision was to preclude any expectation of quid pro quo by the United States. The past relationship had involved Pakistan in an anti-Soviet alignment with the U.S. as the quid pro quo for nonreimbursable U.S. military aid."[100] Thus Pakistan had accepted the 11.5 percent instead of the 8 percent concessional interest rate. Furthermore, it was conveyed to the American side during consultations that Pakistan would be unwilling to become a "conduit of U.S. arms to the Afghan mujahideen."[101] Clearly, however, President Zia and the military, who had independent channels with the U.S. government, had something quite different in mind, as Pakistan had already become engaged in providing military support to the mujahideen. It was an indispensable component of Pakistan's policy to strengthen the Afghan Resistance.

Agha Shahi's experience of nonalignment related to his long association with the United Nations, where the NAM appeared to act as a formidable group and where its positions reflected a touch of idealism. As an active member of the United Nations, but outside the NAM, Pakistan always felt handicapped and somewhat left out. Agha Shahi became a forceful advocate of Pakistan's entry into the movement once the Central Treaty Organization (CENTO) had started crumbling. By 1979 when Pakistan joined it, however, the NAM was a divided house, having lost much of its ideological lustre and credibility as a force on the international scene.

The decision to opt for market interest rates for U.S. credits therefore drew criticism from some military and official circles in Pakistan. First, there was hardly any point in asserting nonaligned credentials, especially when countries fully aligned to one or the other of the superpowers made the same claim to being nonaligned. Second, Pakistan could hardly make a convincing case to prove its nonaligned credentials by talking about its choice of interest rates, which in any event was an unnecessary exercise. A more telling argument was provided by Pakistan's positions in the United Nations on international issues.[102]

Agha Shahi's concern over any weakening of Pakistan's nonalignment or its becoming a conduit for arms betrayed that he was not on the same wavelength with Zia ul Haq or the military. This divergence eventually led to his resignation in February 1982.[103] There were other contributing factors. Agha Shahi had an uneasy relationship with the Americans and the Saudis. On a policy plane, where Pakistan faced a two-front situation, Agha Shahi had doubts over the

success of any policy aimed at placating India and favoured conciliation with the Soviet Union. However, the diplomatic initiatives
pursued by him over the previous two years held out little promise
of securing Soviet withdrawal. The military, on the other hand, were
quite agreeable to making a gesture to India in deference to U.S. concerns and adopting a firm position on Afghanistan.[104]

President Zia's choice of Sahabzada Yaqub Khan as his next foreign minister precipitated yet another change in the Pakistan Foreign
Office. Sardar Shahnawaz, the most senior member of the Foreign
Office and an aspirant for the post of foreign minister, sought reas-
signment as permanent representative to the United Nations in New
York. Being a Mohammadzai and a descendant of Amir Sher Ali, he
was respected for his knowledge on Afghanistan and recognized as
an important supporter of "moderate" Peshawar-based groups and of
the idea of a Loya Jirga. He was a focal point of visiting Afghan émigré
personalities and other prominent Afghans in Islamabad. His departure severed an important, albeit informal, link that the Foreign Office had maintained with the Afghan Resistance.

Yaqub Khan, the new foreign minister, with his impressive credentials as a general and a diplomat, reveled in the classical approach
to diplomatic practice, maintaining a distinction between declaratory aspects of policy and core interests. He had little difficulty in
reconciling Pakistan's nonalignment with seeking a strong security
relationship with the United States as a counterpoise to Soviet hostility, caused by Pakistan's backing of the Afghan Resistance. For
him, the Afghan armed struggle complemented diplomacy, notwithstanding his lack of enthusiasm for the ideological exhortations of
the disheveled mujahideen leadership. For him the prospect of engaging the Soviets to secure their withdrawal, albeit through the
proxy of the Kabul regime and UN mediation, presented a challenge
of historic proportions. In his working style, Yaqub Khan had little
patience with minutiae. His predilection for the broad structure and
logical scheme of things was often skillfully manipulated by Diego
Cordovez in elaborating draft texts at the Geneva rounds. His standing and trust with the military and with President Zia (twice, Yaqub
Khan had been Zia ul Haq's commanding officer) enabled Yaqub
Khan to take decisions on substantial aspects of various drafts without getting too encumbered with the sophistry of detail and nuances.

The change of guard at the Pakistan Foreign Office took place at
a time when ground had already been cleared for the Geneva rounds
of indirect talks. The broad relief of policy choices and desirable

courses of action had become visible. U.S.-Pakistani relations had been revitalized, the direction of President Zia's "peace offensive" with India had been set, and Pakistan was ready to negotiate without a nervous haste on the basis of what it perceived to be reasonable terms for a settlement.

3

Internal Developments:
The PDPA and the Afghan Resistance,
1980–86

Before resuming discussion of the diplomatic process, it would be appropriate to survey developments inside Afghanistan following the Soviet intervention. These constituted the backdrop of the negotiations.

Moscow had anticipated a quick operation in Afghanistan, but its assessment of Afghan resilience in defying an outside aggressor and of its ability to unite the deeply divided People's Democratic Party of Afghanistan (PDPA) turned out to be fatally flawed. There was no parallel to this situation in Soviet experience, contemporary or past. Soviet diplomats and, later, the Soviet media compared it to the "Basmachi rebellion" of the mid-1920s in Central Asia.[1] Yet the similarities did not stretch very far in terms of either domestic conditions or the international environment of Afghanistan.

Throughout their stay in Afghanistan, the Soviets were preoccupied with the task of consolidating the PDPA and pacifying the ubiquitous Afghan Resistance. Their efforts were constantly frustrated in preventing the endemic discord between the PDPA's Khalq and Parcham factions, which pervaded the party and the government structure and caused the DRA army to be dissipated and feckless. Babrak Karmal's deeply doctrinaire policies did little to help Soviet objectives or to broaden the political base of his government. Similarly, the Soviet military campaign failed to quell the Afghan Resistance. Ironically, the Soviet military intervention further spurred the Afghans' historic pattern of uniting against foreign invaders.

Over the years, with gradually built outside support, the Afghan Resistance grew from its bushfire character to a better equipped and better organized guerilla force. Politically, however, the resistance remained deeply divided, afflicted with acute ideological dissensions and the competing political ambitions of individual leaders. Divergent pulls kept Pakistan's policy toward the resistance a hostage to considerations of military expediency and prevented interest in preparing the resistance for an effective future political role, especially in case the Soviets decided to withdraw.

Military support to the Afghan Resistance had reached a new threshold by 1984–85 as Mikhail Gorbachev emerged at the helm of the Soviet political scene. In the following years, no two factors influenced the negotiations more than the transformed military situation in Afghanistan and the steadily changing orientation of Soviet policies under the new Soviet leader.

The PDPA

Since its founding in 1965, the People's Democratic Party of Afghanistan has continually suffered from a running feud between its two constituent factions, the largely Pashtun and comparatively broad-based Khalq faction and the narrower, urban-based Parcham. The phenomenon resurfaced when the party split soon after the Saur Revolution of April 1978.[2] The Taraki-Amin coalition, representing the Khalq faction, carried out large-scale purges of the rival Parcham elements from government positions. Babrak Karmal, for one, was sent as ambassador to Czechoslovakia. Among other prominent Parchamis, Anahita Ratebzad was appointed ambassador to Yugoslavia and Mahmoud Baryalai, Karmal's brother, to Pakistan. Later, Anahita Ratebzad recalled to *Süddeutsche Zeitung* (21 May 1981) that 3,500 Parchamis had been killed by Khalqis.[3]

The Khalq-Parcham rift was therefore deep. When Karmal took power with Soviet backing after Amin's assassination, he was confronted with a near rebellion from the influential Khalq. The DRA army was dominated by the Khalq and had been loyal to Hafizullah Amin.[4] Khalqis were reportedly behind several countrywide disturbances. There were also reports of gun battles between the two factions in early 1980.[5]

Besides the intraparty discord, Karmal was faced with a series of unprecedented demonstrations and the symbolic but potent stigma that he had arrived riding Soviet tanks. Demonstrations against Karmal, which started in February 1980 and involved shopkeepers and civil servants, joined later by students and even schoolchildren, continued intermittently throughout the year.[6] The situation was exacerbated when the Soviet troops joined the Afghan forces in an attempt to suppress the unrest, resulting in several hundred casualties. In the process, Karmal's claim to be a mild alternative to despotic Amin lost credibility.

Another challenge to Karmal was the loosening control of Kabul over tribes, ethnic groups, and the countryside. Before the Saur Revolution, President Mohammad Daoud and his royal ancestors had ruled Afghanistan for a century through a complex balance of tribal alliances and linkages, which the Taraki-Amin government did little to rebuild. Instead, in their revolutionary zeal the government and the party pushed hard for their socioeconomic programme aimed at transforming the existing Afghan societal structure.[7] The result was a series of spontaneous local rebellions and alienation of the tribes. Under Karmal, the visibility of Soviet troops in the countryside, the military campaigns, and the disintegration of the DRA army, triggered by Khalq-Parcham hostility, immeasurably accentuated the problem.

Karmal set for himself two immediate objectives: softening the image of the regime and pulling the PDPA together. He took steps to lower the ideological profile of the regime by laying greater emphasis on its commitment to Islam, its respect for the tribal structure, and its willingness to make adjustments in Marxist reforms of the Taraki-Amin period. Symbolically, the original colours of the national flag were restored, and gestures were made to project the regime as pro-Islam.[8] Within the party and the government, the Parcham faction made a bid for consolidating its control.

The Parcham Gains Shaky Ascendancy

Babrak Karmal had some respite only after he was able to dislodge the most prominent Khalqi, Assadullah Sarwari, a deputy prime minister, whom he dispatched as ambassador to Mongolia in June 1980.[9] By the end of 1980 Karmal began the first major steps toward broadening the political base of the regime. He enunciated plans for the setting up of the National Fatherland Front (NFF), in which non-party masses would be represented.[10] A Preparatory High Commission of forty-four members was set up on 27 December 1980 for this purpose. But the commission did not appear to make headway, mainly because of lack of cooperation from the Khalq.

Karmal faced yet another dilemma over Khalqi representation in the cabinet. The Soviets were pressuring him to assure the Khalq a fair share in the government and to appoint a Khalqi prime minister to effect a genuine rapprochement between the two factions. On the eve of the third anniversary of the Saur Revolution, a beleaguered Karmal announced an extraordinary meeting of the Revolutionary Council to nominate a prime minister and to convene the first congress of the NFF.

The council meeting hastily convened on 20 May 1981 was conspicuous for the absence of Khalqi members and tribal chiefs. In the wake of the meeting a fresh crisis seemed to erupt. There were reports of violent fights in the presidential palace. Karmal rushed to Moscow, apparently to secure fresh assurances of Soviet support in his efforts to consolidate his position. Moscow also summoned the main Khalqi contender for power, Assadullah Sarwari, but was unable to effect a compromise between the two factions.

The outcome of the power struggle underscored further gains by Parchamis and their ascendancy over rival Khalqis in the new state power structure. On 11 June 1981, at the Sixth Plenum of the PDPA Central Committee, Karmal announced a series of changes, the most prominent being the appointment of Sultan Ali Kishtmand, a fellow Parchami, as prime minster.[11] Also, the Presidium, the Politburo, and the Council of Ministers were expanded and reorganized with the inclusion of additional Parchami supporters. Assadullah Sarwari was ousted from all party positions and cast away to continue his ambassadorial exile in Mongolia.

Only pliable Khalqi leaders, willing to accept Parchami dominance, found a place in the principal organs of power. The eleven-member Presidium included only two Khalqi leaders, Saleh Mohammad Zeary and Abdur Rashid Arian. The new Politburo, with nine full and two alternate members, included Zeary as an alternate member. The eighteen-member state council included four Khalqis.[12] Thus, Khalqis had been deprived of effective leadership, and prospects for unity and coexistence between the two factions receded further.

The new appointments, however, reflected a concern to create a support base in the army. The Presidium included two vice presidents, both from the army, Major General Abdul Qader and Major General Gul Aqa; the Politburo included Brigadier Aslam Watanyar and Brigadier Mohammed Rafi; and four ministers had army backgrounds.[13] These inclusions also accorded recognition to the army officers who had been involved in the 1978 Saur Revolution.

Quickly following the PDPA plenum, the First Congress of the National Fatherland Front was convened in a ceremony on 14 June 1981 in Kabul. According to official media, the congress was attended by

940 representatives of "the party, social organisations and national and patriotic forces, tribes, [and] nationalities."[14] As a gesture toward the Khalq, Saleh Mohammad Zeary, who was one of the candidates for the prime ministership, was elected chairman of the NFF.[15] The latter half of 1981 saw the reconstitution of the Ministry of Tribes and Nationalities to organize a series of tribal and ethnic-oriented activities, especially local jirgas to broaden political support for the regime. (A jirga is a traditional Afghan tribal assembly for taking decisions.) Simultaneously there were attempts at reorganization of the PDPA at membership level, as well as the creation of paramilitary party cadre.[16] The functions of the latter encompassed a wide variety of assignments from combat missions to law enforcement and social work.

These political moves did not assuage Soviet anxieties over the Khalq-Parcham rift and the narrow base of the government. In fact, no more than a score of individuals kept being reshuffled to fill top positions in the Presidium, the Politburo, the Council of Ministers, and the newly created NFF.

The last quarter of 1981 witnessed another surge of political and diplomatic activity involving Moscow. A number of Parchami and Khalqi leaders were rumoured to have visited Moscow, including Karmal, Prime Minister Kishtmand, and the Khalqi minister for interior, Lieutenant General Syed Mohammed Gulabzoi. There were also reports that in a fresh move to broaden the base of the government by building a coalition of progressive forces, Kabul had invited back prominent Afghans living in exile.[17] Concurrent with these reports was speculation on Soviet disappointment with Karmal and on his imminent removal. However, Moscow would not have undermined Karmal's position immediately after putting its weight behind him, accepting the ascendancy of the Parcham, and virtual elimination of the Khalq from political power.[18]

The National Fatherland Front

The purpose of the NFF was to enlarge the political base of the party and the government by securing the cooperation of various sections of Afghan society. The Preparatory High Commission for the NFF in December 1980 and Babrak Karmal in his opening address on 15 June 1981 hailed the NFF as a mass organization, "the political foundation of which will be the alliance of workers and peasants."[19] Attention was paid to the Islamic and nationalistic ethos of the society. The statute of the NFF declared that the NFF strictly abides by and respects "the sacred religion of Islam and the specific historical, spiritual and national customs and traditions of all nationalities and tribes of the country."[20]

Notwithstanding these exhortations, the NFF was clearly a doctrinaire institution. As declared by the Preparatory High Commission meeting on 10 June 1981, the NFF was designed to create a broad-based vested interest of "national, democratic, anti-feudal and anti-imperialist classes and strata," encompassing "all categories" of society, to advance the cause of the revolution and to effect a systematic but gradual socialization of the country.[21]

The creation of the NFF and other steps to soften the image of the regime did not evoke enthusiastic response from the Afghans within and outside the country. The rancour among Khalqis did not diminish. The Afghans in exile viewed the NFF as yet another instrument in the hands of Afghan communists. Nevertheless, these measures were part of an overall strategy, based on a combination of political and military approaches, to stabilize the regime. Having taken these steps, a ring of confidence was discernible in Karmal's statements. In a BBC interview on 21 February 1982, he claimed that the situation in Afghanistan "[will] normalize within the next six months and, thereafter, Soviet troops will start withdrawing."[22] Again on 29 March 1982 he told the BBC that the Afghanistan armed forces were "the most powerful armed forces in the history of Afghanistan."[23] Away from Kabul, however, the predicament of Afghanistan suggested a long Soviet engagement to consolidate the PDPA.

Policy Themes under Karmal

Following the temporary resolution of the power struggle between the Khalq and the Parcham, albeit on the latter's terms, Babrak Karmal proceeded to stabilize his position. By late 1982 Kabul had become relatively quiet. Soviet troops had settled in garrison towns and bases and controlled major link roads, and their military tactics had improved. The Afghan Resistance was operative but under increasing pressure, especially from Soviet air power. As a result of the war, population in the countryside had thinned out, migrating in large numbers either to the cities or to bordering Pakistan and Iran.

Against this background, the Karmal government adopted policy measures with four major themes: projecting an Islamic image; strengthening counterinsurgency by building the army, the State Information Agency (the Khad),[24] and paramilitary forces of trusted cadres; establishing links and building influence with tribal and ethnic groups; and pursuing closer political and economic ties with the Soviet Union. Politically, efforts were made to generate activity around the party and the NFF, eliciting support, in particular, by holding local jirgas at tribal and village levels. The political steps were accompanied by considerable propaganda and publicity, a forte of Marxist regimes.[25]

While aimed at achieving political reconciliation, these policies remained highly doctrinaire and lacked credibility. The structure of the party, its orientation, and its style thinly disguised its pro-Soviet, Marxist credentials. Karmal himself could not break out of his revolutionary rhetoric of "undefeatable and irreversible" revolution, nor could he reduce his dependence on Soviet troops and Soviet economic support, which, paradoxically, were both his nemesis and the necessary condition for the survival of his regime. Indeed, the Soviet presence and control in Afghan governmental and other institutions had become considerably pronounced.[26] The following discussion will show how the policies designed to modify the image of the regime suffered from contradictions and served to reinforce the perceptions they were designed to ameliorate.

Education and Islamic image. In accordance with the declared priority attached to projecting an Islamic image, the DRA government allocated funds for the construction and repair of mosques. A large subsidy was arranged to enable pilgrims to perform the Haj. Over one thousand ulema (religious scholars) were placed on the government payroll. A department for Islamic affairs was set up in April 1981.[27] The government also tried to organize international Qirat competitions (recitation from the Holy Quran) and gatherings of Islamic scholars. This effort was soon abandoned because, owing to the OIC censure, participation in these events was limited to a few pro-Moscow Islamic countries and Soviet Central Asia, which highlighted the isolation of the regime in the Islamic world. At the same time, however, the preaching of Islam betrayed the ideological bent of the regime inasmuch as it followed the style of the Central Asian republics. Compatibility between the ideals of Islam and the sociopolitical objectives of Marxism was emphasized.

The educational policies revealed an even clearer bias. At Kabul University, efforts to revise the syllabus, begun after the Saur Revolution, continued. Accordingly, many subjects concerned with Islamic studies and "outdated" material considered repugnant to the new ideology were being eliminated, while more subjects on Marxism and scientific socialism were incorporated. Such changes were carried out even at the secondary school level. Kabul University also entered into exchange programme agreements with Moscow University and universities located in Soviet Central Asia.[28] By 1983 many thousands of Afghan students were enrolled in Soviet educational institutions on scholarships, in addition to large numbers sent to East European countries or receiving technical and military training in the Soviet Union. The media controlled by the Afghan Resistance constantly agitated over the perceived attempt by the Soviets to indoctrinate Afghan youth.

Economy. Since the Saur Revolution, the Afghan economy had become heavily dependent on the Soviet Union. The trend was accentuated by the war and the regime's relative isolation. Kabul relied almost entirely on the Soviet Union and the Eastern bloc countries for its imports, including capital goods, consumer items, and food. In exchange, 95 percent of the gas produced by Afghanistan was sold to the Soviet Union, constituting more than half of the total exports from Afghanistan. While the Soviet military commitment in Afghanistan and its economic assistance to Kabul were a net drain on the Soviet economy,[29] some observers believed that Afghanistan's mineral wealth would make a long-term asset for the Soviets.[30] A large number of Soviet experts had arrived in the country since 1978 to survey its mineral reserves. Agreements were signed for putting up a copper enrichment plant at Ainak and for extraction of iron ore at Hajigak.[31]

An extensive effort to link the Afghan economy to that of the Central Asian republics was under way. The Hairatan Friendship Bridge was inaugurated in May 1982, together with a plan for railway construction up to Pul-e-Khumri. An agreement to construct three more bridges on the River Oxus, connecting Badakhshan Province with Uzbekistan, was concluded in August 1983. Border trade on a barter basis was envisaged through four border points. Similarly, projects were agreed to extend transmission lines from Central Asia to Kabul, Kunduz, Mazar-e-Sharif, and Pul-e-Khumri. These activities were suspect in the eyes of many Afghans as part of a Soviet scheme to develop the option of dividing Afghanistan along the Hindu Kush in the event it became difficult to pacify the entire country.[32]

Nationalities and tribal policies. The restructuring of the Ministry of Tribes and Nationalities[33] and the appointment of its head, Suleiman Layeq, as deputy chairman of the NFF, underscored the regime's eagerness to elicit the support of the Afghan tribes and other ethnic groups. Efforts were made to reach individuals of local influence and to allow a "greater measure of autonomy to various ethnic groups." The regime's programme drew a distinction between the Pashtun and non-Pashtun segments of the Afghan population: the status of "nationality" was accorded to non-Pashtun ethnic groups, and the term "tribes and tribals" used for the majority Pashtun element.[34]

In March 1983 Karmal announced his intent to set up local governments for all nationalities to promote their culture, language, literature, and traditions. In the provinces with majority Uzbek, Turkmen, or Baluch populations, local languages were introduced for primary education. Cultural and economic agreements were signed between bordering provinces for exchange of delegations. For the Pashtuns of Afghanistan, on the other hand, the regime pursued a separate policy aimed at political reconciliation through winning over the traditional tribal leadership and thus undercutting the influence of the newly emerged resistance commanders. Local jirgas were held among the Pashtun and Baluch tribes residing along the Pakistani border in the provinces of Kunar, Nangarhar, Paktia, Ghazni, Kabul, Qandahar, Helmand, and Nimruz. An effort was made to institutionalize local jirgas to perform local administrative functions.

Ironically, this policy, especially the distinction between nationalities and tribes, evoked resentment among Pashtuns, who saw in it an erosion of Afghan (Pashtun) nationalism and influence at the hands of Farsi-speaking Parchamis. Elevation of Kishtmand, a non-Pashtun Hazara, to be prime minister and the exclusion of Khalq, a predominantly Pashto-speaking group, deepened such misgivings. What is more, the nationalities programme was reminiscent of how the Soviets had handled their Central Asian nationalities, fragmenting them into linguistic and ethnic republics, autonomous regions, and autonomous areas.

The Army and the Khad. Besides political consolidation of the party and the government, the main preoccupation of the Parchami leaders was the strengthening of the army and the Khad. The inadequacy of the 1981 conscription measures and continuing defections forced the government in January 1984 to introduce new conscription rules applying to all males above eighteen years of age.[35] Subsequently, the conscription requirement was increased from two to three years.

Addressing an army gathering soon after the announcement of the new conscription measure, Babrak Karmal urged the need for greater alertness and effort against counterrevolution and more sacrifice and devotion.[36] At the Thirteenth Plenum of the PDPA Central Committee in March 1984, he criticized defensive tactics and called for intensification of political work in the army.[37] Increased conscription did little to improve the effectiveness of the DRA army, while producing resentment among the urban population, which represented the principal domain of the regime's authority and control. The DRA army did not grow into a reliable fighting force; military operations inside the country invariably involved a substantial complement of Soviet troops and were conducted under active Soviet guidance.

Counterinsurgency activities organized by the Khad scored some significant successes. Operating in close cooperation with the army and the Ministry of Tribes and Nationalities, the Khad had made inroads within the mujahideen ranks and the tribal areas on both sides of the Durand Line. It was known to have organized "fake mujahideen" to terrorize the local population and discredit the Afghan Resistance. Some of the reported defections from the resistance and voluntary surrenders by "counterrevolutionary bands" were perceived as stage managed and attributed to Khad operatives.[38]

Among the Pashtun, the Khad aimed at inciting local tribes against mujahideen who hailed from other regions. To a certain extent, this policy succeeded with the Shinwaris and Afridis in areas bordering Pakistan's North West Frontier Province (NWFP) and with Achakzais in the vicinity of Baluchistan. A twin facet of this policy was negotiating truces and creating zones of peace through deals with local tribesmen, supplying them with arms and money and promising disengagement of the DRA army from the zone. In return, the tribes were asked not to cooperate with the mujahideen. By 1985 Khad activities also extended across the border into Pakistani territory. A measure of their success was the increase in acts of sabotage and the exacerbation of Shia-Sunni tensions in the adjoining Kurram Agency area of Pakistan, often pitting the mujahideen against the local Shia population.[39]

The 1985 Loya Jirga

Virtually all PDPA Central Committee plenum meetings devoted their time to party organization, improvement of party operations and ideological level, and expansion of the PDPA membership. Despite rhetorical claims, the persisting dissension and weak predicament of the party were evident in Babrak Karmal's statements.[40] At the Thirteenth Plenum of the PDPA Central Committee in March 1984, he called for elimination of "selfishness," "obstructionism," "narcissism," and "lack of enthusiasm" from the party.[41] On the eve of the sixth anniversary of the Saur Revolution, in April 1984, Karmal regretted that "no fundamental transformation" had yet taken place in "revolutionary power" because of "lack of ability" and "passivism" in the party.[42] In May 1984 he decried "factionialism" in a PDPA Politburo meeting.[43] Similarly, the NFF, the other pillar of the regime's political base, failed to serve the intended purpose of a "unifying centre" to bring together all social strata. Therefore, Karmal was obliged to think about the more conservative measure of a Loya Jirga to secure legitimacy for his government.[44]

In July 1983, addressing the Twelfth Presidium of the PDPA Central Committee, Karmal pledged to hold a Loya Jirga within the next two years. By the end of 1983 the NFF was mandated to prepare for the convening of the Loya Jirga. Eventually it was a decree from the Presidium of the Revolutionary Council of the DRA, on 13 April 1985, that established a special commission to organize the Loya Jirga, because by then the NFF had become inactive.[45]

The Loya Jirga, hastily convened 23–25 April 1985, did little to enhance the support base of the Karmal government. In its composition, rhetoric, and overwhelming presence of party and government officials, the gathering was reminiscent of the founding conference of the NFF three years earlier. The objectives set out for the Loya Jirga were equally dogmatic in character. These included development of the tradition of jirgas to achieve the goals of the Saur Revolution and involve the people of all nationalities and tribes in the effort; consolidation of Afghan-Soviet friendship; and endorsement of the fundamental lines of the revolutionary tasks of the PDPA and its role as the "directing force of the society and the state."[46]

Karmal's opening address kept close to these themes, while making a standard reference to the PDPA's policy of respect for Islam. Also emphasizing that Soviet troops would stay in Afghanistan as long as the interference of imperialism existed, he called upon Pakistan and Iran to respond to the 14 May 1980 and 24 August 1981 proposals and accept direct talks. "Counterrevolutionary ringleaders" and the monarchical past were denounced routinely.[47] Following the Loya Jirga, Karmal convened a High Jirga of the Tribes in mid-September 1985 to demonstrate support for his government from the tribes.[48]

However, he continued to exclude any role for non-PDPA elements in the government.[49]

The absence of new policy and the apparent nervousness that characterized convening the Loya Jirga through a decree bypassing the laid-down procedure gave rise to fresh speculation regarding Soviet unhappiness with Karmal. Since the Loya Jirga was held immediately after the change of leadership in Moscow, some surmised that the move was prompted by a warning from Gorbachev to Karmal to consolidate his political position. These conjectures notwithstanding, the Loya Jirga clearly betrayed an effort on the part of Karmal to reassure the Soviets about his political credentials.

The indications of Karmal's willingness to broaden the base of his government by accepting political elements outside the party appeared long after the Loya Jirga, although that occasion might have been better suited for such an initiative. In a ten-point thesis presented to an extraordinary and extended session of the Revolutionary Council of the DRA on 9 November 1985, later adopted on 21 November 1985 at the Sixteenth Plenum of the PDPA Central Committee, Karmal called for the broadening of the social base of his government to construct a new just society.[50] Hinting at his intention to enlarge the composition of the state leadership, he declared that "doors are open" to all "Afghan compatriots" living abroad and that the national democratic nature of the revolution provided "the wide participation by representatives of all social groups" in the running of the state.[51]

The late stage at which these initiatives came from Karmal suggested Soviet encouragement of the new approach. According to later reports, the CPSU Central Committee meeting in mid-October 1985 had reviewed the Soviet Afghan policy and this had accounted for the flexibility in Karmal's ten-point thesis. Moscow now wanted the PDPA government to consolidate its position through political compromise to pave the way for the Soviets to disengage militarily from Afghanistan. It was not Karmal, however, but his successor, Mohammad Najibullah, who was to develop major initiatives in this new direction.

In December *Pravda* endorsed Karmal's efforts to start "a broad dialogue" to secure the expansion of the political base of the Kabul government.[52] Perhaps in an effort to grasp the new direction in Gorbachev's domestic policies, the PDPA Politburo decided to encourage the private sector in early January 1986.[53] In an interview in *Asahi Shinbum*, Karmal stated that those who stopped their armed struggle could participate in state organs;[54] but in a clarification given two weeks later at a press conference he ruled out any forgiveness for "counterrevolutionary leaders."[55]

Babrak Karmal was an inveterate ideologue and carried far too many burdens from the past to prove an effective leader in the new phase of Soviet Afghan policy allowing military disengagement at the minimum political cost to Soviet interests in Afghanistan. Even his ten-point thesis devoted a preponderant part to the irreversibility of the Saur Revolution and the leading role of the party, whereas it would have been expedient to stress themes of reconciliation and nationalism.

Soviet misgivings about Karmal's ability to build political support—which may explain the occasional rumours of Soviet unhappiness with him and of his imminent removal—were publicly confirmed only after the Soviet withdrawal. In a revealing interview in March 1989, the commander-in-chief of the Soviet land forces, General Valentine Varennikov, bitterly criticized Karmal, describing him as a "demagogue of the highest class [who] deserved the trust neither of his colleagues, nor of his people, nor our [Soviet] advisers."[56] In the end, Karmal proved incapable of pulling himself away from Marxist dogma and dependence on the Soviet model and advice for his policies. He did not expect Moscow to flinch from its "internationalist duty" and counted on the continued availability of Soviet military, political, and economic support.

By early 1986 Babrak Karmal had lost Soviet backing. In May 1986 Dr. Mohammad Najibullah, the erstwhile Khad chief, replaced Karmal as PDPA chief. Najibullah had proved his credentials as an efficient organizer who recognized the value of a flexible approach. He had shown facility in dealings with tribes, relying, where necessary, on inciting traditional rivalries or on bribery. His knowledge and control of the Khad network was an additional asset. Some observers saw in him the Soviet choice of a strongman who could consolidate the PDPA and negotiate a broad-based government with the resistance from a position of strength.

Najibullah's test came immediately on his taking over as the new PDPA leader in May 1986. Pro-Karmal Parchamis led by Anahita Ratebzad became restive. Kabul witnessed a new wave of protests and bomb blasts attributed to this new pro-Karmal faction. Najibullah, with his control of security forces, was able to arrest this trend and purge the pro-Karmal elements from party positions. After tentative initial steps, he moved in tandem with the Soviets to launch a pro-

gramme of reconciliation formally enunciated on the last day of
1986.

Politics of the Afghan Resistance

The Afghan Resistance was a generic term applied to disparate Afghan groups inside and outside Afghanistan engaged in an essentially
anticommunist armed struggle, a jihad against the PDPA government
and the presence of Soviet troops. Most prominent among those outside Afghanistan were the Peshawar- and Tehran-based parties and
the amorphous émigré leadership of former Afghan elites, settled
mostly in the West. While staunch supporters of the armed struggle,
they maintained a distinct identity and, by and large, supported the
former king, Mohammad Zahir Shah (living in exile in Rome), and
strongly favoured a political solution. By virtue of Pakistan's crucial
role as a participant in the diplomatic process for a settlement, the
politics and positions of the seven Peshawar-based groups, known as
Tanzeemat until their alliance in May 1985, had a significant bearing
on the process. Accordingly, these groups are discussed in the following section.

Pre-1979 Resistance

The overthrow of Daoud's republic and the establishment of the
PDPA government were not viewed initially by the tribal and traditional Afghan leadership in an ideological perspective.[57] However,
the perception started changing fast as the Taraki-Amin government
pressed for socioeconomic reforms. In a largely tribal society used to
minimal control from rulers in Kabul, the push for radical reforms
spawned local revolts involving sub-tribes and local religious leadership. The activities of PDPA zealots and the visibility of Soviet advisers poured oil on the fire. It was these populist revolts, rather than
the alleged outside inspiration, that created opportunities for ideo-
logically motivated Islamist groups to organize and plan large-scale
rebellion.[58]

The Islamic activists belonging to such organizations as *Jamiat-
e-Islami Afghanistan* (Islamic Society of Afghanistan) and *Hizb-e-
Islami* (Islamic Party or Group), however, had all along treated the
PDPA as a communist party and identified the Saur Revolution with
a Marxist orientation. These groups had been locked for years in a

political-ideological struggle with PDPA intellectuals, especially in educational institutions.[59] These Islamist organizations, known for their fundamentalist bearing, had been suppressed during the early days of the republic under Daoud, who tolerated and sought support from the leftist elements to assure Moscow of his pro-Soviet leaning. It was at that time that two activists who later gained prominence as leaders of the Peshawar-based groups, Gulbuddin Hekmatyar and Burhanuddin Rabbani, came to Pakistan and developed links with Islamic fundamentalist groups there and with the Pakistani security agencies, always on the lookout for potentially important Afghan dissidents.[60]

The most significant rebellion prior to the Soviet intervention occurred in March 1979 in Herat. It was engineered by Jamiat militants, including Ismael Khan, then a captain in the Afghanistan Army and secret member of the Jamiat, later a well-known resistance commander. The rebellion, which left several hundred dead, including many Soviet advisers, led to the stiffening of the hard line within the Taraki-Amin government and to increased Soviet involvement in Afghanistan.[61] Uprisings on a lesser scale followed in areas where Jamiat youth were active, especially in Panjshir and northeastern Afghanistan.

The Tajik and Hazara areas had become restive, largely because of their populations' susceptibility to developments in Iran and their historical experience with the Soviet annexation of Central Asia.[62] Jamiat and Hizb elements with links in Pakistan had long been active in the Nuristani and Pashtun areas bordering Pakistan, causing sporadic local revolts in these southern regions. Resistance to the PDPA policies spread gradually; in the latter part of 1979 significant uprisings occurred in Paktia, Kunar, Nangarhar, and several Pashtun areas.[63] Toward the end of 1979 Hafizullah Amin was becoming increasingly isolated, and large parts of the countryside were in a state of revolt.

Significant numbers of Afghan refugees had begun reaching Pakistan by the end of 1978. Included were Afghan ulema and divines, some of whom became politically active. Apart from Jamiat-e-Islami Afghanistan, headed by Rabbani, and the Hizb-e-Islami of Hekmatyar, three new parties were organized by exiled leaders with substantial, albeit loose, religious followings in the Pashtun areas adjacent to Pakistan. Two of them, Sibghatullah Mojadeddi and Pir Sayed Ahmad Gailani (Effendi Agha), headed, respectively, *Jubha-e-Melli-e Nijat Afghanistan* (Afghanistan National Liberation Front) and *Mahaz-e-Melli Islami Afghanistan* (National Islamic Front of Afghanistan, or NIFA). They belonged to established religious families of Afghanistan who had been close to the monarchy. The third leader, Mohammad Nabi Mohammadi, a traditionalist religious leader, or maulavi, led *Harakat-e-Inqilab-e-Islami* (Revolutionary Islamic Movement) and enjoyed considerable influence within the network of local maulavis and the Sufi brotherhood spread across the country. Pir Gailani was initially a co-leader of the Harkat before he set up his separate group.

The three parties, though Islamist in their character, were traditionalists who favoured constitutional monarchy and were regarded as "moderate." The Hizb was divided in 1979 when Yunis Khalis, a maulavi with tribal links in Nangarhar who enjoyed respect among Islamic activists, developed differences with Hekmatyar over initiating revolt against the government, especially in Nangarhar and Paktia.[64]

The alliances formed between these groups from time to time, primarily to satisfy political or diplomatic expediency, were never more than a facade. The first such alliance was worked out in August 1979, when Hizb, Jamiat, Mojadeddi's Jubha, and Harkat announced a merger into the short-lived *Payman-e-Ittehad-e-Islami Afghanistan* (Covenant of Islamic Unity of Afghanistan). On the eve of the Extraordinary Meeting of the Islamic Conference in January 1980, five of the six parties—the exception being Hekmatyar's Hizb-e-Islami—put up a new alliance under the chairmanship of Abdul Rab Rasul Sayyaf.[65] A theologian fluent in Arabic who had studied in Cairo and Saudi Arabia, Sayyaf had been imprisoned in Kabul until late 1979. With the help of funds from Arab countries, he was soon able to establish his own group, *Ittehad-e-Islami B'rai Azadi-e-Afghanistan* (Islamic Union for Liberation of Afghanistan) with splinter elements from other parties. This alliance lasted until the June 1980 Mont Pélerin meeting with the OIC Standing Committee. It was dissolved in January 1981 when the three moderate leaders, in a joint declaration, made serious charges of corruption and abuse of power against Sayyaf.

Apart from individual differences, the Peshawar-based groups are often loosely distinguished in the Western popular political vocabulary as "fundamentalists" and "moderates." These are not coherent groupings—indeed, rivalry between the Jamiat and Hizb, both known for a fundamentalist disposition, has been more acute than their problems with any of the moderate groups. These expressions are relevant only to certain divergences in outlook that separate the four radical Islamist parties from the three traditional Islamist parties among the Peshawar-based groups.

Although no group possessed a well-defined agenda, the more ideological, pan-Islamist, and politicized fundamentalists aimed at the establishment of an orthodox Islamic government in Kabul. Accordingly, their ambitions went beyond the liberation of Afghanistan and they envisioned a protracted jihad. Their party organization and activities tended to transcend ethnic and tribal divisions.

The Islamic motivation of the moderates was rooted in traditional, populist, and less politicized aspects of Islam, coupled with tribal and nationalistic attitudes. They were preoccupied with the idea of restoring the status quo ante and had no reservations about coexisting with a secular monarchy or accommodating secular elements in a future government. This factor more than any other consideration made for their unbridgeable differences with the fundamentalists.

The affiliations of the moderate groups inside Afghanistan showed lack of structure and formal organization, which proved to be a debilitating weakness, especially as the resistance intensified against the Soviets and acquired an increasingly ideological accent. In the new situation, the Jamiat and the Hizb were quick to develop alliances or to attract local religious leaders to wage a more organized jihad.

The Afghan émigré leadership—mostly former Afghan aristocrats, bureaucrats, and intellectuals who became active after the Soviet military intervention—could not reconcile themselves to the idea of fundamentalists taking over the leadership of the Afghan Resistance. They tended to identify the resistance in terms of tribal affiliations and favoured a leading role by the traditional aristocracy in organizing an effective nationalist struggle combining both diplomatic and military aspects. The émigré intellectuals challenged the fundamentalist agenda, arguing that an orthodox Islamic order could not take root in Afghanistan because it would militate against the nationalistic and tribal ethos of Afghanistan and would be totally unacceptable to the Soviet Union and India. Criticizing fundamentalist indifference to the time factor, they pressed for an early solution instead of a protracted struggle.

Pakistan's Acceptance of Peshawar Groups

The six parties formed inside Pakistan prior to the Soviet intervention, with the later addition of Sayyaf's Ittehad-e-Islami, gained recognition from Pakistan in response to pressures to raise the international profile of the Afghan Resistance and work out arrangements for providing military support to resistance commanders inside Afghanistan. Immediately after the Soviet military intervention, it became expedient to involve the Afghan Resistance at the OIC meetings and, later, with the OIC initiative for a negotiated settlement. This diplomatic activity underscored the question of who could speak for the Afghan Resistance.[66]

Pakistan's position on this question was precipitated by the large influx of refugees into Pakistan and, with it, the proliferation of political groupings each vying for and claiming leadership of the Afghan freedom struggle. By the end of 1981 the number of such groups exceeded forty. Resistance activity inside Afghanistan had developed simultaneously, and its coordination and effectiveness had correspondingly begun to depend on organized parties to discharge logistical functions. There were reports of fighting among contending mujahideen groups and interdiction of supplies.

Such rivalries could be contained only by exercising control over supplies and indirectly encouraging the groups to align with a few selected, recognized parties. Pakistan's acceptance of the Tanzeemat for this purpose was due largely to pre-1979 dealings with its respective leaders by Pakistan's Inter-Services Intelligence (ISI) and the Foreign Office.[67] Many observers ascribe this choice, perhaps unduly, to Zia ul Haq's ideological disposition. Although Pakistan did not actively promote union among the approved parties, it desisted from patronizing other groups. The groupings that had proliferated during 1980–81 gradually faded out for want of resources.

Pakistan's backing of the seven parties and the ISI's preference for the fundamentalist parties among them were deeply resented by pro-monarchist groups and the Afghan émigré leadership. These exerted pressure on Pakistan to encourage a more unified Afghan Resistance leadership through the convening of a Loya Jirga in Pakistan. The proposed jirga was essentially intended to endorse ex-king Zahir Shah as leader of the resistance and authorize him to negotiate a political settlement. Others believed in setting up a "government-in-exile" which could effectively represent and direct the Afghan Resistance. Opinion on these issues was divided within the Pakistani policymaking setup. Sentiment remained weighted against the convening of a Loya Jirga, let alone the establishment of a government-in-exile. Pros and cons were constantly debated, but inertia prevailed, as is characteristic of bureaucracies.

These proposals for Loya Jirga aroused several misgivings, including apprehensions against the creation of a PLO-like body in the shape of a government-in-exile in Pakistan. Besides possible long-term problems, such a body would have limited Pakistani options in virtually every sphere, ranging from negotiations to logistical arrangements and dealings with foreign governments. Pakistan, naturally, desired to retain its freedom of manoeuvre. The Pakistan Foreign Office, despite internal differences on this issue, was concerned that such a move could push Pakistan into an open confrontation with the Soviet Union.[68] There was no indication of Soviet inclination to consider the Zahir Shah card; instead the Soviets showed every intention of staying for as long as necessary to help the PDPA government to consolidate power. In addition, the Iranian factor called into question the advisability of placing the monarchists in the driver's seat.

In addition, a pro-Zahir Shah move had to be assessed in terms of its impact on the Afghan Resistance, chiefly built on Islamic sentiment and maintained through commanders linked mostly to the fundamentalists. The ISI, responsible for maintaining liaison with the Afghan Resistance, could not support a move that would alienate the fundamentalists and thereby damage the Afghan armed struggle. For ISI, the three moderate parties that enjoyed Pakistani support assured adequate representation of monarchist tendencies within the Afghan Resistance. Thus, partly for reasons of choice and partly by default, Pakistan continued to deal with the groups that had cast their lot with it before the Soviet entry on the scene.

The claim by the moderates or the monarchists to the leadership of the Afghan Resistance had been weakened by their relative passivity prior to the Soviet miliary intervention. Most of the former bureaucrats and intellectuals had initially reconciled to the Saur Revolution. Only after the Soviet military intervention did they feel disillusioned and find it necessary to leave Afghanistan. Similarly, the revolt among the Durrani tribes inhabiting southwestern Afghanistan, the stronghold of promonarchist elements, took place after December 1979. Meanwhile, the fundamentalists had already established themselves in the vanguard of the Afghan Resistance. Nonetheless, support for Zahir Shah remained a potent influence among the Afghan refugees and sections of the Afghan Resistance. At later stages, the two issues assumed significance in the context of the negotiations.

Early Pro-Zahir Shah Moves and
a Bid for Loya Jirga

Early moves to pave the way for acceptance of Zahir Shah as the leader of the Afghan struggle can be traced to the visit to Pakistan by Dr. Mohammed Yusuf, a former Afghan prime minister, in July 1980. There were reports that under Dr. Yusuf's guidance, Gailani formed an alliance with the Loya Jirga Party of Umer Barakzai, a Jadran leader from Paktia based in Quetta, provincial capital of Baluchistan. Dr. Yusuf's visit ended by deepening suspicions among the other Peshawar groups and producing the first cracks in the five-party alliance, dissolved, in any event, by the end of the year. An important effort to promote the idea of a Loya Jirga to produce a government-in-exile or, alternatively, a united front of the Afghan Resistance came from refugee groups in Quetta toward the end of 1981.

In September 1981 a number of Quetta-based leaders formally approached the Pakistan government. Included were Umer Barakzai; Azizullah Wasifi, a politician from the Daoud era; Dost Mohammed Gorgaig Baluch, leader of *Sazman-e-Jihad-e-Akbar Islami Afghanistan* (Organization of the Great Islamic Jihad of Afghanistan); and Abdul Quddus Khan, a former senator from Qandahar. They proposed to hold a Loya Jirga in Quetta to establish a shura, the Islamic Solidarity Council, under one political leadership, which could serve as a temporary government and announce a "national policy." The move had a distinct Durrani and monarchist orientation and enjoyed the support of prominent Afghan émigrés from Europe. They held out assurances to Pakistan that the ascendancy of moderate and secular elements, which would enhance the chances for negotiating withdrawal of Soviet troops, would reverse the unfortunate history of past Pakistani-Afghan relations.

The idea of Loya Jirga evoked strong reaction from the Peshawar-based fundamentalist parties, who perceived the proposal as an attempt by monarchists to seize the leadership of the Afghan Resistance and set up a rival centre of power in Quetta. According to some Afghans, a tribal bias attributed to the traditional Durrani-Ghilzai rivalry added to the hostility in the reaction from Peshawar (Hekmatyar and Sayyaf are Ghilzai Pashtuns). In order to preempt the

Quetta move, the fundamentalist parties invoked a call made earlier in May 1980 by a congregation of ulema and religious leaders, supporting the formation of a grand alliance of all groups of Afghan mujahideen. That agreement had been signed by all participants, including the leaders of the Peshawar-based parties. This commitment, and the absence of support from the Pakistan government, restrained the moderate Peshawar groups from participation in the Quetta-based activities. They were obviously careful not to tread on Pakistani sensitivities.

The fundamentalist groups moved to form a new alliance, the "Islamic Unity of Afghan Mujahideen," bringing together five groups, excluding Gailani's NIFA and Sayyaf's Ittehad-e-Islami. In November 1981 the new alliance decided to set up its own forty-member shura, or council, to conduct its affairs. These steps effectively prevented the Peshawar moderates from getting drawn into the Quetta initiative. The new alliance, based as it was on expediency, proved short-lived and split up in February 1982, when the three moderate groups announced another alliance, called *Ittehad-e-Islami-Mujahideen-e-Afghanistan* (Islamic Unity of Afghan Mujahideen). The fundamentalist groups responded by setting up a parallel alliance by the same name. This rival alliance included the four fundamentalist parties and three splinter groups from moderate parties.[69] Known respectively as *Sehgan* (the three-party moderate group) and *Haftgan* (the seven-party fundamentalist group), the split persisted for over one year.

Meanwhile, denied Pakistani backing and suspicious of Pakistani manipulation, some of the dissatisfied tribal chiefs from the Qandahar area and some of the groups based in Quetta gathered in late 1981 to hold a Loya Jirga in the area, at Chashmak near Pishin. At a disorganized and confused meeting, the creation of a council was announced to carry out jihad under the leadership of Zahir Shah and his son-in-law, Prince Abdul Wali. This attempt proved abortive and marked the end of the short-lived prominence enjoyed by Quetta in the politics of the Afghan Resistance. The issue of Zahir Shah's role remained dormant until October 1983, when the former king sent his brother-in-law, Humayun Assefy, to visit Pakistan.

The initiative to send Assefy to Pakistan followed Zahir Shah's interview with *Le Monde* in July 1983, indicating his availability to play a role.[70] In the interview, Zahir Shah had clarified that his objective was to unite the Afghans and to negotiate Soviet withdrawal. He expressed reservations about the Geneva negotiations, saying that the question was between the Afghan people, represented by the Afghan Resistance, and the Soviet Union, the foreign occupying force. Urging direct talks between these two "principal parties," the former king argued that the mujahideen could not vanquish a superpower by force of arms, and once the Soviets withdrew "nothing in the world" could turn Afghanistan into a hostile base against the Soviet Union. Afghanistan would be "neutral, nonaligned, and a member of the Islamic world." Zahir Shah's interview, the first of its kind, appeared to have been prompted by the optimistic mood at Geneva and expectations of an impending settlement during the first half of 1983. Most of the time, however, he remained low-key and shy of taking initiatives.

During his visit to Pakistan, Humayun Assefy visited refugee camps and met with various Peshawar groups and their leaders, but not with Hekmatyar and Sayyaf. He also met Pakistan Foreign Office officials. In Assefy's assessment, the former king had the support of the Pashtuns and representatives of the Hazaras and non-Pashtun tribes in the refugee camps. Among the fundamentalist leaders, he claimed that Rabbani and Yunis Khalis were in agreement with the objective of unity as proposed by Zahir Shah, but were not willing to commit themselves openly, and that their attitude would be determined by Pakistan's view of Zahir Shah's initiative. Assefy made a case for the convening of a Jirga Mamassala (similar to a Loya Jirga), an assembly of representatives of the Afghan tribes, refugees, resistance groups, and mujahideen commanders, to endorse a "Charter of Unity" and form a united front under the former king.

No concrete initiative resulted from Assefy's visit. As the prospects of a settlement receded in the second half of 1983, there was simply no incentive to move in a new direction that would require considerable adjustment and that would risk alienating the Afghan mujahideen groups. The question of the role of Zahir Shah, however, did not disappear, but continued to pose choices for Pakistani policymakers that proved too difficult to make. To explore a possible starting point, however, Pakistan considered it essential to weigh the views of the Soviet Union and those of the Afghan Resistance leadership, both in Peshawar and inside Afghanistan. Lack of clear support for Zahir Shah from these two directions in the critical one-year period following late 1986, when Soviet interest in a broad-based government became visible, hamstrung the Pakistan Foreign Office from effectively developing the Zahir Shah option.

Meanwhile, the exiled Afghan elite provided vocal support to the former king, who also enjoyed popularity among the majority of the refugees. Surveys conducted in July 1987 by Sayed Bahuddin Majrooh's Afghan Information Centre in Peshawar claimed that 70 percent of the Afghan refugees favoured the return of the former king.[71] The ISI, which always showed greater sensitivity to fundamentalist concerns and constantly cautioned against steps that could damage the military capabilities of the Afghan Resistance, conceded that a majority of the refugees supported Zahir Shah, but doubted a similar result inside Afghanistan, where, in their view, the conflict had drastically altered the political scene.

The intelligence agency argued that Pakistan should not induct the former king into Afghan Resistance politics, but should instead support having the Peshawar-based parties and the mujahideen work out an agreed system for an elected assembly, or shura, that would decide on a role for the former king. President Zia kept soft-pedaling the issue, while letting his foreign minister, Sahabzada Yaqub Khan, explore its feasibility with the Soviets. The Zahir Shah option figured prominently in diplomatic efforts undertaken during the course of 1987 and merits detailed discussion in that context in chapter six. Ironically, the best chance of developing this option for Pakistan existed prior to 1986, when the Afghan Resistance was still weak and not yet possessed by the euphoria produced by its subsequent military successes.

The Shia Representation

With the advantage of Pakistani backing, the Peshawar-based seven-party Tanzeemat developed a fairly broad range of contacts, including Afghan émigrés in touch with one or another moderate group. Similarly, mujahideen commanders operating in diverse ethnic zones inside Afghanistan found it possible to align themselves with one of the seven parties for logistical arrangements. However, one area in which the parties were severely deficient was that of Shia representation, a shortcoming that could have been remedied in the early years.

As an exclusively Shia counterpart leadership established itself in Iran, Pakistan missed an opportunity to develop leverage with the resistance movement in the Hazarajat region of Afghanistan. Sheikh Asef Mohseni, who led one of the significant Shia resistance groups, *Harakat-e-Islami* (Islamic Movement), became disillusioned by the infighting among pro-Iranian groups in the Hazarajat and approached

Pakistan in 1982, desiring recognition and support as a separate party.[72] He was advised to join one of the seven parties to receive assistance. This was unacceptable to Mohseni, although for a while he aligned himself with Rabbani's Jamiat on an informal basis.

The Hazarajat had become restive even before the Soviet intervention, but by 1981 the internal politics became ensnarled in conflicts involving traditional Shia leadership, elements inspired by the Iranian Revolution, and the Maoist left, which had taken root among non-Pashtun and Shia communities. The first anticommunist uprising was organized in the Hazarajat in spring 1979 by traditional Shia leadership, which subsequently formed the *Shura-e-Inqilab-e-Ittefaq-e-Islami Afghanistan* (Afghanistan Revolutionary Council of Islamic Consensus), led by Sayed Ali Beheshti. Shura controlled most of the Hazarajat until it suffered splits in 1981. Many of its members were drawn into Nasr, a radical group inspired by the Iranian Revolution. Another pro-Iranian group, known as *Sepah-e-Pasdaran* (Army of Protectors), emerged later. Opponents of Nasr charged that the split in Shura was a consequence of infiltration by the Iranian Communist Party, Tudeh. Asef Mohseni's Harkat was aligned to Shura and was active in areas bordering the Hazarajat.

The struggle against the Soviets in the Hazarajat soon degenerated into internal dissension, and the various groups developed an uneasy, introverted political equilibrium that insulated them from the mainstream jihad. The Soviets and Kabul were content to leave the Hazarajat alone as an autonomous region as long as the groups remained passive. Appointment of Kishtmand, a Hazara, as prime minister also helped the regime to neutralize the Hazarajat.

Pakistan's reluctance to extend recognition to Asef Mohseni, even though a mistake in hindsight, should be judged in the light of circumstances at the time the approach was made. The mushrooming growth of political groups in Peshawar and Quetta, including a splinter remnant of the Maoist left, *Shola-e-Javed* (Eternal Flame), created in the minds of the Pakistani authorities a distrust for new parties.[73] The lack of information on political groups inside the Hazarajat, especially when they appeared to be mixed up with radical or left-leaning elements, posed yet another problem. Concern for a possible negative reaction from the Iranian leadership, who treated the Shia community as their constituency, as well as problems faced by Zia ul Haq from Shia opposition to his Islamization programme, could have influenced the Pakistani attitude on the need to include Shia representation among the recognized parties.

With the passage of time, the Shia resistance against the Soviet intervention lost vitality. Iran became far too preoccupied by the Iran-Iraq War, while the Shia parties in Quetta or those in Afghanistan failed to develop formal linkages with Pakistan. Later, Kabul successfully infiltrated the Shia Turi tribes in the Kurram Agency, creating serious problems for the Pakistani authorities as well as for the movement of the mujahideen through their area. Inclusion of a Shia party in the alliance might have preempted this problem.

The Fragile Alliance

Following the manoeuvring and abortive attempts to forge an alliance in late 1981 and early 1982, the Peshawar-based parties remained divided along fundamentalist (Haftgan) and moderate (Sehgan) lines for most of 1983 and 1984. The hostility was so deep that at the August 1982 Islamic Foreign Ministers Conference at Niamey in Niger, the two groups could not agree on a spokesman to deliver a statement on behalf of the Afghan Resistance. They each met with newly appointed Pakistan Foreign Minister Sahabzada Yaqub Khan, separately staking their claims to represent the Afghan mujahideen and each bitterly denouncing the other group. A plea by Yaqub Khan to set aside their differences temporarily to present the Afghan case before the conference made no impact.

International representation of the Afghan Resistance suffered further from this divisiveness. Contrary to the practice followed in 1980–81, there was no delegation representing the resistance in New York at the time of the UNGA debates on Afghanistan in 1982–84. This was partly due to Pakistan's experience with the Afghan expatriate delegates in 1981, who were critical of the circumspect approach adopted at Pakistan's behest in the General Assembly resolution on Afghanistan. The parties remained unrepresented at other international conferences. An exception was the Casablanca Islamic summit in January 1984, where, under Pakistan's pressure, they agreed on Rabbani to deliver a statement on behalf of the resistance.

In addition to ideological divisions, rivalries ran through the Afghan Resistance along ethnic, tribal, and personal lines. Instances of hostility between mujahideen groups loyal to Ahmed Shah Massoud, the celebrated commander from the Panjshir Valley north of Kabul, and those allied to Hekmatyar's Hizb had strained relations between the Hizb and the Jamiat. In 1984, with intercession from Pakistan, the two parties reached an agreement not to attack each other or interdict each other's supplies. Similarly, Yunis Khalis had serious complaints on the management of financial resources received from affluent Persian Gulf countries, especially Saudi Arabia, that were important in keeping the fundamentalist grouping together.

By the end of 1984 it appeared that greater coordination among the mujahideen groups and a united front for the Peshawar-based parties would help in projecting the resistance internationally. That this was desirable was underscored by a combination of several factors. On the military front, pressure created by the Soviet-DRA campaigns, coupled with the need to supply improved weapons to the mujahideen, necessitated better coordination and organization in Peshawar. The military situation had intensified, and the U.S. commitment was substantially enhanced for the year 1985.[74]

Diplomatically, Pakistan did not expect an early end to the Soviet presence or the Afghan conflict and felt the growing need for the involvement of mujahideen representatives in the increasingly demanding effort to maintain international support. This was underscored by the appointment of Felix Ermacora in August 1984 as UN special rapporteur on Afganistan, at the recommendation of the UN Human Rights Commission. Both right-wing lobbies in the West and Afghan expatriates had generated pressure for a high international profile for the Afghan Resistance. The Loya Jirga organized by Babrak Karmal in 1985 provided the immediate impetus to bring the Peshawar groups together in an alliance.

The new seven-party alliance, called the Islamic Unity of Afghan Mujahideen (IUAM) but usually referred to as the Afghan Alliance, was established in May 1985 with direct intercession from Zia ul Haq. Saudi Arabia's Prince Turki reportedly influenced Sayyaf to accept the new arrangement. As the story goes, Zia ul Haq invited the seven leaders to dinner, where he emphasized the need for unity and asked them to forge an alliance. It was agreed that the Afghan Alliance would have a different spokesman every three months, on a rotating basis. Three months later, the Alliance announced a twenty-one-member "supreme council," or "shura," to direct the jihad inside Afghanistan. Committees for medicine, education, food and agriculture, and other matters were formed under the Alliance umbrella to undertake responsibilities among the refugees and in the "liberated" areas. In order to build the Alliance, Pakistani authorities required Afghan refugees to register themselves with any one of the Alliance parties.

The formation of the Afghan Alliance ensured better disbursement of the increased military and economic assistance for the resistance and fulfilled the elementary requirements of international representation. However, the arrangement remained politically flawed and severely handicapped by internal divisions and constant squabbling. For example, after 1985, although it became possible on a regular basis to send Alliance delegations to New York, Geneva, and elsewhere—headed by its current spokesman—efforts to open Alliance offices in various capitals could not succeed. Individual parties continued to operate their independent offices abroad. Similarly, for over one year, the Alliance leadership could not agree on a director for the Afghan Media Centre, a publicity-oriented project that each of the parties considered politically significant. Pakistan, however, took a conscious decision to help the Alliance build an international profile, especially by encouraging official and nonofficial foreign agencies to associate the Alliance with their activities and by discouraging direct liaison with Afghan refugees or the mujahideen.

The increased Alliance activities and the quantity of foreign assistance inevitably intensified dealings between the Alliance and Pakistani authorities, especially the ISI, generating a new source of complaints and dissension among the Alliance parties. The moderates felt that they were being unfavourably treated in comparison with the fundamentalist parties. The ISI argued that its distribution was determined by the performance of individual parties on the ground and by their effectiveness in the jihad. The split within the Alliance and its lack of central control or political consensus proved fatal when the time came to test its capacity to take political initiatives.

Early Pakistani Concerns

Pakistan's attitude toward the Afghan Resistance in its formative years was largely affected by two basic considerations. First, the irregular character of warfare conducted by the resistance was to be sustained, and it needed time to develop. Second, Pakistan's early diplomatic initiatives for a political settlement envisaged an association of the resistance representatives with the diplomatic process. These considerations were not sufficient to interest or motivate Pakistan to forge a united front of the Afghan Resistance.

In the early years the low level of military assistance required only limited coordination to supply field commanders operating in well-defined zones, obviating the need for centralized leadership. The linkages that the seven parties maintained inside Afghanistan were adequate for sustaining guerilla warfare at the desired intensity in Afghanistan. Also, the proposals for unified leadership mostly envisaged a jirga, which the fundamentalists rejected as a ploy for bringing in the former king. The ISI saw little advantage in pursuing the idea.

Pakistan Foreign Office thinking was focused on securing a settlement based on Soviet withdrawal. The establishment of an Afghan Resistance united front, by no means an easy proposition, was sure to provoke Moscow's ire and could hardly be expected to enhance the prospects of a settlement. Within the Foreign Office, however, Sardar Shahnawaz strongly advocated the convening of a Loya Jirga. The idea was discussed in the "Afghan cell," the highest policymaking body on Afghanistan, chaired by Zia ul Haq himself, but it failed to attract support. After 1982, as the UN-sponsored negotiations developed, the need for promoting a united front of the resistance simply lost its urgency and earlier relevance. The UN format excluded the Afghan Resistance as a party to the negotiations.

Pakistan's handling of the Afghan Resistance has been a cause of grievance to the Afghan émigrés, who felt left out. Over the years it has also attracted negative comments from many Western analysts. At the time Pakistan engaged in the Geneva negotiations, Pakistan's support for the seven Peshawar groups was regarded as a calculated policy to prevent a unified resistance organization in order to monopolize diplomacy. A typical comment reflecting Afghan émigré sentiment was cited in Le Monde of 1 December 1982: "It is obvious that the Pakistanis are leaving to the Afghans the sole responsibility of fighting Soviet occupation forces, keeping to themselves the responsibility of diplomacy."[75] In later years, when prospects of Soviet withdrawal became visible, Pakistan was increasingly blamed for patronizing militant fundamentalist groups to advance its own political and ideological agenda.[76] Military successes in 1986 and afterwards encouraged a thinking among some Pakistani military circles that a victory of the jihad and the establishment of an Islamic government in Afghanistan would provide strategic depth to Pakistan.

Pakistan's military support of the Afghan Resistance was carefully calibrated; it neither permitted other countries to develop independent military relations with the resistance nor did it press for equipping the resistance on an ambitious scale that would thereby raise the temperature.[77] Zia ul Haq believed in keeping the pot boiling, but not letting it spill over. Pakistan demonstrated considerable firmness in keeping control of the arms supplies. At the same time, the myth that Pakistan was not a conduit of arms for the Afghan Resistance had to be maintained, at least in the early years, for diplomatic expediency, especially in the international fora.

Several considerations were responsible for Pakistan's cautious approach in assisting the Afghan Resistance. Pakistan was all along concerned over possible Soviet reprisals and the two-front situation it faced on its eastern and western borders. Concrete and reassuring American response to Pakistan's requirements had taken one and a half years to take shape. Another two years lapsed before the military equipment started reaching Pakistan, especially the much needed squadrons of F-16s, committed along with the 1981 military sales credit and economic assistance package. Until then, the country risked a high degree of military vulnerability.

Another important factor was the universally prevalent perception that by itself the Afghan Resistance could not bring about the reversal of the Soviet advance. On all accounts, at least in the early years, the Soviet military position appeared to be invincible. The resistance was primarily expected to keep military pressure on the Soviets and to thwart Soviet efforts to stabilize the Karmal regime. Combined political and military pressure appeared to stand the best chance of compelling the Soviets to review their Afghan policy.[78]

The War

Contrary to Soviet calculations, the introduction of Soviet troops and their campaigns across Afghanistan intensified rebellion against the PDPA government and provided the Afghan Resistance a visible and unquestionably legitimate target. The deeply religious milieu of Afghan society and its proud tribal espousal of freedom motivated and sustained the armed struggle, which spread with remarkable spontaneity and fervour and, despite setbacks and internal discords, kept the Soviet troops engaged for nearly a decade.

With advance preparations, the Soviet troops moved swiftly following the massive airlift into Kabul and installation of the Karmal government in the fateful closing days of 1979.[79] Within a few weeks they were engaged in Kunar, Nuristan, and Badakhshan. By the end of January 1980 Soviet forces with tanks and heavy equipment were deployed in southwestern and eastern parts of Afghanistan. In February they went into action in Nangarhar and Paktika provinces.[80] This movement appeared to be aimed at securing supply routes leading into Afghanistan from the Soviet Central Asian republics and at sealing Afghanistan's border with Pakistan. By midsummer Soviet troops were engaged in widespread operations in several provinces, with deployments in all major towns.[81]

The heavy armour and equipment brought in by the Soviets were calculated to overwhelm the population. They were also to be used in possible engagements against defecting Afghan regiments or outside military forces. Similarly, the Soviet military resorted to excessive use of firepower to terrorize the population into submission and crush the rebels. There were frequent reports of severe reprisals against villages known to have harboured the mujahideen. When antigovernment protests swept Kabul, Soviet soldiers appeared on the streets in support of the government, and Soviet planes and helicopter gunships reportedly buzzed overhead in a display of strength.[82] Later, in July, when the mujahideen attacked a Soviet military camp north of Kabul, a large force of tanks along with artillery, jet fighters, and helicopter gunships pounded nearby hills for three days, according to eyewitnesses.[83]

These tactics could not subdue the ground swell of resistance, which was widespread and without a centre. It developed as a classical guerilla resistance, finding support and sustenance from the countryside. In fact, the Soviet heavy equipment became a liability; it presented an easily visible target and was ineffective against lightly armed rebels operating in Afghanistan's largely mountainous terrain. Accordingly, after large-scale military offensives in 1980 and 1981, the Soviets were compelled to change tactics. Part of the heavy armour was withdrawn and replaced by more appropriate infantry units. From 1982 onward, the Soviets appeared to settle down for a long haul, mounting less ambitious campaigns and restricting themselves to the defense of military bases, military installations, key cities, link roads, and communication lines. They adopted an "enclave strategy" rather than across-the-board countrywide pacification campaigns.[84] An effort was also undertaken to reorganize the Afghan army, which had dwindled down to nearly 40,000 from its normal strength of 90,000 in past years.[85]

The massive exodus of Afghan refugees into Pakistan and Iran, caused by war and devastation of the countryside, proved to be of critical importance in the growth and development of the Afghan Resistance, nullifying the temporary reprieve that the Soviet forces might have gained as a result of a comparatively "empty" country-side. The refugee population across a porous border provided the resistance with both a safe haven and a dependable recruitment pool. It allowed Pakistan and other countries an enormous advantage in equipping and influencing the organization of the Afghan Resistance. Peshawar assumed unique importance as a focal point of the Afghan struggle against the Soviets.

The early revolts and resistance activity within the Afghan populace relied mainly on the antiquated weapons traditionally possessed by Afghan adults, on arms brought in by defecting soldiers, and on those obtained through interdicting supplies and stores. Outside assistance, channeled in a controlled fashion by Pakistan, remained modest in the early years. It consisted largely of light arms supplied by China or purchased from Egyptian stores with Saudi and U.S. funds.[86] The covert U.S. programme, already set in motion, was restricted in scale, despite U.S. willingness to increase its commitment, indicated immediately after Ronald Reagan moved into the White House.[87] Gradually, Kalashnikovs replaced old Lee Enfield rifles. By 1982 mujahideen started receiving certain categories of shoulder-carried heavy equipment, such as bazookas and heavy machine guns. These arms were effective against heavy armour and for interdicting movement of goods and Soviet troops, but made little impact against Soviet aerial power.

During 1982–83 the Soviet forces engaged selectively in intensified counterinsurgency operations to cripple the resistance. The objective was to wear down the resistance and finish it through attrition in a protracted campaign. Repeated offensives against Panjshir Valley, which commanded the Salang link to Kabul, had resulted in a Soviet advance into the valley.[88] The Soviets had also undertaken military operations, including laying down land mines, in provinces bordering Pakistan, especially Paktia, Nangarhar, and Qandahar,[89] to cut off weapon supplies to the mujahideen, which had become more systematic and regular.

By 1983 Afghanistan was divided into seven military districts, each headed by a Soviet general with an adequate number of Mi-24 helicopter gunships. The Soviets had improved air bases at Herat, Shindand, Farah, Qandahar, Kabul, Bagram, and Jalalabad. Most of the troops were rotated on a six-monthly basis, and their overall number was estimated around 120,000. Following the experience of the early years, air force strength had been increased. The main lesson the Soviets had learned was that ground operations led to heavy casualties. Their tactics were now based on air power, firepower, and the wide use of helicopter gunships. Coordinated deployment of specially trained forces, called Spetsnaz, reported toward the end of 1984, aimed to achieve maximum results in counterinsurgency operations and in protecting communications and supply links.[90] Whenever possible, air transport replaced road convoys, which remained vulnerable to mujahideen attacks even with the improved protection.

The principal aim of Soviet military operations had been to secure key areas in the hope that areas of marginal importance would eventually fall. They appeared to have ceded the countryside to the mujahideen, but there, too, they aimed at narrowing the support base for the insurgency.[91] The policy of massive reprisals against towns and villages harbouring mujahideen was aimed at uprooting the local population, graphically described as "migratory genocide," hurting the mujahideen and curtailing their mobility.[92] This situation prompted the U.S. Congress in 1985 to approve a cross-border humanitarian assistance programme.[93] In addition to helping the Afghans in the mujahideen-controlled areas, the programme was aimed at preventing new flows of refugees and further depletion of local populations.

Throughout 1983 and 1984 repeated military offensives were carried out in the Herat, Panjshir, Mazar-e-Sharif, Qandahar, Shomali (north of Kabul), Urgun, and Baghlan areas.[94] Operations in Shomali and Panjshir were especially significant for strategic reasons, to prevent the mujahideen from expanding the war to Kabul and to keep the Salang tunnel open. Nonetheless, the mujahideen continued to operate around Kabul and Soviet control of the Salang road remained precarious.

Panjshir had been an important front. In 1983, following a determined offensive, the Soviets made some advance in the valley, forcing Ahmed Shah Massoud's forces to retreat farther north to the Rukha Valley. A cease-fire was then arranged between the Soviet and Massoud forces, ostensibly to allow the local population to cultivate the next harvest.[95] Taking advantage of the cease-fire, the Soviets built and reinforced fortifications in the valley. The truce was broken by a new offensive the following summer with the introduction of 15,000 to 20,000 Soviet and DRA troops and the use of high-altitude saturation bombing for the first time, causing extensive damage to villages and crops. In late April 1984 Kabul sources claimed that Panjshir was now "completely secure" from mujahideen control and that Ahmed Shah Massoud had been forced to abandon the valley and evacuate the valley population.[96] It was not until late summer that the mujahideen regrouped and launched a counterattack.[97] The battle for Panjshir continued well into 1986. An important consequence of the failed truce was that it discredited the Soviet and Kabul offers of cease-fire.

Concentrated operations against selected cities and areas, heavy aerial bombardment, and the combination of Mi-24 helicopter gunships and Spetsnaz troops inflicted heavy punishment on civilians and mujahideen alike. In a June 1984 military offensive against Herat, more than one thousand civilians were killed by heavy shelling.[98] Similarly, in retaliatory air strikes carried out a month later on the outskirts of Qandahar, two hundred civilians were killed.[99] In Soviet air and ground assaults in the Shomali region in August 1984, nearly three hundred civilians died in the villages of Istalif, Guldara, and Shakardara.[100] Later during the same month, three hundred mujahideen were reportedly killed in the northeastern half of Panjshir in a Soviet effort to block mujahideen reentry into the valley.[101] Reports of the use of chemical weapons, firebombs, and extensive mining activity by the Soviet forces as part of a "scorched earth policy" appeared amidst the 1984 military operations.[102] Effects of the war were compounded by drought conditions in many parts of Afghanistan.[103]

Having secured limited successes in Panjshir and Shomali, the pattern of heavy aerial bombardment followed by ground assault was repeated during the latter part of 1984 in new campaigns in Logar, Kunar, Ghazni, Paktia, and Paktika provinces. The same period witnessed a sharp escalation in air and ground violations of Pakistani territory, exemplified by the successive attacks for three days on Teri Mangal on the eve of the Geneva round of talks scheduled in August 1984.[104] The cumulative effect of these operations produced a crescendo of demands by the mujahideen commanders and by conservative pro-mujahideen lobbies in Pakistan and the West for the supply of better weaponry to the resistance, especially to counter Soviet-Kabul air power.[105]

Despite its vulnerability to Soviet air power, the Afghan Resistance had gained in experience and demonstrated considerable staying power. Their cooperation in the field in mounting ambushes and attacks had increased, and they had shown their ability to extend the war into Kabul and other major cities of Afghanistan, particularly Herat and Qandahar. The mujahideen had also learned to use comparatively sophisticated equipment effectively and had inflicted significant damage on the Soviet-DRA forces. They had repeatedly overrun government outposts in provinces and were able to lay siege to several garrison towns.

By 1984 it became clear that the resistance had come of age. It possessed the will to fight, and it enjoyed popular support. But these advantages were partly negated by poor equipment, limiting its military capability. Accordingly, in a measured response, Pakistan decided to allow the supply of improved weapons to the mujahideen and, simultaneously, approached the United States to raise its commitment and respond to new military escalation in Afghanistan.

The five years of the Afghan War had swung the mood in the United States decisively in favour of a strong U.S. commitment to help the Afghan Resistance. The unwritten Reagan Doctrine to support anticommunist guerilla movements and "roll back" Soviet advances of the 1970s had become fully operative. In this scheme, Afghanistan occupied the central place. Powerful bipartisan political lobbies had developed on Capitol Hill, spearheaded by the Afghan Task Force—formed in 1982 under the chairmanship of Senator Paul Tsongas. On his retirement in 1984, the chairmanship of the task force went to Gordon J. Humphrey, a Republican senator from New Hampshire. Congressman Charles Wilson was another ardent protagonist of the mujahideen cause, who visited Pakistan on several occasions. His contribution to enhancing the U.S. commitment to the mujahideen, as well as to Pakistan, was highly praised by Zia ul Haq.

At the official level in Islamabad, the liaison between the U.S. Central Intelligence Agency (CIA) and the ISI had improved for the logistical handling of assistance to the resistance. In Washington better coordination had developed between the various U.S. government agencies concerned, namely the State Department, the Pentagon, and the CIA. Following Pakistan's signal of its readiness to raise the temperature, U.S. assistance registered a quantum jump from 1984 onward, when it reportedly crossed the $100 million mark. The allocation of $280 million announced in November 1984 approached the total assistance provided by the United States over the entire 1980–84 period.[106] It was increased to $470 million in 1986 and $630 million in 1987.[107] From 1984 on, Chinese assistance and the flow of Saudi funds to the resistance also stabilized at a fairly substantial scale.[108]

Apart from increased assistance, the single most important step that changed the fortunes of the resistance was the supply of shoulder-borne ground-to-air Stinger missiles. This step was decided in

April 1986, but the ground had been prepared by a different, though related, development. At Pakistan's request, prompted by escalation in violations of its air space and territory, President Reagan in July 1985 approved delivery to Pakistan of Sidewinder air-to-air missiles and basic Stinger ground-to-air missiles.[109] After that, the question of introducing the weapons in Afghanistan was constantly debated in Islamabad and Washington.

During 1985 the Soviet use of aerial power and their military offensives against mujahideen strongholds had continued unabated. Indeed, Soviet military activity appeared to have intensified following the advent of Gorbachev and the appointment of General Mikhail Zaitsev as the new commander of the Soviet forces in Afghanistan. To counter the Soviet-DRA advantage in air power, Stingers were finally introduced in Afghanistan in the second half of 1986.[110] This was a difficult decision for Pakistan and also posed problems for the United States. The introduction of ground-to-air missiles in early 1985 and Stingers late in 1986 had drawn strong private and public protests from Moscow and Kabul.[111] For Pakistan, the implicit danger of escalation revived the fear that the Soviets would resort to hot pursuit and reprisals in the shape of air raids against Pakistani cities or key installations. Nonetheless, neither the powerful pro-resistance forces in Pakistan and the United States nor Zia ul Haq could be expected to acquiesce passively in the systematic decimation of the potentially vigorous resistance by the indiscriminate use of Soviet air power.

The Pakistani military had carefully calculated the military risk of escalation. For nearly six years, despite their failure to wipe out the resistance and their considerable losses in men and matériel, the Soviets had refrained from enhancing their military strength in Afghanistan. Without substantially increasing the number of their troops, the Soviets could not physically extend the conflict to Pakistan. Moreover, internationally, the Soviets were already on the defensive because of their actions in Afghanistan. A major military incursion into Pakistan would have provoked a much stronger international reaction and militated against the new direction of Soviet policies under Gorbachev.

With the network of logistical supplies and coordination developed through the seven-party alliance, the Afghan Resistance became a highly efficient guerilla force by 1986. From late 1986 on, Stingers partly neutralized Soviet-DRA aerial offensives. According to ISI estimates, during the summer of 1987 the mujahideen hit an average of 1.5 aircraft of varied description every day. The mujahideen were also able to launch some of the biggest assaults on Kabul and other major cities during this period. A measure of the confidence gained by the mujahideen was reflected in the audacious strikes they carried out in March–April 1987 across the Oxus River into the Soviet town of Pyandzh, which provoked severe reprisals from the Soviets in the Emam Sahib area in northern Kunduz.[112] By the end of 1987 the military situation had deteriorated for Kabul to the extent that Dr. Najibullah admitted to a daily *Muslim* correspondent that 80 percent of the countryside and 40 percent of towns were outside the control of his government.[113]

During 1986 and 1987 the Soviet and DRA forces undertook major efforts to interdict supply routes and relieve towns and military garrisons from the tightening guerilla siege. They also carried out major operations to capture or destroy large arms caches built by the mujahideen inside Afghanistan in anticipation of a possible settlement and consequent drying up of arms supplies. Some of their successful operations in Paktia and Qandahar and the capture of the mujahideen base in Jawar in April 1986 demonstrated the capability of the Soviet-DRA forces to launch concerted strikes against any point inside Afghanistan. The Khost operation in late 1987 also demonstrated Kabul's determined effort to deny the Afghan Resistance secure control of a major town or base for any length of time, fearing that this would allow the resistance to set up a parallel government inside Afghanistan. Inability of the mujahideen to capture and hold towns or to force major surrenders through siege underscored their weakness in conducting set-piece battles and their failure to develop the necessary organization for that purpose.

Western Media Coverage

As compared to 1980, the media coverage of Afghanistan dropped significantly in the following year, yet the Afghan story continued to be featured in international media and helped sustain moral pressure on the Soviets to withdraw. Lack of access to the theatre of war by the Western media and their distaste for partisan versions of the war given out by the various Afghan Resistance groups or by Western and Pakistani sources largely accounted for the early decline. Both the reaction of horror to the Soviet action and interest in international deliberations and diplomatic activity on Afghanistan lost their early intensity.

As the resistance groups became better organized, it became possible for Western correspondents to visit inside Afghanistan. Simultaneously, some nongovernmental humanitarian organizations, such as Médecins sans Frontières, were able to establish their networks in areas controlled by the mujahideen. Accounts from these sources served to refocus international media attention on the conduct and brutality of the war and the tragedy it caused the Afghan people.[114] Eyewitness accounts of military campaigns and of mujahideen operations and control of the countryside imparted a degree of credibility to official briefings, which started receiving attention.[115] Mobilization of conservative support for the Afghan Resistance also helped stimulate a steady coverage of the war. Indeed, during 1984, media interest was once again on the upswing and contributed significantly to support for the mujahideen clamour for better weapons in the face of Soviet military pressure.

Lack of access to the conflict areas inside Afghanistan turned Peshawar into a focal point for the international media's coverage of the Afghan War. This introduced an anomaly, inasmuch as the media coverage became overly preoccupied with the activities on the periphery, such as Pakistani control over supplies, discord among the seven Peshawar-based parties, instances of corruption or pilferage from relief assistance, and a negative view conditioned by local problems. Such reports often caused complications for Pakistani diplomacy. In international fora, the DRA representatives invariably cited the Western press to substantiate Pakistan's complicity in the internal situation of Afghanistan.

Other notable themes developed between 1982 and 1984 underscored the weak predicament of the Afghan Resistance. An impression gained strength that time was not on the side of the Afghan Resistance, that the Soviets had succeeded in transforming the conflict into an Afghan-versus-Afghan struggle, and that it was futile to help the fractious Afghan Resistance because it would only prolong the Afghan tragedy.[116] Left-liberal elements subtly but systematically exploited these themes to accuse the United States and Pakistan of fighting to the last Afghan. The opposition in Pakistan criticized Zia ul Haq for pursuing an Afghan policy at the behest of the United States.[117] Although the Pakistan Foreign Office showed sensitivity to this criticism, it did not appear to upset Zia ul Haq, whose commitment to supporting the Afghan Resistance needed little outside impetus.

4

The Geneva Negotiations, 1982–86

The first round of indirect talks between Afghanistan and Pakistan in June 1982 through the United Nations intermediary could not accomplish more than a sketchy annotated agenda, and for the most part grappled with complicated issues of legitimacy, recognition, and *locus standi* (legal standing). The Afghans focused on direct talks, a bilateral agreement with Pakistan on noninterference, and international guarantees limited to noninterference. For them, withdrawal was outside the purview of the UN negotiations. For the Pakistani negotiators, their nonrecognition of the Kabul government—formally tied to the OIC position—ruled out the signing of a bilateral agreement. Pakistan desired a balanced, comprehensive settlement that provided for irreversible withdrawal within a short time frame and guarantees to cover the entire settlement. It insisted on UN consultations with "Afghan refugees"—a euphemism for the Peshawar-based Afghan groups—and remained preoccupied with the internal aspect of the Afghan conflict.

The external environment was not conducive to progress in the negotiations either. By all indications the Soviets had become deeply embroiled in Afghanistan. Washington showed little enthusiasm for negotiations, while bipartisan political lobbies had become active in support of the Afghan mujahideen.

The brief interregnum under Brezhnev's successor, Yuri Andropov, who for the first time admitted the pressures exerted on the Soviet Union by the Afghan conflict, raised hopes in early 1983 that an Afghan settlement might be possible. The promising signs quickened the pace of the negotiations. At the April 1983 Geneva round, Diego Cordovez first pushed for a comprehensive draft settlement, but, confronted with a variety of irreconcilable issues, later attempted to work out an understanding linking Pakistan's acceptance of provisions on noninterference to a Soviet offer of a short time frame. Despite uneven progress on the draft texts and a number of outstanding substantive and political issues germane to a negotiated settlement, the April 1983 round was suspended on an optimistic note, to be resumed in late June 1983.

The resumed Geneva round proved an anticlimax to the stirred-up expectations, which in any event were premature if not unwarranted. A preview of the later impasse was provided by Sahabzada Yaqub Khan's meeting with Gromyko in Moscow on the eve of the resumed talks. The Soviet foreign minister reiterated familiar demands and showed little evidence of Soviet movement toward the concept of a negotiated settlement that Yaqub Khan thought had been developed at Geneva. The apparent regression in the Soviet position might have resulted from the reported stroke suffered by Andropov in early June. Nonetheless, even had he remained active, it would have taken more than one Geneva round to reach a settlement, as events later proved following the end of Moscow's crisis of aging leadership and the rise of Mikhail Gorbachev to power in March 1985.

Until then the deteriorated international climate conditioned the negotiating process, although there was some notable progress on draft texts and a softening of the Pakistani position on signing a bilateral agreement with Kabul. The extent of the extraordinary changes in Soviet policies under Gorbachev was not immediately visible, yet his overtures to the West and a fresh outlook at home reactivated negotiations on Afghanistan. The negotiations progressed and scored a major success in eliciting U.S.-Soviet agreement on the text of guarantees. In late 1985, however, the process stalled on Afghan demands for direct talks to tackle the several remaining issues, especially the time frame for withdrawal. This politically loaded issue was resolved only after political changes in Kabul that appeared to have been encouraged by Moscow.

As it did in other sectors of policy, the new Soviet leadership seemed to have reviewed Moscow's involvement in Afghanistan by late 1985. Such a review was reflected in Gorbachev's report to the Soviet Communist Party Congress in February 1986. Meanwhile, Moscow encouraged the Kabul leadership to broaden its political base. A clear lead in this direction came, once again, from Gorbachev, in his Vladivostok statement in July 1986. By then, the doctrinaire Parchami leader, Babrak Karmal, had been replaced by Najibullah.

At Geneva, the negotiations came to a head on the time-frame issue in July 1986, but the Soviets seemed in no hurry to settle this issue, which was necessary to wrapping up the settlement. Their position unraveled later in the year when Moscow sought internal political reconciliation in Afghanistan before undertaking withdrawal, in practical terms linking the two issues. At the close of 1986, for domestic and external reasons, Moscow had decided to terminate its military engagement, but it did not wish to do so without giving the PDPA regime a chance to shore up its political position. Meanwhile, the military situation had changed in favour of the Afghan Resistance, carrying profound implications for the negotiating process and the new diplomatic efforts to address the internal dimension of the Afghan conflict.

Concerns Preceding Geneva

Unlike the OIC and EC initiatives, which tended to address both the external and internal aspects of the Afghan situation, the Geneva negotiations segregated and compartmentalized the two issues. Until the final phase, the negotiations focused only on the external aspects—withdrawal, noninterference, guarantees, and refugees. The internal aspect of political reconciliation within Afghanistan was a taboo for Moscow and Kabul. Their approach conformed to the 14 May 1980 and 24 August 1981 proposals; and they viewed the Geneva negotiations as a vehicle to bring about direct talks—to engage Pakistan in a discussion of "guarantees of noninterference" and normalization of relations. Babrak Karmal reaffirmed this objective at a press conference in Moscow in December 1982: "We consider this step (U.N. mediation) as a good beginning. We hope that this process of indirect dialogue will ultimately lead to direct talks. . . . We have patience and are in no hurry."[1]

Pakistan approached the Geneva negotiations taking withdrawal to be the key to a settlement, but without losing sight of the internal aspect of the problem. The concession implicit in its agreement to drop self-determination from the agenda was regarded by Pakistan as essentially formalistic. It believed that Moscow would not discuss withdrawal without simultaneously showing willingness to accept replacement of Karmal by a broad-based government of national reconciliation, and assumed that progress in the negotiations would elicit moves from Moscow to address and resolve the internal aspect.

Politically, Pakistan came under criticism for accepting the Geneva negotiations without the participation of the mujahideen, who were popularly seen as the real party in the Afghan conflict. For that reason, Pakistan kept insisting on consultations with the refugees as a means to ensure that the mujahideen were associated with the Geneva negotiations.

Geneva I, 16–24 June 1982

At the first round of Geneva negotiations, held 16–24 June 1982 and known as Geneva I, the challenge for Diego Cordovez was to develop the structure for a settlement from the agreed agenda. He also tried to resolve the procedural issue of the format of the negotiations. To avoid confusion, this issue will be referred to herein as the negotiating procedure, to distinguish it from the separate issue of the format of the negotiated settlement.

Cordovez had to tread carefully between the seemingly irreconcilable positions of Islamabad and Kabul, but he was not pressed for time. No one expected quick results. In practical terms, Cordovez adopted a method of holding discussions in formal and informal sessions and of presenting draft texts to the two interlocutors himself. Formal sessions largely focused on the agenda-related questions, the informal sessions on initial soundings and off-the-record exchange of views. From these discussions, Cordovez intended to draw material, to fill in what he called "pigeonholes" under each separate item, that could eventually provide texts for a settlement with an agreed format and structure. Also, he introduced a "Note for the Record" at the end of each Geneva round to tie down understandings and agreements on the progress achieved and the course of action for the next session. Cordovez's idea of doing the drafting himself was readily agreed by Yaqub Khan, who was never comfortable with technical drafting.

Positions and Perceptions Relevant to the Agenda

The first Geneva round discussions helped in expanding the annotations already agreed under the four agenda items, but stopped short of evolving a structure and text of a settlement. The dialectics and development of ideas during discussions on the four agenda items are summed up below.

Interrelationships and the issue of withdrawal. For Pakistan, the return of refugees was linked to Soviet withdrawal, while the Afghan position linked withdrawal to stoppage of outside (non-Soviet) interference. This line of argument could obviously yield no results. Accordingly, the interrelationships between the various elements needed to be defined in a neutral manner and chiefly in terms of time frames and dates. Pakistan absolutely insisted on the inclusion of the time frame for withdrawal and its modalities in the text of the comprehensive settlement. These could not be dependent on Moscow and Kabul alone. Under modalities, Pakistan tentatively suggested the idea of phasing the withdrawal by territorial sectors with a view to facilitating refugee return and a commitment that the troops would not reenter following withdrawal. Also, according to Pakistan, "foreign troops" had to be interpreted in a generic sense to apply equally to Soviet military advisers.

The Afghan side, on the other hand, maintained the withdrawal to be an exclusively bilateral matter with Moscow. Cordovez interpreted this position to suggest that it was only in a military sense that the Afghans regarded the decision for withdrawal to lie within a bilateral jurisdiction. He felt that the decision could be reflected within an appropriately devised format for the comprehensive settlement. This raised the issue of format.

Noninterference. Pakistan accepted commitment to the principle of noninterference and such assurances as would not imply that interference was taking place. By the same token, Pakistan rejected any linkage between noninterference and withdrawal. The assurances, in Pakistani perception, had a future orientation and, by virtue of reciprocity, would apply in equal measure to the Afghans' raising in future the Pashtunistan issue and to the issue of harbouring dissidents, which had been a source of constant friction in Pakistani-Afghan relations in the past. The Pakistani side also formally proposed that the assurances should provide for "inviolability of frontiers," a euphemism for implicit recognition of the Durand Line by Afghanistan. It was argued that a settlement laying down principles and assurances of noninterference would mean little without a reference to the international border.

For the Afghan side, interference was the starting point of the entire issue and cessation of interference the key to normalization of relations, as well as to a decision on withdrawal. Again and again, Afghan Foreign Minister Shah Mohammad Dost dwelt at length on alleged instances of Pakistani-sponsored activities to overthrow the

Kabul regime with the complicity of the United States, China, and others. He demanded that the item on noninterference should be taken up first for consideration and proposed specific measures for acceptance by the Pakistani side. The list of measures included closure of "camps and bases," restrictions on freedom of movement of mujahideen leaders, closure of their offices, depriving Afghans of "the right of sanctuary," termination of the supply of arms, closing down of "radio transmitters," and preventing foreign journalists from accompanying the mujahideen into Afghanistan. As for inviolability of frontiers, the Afghans stated that the issue was not germane to the negotiation, but that they were ready to take up the dispute over the Durand Line after a settlement had been reached at Geneva. For Afghans, normalization of relations could proceed without "demarcation of the border."

International guarantees. At the first Geneva round the concept of guarantees remained ambiguous, almost undefined. The Pakistani side wanted to know what the Afghans had in mind. Several questions were raised, for example, the identification of guarantors and modality of guarantees. Should the guarantees include the five permanent members of the Security Council? Should they be in the form of declarations or a resolution of the Security Council? What should be the scope, content, and timing of guarantees? The Afghan side limited the guarantees to third party commitment to noninterference. The Pakistani side suggested the idea of an international conference, as outlined in Lord Carrington's proposals, as a modality for working out guarantees. Cordovez, however, favoured an approach under the UN umbrella.

Return of refugees. The position of the Pakistani side was based on discussions that had already taken place during the shuttle preceding the Geneva round. It emphasized (a) the conditions to be offered by Kabul for voluntary return of refugees;[2] (b) practical plans for repatriation of the refugees so that proper arrangements existed on the other side on their return; and (c) UN-sponsored consultations with the refugees, which in Pakistan's view provided an opening for the involvement of the "refugee" (Tanzeemat) leadership with the negotiating process. Pakistan perceived the requirement of consultation with the refugee leadership as a moral requirement and a political necessity. The question of consultations also implied a linkage between the time frame for withdrawal and the voluntary return of refugees. The assumption was that without the provision of an acceptable time frame for withdrawal, the refugees were unlikely to agree to any conditions for return. Similarly, it was necessary that the consultations should appear credible to the refugees and that the refugees be assured that the conditions offered would be met. This criterion had to be satisfied by the modality of consultations. The UNHCR was acceptable at the initial stage, but, later on, Pakistan stressed a direct involvement of the UN mediator.

The Afghans first took the line that the bulk of the refugees were nomads.[3] The Afghan side then accused Pakistan of forcibly holding back these nomads and refugees to make propaganda against Kabul and to benefit from international relief assistance. Behind this Afghan propaganda screen was a desire to plug in the issue of nomads as a possible bargaining chip and to draw a distinction between "genuine refugees" and "armed mujahideen." The Afghan side objected to a UN or UNHCR role, without challenging the need for ascertaining the wishes of the refugees. They provided a precise list of conditions to be offered for voluntary return, which included "freedom and immunity" to the repatriates; the right to use pastures on "a just basis and [with] free movement of tribes and nomads"; guarantee of security, freedom of choice of domicile, and equal participation in "the solution of the land question on the basis of agrarian reforms"; and necessary conditions for "living, fruitful labour and social activities for the welfare of the homeland." Amnesty could be granted only to those returnees who laid down their arms, raising the question of the personal arms customarily carried by the Afghans and tribesmen inhabiting both sides of the Durand Line.

Format of the political settlement. Discussion on the agenda items underlined the question of the format, or structure, of the settlement, that is, whether it would be in the form of a legal treaty or treaties or in some other form. The question was first raised in the context of the Afghan position on withdrawal. At the outset, Cordovez did not fully reveal this position to the Pakistani side, although he did indicate that the requirement of reflecting the time frame for withdrawal in the settlement necessitated consideration of an appropriate format. Later during the round, Cordovez interpreted the Afghan position as suggesting that while the Afghan side saw the time frame as part of a comprehensive settlement, it insisted that the subject could only be discussed and decided bilaterally with Moscow. Pakistan objected to this position, which would prevent a negotiated time frame from becoming part of a formal multilateral agreement. The issue forced consideration of an appropriate format, which was pertinent also because of Pakistan's refusal to consider a bilateral agreement on noninterference, based on its nonrecognition of the Kabul regime, and because of ambiguity over the character and form of international guarantees.

Among the possible formats discussed at Geneva I were a Security Council resolution consecrating various understandings, declarations, and agreements, to be integrated, for example, in a secretary general's report. An alternative was a combination of international agreements, unilateral declarations, and other forms of understandings mutually linked together to bring about a comprehensive settlement. These were tentative ideas and it was agreed to keep an open mind and to defer the issue until the structure and texts of the component elements of the comprehensive settlement took some shape. The Pakistani side was concerned, however, that the format for the settlement or for each of its components should be legally binding and command equal legal status.

A Theoretical Framework and Embryonic Structure

The Afghan positions on the agenda items and the settlement were anchored in the 14 May 1980 and 24 August 1981 proposals, whereas the Pakistani side did not have a fully developed concept of a settlement. The issues were new and Yaqub Khan did not have the benefit of authoritative advice; at the last minute Sardar Shahnawaz, who had until then been engaged with the Afghan policy, could not join the delegation in Geneva. Once at Geneva, the Pakistan delegation developed a seminar-like working style with Yaqub Khan presiding. Gradually a logic and a concept emerged to provide moorings for Pakistan's positions in negotiating the texts presented by Cordovez.

Two considerations dominated Pakistani perceptions. First was the desire for an equitable settlement; the settlement must avoid pointing a finger at any of the parties or endorsing either side's point of view, implicitly or explicitly. The sequential relationship implied in Kabul's demand for stoppage of interference as a precondition for withdrawal was, therefore, unacceptable to Pakistan. Second was Pakistan's fear that Moscow might use the negotiations or a settlement as a tactic to confuse and weaken the Afghan Resistance, as well as international opinion. It was felt that once the assurances of noninterference came into force and a settlement was enunciated, there would be an automatic diminution of international pressure on Moscow and a break in the momentum of the Afghan Resistance. These two concerns yielded the basic ideas of an "equitable, integrated

and comprehensive" settlement, and "simultaneous rather than sequential" implementation of various aspects of that settlement.
Similarly, Pakistan insisted on firm assurances for uninterrupted implementation of the settlement, sometimes described as the "unconditionality principle," which figured in several discussions on
various textual issues during successive Geneva rounds.

Amidst discussions verging on thinking out loud, Yaqub Khan ca-
tegorized the four elements comprising the agenda into acts and processes. Assurances of noninterference and guarantees were precisely
timed acts, whereas withdrawal and return of refugees, the two elements of interest to Pakistan, were processes spread over a period of
time. The settlement was required to synchronize these acts and processes and to provide for the uninterrupted continuation of the processes, especially withdrawal, ensuring that Moscow fulfilled its part
of the bargain.

Meanwhile, Cordovez was anxious to identify ideas that could
help in evolving a structure and text for a settlement. He started by
expanding the annotated agenda by developing new opening themes—
"chapeaus," in diplomatic parlance[4]—and inserting ideas the two interlocutors could live with in the light of their own interpretations.
Yaqub Khan's abstract exegesis perceiving the four items as acts and
processes helped Cordovez to conceive correlations of dates as a practical means to define interrelationships and linkages. He started
thinking in terms of dates for the agreement, for the enforcement of
assurances of noninterference, and for the commencement and completion of withdrawal and repatriation of refugees. The blueprint for
addressing the withdrawal question was thus characterized as including "definition" of the interrelationship between "the circumstances, modalities and timing of the withdrawal," "measures" of
noninterference, and the various stages of voluntary return of refugees.

Under noninterference, Cordovez attempted to accommodate both
Pakistan's insistence on restricting assurances of noninterference to
a reaffirmation of principles and the Afghan demand for delineating
specific measures. Carefully crafted language stated that "guidelines
for these measures" would be found in the generally accepted principles of international law relating to noninterference and nonintervention, particularly in the principles contained in two General
Assembly declarations—the Declaration on Principles of International Law Concerning Friendly Relations and Co-operation among
States in Accordance with the Charter of the United Nations,

adopted in 1960 by consensus, and the Declaration on the Inadmissibility of Intervention and Interference in the Internal Affairs of States, adopted in 1981 chiefly with the sponsorship and vote of the nonaligned members of the United Nations.[5]

The 1981 declaration, in particular, came in handy to Cordovez, because it was drafted through long deliberations among nonaligned countries in the period following Soviet intervention in Afghanistan and included many clauses underlining specific concerns of the spectrum of interests represented within the NAM. The 1981 declaration also contained a clause on the principle of inviolability of international boundaries. Cordovez made a specific reference to this principle, understandably anticipating that the issue was of fundamental importance to Pakistan and could be used to draw concessions from the Pakistani side.

In deference to the Afghan position, Cordovez introduced a more direct reference to the possibility of including measures to prevent actions that disrupted good neighbourly relations among states. Under Afghan pressure, Cordovez also wanted to refer to the measures listed by the Afghan side in a "neutral form such as a footnote." Pakistan, however, firmly rejected any reference to the Afghan list. It also objected to the use of the term "measures" under noninterference, but deferred its final reaction until it had seen the text which was to be evolved later.

The chapeau for arrangements for the voluntary return of refugees referred to several details, most importantly to conditions offered by the Afghan side and to "consultative mechanisms to ensure that the arrangements are satisfactory to the Afghan returnees." To make it palatable to the Afghan side, the "consultative mechanisms" were also to ensure the absence of impediments to the voluntary return of refugees. Furthermore, it was contemplated that the settlement would set out functions to be discharged by international agencies such as the UNHCR, in agreement with the governments concerned.

In expanding the annotated agenda items, Cordovez injected the principle of the integrated character of the settlement and of simultaneity in the implementation of each component element. A "Note for the Record," prepared at the conclusion of Geneva I, provided that the settlement would be developed as "an integrated set of agreed provisions." For simultaneity, Cordovez provided that the dates and time frame for each component would be determined taking into account the time frame for the implementation of the other component elements of the settlement. To accommodate the Afghan side's concern that the aim of the negotiations should be the normalization of relations between the concerned states, Cordovez defined the objective of the comprehensive settlement to include the promotion of good neighbourly relations and cooperation among states in the area, and the strengthening of international peace and security in the region on the basis of certain unexceptionable principles derived from UN declarations. With some modification, these principles survived the numerous transmutations of the draft settlement and appear in the Accords signed six years later at Geneva.[6]

Nontextual Issues at Geneva I

Among nontextual issues, the question of negotiating procedures received considerable attention. In addition, during informal tête-à-tête meetings, Cordovez frequently exchanged views with Yaqub Khan on, among other subjects, the internal dimension of the Afghan problem.

Cordovez faced the difficulty of satisfying the Afghan demand for direct talks. The promise of change of format to direct talks had to be kept alive. At Geneva I, Cordovez only succeeded in obtaining agreement that "his understanding" of the procedure, as detailed in his letter addressed to the two sides following his April 1982 shuttle, would be incorporated in the Note for the Record as the understanding shared by the interlocutors.[7] The vague character of the understanding was obviously unsatisfactory to the Afghan side, which maintained the pressure for direct talks in the subsequent rounds of Geneva negotiations.

Pakistan showed some anxiety about its decision to enter into negotiations with Kabul without Iranian participation. The Iranians, steeped in their revolutionary creed, had rejected the Geneva talks, asserting that only the mujahideen were entitled to negotiate the terms for Soviet withdrawal. Pakistan, however, sought a token association of Iran with the process for the sake of appearance and to minimize domestic criticism from pro-mujahideen religious groups.

The Iranians were persuaded to agree to be kept informed by the Pakistani side through their chargé d'affaires in Geneva. In June 1982, after awaiting the return of the chargé from New York and then receiving confirmation of his arrival in Geneva from the Iranian permanent mission in New York and the Swiss authorities, the Pakistan delegation made hectic efforts to get in touch with him. The chargé, however, remained incommunicado for two days; meanwhile, his deputy declined to receive any briefing. It took several messages back and forth between Geneva, Islamabad, and Tehran before the Iranian chargé d'affaires could be briefed. It became clear, if ever there was any doubt, that Iran could not be brought into the fold of Geneva negotiations. Nevertheless, Pakistan maintained the ritual of regular briefings and also passed on to the Iranian side the documents and drafts evolved during the course of the negotiations.

The question of a broad-based government in Kabul, which had been touched upon during the shuttles by Pérez de Cuéllar and Cordovez, received cursory attention at Geneva I in informal contacts. During one of the formal sessions, however, Yaqub Khan pointed to the requirement of a cease-fire in Afghanistan as a necessary condition for smooth implementation of any negotiated settlement. The remark was not intended to put forward a precondition, but reflected a concern that continuation of indigenous resistance, over which Pakistan could exercise little control, might provide the Soviets with a pretext to accuse Pakistan and scuttle the settlement to revive the military option.[8]

Despite the limitations of the Geneva format, which excluded discussion of the internal aspect, Yaqub Khan shared with Cordovez, during informal contacts, the view that the fate of the negotiated settlement was ultimately tied to Soviet willingness to accept changes in Kabul. This issue was premature, however, because the prospect of a settlement had not yet emerged. The first Geneva round had helped to shape only an embryonic structure of a settlement. The principal accomplishment seemed to be that the negotiations had started.

The External Environment and the Mediator's Concerns

The international environment and the situation on the ground in Afghanistan offered little encouragement for an early settlement. East-West polemics on arms control and regional issues were acute. In Afghanistan the Soviets had finally decided to throw their weight behind Babrak Karmal. Their military operations continued without letup throughout the northern, northeastern, and southern provinces. There were reports that the Soviets were constructing and expanding six airfields in southwestern Afghanistan.[9] Most military analysts agreed that the Soviets were preparing for a long stay in Afghanistan. Soviet statements showed little change; in public at the UN General Assembly and privately with Yaqub Khan, Gromyko insisted on prior cessation of interference as a condition for withdrawal.[10]

Meanwhile, buoyed by the circumstances and rhetoric of the early days of the Reagan administration, conservative political lobbies in the United States were becoming active in support of the Afghan Resistance. The emerging picture was sometimes overdrawn as a tussle between "the bleeders," who wanted to "avenge Vietnam" by raising the cost of the Soviet transgression and keeping the Soviets bogged down in Afghanistan, and "the dealers" favouring a political settlement.[11] The latter category, known to include the U.S. State Department, took a more circumspect view of the capacity of the resistance to exert military pressure on the Soviet troops. The U.S. media also intermittently reported increasing U.S. involvement in covert operations to assist the resistance. Overtly, the $3.2 billion aid package represented a far greater U.S. undertaking to strengthen Pakistan against the perceived threat from Moscow.

Within the United Nations, support for the UNGA resolution on Afghanistan had stabilized. A new issue of the use of chemical weapons had figured at the debates, injecting extra bitterness.[12] In September 1982 the UN secretary general publicly cited the "failure" of the United Nations to obtain Soviet withdrawal as one of the failures of the organization.[13]

Under the circumstances, Diego Cordovez became obsessively concerned with the need to draw public support from the concerned states for the UN initiative and for his role. Islamabad and Kabul had their own reasons to support the UN-sponsored negotiations. Occasionally, Moscow paid lip service to the process.[14] However, the Soviet position remained firmly rooted in the precept of "irreversibility" of the Saur Revolution and the terms of the 14 May 1980 and 24 August 1981 proposals for a settlement.[15] The U.S. attitude caused Cordovez the most concern. He feared growing support for the Afghan Resistance and conservative backlash in the United States as a potential obstruction to his efforts; and he discerned in the press reports and leaks about military supplies to the resistance a calculated ploy to encourage hard-liners in Pakistan and to undercut the diplomatic process. In practice, quite to the contrary, these leaks caused considerable embarrassment to Pakistan and were resented by the resistance leaders.[16]

Following Geneva I during the second half of 1982, Cordovez often elicited Pakistan's help in persuading the United States to make public statements supporting the UN role.[17] Behind this prodding was an unrealistic expectation that the United States and Pakistan would commit their unreserved support to Cordovez to enable him to convince Moscow to be cooperative. On its part, the United States, being constantly on the defensive in the United Nations, maintained a cynical attitude toward the organization, reflected in its general lack of interest in UN-sponsored proposals. The progress at Geneva I or in the earlier shuttles, about which Pakistan had kept the Americans informed as a matter of policy, did not evoke substantial comment.

The United States, furthermore, was not required to respond to any specific element of the negotiated settlement, which so far existed in the realm of abstract and general principles. On the issue of guarantees, U.S. Under Secretary of State Lawrence Eagleburger initially took a legalistic view with Cordovez and with Pakistan, drawing attention to the U.S. constitutional requirement for ratification of international agreements. The State Department refrained from playing an activist role. Sharing the prevalent assessment about basic inflexibility in the Soviet position, it cautioned Pakistan against overcommitment. U.S.-Pakistani contacts during the fall of 1982 dwelt mainly on issues related to the aid package, its processing on Capitol Hill, and, in that context, Pakistan's defense requirements.[18]

For Pakistan, Soviet willingness to withdraw, accepted at face value by Cordovez in the interest of advancing the negotiations, needed to be reflected in Soviet actions on the ground and Soviet readiness to accept political realities in Afghanistan. Pakistan's channels with Moscow were open, and it had no reason to believe that the Soviets would move toward a settlement without first sending the right signals. Pakistan also kept in close touch with friends and allies to test its assessment. Its soundings with the United States, China, West Europeans, especially France, and a large number of Islamic and nonaligned states only served to reinforce skepticism about Soviet interest in negotiated withdrawal. While playing a lead role in the conduct of the negotiations, Pakistan saw no advantage in moving far ahead of its allies on the Afghan issue. This did not imply a closed mind. When signs of change appeared on the Soviet scene, Pakistan acknowledged them.

Geneva II, 11–22 April and 12–24 June 1983

The brief interregnum under Brezhnev's successor, Yuri Andropov, was marked by heightened optimism and a fresh impetus to the negotiations of the second round of Geneva Talks (Geneva II), conducted in two sessions held successively in April and June 1983. The early optimism of April and the disappointment at the conclusion of the June session have been the subject of considerable argument in the media, as well as in political and academic circles. This section will survey the developments and status of the negotiations during the period and provide a basis for examining the surrounding controversy.

New Expectations from Change in Moscow

In November 1982, when President Zia ul Haq visited Moscow to attend the state funeral of Brezhnev, he was received by the new Soviet leader, Andropov. The cordial nature of the meeting and a positive reference to it in the Soviet press[19] were viewed by the Pakistani side as a significant gesture.[20] More important, Andropov spoke of Soviet preference for a political settlement, disclaimed any Soviet intention to absorb Afghanistan, and expressed desire for better relations with Pakistan. Zia ul Haq reaffirmed Pakistan's commitment to a political settlement and the belief that the situation in Afghanistan could not be resolved through military means.

The meeting did not address the issue in any specific details, but its tenor was encouraging. In a press conference in Moscow following the meeting, Zia declared that he perceived "some freshness" in the new Soviet leadership's approach to Afghanistan.[21] Addressing the U.S. Foreign Policy Association in New York a few weeks later, he reaffirmed this assessment, suggesting "a hint of flexibility" in the Soviet attitude, adding, however, that there was yet "no proof, no indication" of an early solution to the problem.[22] The Soviet press also carried faint indications of Soviet disaffection with the conflict, implying an interest in a political settlement.[23] The muted character of the overtures engendered hope and expectation rather than euphoria.

During his visit to Washington, 6–8 December 1982, Zia ul Haq received no clear assessment of change in the Soviet position. The advisable course appeared to be to watch for developments and proceed on the basis of concrete indications and proposals. The closed character of the Soviet system always left negotiators and observers guessing, with little information to test a new surmise, and experience dictated that gambling did not pay in dealing with the Soviets, especially on issues so grave and fundamental as Afghanistan. If the

Soviet position had really undergone a change, it was prudent to wait for the change to become visible. Nonetheless, it was significant for Pakistan that the first signal from the new Soviet leadership had been conveyed to Zia ul Haq. Clearly, it showed that on the Afghan issue, Moscow had no inhibition in dealing directly with Pakistan.

The ascent to power of Andropov quickened the pace of the negotiating process, and Cordovez launched another visit to the area, 21 January–7 February 1983.[24] During this shuttle between Islamabad and Kabul, Cordovez obtained an agreement for convening the second round of Geneva talks in April, soon after the Seventh Non-Aligned Summit in New Delhi in the third week of March and a visit in late March to Moscow by Pérez de Cuéllar and Cordovez.

The secretary general and Cordovez returned from Moscow elated and full of optimism. Pérez de Cuéllar said he had received "renewed encouragement" from Andropov to pursue UN mediation.[25] An unequivocal endorsement for the UN role by the Soviet Union, a superpower, generated hope at a time when the secretary general had been lamenting the ineffectiveness of the United Nations and the breakdown of multilateralism in international affairs.[26] Later in April, at Geneva, Cordovez attached considerable importance to Andropov's admission that the Soviet presence in Afghanistan was hurting the Soviet Union. With a touch of drama, he narrated how Andropov raised his hand and counted the damages on his fingers: loss of life; unnecessary financial expenditure; regional tensions; setback to détente; and loss of Soviet prestige in the Third World.[27] This was a new theme, echoed in Kabul, where Prime Minister Kishtmand gave a long account of the damage caused to the economy as a result of "counterrevolutionary" activism.[28]

Andropov's argument clearly reflected a reappraisal of Soviet involvement in Afghanistan, contributing to a change of atmospherics, but did not yet indicate a modification of Soviet terms for withdrawal. Even after the Moscow meeting, Cordovez had conceded that the Soviet Union continued to endorse the Afghan position that the Soviet troops would be withdrawn only after "the rebel threat" was ended.[29] Nonetheless, the April Geneva II round of talks had an upbeat start. At New Delhi President Zia assured the UN secretary general of Pakistan's support of the UN initiative and its seriousness in seeking a political settlement.

Uneven Progress on a Text

Cordovez's immediate task was to put together a draft text for a settlement, however preliminary, so that he could zero in on issues requiring political decisions on the part of the interlocutors. During
his shuttle to the area from 21 January to 7 February 1983, he attempted to delineate structure and guidelines for elaborating a draft
text, which he later presented to the Afghan and Pakistani sides at
the end of March 1983 in New Delhi. (Table 2 depicts the evolution
of the agenda into a draft settlement and, eventually, the Geneva
Accords.)

The first draft provided by Cordovez was divided into four sections, corresponding to the four agenda items, and a preamble setting
out the objective and principles of "the comprehensive settlement."
Structurally, Section I on interrelationships and withdrawal represented the heart of the comprehensive settlement. This section spelt
out

1. the integrated nature of the settlement;
2. a distinction between the date of the comprehensive settlement (either
the date of enunciation or of signature, depending on the form) and the date
on which withdrawal and return of refugees would begin and commitments
on noninterference and declarations of guarantee would enter into force;
3. a condition to complete all steps required toward fulfilling the provisions of the comprehensive settlement by a certain date;
4. provision for consultations to deal with questions arising during the
course of implementation of the settlement.

Out of Section I's seven sketchy paragraphs, the one paragraph on
withdrawal, the only reference to the subject in the entire draft,
stated that "the gradual withdrawal of foreign troops will commence
_____days from the date of (this) comprehensive settlement" and left
a blank space for defining modalities for withdrawal. This was obviously unacceptable to Pakistan. It did not even indicate a provision
for a time frame for the completion of withdrawal. In comparison to
this reference, the other sections, especially Section II on noninterference, were far more elaborate.

During the preceding shuttle, Cordovez had obtained the consent
of Kabul and Islamabad that provisions under Section II on noninterference would be based, in all essential respects, upon the 1981
Declaration on the Inadmissibility of Intervention and Interference
in the Internal Affairs of States, which was supported by both Af-

ghanistan and Pakistan. This declaration had originated in a decision at the Havana NAM summit in September 1979 before the Soviet military action, and was finally adopted after a contentious debate at the 1981 UNGA session with the support of NAM and East bloc members.[30] At that time, no one had envisaged that this loosely formulated declaration, drafted in the cavalier style of the NAM documents, would furnish the basic material for the comprehensive settlement to be worked out by Cordovez two years later.

Cordovez lifted eleven clauses from the 1981 declaration and placed them in Section II as obligations, under the implementation of the principle of noninterference and nonintervention. He had introduced some changes, mostly of minor importance, such as reversing the order of the standard UN phrase "nonintervention and noninterference," something dismissed by Yaqub Khan as a minor technicality. There was one significant change, however. The phrase "existing internationally recognized boundaries," appearing in the corresponding clause of the UN declaration, was substituted by "the international borders" in the text of Section II.

Another significant aspect of the draft text of Section II was its last paragraph (paragraph 3), stipulating completion of all measures required to ensure full implementation of the obligations by the date these obligations were to take effect. That date was to be the same as the date for the commencement of withdrawal. It was agreed that the settlement would come into effect thirty days after the date of signature or enunciation of the settlement, sometimes referred to as the D-day. The date of implementation was noted as D + 30. This clause fitted the philosophy of simultaneity, yet its interpretation could be stretched to establish a sequential relationship between cessation of interference and commencement of withdrawal, a subtle distinction exploited by Cordovez to satisfy the logical requirements of the divergent positions of the two interlocutors.

Under Section III on guarantees, Cordovez presented a draft declaration that focused exclusively on third-state support for the commitments on noninterference elaborated in Section II, and an undertaking on the part of each such state to respect those commitments. The draft also included a provision for consultation among guarantor states with a view to ensuring observance of these commitments. Pakistan could not agree to this draft because, in its view, the guarantees must apply to all aspects of the settlement and their scope must especially include withdrawal along with observance of noninterference.

Table 2: Evolution of the Texts
of the Geneva Accords on Afghanistan

Agenda Items (April 1982)	Annotated Agenda: Geneva I (June 1982)	Draft Comprehensive Settlement: Geneva II (April, June 1983) Geneva III (August 1984)
Withdrawal	Consideration of withdrawal in terms of interrelationships with measures under other items.	Section I. Interrelationships elaborated as coincidence of dates for implementation of various elements; a blank for time frame for withdrawal; definition of component parts of the comprehensive settlement.
Noninterference	Consideration of "measures" to ensure principles of nonintervention and noninterference.	Section II. Obligations drawn from 1981 UN General Assembly (UNGA) Declaration on Inadmissibility of Intervention and Interference in the Internal Affairs of States. (At Geneva III, a draft bilateral agreement based on Section II was proposed to supplement the draft settlement.)
International Guarantees	Discussion on guarantees and identification of guarantors.	Section III. Undertakings to respect provisions of Section II. Later scope was broadened by adding expression of support for the settlement.
Voluntary Return of Refugees	Discussion on conditions and modalities of voluntary return of refugees.	Section IV. Conditions for voluntary return; modalities for UN High Commissioner for Refugees' (UNHCR) role, etc.

Draft Instruments: Geneva IV, V, VI (1985), Geneva VII A, B (1986)	Geneva Accords, 14 April 1988
Instrument IV. Discussed and finalized in 1986 on the basis of text of Section I; legal format and UN monitoring were the last issues to be resolved, leaving time frame to be settled later.	Agreement on Interrelationships for Settlement of Situation Relating to Afghanistan (includes time frame for withdrawal).
Instrument I. Draft bilateral agreement on noninterference and nonintervention; Kabul's reservation on "border formulation" revived.	Bilateral Agreement between Afghanistan and Pakistan on Principles of Mutual Relations, in Particular on Noninterference and Nonintervention.
Instrument II. Draft declaration of guarantees; text finalized and agreed upon in 1985.	Declaration on International Guarantees.
Instrument III. Draft bilateral agreement on voluntary return of refugees. The issue of consultation with the refugees remained unresolved until it was dropped in late 1986.	Bilateral Agreement between Afghanistan and Pakistan on the Voluntary Return of Refugees.

Section IV on voluntary return of the refugees was fairly elaborate, indicating

1. conditions for voluntary return, which were an improvement over the six conditions offered by the Afghan side at Geneva I;
2. provision for appropriate consultations with the Afghan refugees to ascertain that these conditions were satisfactory to them;
3. undertakings on the part of the governments concerned to facilitate the repatriation process;
4. provision for the establishment of a "mixed commission," with the participation of UNHCR, for organizing, coordinating, and supervising the repatriation process;
5. functions and responsibility of the UNHCR.

Besides several issues requiring clarification, Pakistan had a major difficulty with the idea of mixed commissions. It could not accept any joint operation involving Kabul officials. Also consultations with the refugees needed further elaboration. This was especially important in the light of Pakistan's reluctance to negotiate the conditions for voluntary return, which could only be addressed legitimately by the refugees and their leadership. The Afghan side, on the other hand, took issue with the concept of consultations with the refugees and raised the issue of nomads.

The draft text represented a significant advance, but it became evident in preliminary discussions at Geneva II that apart from the issues requiring political decisions, the two interlocutors had major difficulties with the substance of the text, which did not appear amenable to easy or early solutions. The Afghans had problems with the structure, because they could not accept withdrawal to be part of any document comprising the comprehensive settlement. Similarly, they wanted Section II to be lifted out of the text and redrafted in the form of a bilateral treaty between Pakistan and Afghanistan. The Pakistani side accepted the structure, but it had major problems with the text, especially the absence of a time frame and modalities for withdrawal, the one-sided nature of the guarantees, and ambiguity about consultations with the refugees.

Cordovez quickly realized the problems in attempting to elaborate Section I, as the Pakistani side was asking, and proposed a new approach. He suggested parallel discussions on finalizing the text of Section II (noninterference and nonintervention) and on the format of the comprehensive settlement and the remaining three sections, with a view to developing their texts. Yaqub Khan accepted the proposal on the explicit understanding that the comprehensive settlement was of an integrated character and that, without an overall agreement, none of its component elements, even if finalized, would be regarded as agreed or operational. Since this approach departed from the requirement of simultaneous and balanced development of the text, its acceptance was regarded by Pakistan as a major concession in the interest of progress in the negotiations. Yaqub Khan was also persuaded by Cordovez's argument that finalization of Section II would serve as an earnest of Pakistan's seriousness and convince the Soviets to deliver a time frame for withdrawal.

During Geneva II, the Soviets sent to Geneva a special representative, Ambassador Stanislav Gavrilov, something that Cordovez regarded as a proof of Soviet sincerity in seeking a political settlement. He had a highly positive view of Gavrilov, whose difficulties Cordovez attributed to apparent inflexibility in the Afghan position, thereby hinting at a divergence of views developing between Moscow and Kabul. Yaqub Khan shared this assessment, because he not only believed that Moscow held the key to a settlement, but intuitively expected a change in Moscow's attitude. Like Cordovez, he too had a personal interest in being the author of a settlement that would secure Soviet withdrawal.

Informal Diplomacy and Mixed Signals Raise Optimism

Two parallel sets of discussions and exchanges developed at Geneva II: formal discussions on Section II and the remaining text, and informal, off-the-record exchanges involving Cordovez, his principal interlocutors, and Soviet representative Gavrilov. Having obtained Pakistan's agreement to discuss Section II before Section I, Cordovez pressed for the completion of Section II, considering it a vital condition for a breakthrough. On the same premise, Cordovez tried to work out understandings through informal exchanges, which prematurely raised hopes of an impending settlement.

The text of Section II proposed by Cordovez posed several problems to the two interlocutors. The Pakistani side asked for the restoration of the phrase "existing internationally recognized boundaries," arguing that it accepted the eleven clauses placed under Section II only because these were taken from the 1981 UN declaration and that any deviation from the original in regard to the phrase on boundaries would be indefensible. The Afghan side, on the other hand, demanded deletion of the reference to "the international borders" from the text and rejected Cordovez's plea that the reference, appearing as it did as part of a general principle, would not imply the Durand Line. Cordovez posited the importance of the issue to Pakistan and not only retained the reference but incorporated the relevant phrase from the 1981 declaration in the revised text of the draft comprehensive settlement. The Afghans, nevertheless, maintained their objection.

The Afghans considered the text based on the clauses of the 1981 declaration as inadequate and wanted to augment it with specific measures similar to those conveyed by them to Cordovez at Geneva I. Their proposed additions called for the expulsion from Pakistan of leaders of opposition groups (the resistance leaders) and disarming and refusing shelter to all individuals opposed to the other party, that is, the Kabul government. Pakistan could not accept such references in the text. Nonetheless, under Afghan pressure, Cordovez modified one of the provisions to read as follows:

> . . . to prevent within its Territory the presence, harbouring, in camps and bases or otherwise, organizing, training, financing, equipping and arming of individuals and political and ethnic groups for the purpose of creating subversion, disorder or unrest in another State and accordingly also to prevent the use of mass media and the transportation of arms, ammunition and equipment by such individuals or groups.

(This provision was eventually retained substantially unchanged and appears in Article II, paragraph 12, in the bilateral agreement on noninterference and nonintervention signed at Geneva.)[31]

Although Yaqub Khan was undecided, the rest of the Pakistan delegation opposed the new formulation, which appeared to be placing Pakistan in the dock. Stepping beyond the 1981 UN declaration seemed unreasonable. Furthermore, the Afghans still insisted on an understanding, albeit outside the text of the settlement, on the measures they had demanded. As a drafting tactic, Pakistan suggested inclusion of one of the provisions from the 1981 UN declaration, omitted by Cordovez, calling for nonrecognition of situations brought about by military intervention. As expected, both the Afghans and the Soviets reacted strongly to this clause, later referred to as "the Naik clause" (after Pakistan Foreign Secretary Niaz Naik). As the discussion of Section II became increasingly focused on details, the Pakistan delegation became nervous about other sections that remained sketchy and vague. Apart from time frame and modalities for withdrawal, the Pakistani side wanted to settle the scope of guarantees and arrangements for consultations with the refugees.

Meanwhile, in the informal, off-the-record conversations with Yaqub Khan, Cordovez developed an entirely new focus for negotiations. Basing his assessment on exchanges with Gavrilov, Cordovez became convinced that Moscow could be persuaded to give a time frame for withdrawal, provided Pakistan accepted a final text of Section II. Cordovez embarked on developing an understanding linking the two crucial issues. Relentlessly pushing the idea, Cordovez argued for concessions by the Pakistani side in order to finalize the text, stressing the need to proceed expeditiously and to build confidence with the Soviets. This was a sudden and audacious proposition. If the Soviets were indeed willing to give a time frame, then a number of questions needed to be addressed urgently.

First and foremost was the time frame itself. Pakistan could not simply agree to any terminal date the Soviets might offer. It had to be a date acceptable to Pakistan and agreeable to the guarantors (other than the Soviet Union) and the refugees (the Afghan Resistance). Also, modalities had to be spelt out. Second, consultations with the refugees were a political requirement for Pakistan. While Cordovez was assured that Pakistan would not permit the refugees to exercise a veto on the settlement, they could not be left out. Cordovez was ready to discuss the matter, but remained unwilling to make any commitment.

On international guarantees, Cordovez argued against a wider scope, saying that the Soviets would never agree to give a commitment of withdrawal to a third state, much less allow guarantees to cover withdrawal. He felt that once Pakistan accepted Section II, the potential guarantors, especially the United States, would be under pressure to go along with the language of limited guarantees. For Pakistan, restricting guarantees to noninterference, coupled with the specific language of Section II, were like an admission of guilt by Pakistan and the United States. In order to be balanced, guarantees had to apply to the entire settlement. Furthermore, Yaqub Khan felt that Pakistan could not concur in manifestly one-sided guarantees on behalf of the United States, just as, morally, it could not negotiate conditions for voluntary return on behalf of the refugees by discarding the requirement of consultations with them.

Under pressure from Cordovez to agree to the text of Section II, the Pakistani side tried to address without much success the major unresolved issues. At Pakistan's insistence, Cordovez improved the withdrawal paragraph in Section I to make room for a terminal date, but he avoided discussing modalities. Similarly, there was no progress on the text of guarantees and the issue of consultations with the refugees. Yaqub Khan was tempted to accept the text of Section II to enable Cordovez to put pressure on the Soviets to give a withdrawal date. But he desisted from taking a decision to drop the border formulation and accept the new provision referring to "camps and bases" and "transportation of arms" without first having detailed consultations with Islamabad. Meanwhile, the Afghan side maintained its refusal to accept the border formulation. When discussion stalled on Section II, Cordovez proposed a short break in the round and a tentative understanding.

According to this understanding, which Cordovez shared with Gavrilov and Yaqub Khan, when Geneva II resumed Pakistan was to accept Section II of the draft settlement; it was to give a date on which it would be ready to conclude the comprehensive settlement; and it was to give an undertaking, as provided in the text, that it would take all steps necessary for the implementation of the provisions of Section II by D + 30 (that is, thirty days from the date of conclusion, as explained earlier). Reciprocally, during the resumed Geneva II, the Soviet Union, on the basis of an agreement between Kabul and Moscow, would provide the terminal date for the withdrawal of "foreign troops," which would be indicated in the text of the settlement. In this context, major differences on the text of Section II were noted in the expectation that these would be resolved at the resumed Geneva talks, scheduled to convene two months later, in mid-June 1983. A different version of this understanding, mentioned later in June, had Gavrilov promising only to go to Moscow to discuss the issue of time frame on the basis of the understanding proposed by Cordovez.

Outside the text, the off-the-record conversations between Yaqub Khan and Cordovez reflected upon the issue of a future government in Kabul. Exchanges on this issue were entirely informal and extremely fuzzy, looking through a dense future landscape to clarify ideas. To begin with, in Pakistan's perception, Soviet willingness to withdraw subsumed Soviet readiness to promote a stable government in Kabul. Further, a settlement was to be workable only if there was a cease-fire within Afghanistan, which could not be envisaged without a broad-based acceptable government. The logic of this hypothesis posed an intriguing anomaly that the Karmal regime would be negotiating a settlement that would lead to its own demise. Accordingly, in an academic sense, Yaqub Khan's thinking was receptive to suggestions of a cleavage developing between Kabul and Moscow as the latter moved toward a settlement.

At the practical level, there was the question of the nature of change required: Would a change of face at the top—removal of Karmal—help to bring about a cease-fire and create conditions necessary for the implementation of the settlement, or would a more substantial change in Kabul be necessary? Cordovez wanted to find out if a cosmetic change would help move Pakistan to recognize and enter into direct talks with the Kabul government or sign a bilateral pact with it.[32] According to Cordovez, Gavrilov had told him that Zia ul Haq did not agree to a Soviet offer to replace Karmal by Kishtmand. Zia denied any knowledge of such an offer; on the contrary, the Soviets had been extremely sensitive to any suggestion of a need for change in Kabul.[33] Nonetheless, Cordovez's information, taken at face value, was perceived as an indication that the Soviets were thinking of a change. From Pakistan's point of view, a meaningful, broad-based government marked by political compromise, possibly involving Zahir Shah, was obviously most desirable. But it was felt that a cosmetic change, Kishtmand for Karmal, would make it difficult for Pakistan to refuse to conclude an agreement or resist direct talks with the new Afghan government.[34]

The unstructured informal discussions on the future government in Kabul were propelled more by considerations of logic than by any serious corroborating evidence of Soviet thinking on the issue. Soviet interest in a settlement and hence in a change of government in Kabul was taken for granted, along with the presumption that Moscow had the capacity to bring about such a change. The Pakistani side also felt convinced, and not without justification as developments in early 1987 showed, that if ever the Soviets would want to discuss the question of a change in Kabul, they would do so first with Pakistan, in view of its relations with the Afghan Resistance. In retrospect, the informal discussions on the subject at the April 1983 Geneva round served to raise undue expectations, and even led to the reported misunderstanding on the part of Cordovez, although he never mentioned it to the Pakistani side, that Pakistan accepted a cosmetic change for the purposes of a settlement.[35]

The progress on Section II and the atmosphere created by informal diplomacy, against the backdrop of perceptible change in the Soviet attitude favouring a negotiated settlement, generated a sense of euphoria. This was exemplified by Cordovez's statement to the press in early May that the settlement was "95 percent ready," a statement he later regretted.[36] Cordovez's statement stirred interest all around. It alarmed the Afghan Resistance leadership and pro-resistance political circles over the possibility of a sellout at Geneva, and it both intrigued and agitated the Pakistani negotiators, because most of their concerns were still unresolved. The more circumspect Pakistani assessment was made by Yaqub Khan at a press conference in Islamabad on April 26, when he stated that it would not be right to talk of a qualitative change, but only that "the talks have moved a stage further."[37]

Resumed Session: The Illusion of Missed Opportunity

The Pakistan delegation left Geneva on 25 April with the impression that the negotiations had entered a serious phase, that the apparent indication of Soviet willingness to give a terminal date for withdrawal at the resumed session was a tangible signal of Soviet intention to seek a settlement, and that a close examination at home and consultations with friends and allies abroad were needed to assess the emerging prospects of a settlement. In Islamabad, high-level Afghan cell meetings, presided over by Zia ul Haq, examined a wide range of possibilities. But, in his characteristic style, wherever he could postpone, Zia ul Haq avoided taking hard decisions. One concrete outcome was a decision to send Yaqub Khan to visit Riyadh (because Saudi Arabia then chaired the OIC) and the capitals of the five permanent members of the Security Council. The purpose was to sound out Moscow on the critical issues of the time frame and the need for a broad-based government in Kabul and to take allies and friends into Pakistan's confidence.

On specifics, the Afghan cell approved the modified paragraph proposed by Cordovez in Section II, but opinion was divided on the issue of the border. While one point of view favoured seeking recognition of the Durand Line, the other regarded the issue as marginal and questioned the advisability of obtaining recognition for the Durand Line from an "illegal" regime. Another issue examined by the cell in the context of Section II was the need for an earnest from the Soviets to match the steps required on the part of Pakistan to observe noninterference by the date of implementation, D + 30. It was argued that Soviet military activities must stop by D + 30 or Pakistan should ask that Soviet troops be confined to designated areas prior to withdrawal. The complicated issues of the date for concluding the settlement and the format of the settlement were left unaddressed.

The discussions in Islamabad brought up several vexing questions. The refugees needed to be consulted, yet if they were to be consulted on every issue nothing would get off the ground. A broad-based government was desirable, yet it imposed on Pakistan the difficult task of promoting those elements within the Afghan Resistance who would be amenable to a political compromise. The U.S. attitude toward a settlement was unclear. It was agreed that Pakistan should guard against isolation and against any settlement that would blame Pakistan for interference.

Yaqub Khan undertook immediate visits to Riyadh, Peking, London, Paris, Washington, and Moscow, with Moscow his last stop before the resumption of Geneva II.[38] In the first four capitals the assessment of Soviet intentions was marked by skepticism, even though each capital affirmed support for the UN negotiating process. In Peking and Paris doubts were quite palpable that Moscow would let Afghanistan slip from under its control. Peking even suggested that a guarantee of noninterference should follow withdrawal. In Washington Yaqub Khan held extensive consultations with Secretary of State George P. Shultz and Under Secretary Eagleburger, in addition to meeting Vice President George Bush.[39] Shultz and Eagleburger asserted that the United States did not want to bleed the Soviet Union and viewed the UN process in a positive light, pointing out that success of these negotiations could become a catalyst for better East-West relations. Shultz even volunteered to send a message to Gromyko, which he did.

The discussion with Eagleburger went into the details of guarantees and the overall format and content of a settlement. Eagleburger affirmed that guarantees should cover the entire document and should refer to the nonaligned status of Afghanistan. Regarding form, he expressed apprehension that any resemblance to a treaty would attract constitutional procedures and cause difficulties. Apart from these comments with respect to guarantees, the U.S. officials did not take issue with any other aspect of the partially evolved draft text of the settlement, which in any event mainly concerned Pakistan.

Contrary to the somewhat withdrawn attitude of the U.S. officials, Yaqub Khan was faced with an excited press, spurred by Cordovez's statement. On the eve of his visit to Washington, there were "leaks" to the press about the expanding U.S. covert assistance to the Afghan Resistance and Pakistan's complicity in facilitating the operation.[40] These leaks were interpreted by many observers as signals from hard-liners within the Reagan administration that the United States was not ready for a political settlement. If that was indeed the purpose, however, Washington did not have to resort to the press to convey it to Pakistan.[41] Leaks to the press are generally regarded as part of Washington's political culture rather than as instruments of policy. Nonetheless, the media viewed with skepticism the "real" intentions of the administration and of Pakistan. In response to questions doubting Pakistan's ability to act independently of the United States, Yaqub Khan was often obliged to make strong assertions of Pakistan's interest in a settlement.

Yaqub Khan arrived in Moscow on 9 June 1983 with the expectation that he would clinch an understanding on time frame and Soviet blessing for the idea of a broad-based government in Kabul. The meeting with Andrei Gromyko, held the following morning, dashed these hopes. Yaqub Khan's assumption that Moscow had accepted the philosophy of the settlement that he thought he had developed with Cordovez at Geneva also turned out not to be true.

In a meticulously prepared presentation, Yaqub Khan began by stating Pakistan's seriousness in pursuing a political settlement, emphasizing the Soviet-Pakistani interest in a political settlement. He spoke of his efforts to seek the support of the other permanent members of the Security Council for the UN process and to explain to them the elements of a "package deal" being forged at Geneva. With his flair for the quintessential, Yaqub Khan spoke of the equitable and integrated character of the settlement and the need to avoid apportioning blame to either side. He then declared the major outstanding issues to be a short time frame, guarantees, and consultations with the refugees. Yaqub Khan had hoped to build on this foundation, expecting a supportive response from Gromyko. What followed, however, derailed the exchange.

Appreciating that Yaqub Khan had taken the trouble to visit various capitals to explain Pakistan's position, Gromyko proceeded to reiterate the well-known Soviet view emphasizing interference from Pakistan as the basic issue. He likened Pakistan to someone who had given his apartment to "bandits" to fire upon his neighbours, and stated in clear terms that the question of withdrawal of the Soviet contingent would not arise until Afghanistan felt fully secure—that is, until interference against the Kabul regime was fully ended and its nonresumption guaranteed. The aim of Pakistani interference,

Gromyko asserted, was to influence the internal situation of Afghanistan. He dismissed such aspirations as "unrealistic fantasies."

In response, Yaqub Khan disavowed any policy on the part of Pakistan to determine the nature of the government in Kabul, which he said was the business of the Afghans. Later in the meeting, however, he delicately made the point that a future regime in Kabul required a wide support base in the interest of peace in Afghanistan. Yaqub Khan then turned the argument to Pakistan's interest in Soviet withdrawal, because it was a necessary condition for return of the refugees. He also repeated Pakistan's readiness to give assurances of noninterference if, simultaneously, a firm commitment for commencement and completion of withdrawal was made by Moscow. Gromyko found the withdrawal–return of refugees link "illogical" and ruled out coupling withdrawal to mere assurances of noninterference. Pakistan was required to adopt a "clear-cut and precise policy" to end interference and reach an agreement with Afghanistan.

Yaqub Khan attempted again to focus on the outstanding issues in the Geneva texts, recalling that in other capitals, including Washington, he had found support for the UN process, and emphasizing the centrality of the time-frame question to the negotiated settlement. Nonetheless, a dour Gromyko firmly maintained that inclusion of withdrawal in a UN document was unacceptable. "These were Soviet troops, not Afghan or Pakistani," he said. As the Soviets had no right to negotiate Pakistani-Afghan differences, Pakistan could not discuss Soviet withdrawal, which had to be treated separately since it concerned Moscow and Kabul alone. The same applied to the scope of guarantees, even though Gromyko did not specifically address this issue. The meeting remained stuck in the familiar grooves of divergent perceptions, with but one concordant note. Gromyko agreed that the negotiations were making progress and their momentum needed to be maintained, adding that indirect talks were better than no talks, but not as good as direct talks.

A subsequent conversation the same afternoon between Yaqub Khan and Soviet Deputy Foreign Minister Georgi Korniyenko en route to the airport deserves a mention here. Korniyenko made some precise enquiries. He asked whether Pakistan had agreed to complete all steps to ensure noninterference between D-day and D + 30. Yaqub Khan clarified that this required a counterpart provision (preparatory steps for withdrawal) in order to ensure balanced obligations under the settlement. In response to another query, Yaqub Khan confirmed that Pakistan wanted the scope of guarantees to cover all aspects of the settlement. Another clarification given to Korniyenko related to Pakistan's insistence on retaining the border phrase in Section II.

In regard to the format of the settlement, as Yaqub Khan spoke of the comprehensive draft being developed at Geneva, Korniyenko for the first time revealed Soviet thinking on this matter. The Soviets envisaged four separate agreements: on noninterference, between Afghanistan and Pakistan; on withdrawal, between Afghanistan and the Soviet Union; on guarantees, involving the Soviet Union and the United States; and on return of refugees, between Afghanistan and Pakistan. This thinking was reasserted more than a year later when, under Soviet-Kabul pressure, Cordovez was obliged to split up his four-part draft comprehensive settlement.

The exchanges in Moscow confirmed Pakistan's suspicions that the Soviets were unaware of what Pakistan now regarded as the agreed underpinnings of an integrated, comprehensive, balanced, and equitable settlement. The Soviets appeared to be under the impression that Pakistan had accepted the text of Section II on interference without any qualification and without any reference to the requirement of overall agreement on the comprehensive settlement. On this and other important issues germane to the settlement, the positions and perceptions of the two sides thus revealed fundamental divergences which could not be bridged by skilled diplomacy alone.

Against the backdrop of optimism generated at Geneva, the Pakistani side found the meeting with Gromyko and the apparent inflexibility in the Soviet position intriguing. Yaqub Khan put the best construction on it, attaching importance to Gromyko's acquiescence in the continuation of indirect talks and explaining the inflexibility as tactical play. "The Soviets are not known to reveal their hand in the first move," he explained. But there could be no doubt that the Soviets were not ready to provide a time frame for withdrawal. Proceedings at the resumed Geneva II later served to confirm this conclusion. Yaqub Khan's expectations from resumed Geneva II were dashed, as evident from his press briefing in Paris on his return from Moscow.[42]

At those resumed Geneva II negotiations, 12–24 June 1983, the exchanges soon lapsed into a stalemate. The Afghan side started by demanding direct talks. Pakistan complained that there was virtually no progress on the withdrawal question or on resolving other outstanding issues. Having conceded the modified paragraph (regarding camps and bases and transportation of arms) in Section II and the deletion of "the Naik clause," Yaqub Khan invoked the April understanding, asking whether the Soviets would give a time frame. The new Soviet representative, Vasili S. Safronchuk, instead took the earlier Afghan position asking for the removal of withdrawal from the text. Cordovez now insisted that Pakistan must first agree to the entire text to enable him to obtain a time frame from the Soviet side. Only when the Soviets could see the entire text ready could they be persuaded to give "a date for a date"—a date on which Pakistan would be ready to conclude the settlement and a terminal date for completion of withdrawal by the Soviet Union.

Cordovez started pushing Pakistan to remove its opposition to the limited scope of the text on guarantees. By now, the Pakistani side had developed its own set of misgivings, further reinforced under pressure. For several reasons, Pakistan insisted on guarantees to cover the entire settlement. First, such guarantees would ensure that the Soviets would make a commitment on withdrawal, not only to Pakistan but to other powers as well. Second, the limited scope of guarantees, if agreed by Pakistan, would drive a wedge between Pakistan and the United States. Third, on a point of principle, the text had to be balanced and equitable and not implicate either of the parties. Fourth, in purely textual terms, the Pakistani side reduced its requirement for the scope of guarantees to a minimum and only asked for a provision underlining the "support and commitment" of the guarantors to the "principles and provisions of the comprehensive settlement." The Pakistani side felt that such a provision could not justifiably draw objection from the Afghans or the Soviets if they had accepted the comprehensive and integrated nature of the settlement. Cordovez argued that even this innocuous language implied that the Soviets were being asked to make a commitment to Pakistan and the United States on withdrawal, which, he insisted, the Soviet Union as a superpower would never agree to.

Pressure engendered tension as Cordovez, unable to break the impasse, felt increasingly frustrated and even stretched his argument to imply that, by withholding acceptance of his text on guarantees, Pakistan was, in fact, relying on the United States to reopen Section II. He also showed reluctance to consult the refugees, suspecting that such a procedure could also reopen the document, despite Pakistani assurances to the contrary. On the other hand, the Pakistani negotiators saw that, subsequent to their agreement on Section II, instead of making progress on such issues relating to withdrawal as time frame and modalities—which Cordovez had now dropped altogether

—new demands and issues had been raised and there was backtracking on consultations with the refugees. Pakistan wanted an equitable settlement and not a settlement on any terms. Regrettably, the drama of tension and pressure tactics did little to advance the negotiating process, while causing harm to mutual trust, the need for which Cordovez almost ritualistically stressed at every Geneva round.

Indeed, Geneva II had resumed on an inauspicious note. Gavrilov, with whom Cordovez had developed a confident working relationship in April, had suffered a heart attack and was replaced by the reputedly tough and stolid Safronchuk, who had served in Kabul with special status from 1979 to 1982.[43] In addition, before his departure for Geneva, when pressed to comment on Cordovez's statement claiming 95 percent completion of the text, Pakistan Foreign Secretary Naiz A. Naik had remarked that "everything was open."[44] Somewhat impulsively, he had reflected the general feeling within the Pakistan team that none of Pakistan's concerns had yet been addressed.

Cordovez reacted strongly to this statement, saying it had upset the Soviets and aggravated distrust on their part. Yaqub Khan pleaded to no avail that negotiations should proceed from concrete positions rather than press statements, and that if statements were to be counted, Zia ul Haq had publicly expressed satisfaction with progress made at Geneva and had praised the Soviets for adopting "a very positive approach" on the eve of the resumption of Geneva II.[45] Cordovez was also agitated over Yaqub Khan's visits to the five capitals, even though in the formal sessions he described them as a "brilliant move." He invariably emphasized the centrality of his own role and was highly sensitive on this point.

During the April round, spurred by the changed tone of Moscow under Andropov and an understandable personal ambition, Cordovez had targeted time frame and Pakistan's commitment to noninterference as the key issues. According to his calculation, these issues, if secured, would become the locomotive for a settlement, generating irresistible political pressures and dwarfing the remaining issues of procedure, format, and substance. He attempted to develop the text and the relevant understandings as far as he could; through a complex of innuendos and typically half-said remarks, he conveyed the impression to each side that the other was close to its own point of view. In his view, such illusions needed to be sustained until he was able to push his interlocutors into concrete commitments. This proved impossible after the Gromyko-Yaqub Khan meeting.

Having agreed to the text of Section II, Pakistan had expected a more understanding approach from Cordovez. Instead, he launched into the theme of Soviet distrust of Pakistani intentions, and the need for Pakistan to do more by accepting guarantees of limited scope and by setting aside the requirement for refugee consultations. In addition, Pakistan was advised not to insist on legal or formal assurances on withdrawal, since the Soviet Union, as a superpower, expected its word to be taken seriously. Making matters worse were Cordovez's reminders about Soviet accusations against Pakistan, suggesting that Naik's statement had damaged Pakistan's credibility in Soviet eyes, coupled with indirect hints that while in Moscow Yaqub Khan had not forcefully demanded a terminal date for withdrawal and that Pakistan was under U.S. pressure. Pakistan felt that Cordovez showed less sensitivity to its concerns and was pushing for a "quick fix."[46] It had become apparent that the negotiations were in for a long haul—a *"lamba chakkar,"* as Zia ul Haq said when he received reports of the proceedings of the first days of resumed Geneva II. When Cordovez pressed Safronchuk for a notional time frame, the latter plainly ruled it out, saying the negotiations had not reached the appropriate stage.

A new element introduced by Safronchuk and the Afghans at resumed Geneva II was the Iranian dimension. Declaring that the interference was being shifted from Pakistan to Iran, they asserted that Iran, too, should therefore be asked to undertake a commitment to noninterference. Ironically, the circle thus turned 180 degrees on the issue of Iranian participation. The Soviets had obviously felt concerned over the visits to Tehran of Hekmatyar and Rabbani, who, reacting to optimistic noises resulting from Geneva II, wanted to secure an alternative support base. The issue kept surfacing at subsequent rounds.

The resumed session turned out to be inconclusive; it was tense, and it raised more questions than it settled. Cordovez felt that an opportunity to clinch a settlement was lost between the two split sessions of Geneva II. Later on, some journalists also picked up this theme. Skeptics who could not credit Pakistan with independence of action ascribed it to "the hidden U.S. hand" restraining Pakistan.[47]

The truth was that the elusive opportunity had disappeared before it had matured. Undoubtedly, the hard-liners in Pakistan and the

United States had little interest in promoting a settlement. But it is only an academic question whether they would have prevented a settlement from materializing in 1983 had the situation come to a head. The Gromyko-Yaqub Khan meeting demonstrated that the Soviet position had hardened before the resumption of Geneva II. Speaking to Pakistan Ambassador Shahnawaz, Secretary General Pérez de Cuéllar had affirmed this assessment. Surely, the Soviets could not have been so naive as to expect Pakistan to agree to a settlement completely on the terms the Soviets had publicly demanded, terms which Gromyko had repeated privately during the Moscow meeting.

A plausible explanation of this development could be found in the first reports of the stroke suffered by Andropov, resulting in the loosening of his grip on state affairs. The *Times* of London of 8 June 1983 had reported "rapid decline" in Andropov's health. "A sharp turn for the worse" was noticed when the Soviet leader came to a dinner in honour of President Mauno Koivisto of Finland, two days before Yaqub Khan's arrival in Moscow. He was supported by two aides at either elbow and his right hand shook "uncontrollably." Andropov's paralysis and the possible influence of old guard hard-liners led to nearly two years of inertness in Soviet policy.[48] Even if Andropov had remained active, it would have taken much more than one Geneva round to finalize the settlement. Gorbachev, who picked up Andropov's testament describing Afghanistan as "a bleeding wound," took nearly three years before making a serious offer of a time frame, despite the fact that by then the format of the settlement had already been shaped to Soviet liking and the text of guarantees had been settled.

Even though marred by deteriorated atmospherics, the resumed session was not devoid of certain significant results. It whittled down Pakistan's expectations on issues it considered important. The issue of modalities for withdrawal, for which a blank, numbered paragraph was provided in the text, was obfuscated in the heat of the session. On refugee consultations, Pakistan virtually conceded that it could live with a pro forma exercise. Cordovez also planted the idea that the existing format of the comprehensive settlement could be split up to shape a bilateral agreement based on the provisions of Section II. Implied was the issue of Pakistani readiness to sign such an agreement with the Kabul regime.

As for the Soviets and the Afghans, Cordovez had some success in impressing upon them the imperative of preserving the reference to time frame in the text of the settlement, and the need to include an expression of support to the entire settlement in the text on guarantees. On the last day of the resumed session he even proceeded to add a paragraph to his text on guarantees affirming "support for the comprehensive settlement" by the guarantors, which inevitably drew objection from the Afghans. Cordovez also obtained an unambiguous agreement from the Afghans and the Soviets on the package nature of the settlement—that agreement reached on any component part would only be deemed to be "definitive" when the text was completed. The resumed session helped in improving the text of the draft settlement, through editorial changes and by removing minor differences. The single most important achievement was an agreement in principle not to reopen the text of Section II.

Given the degree of Pakistan's support of the Afghan Resistance, a comment is warranted to explain Pakistan's acceptance of Section II, whose provisions so obviously militated against the entire range of Afghan Resistance activities inside Pakistan. Technically, in those early years, Pakistan described the Afghan Resistance leadership based in Peshawar as "refugee leadership," by definition governed by the principle of voluntary return. Therefore, Pakistan felt that it was not obliged to carry out drastic measures of closing down the offices of the Peshawar groups or asking their leaders to leave Pakistan.

Quite apart from relying on such a minor technicality, the political consideration underlying the acceptance was the belief that the regime in Kabul would either become broad-based or not survive the exit of the Soviet forces. Either outcome would circumvent any juridical snags developing in the implementation of the provisions on noninterference. Yaqub Khan was, therefore, less concerned about the status of the Peshawar-based leaders in Pakistan in the post-settlement scenario than over possible technical objections by UN agencies to the returnees' carrying personal arms, assuming that the Kabul regime would survive during the period of withdrawal.

Following the anticlimax of the June round, Cordovez was reluctant to set a date for the next round or shuttle, although he agreed to have exchanges with Pakistani officials in Geneva on modalities for consultations with the refugees. Further discussion on resumption of the process had to await the commencement of the General Assembly session. The UN secretary general, in his report to the General Assembly, expressed concern at "the slow pace of the negotiations and at the difficulties encountered in overcoming existing obstacles," adding, however, that "the diplomatic process [had] moved in the right direction and that a settlement [was] possible on the basis of what [had] already been accomplished."[49]

On a broader plane, with the exit of Andropov and the crisis of aging leadership in Moscow, the inertia of settled policies prevailed with ease. Skeptics of Soviet intention to withdraw started treating the Geneva process as a diplomatic ritual, hardened in their belief that the Soviets, true to their past record, were unlikely to give up a piece of real estate. The Afghan Resistance leadership and exiles, left out of the Geneva process, as well as conservative political elements, especially within the United States, maintained their opposition to the negotiating process, calling it a Soviet tactic to weaken international opinion.

In contrast, the opposition press in Pakistan blamed the United States and the military regime of Zia ul Haq for stalling progress at Geneva. Cordovez sometimes used such press reports to play on the sensitivities of the Pakistani negotiators. Nonetheless, they made little impact on the Zia government and barely affected the larger canvas on which Pakistan fought propaganda battles and struggled to maintain international support for its position. At the 1983 UN General Assembly the vote in support of the resolution on Afghanistan registered an increase over the previous record.

Geneva III, 24–30 August 1984

After the June session, the negotiating process shifted into slow gear. Only after a gap of more than one year was the next round, Geneva III, convened, from 24 to 30 August 1984. Chastened by the experience of Geneva II and acknowledging the stagnant international political climate, which did not encourage prospects of an early settlement, Cordovez used the intervening period to consolidate understandings already developed and to make adequate preparations for the next step.[50]

Steady Stocktaking

The exchanges held during the 1983 UNGA session were comparatively relaxed. They soon focused on the need to reaffirm, in writing, understandings on the conceptual framework and operation of a "policy mechanism" for the comprehensive settlement, and on a future agenda for the diplomatic process. This systematic approach—

articulated in a Note for the Record compiled in December 1983 on the basis of New York discussions held from September to November 1983 between Cordovez and his two principal interlocutors— yielded a clearer statement on the integrated and interrelated character of the settlement, ruling out definitive agreement on any component prior to the completion of the whole settlement. Furthermore, it was stipulated that the format of the comprehensive settlement, which was yet to be determined, would not alter its integrated character or the interrelationships conceived for the implementation of the various elements.[51]

The specific understanding on the future course of action included agreement not to reopen the provisions of Section II and to complete the formulation of all the provisions of Section I. This was an important advance for Pakistan since Section I addressed its central interest, namely the time frame for withdrawal. Other steps called for the resolution of issues relating to guarantees, including the identification of all possible guarantors, and finalization of arrangements for consultations with the refugees to "ascertain the voluntary and unimpeded character" of their return. Responding to the constant Afghan pressure, a provision was included to review the negotiating procedure, in particular an "arrangement that might be considered for the holding of direct talks." Insofar as the provision did not call for direct talks, Pakistan could live with it.

Cordovez visited the region 3–15 April 1984 to pave the way for the next Geneva round. He had moved slowly, arguing that the UN process could not afford a setback and every step had to be well prepared to ensure progress. The long gap had bred some concern among the Pakistani negotiators, who desired the continuation of the Geneva process to avoid domestic perception of a failure of diplomacy and to preempt new and less attractive international initiatives taking shape. Cordovez knew that delay in undertaking an early round could be used to soften the positions of the interlocutors. But he, too, could not afford to postpone the resumption of the process for very long. Stakes for the United Nations and for him personally were considerable.

During the April 1984 shuttle, Cordovez obtained an understanding in Islamabad and Kabul that legally binding forms for the agreements under the comprehensive settlement could include bilateral agreements and that the next round would endeavour to finalize outstanding issues, especially guarantees and arrangements for ascertaining the "voluntary and unimpeded" character of refugee return.

To accommodate Pakistan's insistence on the need for progress on withdrawal, he persuaded the Afghans to accept an understanding that Kabul and Moscow would engage in discussion for an agreement on withdrawal. On procedure, he created an optical illusion to placate the Afghans by proposing that the next round would be held on the basis of a new format of "proximity talks." This was essentially a change of semantics. In practical terms, it meant that the two delegations would sit in separate rooms at the same time, instead of holding alternate meetings with Cordovez at different times. He had thus temporarily staved off the brewing crisis on the issue of direct talks.

Besides these agreements, the shuttle had provided an opportunity for detailed exchanges on the issue of withdrawal. The most obvious difficulty was to reconcile the Soviet-Afghan insistence that the withdrawal was an exclusively bilateral issue with Pakistan's demand that the issue be addressed within the legally binding format of a comprehensive settlement. Cordovez was convinced that Moscow would not provide the time frame until the very end of the process. He argued that the time frame was a strategic decision that Moscow was unlikely to take unless it was fully satisfied with all aspects of the settlement. The critical requirement, in his view, was the completion of an agreed text and an understanding on the format.

On the eve of Geneva III Cordovez made new proposals for paragraphs relating to withdrawal and the format for the settlement. He based these proposals on his assessment of the fundamental concerns of the two sides. On the Moscow-Kabul side, the time frame for withdrawal was to be decided bilaterally and Section II converted into a bilateral treaty between Pakistan and Afghanistan. On the Pakistani side, the time frame had to be acceptable.

Accordingly, Cordovez presented a revised text of the draft comprehensive settlement with its four sections intact, along with a draft bilateral agreement based on Section II. In Section I he introduced a new paragraph to say that withdrawal of the foreign troops would be "in accordance with an agreement between Afghanistan and the Union of Soviet Socialist Republics." That paragraph was in addition to the paragraphs stipulating that withdrawal, like other operations, would commence thirty days after the conclusion of the comprehensive settlement and would be completed within a definite time frame that had to be specified.

The third Geneva round, 24–30 August 1984, was comparatively short. It had an inauspicious start but ended up providing an important impetus to the negotiations. For two successive days between 18 and 20 August, Afghan artillery and aircraft had shelled the Pakistani border area in the Kurram Agency, killing thirty-four persons and wounding many more.[52] The shelling resulted in a slow start for Geneva III as the Pakistani side had to go through the motions of protest. The Pakistan delegation had been contemplating an important initiative, but put it off for a few days so that it did not appear to be acting under intimidation.

The first two days were spent mostly on the issue of time frame and on Pakistan's suggestion that, if the Soviets considered the time frame to be the "trump card" to be disclosed at the very end, they should start by discussing modalities. The format of the settlement also came under discussion, since Cordovez had introduced the draft bilateral agreement in addition to the draft comprehensive settlement. Pakistan insisted on a legally binding form for the comprehensive settlement, while still withholding its acceptance to concluding a bilateral agreement with Kabul.

Pakistan Unlocks Its Position on Signature

On the third day Yaqub Khan offered to sign, together with the Kabul government, the draft bilateral agreement and the draft comprehensive settlement, *provided* an acceptable time frame was filled in. The move was intended to draw out the Soviets on a time frame and to put them on the defensive in the likely case of their unwillingness. The last draft prepared by Cordovez had facilitated this initiative by satisfying some of Pakistan's principal concerns, especially on guarantees. Also, Cordovez's hints during the April shuttle, regarding the demand by the other side for a bilateral agreement on noninterference, had given Pakistan sufficient notice to consider the matter and enabled Yaqub Khan to dilute Zia ul Haq's opposition to signing an agreement with the Kabul regime, provided the Soviets offered a short time frame.

Following Geneva III, Yaqub Khan strongly felt that the Soviets, having secured Pakistan's consent to the text of Section II, were engaged in a kind of "salami tactic," treating every situation as a new starting point and every concession by Pakistan as a platform to raise new demands. Also, in the assessment of the Pakistani side, the Afghan-Soviet side was not in a position to move on the time frame, and Pakistan was being unjustly blamed for lack of progress in the negotiations. For his part, Cordovez kept complaining about deep mistrust between the two sides, for which he seemed to hold the Pakistani side somewhat more responsible. Thus, the offer to sign, together with Kabul, the text prepared by Cordovez simultaneously met the requirement of an earnest—stressed by Cordovez—and countered the criticism that Pakistan was dragging its feet on the text of the settlement.

The offer hit the target. It took both Cordovez and the Afghan side by surprise. On hearing it from Yaqub Khan in a formal meeting, Cordovez sought clarification twice and, following a few minutes' silence, left the conference room to consult with the other side. He returned after a long session with the Afghans and admitted that their positions were unclear and confused.

Pakistan's move, even if tactical in character to deflect pressure and criticism, carried significant implications for the negotiations. As expected, it exerted considerable pressure on Kabul and the Soviets to clarify their position on the format of the settlement. Furthermore, the onus of objecting to the text, now acceptable to Pakistan, was on the Afghan-Soviet side.

The Afghan position came out in the open when they described the draft comprehensive settlement as an "interrelationships paper," which they were not prepared to sign. Pakistan could not become a party to an agreement on withdrawal. Similarly, in the Afghan view, the United States was an important party only insofar as interference was concerned, but it could not be involved with the settlement. In that case, remarked Yaqub Khan, "the comprehensive settlement goes in a limbo." Cordovez now had the clear task to persuade the Afghans to accept a legally binding format for the comprehensive settlement to which the United Nations was firmly committed in public statements, as well as in the secretary general's annual reports to the Security Council and General Assembly.

The Afghan vicissitude over the draft comprehensive settlement allowed Pakistan to further harden its position on direct talks. Although Pakistan had never accepted direct talks, at Geneva I and in a subsequent Note for the Record Cordovez had managed to secure Pakistan's acquiescence in considering changes in the negotiating procedure after sufficient progress had been made. Under Afghan pressure, Cordovez tried to draw in the Pakistani side on this point, constructing various hypothetical scenarios, but Pakistan never defined its position on the subject clearly. After Geneva III, Yaqub Khan took the position that Pakistan's readiness to sign an agreement had obviated the need for direct talks.

An important consequence of Yaqub Khan's move was that Pakistan could no longer raise new textual issues beyond the text presented by Cordovez in August 1984. That text, ipso facto, became Pakistan's basic position. The obvious casualty was the question of modalities for withdrawal; but the long discussions during the earlier rounds had convinced the Pakistani negotiators of the futility of asking the Soviets to agree to provide details of withdrawal in the text of the settlement. Furthermore, Pakistan did not envisage a time frame longer than six months. This expectation was encouraged by the fact that Cordovez would normally assume a six-month notional time frame to explain the operational mechanism of the draft settlement. Hints by Cordovez that he could guess the time frame the Soviets had in mind from his conversations with Gavrilov and other Soviet contacts created the impression that the notional figure of six months used by Cordovez could not be shorter than the time frame indicated to him by the Soviets.

Lack of response from the Afghan side to Pakistan's move obliged Cordovez to terminate Geneva III. This was followed by a hiatus in the negotiation until the death of Konstantin Chernenko in March 1985, which marked the end of the lingering crisis of succession in Moscow. Cordovez ascribed this predicament to deterioration in East-West relations.[53] Inside Afghanistan, the Soviet war effort had seen new escalation.[54] A long-term programme of Sovietization of Afghanistan appeared to have been set into motion.[55] Air raids along the Pakistani border were intensified.[56] At the same time the end of 1984 was a turning point, marking substantial increases in U.S. support to the Afghan Resistance.[57]

Negotiations in 1985: Geneva IV, V, and VI

The advent of Mikhail Gorbachev following the death of Chernenko on 10 March 1985 generated upbeat expectations that the dynamic new Soviet leader would bring about a movement in the stagnant Soviet policies identified with the erstwhile aging Soviet leadership. Gorbachev's early initiative on arms control[58] and his swift moves on the domestic political and economic front[59] began to have a favourable impact in the West.[60]

Although tangible signs of evolution in Soviet policy did not appear until early 1986, the change of leadership in Moscow and the concomitant improved atmosphere revived the Geneva negotiating process. Cordovez undertook a shuttle in the region and successively convened three Geneva rounds of talks between May and December 1985, even though signs for the anticipated change in Moscow's Afghan policy came slowly. These three Geneva rounds were registering progress on the format of the settlement until a new deadlock emerged when the Afghan-Soviet side linked the consideration of withdrawal to the issue of direct talks.

At Chernenko's funeral in March 1985, Zia ul Haq had been received by Gorbachev, but the meeting was harsh. A TASS report of the meeting carried a comment that "from the Soviet side a frank principled assessment was given of the policy being pursued in the matter by the government of Pakistan from whose territory aggressive actions are being launched against the Democratic Republic of Afghanistan."[61] Zia ul Haq later described the meeting to Cordovez as "intense."

Nevertheless, Gorbachev supported the Geneva process and accepted the role of the United Nations. The Pakistani side also discerned a positive signal in the fact that, unlike Chernenko, Gorbachev had decided to meet Zia ul Haq. Another noteworthy development was an indication of Soviet willingness to activate official Soviet-U.S. senior-level talks on Afghanistan following a break of three years.[62] The talks were held in Washington in June 1985. These positive signs gave rise to an expectation for movement in the Soviet position on Afghanistan and provided a fresh impetus to the Geneva negotiations, even though Moscow's military effort in Afghanistan had shown no sign of relenting.

Format of the Settlement

Cordovez resumed the UN-sponsored diplomatic process with a shuttle to the area 25–31 May 1985. His objective during the shuttle was to secure an agreement on the format of the settlement. He wanted Pakistan formally to accept the format of a bilateral agreement for noninterference to be signed by the two parties and to leave the remaining part of the comprehensive settlement, especially Section I, to be treated separately in an appropriate, mutually satisfactory form, such as a summary by the secretary general or letters to be addressed to the secretary general by the interlocutors. Such options for the format of Section I, which represented Pakistan's core interest in the body of the settlement, appeared unsatisfactory to Pakistan.

Time and again, Cordovez stressed that the Soviets could not make a commitment to Pakistan on withdrawal and that, in Soviet eyes, Pakistan, like Ecuador or Argentina, had no *locus standi* to demand a time frame, much less negotiate an acceptable time frame. On withdrawal, Pakistan should take the Soviet word at its face value. If Pakistan agreed to sign a bilateral agreement on noninterference with Kabul, and if the Soviets regained confidence in the credibility of Pakistan's commitments under the bilateral agreement, the Soviets would withdraw. It should not matter to Pakistan if they did so in pursuance of a legally binding arrangement or a unilateral press release, Cordovez insisted, citing the French position in Chad to suggest that withdrawal by definition was a unilateral act. By the same token, if, despite the bilateral agreement, the Soviets did not proceed with withdrawal, Pakistan would not be obliged to observe the bilateral agreement.

This argument ignored Pakistan's concept of an equitable settlement and its demand that commitments be sufficiently binding to minimize the possibility that the Soviets might use the settlement as a tactic to break the momentum of the resistance. Another point emphasized by Cordovez was the strategic significance of the time frame. He cited an article by George Ball, "Block That Vietnam Myth," which argued that President Nixon had destroyed U.S. bargaining leverage by prematurely announcing a major troop withdrawal and indicating U.S. intention to withdraw all forces.[63] After that, according to Ball, Hanoi only needed to wait and to stall on negotiations.

Pakistan could not accept this reasoning and recalled all previous understandings reached with Cordovez that an acceptable time frame would be part of the settlement. Yaqub Khan recounted the concessions that, in his view, Pakistan had made to facilitate the settlement, including its willingness to transform Section II into a bilateral agreement, and criticized Afghan recalcitrance in addressing the central issue of withdrawal. He reminded Cordovez that Kabul needed to be prodded about the follow-up on the understanding reached in April 1984 that Kabul and Moscow would hold discussions concerning an agreement on withdrawal. In formal meetings during the May 1985 shuttle, as during the earlier Geneva round, Yaqub Khan had to affirm Pakistan's right to demand a reasonable time frame, underscoring the change in Pakistan's security environment, the presence of refugees, and the border violations as direct consequences of the Soviet military presence in Afghanistan.

Cordovez's talks in Kabul made some advance. On his return to

Islamabad, Cordovez presented his idea of splitting the draft comprehensive settlement into four separate instruments for which legally binding forms could be developed. Pakistan agreed, *provided* all instruments were legally binding, possessed equal status, and preserved interlinkages and simultaneity, as envisaged in the existing draft comprehensive settlement. Geneva negotiations once again picked up momentum. Cordovez moved fast and scheduled three successive rounds at Geneva during 1985 in order to finalize the text.

At the fourth Geneva round of proximity talks (Geneva IV) convened 20–25 June 1985, Cordovez presented four separate instruments, with texts based on the four sections of the draft comprehensive settlement, except that Section I, which had presented the major difficulty, had now been retitled Instrument IV, with the obvious intention that it would be the last to be tackled. These instruments, later referred to in the secretary general's 1985 report[64] and enumerated as component parts of the settlement, included

1. A bilateral agreement between Afghanistan and Pakistan on the principles of mutual relations, in particular on noninterference and nonintervention.

2. Declaration(s) on international guarantees (by the Soviet Union and the United States).

3. A bilateral agreement between Afghanistan and Pakistan on the voluntary return of refugees.

4. An instrument setting out the interrelationship between the above instruments and the solution of the question of the withdrawal of foreign troops in accordance with an Afghan-Soviet agreement.

The formal title of Instrument IV was to be discussed along with its text at a later date. In transforming the sections into instruments, Cordovez made two technical provisions to preserve the agreed principle of the integrated nature of the settlement. He added in the first and the third instruments a preambular, or linkage, paragraph stating that the respective instrument was being concluded in the context of a comprehensive settlement defining interrelationships between withdrawal and other elements. The text on guarantees already included a reference to "commitment and support" to the comprehensive settlement. The Pakistani side conceded that the linkage paragraphs, which had drawn Afghan objections, could be dropped once a satisfactory text of Instrument IV preserving the integrated nature of the settlement had been agreed. Additionally, Cordovez provided a space for signatures under Instruments I and III that foreshadowed their bilateral nature, as Pakistan had in principle conceded at Geneva III.

Geneva IV began with the usual overture: Pakistan stressing discussion on time frame, Cordovez pushing for the finalization of the text, and the Afghans and Soviets refusing to deal with the issue of withdrawal in a manner that would legally appear to commit them to Pakistan or the United States. Cordovez started by identifying areas of divergence in the texts. By the end of Geneva IV, the following issues stood out clearly.

In Instrument I, the bilateral agreement on noninterference, the Afghan side revived its objection to the reference to "existing internationally recognized boundaries" that they had previously agreed under Section II. According to the Afghan argument, since Section II had been converted into a bilateral agreement, retention of the phrase in the new context would accord recognition to the Durand Line.

In Instrument II on international guarantees, the Afghans and Soviets objected to the paragraph, introduced by Cordovez at the behest of Pakistan toward the end of Geneva III, that referred to "commitment and support" to the comprehensive settlement. The text on international guarantees, in fact, became a major focus of discussion at Geneva IV.

In Instrument III on the voluntary return of refugees, Pakistan had one major demand and one textual difficulty. It continued to emphasize the requirement of consultation with the refugees to "ascertain" whether the arrangements and conditions incorporated in the text for voluntary return were acceptable to them. Furthermore, Pakistan was unhappy about the provision of "mixed commissions," as yet undefined. Pakistan rejected any arrangement involving "Pakistani and Afghan government personnel" as impractical and instead called for Pakistani-UNHCR and Afghan-UNHCR commissions operating separately on either side of the border. The Afghans, on the other hand, opposed UN consultations with the refugees. They also proposed a trilateral mixed commission comprising officials from Afghanistan, Pakistan, and the UNHCR.

Instrument IV was wide open. The Afghan side refused to consider either the text or the format and instead demanded vigorously that this instrument could be discussed with Pakistan only through direct talks.

Geneva V, on 27–30 August 1985, and Geneva VI, on 16–19 December 1985, remained preoccupied with the issue of direct talks and the related question of procedures and understandings needed to initiate discussion on Instrument IV. As the negotiations progressed, however, Soviet-Kabul resistance to dealing with the withdrawal issue in the framework of a legally binding instrument gradually weakened. Geneva V marked the last occasion when Yaqub Khan was again obliged to justify Pakistan's *locus standi* to ask for an acceptable time frame.

An Airport Meeting in Moscow

On the eve of Geneva V, when Yaqub Khan passed through Moscow en route to Geneva, the Soviets for the first time sought direct high-level contacts to discuss Pakistan's position on the instruments being negotiated and to seek clarifications. At Geneva, the Soviet representatives had studiously shunned contacts with Pakistan, a stance maintained until the final Geneva round in 1988. This unexpected gesture in August 1985 came from Soviet Deputy Foreign Minister Georgi Korniyenko, who received Yaqub Khan during his short stopover at Moscow airport, and suggested a private meeting with him to discuss Geneva-related issues.[65]

Korniyenko was interested in finding out from Yaqub Khan Pakistan's position on direct talks and the status of Instrument I (on noninterference). Pakistan's position on direct talks had by then been articulated in response to a formal query from Cordovez. Frustrated in its efforts to start discussion on time frame or Instrument IV, the Pakistani side now maintained that only after all the instruments had been finalized would they deem "sufficient progress" to have been made to justify consideration of direct talks. Yaqub Khan conveyed this position to Korniyenko.

On the second issue, Korniyenko wanted to confirm whether Pakistan had accepted the format of a bilateral agreement for Instrument I. According to Yaqub Khan, Korniyenko pulled the draft instruments from his pocket and, placing them on the table, pointed to the space for signatures under Instrument I. He asked if Pakistan would sign the agreement with the representatives of the DRA, and Yaqub Khan responded in the affirmative. The meeting elated Yaqub Khan, and, once again, the Pakistan Foreign Office looked for signs of Soviet interest in a settlement and actively sought contacts with the Soviets.

International Guarantees

The Afghan-Soviet objection to the inclusion of a paragraph affirming "support for the comprehensive settlement" in the text on guarantees at the conclusion of Geneva II had led to a protracted drafting exercise at Geneva III and Geneva IV. Several formulations were considered, such as "noting with satisfaction and support" for the settlement or a negative assurance stipulating that the guarantors would "do nothing to frustrate the objectives" of the settlement, but all were disagreeable to the Soviet-Afghan side, which did not want the text to go beyond noninterference. Cordovez was appreciative of Pakistan's view but was hamstrung, especially by the rigidity of the Soviet position.

A tentative compromise was reached at Geneva IV on a somewhat strained phraseology, with the understanding that the final say in the matter rested with the guarantors. This phraseology has survived and is preserved in the first two paragraphs of the Declaration on International Guarantees signed at Geneva in April 1988:

Expressing *support* that the Republic of Afghanistan and the Islamic Republic of Pakistan have concluded a *negotiated political settlement* designed to normalize relations and promote good-neighbourliness between the two countries as well as to strengthen international peace and security in the region; Wishing in turn to contribute to the achievement of the objectives that the Republic of Afghanistan and the Islamic Republic of Pakistan have set themselves, and with a view to ensuring respect for their sovereignty, independence, territorial integrity and non-alignment [emphasis added].[66]

It was also agreed at Geneva IV that Cordovez should transmit the text to the Soviet Union and the United States. At one point, China was suggested as a possible guarantor, since the Afghans also accused that country of interference, but the idea was dropped by Cordovez when the Afghans proposed India in addition, advancing a curious argument that the proposal was intended to balance China.

The Soviets responded quickly and presented a series of amendments to the compromise text during the August session. While asking for the replacement of the reference to the "negotiated political settlement" with "the Bilateral Agreement" on noninterference, the Soviet amendments introduced two significant concepts: first, an undertaking on the part of the guarantors, by virtue of "their standing," to prevent others from interference in the affairs of Afghanistan and Pakistan; and second, a provision for consultations with a view to considering measures for compliance. These amendments obviously carried far-reaching implications. Seen in the context of the history of the Pakistan-India conflict, they even possessed an attractive facet for Pakistan. And yet, they seemed to be a recipe for limited sovereignty, something unacceptable to Pakistan.

The Soviet comments also raised an intriguing question as to why the Soviet Union should confer upon the United States, its rival superpower, a treaty right as a guarantor for the security of an area in its own backyard. Indeed, one of the Iranian objections to the Geneva negotiations was to the involvement of the United States as a guarantor. During the final phase of the negotiations, the Soviets had become less enthusiastic about U.S. guarantees and even proposed that the Geneva Accords be concluded without the United States.

Toward the end of 1985 the formal acceptance of the United States was conveyed to Cordovez in a State Department communication. The United States could accept the draft guarantee instrument, it stated, provided that "the central issue of Soviet troop withdrawal and its interrelationship with other elements in the comprehensive settlement were effectively addressed and resolved." Soon after, the position was made public by U.S. Deputy Secretary of State John Whitehead.[67] The U.S. agreement on guarantees, which later came under hard-line criticism, was decided primarily by the State Department and cleared by the White House, though it was not seen by President Reagan personally.[68]

Conversations with State Department officials revealed that the decision was influenced by several arguments. One was that such guarantees were affordable, in view of the short, three- to four-month time frame that Pakistan then had in mind for withdrawal. Also, it was felt that U.S. hesitation to accept guarantees could detract attention from the real issue of withdrawal and attenuate diplomatic pressure on Moscow.

Cordovez appraised the U.S. decision in highly positive terms, but worried about public debate and a conservative backlash. Since the U.S. government had accepted the compromise text as agreed by the two interlocutors, Cordovez persuaded the Soviets to withdraw their amendments.

Direct Talks and Instrument IV

As confirmed by the secretary general's report of October 1985, when Geneva V convened in late August most of the textual issues were settled, except Instrument IV.[69] Texts of the two bilateral agreements were virtually completed. As noted, a text on guarantees, finally agreed between the two interlocutors in June, had been transmitted to the two guarantor states, namely the Soviet Union and the United States, for their concurrence. Pakistan insisted on starting discussion of Instrument IV and finalizing arrangements for consultations with the refugees. Cordovez wanted to push the pace of the negotiations, but soon these were stuck when Shah Mohammad Dost demanded direct talks as a condition for the discussion of Instrument IV.

The impasse revived Cordovez's chronic concern over distrust between his interlocutors. This time, he even sounded out Pakistan to consider deferment of the UNGA debate on Afghanistan as a gesture to the Soviet Union. Cordovez had always felt uneasy with these "annual carnivals" and worried about their impact on the negotiating process. Notwithstanding his irrepressible desire to explore new ideas, however improbable, Cordovez would hardly have expected Pakistan to give up on the UNGA debate, the single most visible occasion for demonstrating international pressure on the Soviet Union. The Soviets had just begun paying attention to the UNGA debate to gauge the impact of their moves on Afghanistan. At the Fortieth UN General Assembly session, in 1985, their stand on direct talks was put to the test.

In contrast to the growing signs of Soviet interest in a political settlement, the Soviet moves at the negotiating table were measured, circumspect, and closely coordinated with the evolving situation on the ground. Accordingly, the negotiations made steady but slow progress. While the discussion on the text of international guarantees had been wrapped up at Geneva IV, the succeeding two rounds in August and December 1985 remained dominated by the questions of direct talks and Instrument IV.

Confronted with the Afghan demand for direct talks at Geneva V, Cordovez attempted to work out an understanding for holding of direct talks immediately on completion of the texts of all instruments, including Instrument IV.[70] Both Pakistan and Afghanistan entertained reservations on the proposal, which was further pursued in December 1985 at Geneva VI. Meanwhile, the focus of the diplomatic process shifted to the UN General Assembly. The Afghan government, supported by the Soviets, waged an all-out campaign to build pressure on Pakistan for direct talks. At the United Nations they took the position that a settlement was in sight if only Pakistan were to agree to direct talks. Apart from the UN General Assembly, the main target of their effort was public opinion in Pakistan.

During 1984–85, with the escalation in bombing raids along the border, acts of sabotage in urban areas, and socioeconomic pressures inside Pakistan caused by the prolonged presence of the Afghan refugees, the critics of Zia ul Haq's Afghan policy had become increasingly vocal.[71] Besides the traditionally pro-Moscow elements exemplified by Pashtun leader Abdul Wali Khan, important sections of the opposition accused Zia ul Haq of using the Afghan issue to perpetuate his rule. The secular segment of the opposition had little truck with the Afghan parties based in Pakistan, nor did it have qualms over dealing with Babrak Karmal, particularly if this could promise a settlement based on withdrawal and return of refugees. This opposition, along with important sections of the domestic press, therefore, vigorously advocated direct talks and challenged the government argument that such a step could accord recognition or confer legitimacy on Karmal. The argument of legitimacy did not carry conviction, given the circumstances of the Zia government, as well as historical precedents. Direct talks had been held between many nations without implication of recognition, the U.S.-Hanoi negotiations being the most prominent example.

Pakistan's rejection of direct talks was politically motivated, but it also made good tactical sense. Direct talks would have politically damaged the resistance and bolstered the international standing of the Kabul regime. Tactically, it was feared that the Afghan side would try to turn direct talks into a series of bilateral meetings and, at the same time, make propaganda against Pakistan for lack of progress. The Afghan conflict would thus have gradually assumed the appearance of a bilateral issue between Pakistan and Afghanistan. Further, the inflexibility and reticence shown by the Afghan side on the issue of withdrawal convinced Yaqub Khan that negotiating a time frame for withdrawal would be impossible without the United Nations, which was committed to treating withdrawal as a component part of the settlement.

The rationale of Pakistan's opposition to direct talks was the principal theme of Yaqub Khan's address to the UN General Assembly at the time of the November 1985 Afghan debate and of his speech in the Majlis-e-Shura (parliament) that discussed the Afghan policy toward the end of December 1985. At the General Assembly he enumerated the considerations he had outlined during the preceding Geneva round to explain why Pakistan considered the demand for direct talks unreasonable and untenable. He argued that when three of the four instruments had been completed through indirect talks, it was illogical to ask for a change in negotiating procedure for the fourth instrument. Kabul's demand, he stated, was aimed at securing for itself a political advantage that had no relevance to the finalization of the political settlement.[72]

Addressing the domestic constituency in the Shura speech, Yaqub Khan was less restrained and spoke candidly of Pakistan's misgivings and fears:

There are those who call for direct talks with the Karmal regime not because they regard it as a legitimate regime, but because they feel it is the only way to facilitate a solution. The truth, however, is that there is no reason whatsoever to believe that such a move would lead to the withdrawal of Soviet troops and return of the refugees. . . . A resort to direct talks with Babrak Karmal would not change the objective situation in Afghanistan. It would only confuse and disappoint our own people, isolate us from our friends, encourage our adversaries and demoralise the Afghan refugees. Once you accord de facto recognition to [the] Babrak Karmal regime—and that is what direct talks would mean—you really have no basis to question whom he should or should not have invited, including foreign military forces, into his country. In effect, we would have legitimized the present situation including the presence of foreign troops in Afghanistan as a fait accompli. We would thus have made a unilateral concession, alienated domestic and external support, and weakened our position morally as well as materially. We would have in fact moved even further away from our objectives of securing the withdrawal of Soviet forces from Afghanistan and the voluntary return of Afghan refugees to their homes.[73]

At the 1985 General Assembly session, the Afghanistan delegation accused Pakistan of going back on an understanding to hold direct talks. While the Pakistani position had demonstrably stiffened on this issue, the fact remained that Pakistan had never specifically agreed to hold direct talks.[74] The possibility that the Afghans had got this impression from Cordovez could not be ruled out. To counter the accusation, nevertheless, Pakistan proposed that the United Nations make the Geneva record public in order to clarify the matter.[75]

The General Assembly vote on Afghanistan maintained and marginally increased its level in favour of the customary resolution calling for withdrawal. The direct talks issue had failed to make an impact, thus strengthening the hand of the Pakistan government in dealing with domestic pressure. The December debate in the Shura resulted in the predictable endorsement of the government position, thereby ruling out any possibility of Pakistan's acceptance of direct talks. The fate of the Afghan demand had already been sealed, however, earlier in November at a meeting in New York when Zia ul Haq conveyed to Secretary General Pérez de Cuéllar Pakistan's rejection of direct talks, foreclosing any flexibility by the Pakistani negotiators.

At Geneva VI, on 16–19 December 1985, Cordovez started looking for ways to lock the two sides into a discussion of Instrument IV, while circumventing the question of direct talks. He discerned a narrow opening in the Afghan position when Dost suggested that an indication of a date for direct talks would enable him to disclose the contents of the draft of Instrument IV prepared by the Afghan side. According to Cordovez, Dost pointed to a red folder that contained, he said, a complete draft. He claimed that this draft was better than the one Cordovez based on Section I, and that it defined all interrelationships in clear terms and gave dates for withdrawal. Cordovez proceeded to prepare a memorandum incorporating an understanding on elements of Instrument IV. He hoped that an agreement on the essential elements, including a notional time frame acceptable to Pakistan, could persuade the latter to acquiesce in direct talks.

Simultaneously, Cordovez explored ways to further tie down the Pakistani position on implementing Instrument I (the bilateral agreement on noninterference), with a view to softening the Soviet position. He sensed that the Soviets were not insistent on direct talks. Instead, to facilitate progress, they wanted positive assurances or evidence on the ground of Pakistan's capability to implement Instrument I.[76] As on past occasions, Pakistan had no intention of making any commitment on such specifics. Cordovez also asked for a definitive date for the implementation of Instrument I to establish credibility with the Soviets. Once again, in Pakistan's view, this date was linked to the date of the entire settlement. The Pakistani side, however, agreed to expand the thirty-day preparatory period, which, according to Cordovez, the Soviets found insufficient to complete the preparatory tasks required of Pakistan. The period was increased to sixty days.

The parallel discussions on the Cordovez memorandum remained inconclusive. Cordovez incorporated in it the essentials of his draft Instrument IV, which provided that the political settlement comprised the four instruments (integrity of the settlement); that all instruments would be signed on the same date (simultaneity and legally binding character); and that all preparatory steps would be completed by the date of entry into force of all instruments (balanced implementation). Specific reference was made to withdrawal, with a blank space meant to indicate time frame. These elements were all acceptable to Pakistan, but it was not ready to agree to negotiate Instrument IV in direct talks, because of its publicly stated fears. Hints from Cordovez that he had been shown a time frame that Pakistan would find acceptable did not convince the Pakistani side to give a date for direct talks as a quid pro quo. Nor was Pakistan moved by his pressure tactic suggesting that its inflexibility might blow up the opportunity for a quick settlement.

On the third day of Geneva VI the Afghan side made an advance by conveying to Cordovez the elements of the Afghan draft of Instrument IV and asking him to transmit these to the Pakistani side. Cordovez admitted that he had complied with the Afghan request only reluctantly, because these elements confirmed (as did the Afghan draft later transmitted in March 1986) the Pakistani suspicions that the Afghan side had not conceded the principles Pakistan had assumed to be the basis of Instrument IV. The Pakistani side would have found itself in an impossible position to discuss this instrument in direct talks that would have drastically curtailed, if not eliminated, the role of the UN intermediary.

The Afghan draft elements for Instrument IV included the following essential points:

1. Description of the objective of the UN diplomatic process as an effort for the achievement of settlement of the situation *around* Afghanistan.

2. Consent of the parties that the political settlement was based on generally recognized principles referred to in the bilateral agreement on noninterference and the right of the refugees to voluntary return.

3. Enumeration of the three agreements on noninterference, guarantees, and refugees (excluding instrument IV concerning withdrawals) as component parts of the accord.

4. Interrelationship between the three agreements and solving the question of the withdrawal of Soviet troops in accordance with a separate agreement between Afghanistan and the Soviet Union, including a time frame. (The draft had stipulated that the withdrawal would start on the entry into force of the other three agreements provided all steps required for their compliance had been completed. The withdrawal was envisaged in two phases, and the commencement of the second phase depended on the assurance that commitment to noninterference was being thoroughly observed and the "material basis" for such interference had been eliminated.)

5. Provision of consultations concerning the implementation of the bilateral agreement on noninterference.

Cordovez had by then also seen the detailed text of the Afghan proposal and found no point in continuing Geneva VI. He suggested adjournment and asked the two interlocutors to carry with them his memorandum, in which he had now filled in the figure of six months for time frame. He planned a shuttle to the area to start preliminary discussions on Instrument IV, pending the resolution of the issue of direct talks. Cordovez had also become more convinced of differences between the Soviet and the Afghan positions, although he conceded that the Soviets had to show solidarity with the Afghans.

This assessment was shared by Yaqub Khan, who theorized that the Soviet core interest was noninterference, while Kabul's core interest remained legitimacy, which explained its emphasis on direct talks. The revelation of the ideas that the Afghans had in mind for Instrument IV reinforced Pakistan's contention that direct talks would snarl up negotiations by allowing the Afghans to make untenable suggestions. Pakistan now insisted that direct talks could be considered only when all the instruments were finalized and ready for signature, or in Yaqub Khan's more graphic words, "when all the *i*'s are dotted and all the *t*'s are crossed."

Negotiations in 1986: Geneva VIIA and VIIB

The year 1986 brought forth increasingly visible signs of Soviet difficulties in Afghanistan and Soviet desire for a political settlement. The most significant indication came in Gorbachev's famous statement to the Twenty-Seventh Soviet Communist Party Congress on 26 February 1986. Describing Afghanistan as a "bleeding wound," Gorbachev stated:

We would like in *the nearest future* to bring the Soviet forces—situated in Afghanistan at the request of its government—back to their homeland. The schedule has been worked out with the Afghan side for a step-by-step withdrawal, as soon as a political settlement has been achieved which will provide for a real end to, and reliably guarantee a non-renewal of, the outside armed interference in the internal affairs of the DRA [emphasis added].[77]

Accordingly, the negotiations entered a new phase of expectations similar to but less euphoric than the early 1983 period. Progress on the vital issue of time frame proved to be slow, as a new direction in the Soviet policy emphasizing the internal dimension of the Afghan issue began to emerge. Meanwhile, the removal of procedural hurdles facilitated the finalization of the texts of all four instruments.

In March 1986 Cordovez set out to the area to pave the way for discussion of Instrument IV. He had yet to overcome the issue of direct talks. Gorbachev's statement, which conspicuously avoided any reference to the issue, held out encouraging prospects. Further, Cordovez needed to persuade the Afghans to abandon their draft Instrument IV and to accept his own draft, incorporating the formulations of Section I, as the basis for future discussion.

During the shuttle of 8–18 March 1986, Kabul finally dropped its insistence on direct talks and agreed to the finalization of the instruments through the existing procedure. On the face of it, the Afghan concession came when Cordovez introduced in his draft text of Instrument IV, under the paragraph recounting the history of negotiations, a sentence providing that after the finalization of the instruments, the procedure would be changed to direct talks on a certain date.[78] The sentence did not commit the parties to any specific date. Rather, it was agreed that the next round, namely the seventh, would be the last to be convened on the basis of proximity talks. However, it took more than one round before the instruments were finalized. The five rounds of talks held in Geneva between 1986 and 1988 were thus technically regarded as one continuing seventh round.

Why did the Afghans climb down from their demand? It is difficult to determine whether it was the result of Soviet pressure on Kabul or the consequence of a decline of the political position of Babrak Karmal. The chief protagonist of direct talks between Afghanistan and Pakistan, he had all along maintained that bringing about such talks was the aim of the UN secretary general's good offices.[79] In late March Karmal had reportedly left for Moscow for medical treatment;[80] and on 5 May 1986, virtually on the eve of the seventh round of Geneva talks, Karmal's resignation and his replacement by the Afghan security chief, Dr. Najibullah, were announced in Kabul.[81]

Premature Expectations for a Time Frame

Gorbachev's February statement, Kabul's consent to drop its demand for direct talks, rumours of impending change in Kabul that materialized just before the start of Geneva VII, and Cordovez's assertion that the seventh round would be the last proximity talks to complete the texts, all strengthened the belief that the Soviets were serious in seeking a settlement and could be expected to put forward a time frame. The Americans also expected the Soviets to make a move. Cordovez received positive vibrations both from the U.S. State Department and from Soviet representative Safronchuk, who had now joined the Soviet permanent mission in New York.

The international press had also picked up on speculation about a time frame. As early as 1 January 1986 the *New York Times* had mentioned one year as the time frame that the Soviets were expected to settle for.[82] The same figure appeared in the Pakistani press.[83] A *New York Times* story by Bernard Gwertzman quoted a senior State Department official as saying that Dost, at the December 1985 Geneva round, had shown Cordovez a "timetable" that planned withdrawal "within one year." It later transpired that this "leak" was based on confusion caused by Cordovez's memorandum and the summary of the Afghan draft Instrument IV given to Cordovez by Dost.

Within Pakistan, the newly elected government of Prime Minister Mohammad Khan Junejo was far more susceptible than the military government of Zia ul Haq had been to pressures exerted on Pakistan by the Afghan War. The Junejo government had also begun asserting its authority on matters of state vis-à-vis Zia ul Haq, now president and thus head of state in Pakistan's parliamentary system. At the high-level Afghan cell meeting in Islamabad in late April 1986, in which both the prime minister and the president now participated, the main agenda was the review of the pre-Geneva VII scenario and the upper limit of Pakistan's position on a time frame. The discussion largely meandered over the internal situation in Afghanistan and the need for the Soviets to accept a political change in Kabul for an implementable settlement.

One important outcome, however, was a somewhat controversial decision to mandate Yaqub Khan to accept a time frame with a maximum limit of one year. In response to Yaqub Khan's articulation of the issue, Junejo had remarked that Pakistan could live with a one-year time frame, while Zia ul Haq did not comment. Once the anticipated discussion on the time frame started at Geneva, however, Yaqub Khan took it upon himself to negotiate the shortest possible time frame and to seek Islamabad's guidance on every offer and counteroffer. Since cipher communication took time, a code was devised to seek instructions on the telephone.

Before Yaqub Khan's departure for Geneva, the Pakistan Foreign

Office conveyed on his behalf an interest in another airport meeting in Moscow with Korniyenko during Pakistan International Airline's convenient stopover there. This time Korniyenko was accompanied by Deputy Foreign Minister V. G. Komplektov, the new principal Soviet foreign ministry official dealing with Afghanistan. Yaqub Khan wanted to draw out the Soviet side on time frame, but Korniyenko appeared to be inhibited and Komplektov was not communicative. The meeting provided Yaqub Khan an opportunity to convey Pakistan's views on Instrument IV, the rationale for a short time frame, Pakistani commitment to sign the instruments with the DRA, and its desire for an early settlement. Yaqub Khan had presumed that the Soviets were ready to negotiate a reasonable time frame. The reserve on the part of the two Soviet officials was seen as mutual restraint that the two appeared to impose on each other (glasnost had not yet caught on), rather than as the absence of a definitive position on time frame and allied issues. As subsequent events revealed, the latter was closer to the truth.

Geneva VIIA was the single longest round, lasting from 5 to 23 May 1986. It was spent mostly on cleaning up the text of Instrument IV and various auxiliary issues, while waiting for a time-frame offer from the Soviet-Afghan side. The informal talks between Yaqub Khan and Cordovez during Geneva VII dwelt on the significance and implications of the change at the top in Kabul, which Cordovez tended to regard as the anticipated harbinger of Soviet moves toward a negotiated settlement. Najibullah could be trusted by the Soviets to keep an effective grip on the situation during the critical period of withdrawal.

Cordovez had expected the Soviets to offer a time frame on a take-it-or-leave-it basis. In his inimitable manner, he had tried to prepare the Pakistani side mentally for such an eventuality. During the March shuttle, he went to great lengths to explain the superpower psyche, concluding that, technically, the Soviet Union could not offer a time frame to either Pakistan or the United Nations, much less agree to discuss the time frame with Pakistan.

Cordovez was also troubled by the reference to a four-year time frame mentioned in the Afghan draft of Instrument IV, which he had passed on to Pakistan at Afghan insistence. That draft contemplated withdrawal of one-third of the forces in the first year and the remaining two-thirds in the next three years, provided compliance with the provisions on noninterference and the guarantees proceeded satisfactorily. However, Cordovez had asked Pakistan not to attach any significance to this "unreal" time frame and argued that the "true" time frame would come from the Soviets when everything was finalized.

Expecting an offer of one year, which he felt convinced was agreeable to the Americans, Cordovez wanted to tie down Pakistan's position to this figure. Pakistan, keeping in view Cordovez's notional figure of six months, talked of a three- to four-month time frame, asserting that this was sufficient from a logistical point of view. At the same time, like the Americans, the Pakistani negotiators shared the view that the Soviets would not want to take long to withdraw once they decided to do so.

While awaiting the time frame, Cordovez pushed for the finalization of Instrument IV and scored quick successes, except on the issue of monitoring the settlement. He simply squelched Pakistani reservations on the other parts of his draft text by characterizing them either as not basic or as attracting Soviet-Afghan objections. His task was facilitated by Yaqub Khan, who showed little tolerance for details of secondary importance and believed that "to add frills and gild the lily was going too far when dealing with a superpower."[84] A practical result, namely a short time frame, was what counted.

As the text developed, Yaqub Khan pressed Cordovez on the time frame. But their high expectations, which both genuinely entertained for different reasons, were soon to be disappointed. The initial delay was explainable in terms of lack of progress on the text of Instrument IV and possible confusion among the Afghan delegation as a result of the political change in Kabul. By the end of the second week, however, Dost started raising the issue of Iran with intriguing vehemence. Pakistan, in turn, pointed to the requirement of consultations with the refugees, stressing, at the same time, that a short time frame would be key to the attitude of Iran and the refugees toward the settlement. The new Soviet representative at Geneva, Nikolai Kosyrev, regarded as a more affable person than his predecessor, made no specific proposals. Instead, according to Cordovez, he criticized the Pakistani position of three to four months.

The issue came to a head when, despite reluctance on the part of Cordovez, the Afghan side asked him to formally convey the four-year time frame to the Pakistani side. Their proposal was accompanied by an elaborate rationale that Afghanistan had been under attack from Pakistan for more than seven years and that a long time was needed to undo the impact, neutralize the "political brainwashing" and "military capacity" of the resistance, and dismantle the resistance activity generated from Pakistani territory. Yaqub Khan reacted sharply, decrying the Afghan position as an attempt to "torpedo the whole basis of the negotiations" and as evidence that the Afghan side had treated the negotiations merely as a propaganda device. He threatened to break off the talks and make the Afghan position public. The same evening, Yaqub Khan asked the Pakistan delegation to go through the motions of finding appropriate flight connections and making tentative reservations for departure.

Cordovez, surely, saw no danger of a breakup of what had become a long, drawn-out negotiating process. Pakistan could hardly have a good reason to discontinue it. Nonetheless, the offer of a four-year time frame had given Pakistan a propaganda advantage and placed it in a position to expose the "lack of seriousness" on the part of Kabul and Moscow in negotiating a reasonable settlement. This could in turn relieve Pakistan of the pressure generated by press speculation about Soviet willingness to offer a one-year time frame.

Public disclosure of the Kabul offer would have embarrassed Cordovez, revealing his proclivity to make excessively upbeat projections.[85] At stake also was the credibility of the negotiations.[86] Accordingly, Cordovez proceeded to contain the damage, sympathizing with Pakistan's apparent disappointment and saying that the United Nations had formulated its own position of six months, as incorporated in the memorandum prepared by him in December 1985. Time frame, he agreed, had to be a matter of months, not years. He lamented official-level changes in Moscow,[87] slow communications, and uncertainty on the Afghan side, and asked Yaqub Khan to postpone his departure until Kosyrev was able to receive word from Moscow.

Cordovez admitted his perplexity when, three days later, Kosyrev endorsed the Afghan position as reasonable. Meanwhile, however, Cordovez had managed to cool temperatures. Dost had called the time frame negotiable and, as a token, had reduced the four years by six months. The taboo against Pakistan's *locus standi* to discuss time frame for withdrawal, stressed by Cordovez for nearly four years, had suddenly given way, thereby initiating a new phase of political and diplomatic manoeuvring centred around the time-frame issue.

Yaqub Khan had drawn his own conclusions: the Soviets had taken an initial negotiating position that could never be their final one if they wanted an agreement, which they did. They would now seek a compromise that depended on the objective circumstances and on the incentive for, and pressure on, the other side to come to terms.

During the August 1986 round, Geneva VIIB, Cordovez claimed that Kosyrev had bureaucratic problems and that Pakistan's insistence on a UN monitoring role was responsible for preventing the real time frame from coming through. To push the negotiation forward, Cordovez even turned up the pressure on Pakistan to draw out its minimum position on time frame. Given the unsound position taken by the Afghan side, Yaqub Khan refused to go beyond Pakistan's declared position of three to four months justified on logistical considerations. As it happened, the Soviets were in no hurry to settle the time frame. Their approach was shaping up in a new direction.

By July, contours of a new Soviet approach had begun to be visible, foreshadowing the search for an internal Afghan political settlement. In a Vladivostok address on 28 July 1986, Gorbachev enunciated wide-ranging policy initiatives toward China and the Asian Pacific and an important detailed statement on Afghanistan. Announcing the withdrawal of six regiments from Afghanistan by the end of 1986 and demanding reciprocity through the curtailment of outside interference there, he indicated Soviet preference for a resolution of the internal dimension of the Afghan issue, as follows:

We support the line of the present Afghan leadership [for] national reconciliation [and] widening of the social base of the April national democratic revolution, including the creating of a government with the participation in it of those political forces that found themselves beyond the country's boundaries but are prepared to participate sincerely in the nationwide process of the construction of new Afghanistan.[88]

By the end of 1986 the Soviet position on withdrawal and the provision of an acceptable time frame had become linked to progress toward an internal political settlement.

Finalization of the Texts

Cordovez found it prudent to try to settle the various outstanding issues in order to bring the time-frame issue under even sharper focus. Apart from textual issues like monitoring, the two political questions that received considerable attention during Geneva VIIB in August and the diplomatic shuttle of 20 November–3 December 1986 were the issue of consultations with the refugees and the intermittent Kabul-Soviet demand for Iranian support of the settlement.

Textual issues in Instrument IV. Five textual issues in Instrument IV that were subject to extensive discussion and drafting deserve to be highlighted for the nuances underlying divergent positions: (1) the phasing of withdrawal; (2) the "unconditionality paragraph," included in Cordovez's original draft of the comprehensive settlement, which provided that alleged violation of any of the provisions would not affect the continued implementation of all provisions of all instruments; (3) the requirement of balanced obligations (symmetry), to be incorporated in a separate paragraph stating that all steps required toward fulfilling the provisions of all the instruments would be taken, in good faith, by the date of implementation of the settlement (this was a mirror image of a similar paragraph already provided in Instrument I, the Bilateral Agreement on Non-Interference); (4) the form of Instrument IV; and (5) the monitoring of the settlement.

These were old issues; from Pakistan's point of view they were resolved in the text of Section I of the draft comprehensive settlement. But, as became evident at Geneva III in August 1984, that text was acceptable to neither the Afghans nor the Soviets. The crux of the Soviet-Afghan problem with Section I lay in Soviet-Afghan opposition to the idea of treating withdrawal as part of a package. As the Soviet position on this point relaxed, an agreement on the related textual issues became correspondingly possible. On each of these issues, especially that of monitoring, the Soviets started by taking a tough posture, but climbed down wherever Pakistan refused to compromise, because Pakistan could not do so without damaging the precariously balanced text proposed by Cordovez on the basis of Section I.

Pakistan had given up on modalities, but it continued to insist on a definition of phases. The years of discussion had reconciled Pakistan to the idea that, as long as the time frame was short, it did not matter how the Soviets withdrew in terms of modalities. The draft text, however, had qualified "withdrawal" variously as "phased" or "gradual."[89] Accordingly, Pakistan called for defining the phases for the purpose of monitoring and because refugees might be induced to return if the Soviets were seen to be withdrawing. Without such definition, the Soviet troops could theoretically stay until the last day of the time frame.

During 1986 Cordovez suggested to Pakistan that phases and broad modalities could become part of the Soviet-DRA agreement, which could be included as an annex to Instrument IV. Pakistan disagreed, fearing that such an agreement could contain other provisions unacceptable to Pakistan. A couple of variants on the same proposal were considered and rejected. In fact, the same logic had prompted a change in the paragraph on withdrawal and the phrase "in accordance with the Agreement between USSR and DRA" was replaced by "in accordance with the time frame agreed between USSR and DRA."

The idea of phases was finally introduced by Cordovez during the May 1986 session of Geneva VII, taking advantage of the Afghan draft of Instrument IV, which contemplated the withdrawal of one-third of the troops the first year, the remainder during the next three years. Accordingly, Cordovez introduced an additional sentence stating, "One-third of the troops will be withdrawn by ＿ and the withdrawal of all troops will be completed within ＿." The sentence was ultimately modified and completed on the basis of the Soviets' concrete offer made in 1988 for "front-loading" of withdrawal.

A paragraph on "unconditionality," or uninterrupted implementation, was originally introduced in Section I by Cordovez in conjunction with the paragraphs addressing alleged violations and clarifications that might arise in the course of implementing the settlement. The Pakistani side attached importance to this paragraph in view of its apprehension that the Soviets might use the continuing armed struggle inside Afghanistan as a pretext to stop withdrawal, thus using the settlement as a political manoeuvre to break the momentum of the Afghan Resistance and defuse international pressure.

Pakistan regarded the paragraph as an additional assurance of Soviet commitment to withdrawal, notwithstanding the military logic that a Soviet decision to withdraw would affect the morale of the Soviet troops, diminishing their interest in fighting and increasing their desire to leave at the earliest possible time. However, Pakistan was more concerned with the problems the seemingly fragile and amorphous resistance might face than with those of the Soviets in renewing their military engagement in a post-settlement period. The Afghan and Soviet objection to the paragraph, even though linked with their stand on the whole issue of withdrawal, served to aggravate Pakistani suspicions.

Faced with the Soviet-Afghan objection, Cordovez proposed deletion of the unconditionality paragraph. The best guarantee of uninterrupted Soviet withdrawal, Cordovez would argue, was the scrupulous observance by Pakistan of the provisions of Instrument I on noninterference. At one point he also pointed out that both the Soviet Union and the United States had reservations about the paragraph, which was perceived as a double-edged sword. Cordovez also made a legalistic argument, one he said was shared by the Soviet and U.S. legal experts, that, under customary international law, alleged violations could not be used by treaty parties to suspend implementation. This did not make much impact—first, because the paragraph had been introduced by Cordovez's own principal legal aide, and second, because the Pakistani negotiators had little claim on legal expertise and were more sensitive to political considerations. Nonetheless, the Pakistani side gradually relented, especially in view of its increasing insistence on an effective monitoring system, which appeared to undercut the logic of its demand for the retention of the unconditionality paragraph.

The Soviets and the Afghans had also asked for the deletion of the paragraph ensuring balance, or symmetry, in the preparatory steps to be taken by the respective parties to fulfill their obligations under all the instruments by the date of implementation. Pakistan, on the other hand, insisted on retention of the paragraph. From a conceptual point of view, it reasoned, the settlement must preserve equity not only in the implementation of the various elements, but also in the preparatory steps leading to their implementation. Absence of this paragraph from Instrument IV while the Bilateral Agreement on Non-Interference, Instrument I, included a specific provision for preparatory steps would have been detrimental to Pakistan's concept of an equitable settlement. More than for its practical utility, Pakistan needed the symmetry paragraph to defend the settlement domestically. It had to be able to say publicly that preparatory steps were required in respect of both noninterference and withdrawal.

In the final text Cordovez accommodated Pakistan's concern in a consolidated paragraph, defining simultaneous operations for the implementation of the various elements of the settlement, as well as completion of preparatory steps in all aspects prior to the implementation. An optical illusion of a compromise was thus created by retaining the idea but dropping reference to it in a separate paragraph, as Pakistan had originally wanted in order to balance the similar paragraph in Instrument I.

The resolution of the question of the legal status and format of Instrument IV became easier with the Soviet readiness to discuss withdrawal and time frame in the context of the Geneva negotiating process. Prior to 1986 the Soviets and the Afghans had vaguely conceded the need for a "mother" document, of a less than formal status, to define interrelationships between the various elements and withdrawal, the latter to be decided separately between the Soviet Union and Afghanistan. It was even conjectured that, like salmon, this informal mother document would dissipate after spawning separate independent agreements. The Afghan draft of Instrument IV provided for its separate certification by the interlocutors and the state-guarantors and for its transmission to the secretary general. Pakistan, on the other hand, insisted on the legally binding character and equal status of all instruments, while showing flexibility on their specific form. Theoretical options such as an endorsement by the Security Council or formal transmission to the secretary general were considered, but Pakistan preferred formal signature for Instrument IV, if it were to sign Instruments I and III as bilateral agreements. An auxiliary question was the appropriate form of guarantees that could avoid difficulties arising from U.S. constitutional procedure.

Like the Pakistani side, Cordovez favoured a neat, document-signing format to conclude and formalize the agreements. Noting the change in the Soviet attitude on the question of withdrawal, Cordovez proposed a paragraph laying down that the representatives of the parties to the bilateral agreements (Afghanistan and Pakistan) would affix their signatures in the presence of the secretary general, while the state-guarantors would signify their consent to the provisions of Instrument IV. Following his shuttle to the area in November–December 1986, when the text of Instrument IV was finalized following an agreement on monitoring, Cordovez put forward a text with space for four signatures, identifying the interlocutors and the state-guarantors. He also included a provision for signatures under Instrument II on guarantees. The proposal did not draw reservations. The main question raised before the final round in 1988 was the level of representation.

Monitoring. A mechanism for regular review of progress in implementation and for addressing any issues or alleged violations arising in the process of implementation had been envisaged in Section I of the draft comprehensive settlement. It was predicated on the continuing role of the personal representative of the secretary general, namely, to "monitor the on-going implementation process," as well as to assist the parties and propose specific measures to ensure complete observance of the provisions of the comprehensive settlement. The same provision, acceptable to the Pakistani side, was brought into the draft text of Instrument IV by Cordovez during Geneva VII.

The Soviets and the Afghans objected to a UN role in monitoring withdrawal, raising the question of the UN's *locus standi*. They proposed restricted bilateral consultations between Pakistan and Afghanistan to look into complaints regarding implementation of the agreements. Only in that context could assistance be sought from the personal representative of the secretary general or the state-guarantors.

In response, Pakistan asked instead for a viable and central role for the United Nations, one that would require the UN mediator to remain in touch with all parties, including the state-guarantors, and to provide or obtain information that could enable him to recommend specific measures to ensure implementation. Pakistan conceded bilateral consultations only if these were to be organized by the UN mediator with the consent of the parties. Yaqub Khan argued that bilateral consultations could easily lapse into a counterproductive exchange of accusations and, further, that complaints and their adjudication required a neutral mechanism. The underlying motivation, however, was to avoid commitment to establishing formal contacts with Kabul, which could place the Pakistan government in a difficult position with the Afghan Resistance. Also, effective monitoring could help assure uninterrupted implementation of withdrawal. These considerations prevailed over misgivings within the Pakistani side that a strong monitoring mechanism with UN involvement could become an instrument of pressure on Pakistan.[90]

The early Soviet objection to the UN's *locus standi* to monitor withdrawal made Cordovez pessimistic about the Pakistani demand.[91] He cited traditional Soviet opposition to a UN peacekeeping role and believed that the Soviets would not even agree to keep the UN secretary general informed about withdrawal. If Pakistan desired effective monitoring, then it would have to exclude withdrawal from the monitoring purview.

Cordovez also tried to play down the need for UN monitoring, because he felt that Moscow would not backtrack on withdrawal and that the United States possessed the means to monitor and ensure continued Soviet withdrawal. In any event, Cordovez would argue, Article 33 of the UN Charter could always be invoked to seek intercession by the UN secretary general. In Yaqub Khan's view a short time frame could circumvent the need for credible, effective, and impartial monitoring, but since an acceptable time frame was nowhere in sight, a substantial UN role in monitoring appeared essential. Kosyrev reportedly complained that Pakistan had first asked for monitoring and then raised impossible demands. By the end of Geneva VIIB in August 1986, however, he indicated to Cordovez Soviet readiness to accept a UN role.

Cordovez had all along wanted the continuation of his role after the settlement. The green signal from the Soviets enabled him not only to obtain an agreed text for monitoring, which was referred to as "arrangements for the implementation of the settlement," but also to propose an elaborate memorandum containing a plan for the stationing of an observer group in Kabul and Islamabad to oversee the implementation. The memorandum eventually became an annex to Instrument IV. Agreement on monitoring completed the text of Instrument IV, sharpening the focus on the time frame for withdrawal.

Cordovez had proposed the stationing of two five-member teams in the respective capitals, headed by a senior military officer as deputy to the secretary general's representative. If necessary, the number of personnel could be raised to twenty-five in each capital. The logistical support was to be provided by the host government. For the duration of the arrangement, Cordovez had first suggested that it coincide with the time frame for withdrawal, but he later modified the duration to cover the longest time frame available in the instruments, namely, the eighteen months specified for arrangements for repatriation of the refugees. To avoid the need for prior approval of the Security Council, the personnel for the teams were to be drawn from the existing UN peacekeeping operations. For the same reason, the nomenclature for the arrangement was changed from observer group to the UN Good Offices Mission in Afghanistan and Pakistan (UNGOMAP).

All along, Cordovez was anxious about Security Council endorsement of the arrangement. He feared a debate in the council, especially on mandate, and advocated that it should be avoided in the interest of preserving a congenial atmosphere for the implementation of the Accords. Besides, he worried that the Security Council would raise technical questions on placing UNGOMAP under the relevant department of the United Nations, excluding his direct control.[92]

The elaborate structure of UNGOMAP, which was in place until March 1990, was attributable initially to Cordovez's preference.[93] After the signing of the Geneva Accords, however, the Soviets wanted to strengthen UNGOMAP to undertake more vigorous inspections. For Pakistan, the original sponsor of the idea, UNGOMAP was beneficial only in one unexpected way. The UNGOMAP inspections and findings provided Pakistan with the best defense against the ceaseless Soviet-Kabul complaints accusing Pakistan of violating the Geneva Accords.

The Issue of Consultations with the Refugees

The provision for consultations with the refugees was made in the Note for the Record agreed in June 1982, following the first Geneva round. Since the UN format precluded the Afghan mujahideen and refugees from becoming a party to the Geneva negotiating process, Pakistan had sought their involvement with the process through this provision conceived under Instrument III. The promise of consultations helped Pakistan to soften criticism from the Afghan refugees, expatriates, and the resistance, who did not agree that Pakistan could represent their interests in the negotiations.[94]

For Pakistani negotiators, the requirement of consultations was essentially a matter of form; they had no illusions about substantial involvement in the negotiations by the refugees or the Tanzeemat, as the Peshawar-based parties were referred to before their alliance in May 1985. It was felt, however, that a short time frame would mitigate opposition to the Geneva process and bring about Tanzeemat acquiescence in the Geneva settlement. The confidence that the outcome of the negotiations would be accepted by the Tanzeemat was based on assurances given by the ISI chief, Lieutenant General Rahman. (The Pakistan Foreign Office became skeptical about these assurances after October 1985 when Gulbuddin Hekmatyar, who was leading a mujahideen delegation in New York, refused to proceed to Washington to meet President Reagan. Despite a long telephonic effort by General Rahman to persuade him to change his mind, Hekmatyar insisted that he had not been mandated by the Tanzeemat shura to visit Washington.) The principal concern of the Pakistani side was that consultations must look credible.[95]

Cordovez had his reservations on consultations. He showed deep sensitivity about making any commitment that could embarrass him with Moscow or Kabul, which firmly vetoed any contacts between the United Nations and the Tanzeemat—later the Afghan Alliance—or the refugees, with the exception of the UNHCR. In August 1984 Dost made a strong demarche to Cordovez, asking him to denounce a statement by an Afghan expatriate group that designated Zahir Shah as their representative to conduct negotiations with the

United Nations. Accordingly, prior to 1986, Cordovez treated his contacts with Afghan expatriates as highly confidential.[96]

Cordovez also suspected that through consultations with the refugees, Pakistan was keeping to itself an option to stall on a negotiated settlement. He did not find convincing the repeated Pakistani assurances that neither the refugees or the Tanzeemat would be allowed to exercise a veto on the settlement. Furthermore, he felt that he need not oblige Pakistan on an issue which, from his point of view, was unlikely to contribute to the negotiating process but which risked the annoyance of Kabul and Moscow. Nonetheless, the long, drawn-out Geneva rounds provided ample opportunity to discuss the subject and explore the feasibility of consultations.

The first exclusive discussion to outline an understanding on consultations with the refugees took place in August 1983, following the resumed Geneva II. The basic questions to be addressed included (1) who would carry out the consultations; (2) who was to be consulted, and whether the Tanzeemat leadership would be involved; (3) what would be the scope of consultations, the entire settlement or only Instrument III; (4) what would be the status of the refugee responses and how would these be interpreted; and (5) what would be the modality of consultations.

For the Pakistani side, the minimum condition for credible consultations required some form of direct association of Cordovez with the process, participation of the seven Tanzeemat leaders, and inclusion of a general briefing to the refugees and Tanzeemat representatives about the settlement. With these caveats, the Pakistani side had virtually committed itself to stage-manage the consultations in deference to concerns on the part of Cordovez.

Timing posed a dilemma. With no reasonable time frame available, no positive outcome was likely to result from consultations. After Geneva II, when the difficulties in obtaining a time frame had become increasingly evident, Pakistan suggested that consultations be initiated positing the availability of an acceptable time frame, with a view to ascertaining refugee comments on Instrument III, so that it could be finalized. Another possibility was to organize consultations in two or more stages.

Aware of the Kabul-Soviet sensitivity, Cordovez tried to persuade Pakistan to accept exclusive UNHCR responsibility for consultations, with their scope limited to Instrument III. The UNHCR, in any event, had shown reluctance to undertake consultations that, it rightly suspected, were politically loaded. In addition, Cordovez could not agree to the participation of the Tanzeemat leaders. He pointed to technical grounds invoked by the Afghan side that the Afghans residing in Pakistan prior to December 1979 could not be counted among refugees.

Following detailed discussions in August 1983, Cordovez presented his first tentative ideas on arrangements for consultations, which envisaged a small UN/UNHCR team to be selected in consultation with Islamabad and Kabul. The team was supposed to consult a wide cross section of refugees, to be selected by the teams on the basis of information provided by the two governments. The scope of consultations was to be limited to illustrating to the refugee representatives the structure of the comprehensive settlement, the conditions of voluntary return (then contained in Section IV), and the role of the United Nations and relevant agencies in repatriation and rehabilitation of refugees. The team was supposed to submit a report to Cordovez, who would then inform the two interlocutors of the conclusions reached in regard to the specific question whether the conditions of voluntary return were acceptable to the refugees or needed some modification.

This blueprint fell far short of Pakistan's minimal position, which, at the least, required Cordovez to inaugurate consultations, leaving their actual conduct up to his team. The deadlock persisted, so much so that at Geneva VIIA in May 1986, the Kabul side interpreted the clause "having ascertained that the arrangements for the return of the Afghan refugees are satisfactory to *them*" (emphasis added) to imply that the arrangements were to be satisfactory only to Pakistan and the DRA.[97] In case Pakistan wanted to consult the refugees or any other Afghans, in this reading, it could do so on its own without involving the United Nations.

The question of legitimacy was at the heart of Kabul's strong objection to any contact between Cordovez or the United Nations and the Tanzeemat/Alliance leadership. Cordovez had therefore ruled out his participation in consultations or contact with the Tanzeemat/Alliance leadership. At Geneva VIIA he admitted that there was a clear understanding between the United Nations and Kabul that the UN team would neither be involved in anything like a real or perceived dealing with the seven Alliance leaders nor could it be involved with the refugees in political negotiations. While waiting for an Afghan move on time frame at Geneva VIIA, Cordovez attempted yet another memorandum along the lines of his suggestions of August 1983. His new proposals further narrowed the mandate of the

UN team, requiring consultations to focus exclusively on Instrument III.

Until late 1986 Kabul continued to demonstrate extraordinary sensitivity over any dealings between the United Nations and the Afghan Resistance. In November 1986, prior to the UN General Assembly debate on Afghanistan, members of the Afghan mission in New York physically assaulted the Alliance representatives when they entered the UN building in New York at the invitation of the UN Correspondents' Association.[98] Cordovez's extra, albeit understandable, caution in maintaining a distance from the Tanzeemat/Alliance leadership engendered a feeling of bitterness, especially among its fundamentalist component. This gravely impaired Cordovez's capacity to deal with them in pursuit of his subsequent second-track negotiations on the question of a future government in Kabul.

The change in Kabul's attitude that allowed Cordovez to establish contacts with the Alliance leadership came late and virtually coincided with Najibullah's enunciation of his policy of national reconciliation. By then, military successes scored by the mujahideen during the course of 1986 compounded the grievances of years of neglect and further toughened the Alliance attitude toward the Geneva negotiations. The Alliance leaders no longer asked for their participation in the Geneva process; now they called for direct dialogue between the Soviet Union and the mujahideen, which they regarded as the two real parties to the conflict.[99] Sensing these changes, the Pakistani side no longer raised the issue of consultations after May 1986. That the issue had lost its relevance was suddenly revealed during Cordovez's shuttle to the area, 20 November–3 December 1986.

On returning to Islamabad from his first visit to Kabul during that shuttle, Cordovez expressed his willingness to meet the Alliance leadership, emphasizing that he wanted to do so at his own risk and off his own bat. Yaqub Khan undertook to arrange the meeting but reminded Cordovez that neither Pakistan nor the Alliance could accept it as the only meeting nor as a pro forma fulfillment of the obligation under the provisions of Instrument III. Cordovez made no commitment, but showed visible excitement over the prospect of meeting the Alliance leadership.

The meeting, however, did not materialize. According to ISI, the liaison agency, four of the seven leaders were outside Pakistan and the other three required prior approval by the Alliance's shura, its consultative assembly. All this could not be accomplished at short notice. The Pakistan Foreign Office, convinced that the meeting would add to the international stature of the Alliance, tried to seek Zia ul Haq's intercession. He appeared to share the Foreign Office view, but after Cordovez departed without meeting the Alliance, he remarked that the Alliance leaders carried many responsibilities and could not be summoned at short notice.

Cordovez felt disappointed and unhappy. He conveyed his feelings in a formal meeting with Yaqub Khan in strong terms, virtually accusing the Pakistani side of playing games and disclaiming all obligation on the part of the United Nations to carry out consultations with the refugees. Puzzled by its failure to arrange the meeting, the Pakistan Foreign Office found itself out of tune with the thinking within the Alliance, as well as that of the ISI. After the November–December 1986 shuttle, the issue of consultations was quietly dropped. The Pakistan Foreign Office decided to share with the Alliance leaders the contents of the agreements being formulated at Geneva, and in January 1987, for the first time, provided them a detailed synopsis of the texts.

The political climate changed rapidly with Soviet support and the push for national reconciliation in Afghanistan enunciated by Dr. Najibullah on 31 December 1986. The Alliance leaders had gained the status of armed opposition in the eyes of the Soviets, and their support was considered crucial for the success of the national reconciliation policy. Cordovez was quick to grasp the implications of the policy shift and tried to establish direct contacts with the Alliance leaders at the first opportunity, which became available at the Islamic summit conference held in Kuwait in late January 1987. His overtures, however, did not elicit a meaningful response beyond handshakes and perfunctory exchanges in the Conference Hall lobbies.

The Issue of Iran

The Iranian question had undergone a metamorphosis from the early Pakistani position seeking Iranian participation in the negotiations to the later Kabul-Soviet demand for involving Iran as a party to the Geneva process and securing its commitment to the provisions of noninterference. Apparently, the Soviet failure to pacify western Afghanistan, especially Herat, and intermittent visits by some of the Alliance leaders to Tehran fed suspicions that if Pakistan accepted a settlement, the centre of interference would shift to Iran. The draft of Instrument IV presented by the Afghan side toward the end of 1985 had specifically envisaged separate bilateral agreements on noninterference with Pakistan and Iran as part of the political settlement.

Notwithstanding the rejection by Iran of the Geneva negotiating process and its strong support for the mujahideen as the legitimate representatives of the Afghan people, Pakistan had always believed that once a settlement acceptable to Pakistan had been worked out, Iran would go along with it, even if not endorsing it. On its part, Pakistan kept in close touch with Iran and encouraged Cordovez to do the same. For obvious reasons, however, it could not undertake to ask Iran to accept a framework for the settlement that Pakistan had negotiated at Geneva.

The first tangible progress with Iran was achieved by Cordovez during the April 1984 shuttle when, at Pakistan's request, Iran had received Cordovez. The outcome was the first and only Note for the Record containing the paraphrased version of the well-known Iranian position. In its essence, the Note for the Record referred to Iranian support for the legitimate interests of the Afghan people; the Iranian policy with regard to withdrawal of Soviet troops, return of refugees, and the need for the Afghan people to freely determine their own future; and an Iranian commitment to endorse a political settlement consistent with these interests and principles.

From early 1985 Iran began to figure as one of the major concerns expressed by the Afghan side and the Soviet representative to the Geneva negotiations. During Geneva VII the issue was raised with considerable seriousness.[100] Dost even proposed that Afghanistan agree only to withdrawal of one-third of the Soviet contingent initially, withdrawal of the remaining two-thirds to be withheld until Iran had endorsed the settlement.

While such propositions could not be considered, the issue of Iran remained a constant irritant for Cordovez. He agreed that Iran could not be asked to accept the agreements negotiated between Pakistan and Afghanistan, and he tried to work out language embodying a formal Iranian commitment along the lines of the Note for the Record of April 1984. He thought of negative assurances from Iran in terms of a commitment not to do anything contrary to the objectives of the settlement. Another alternative was to obtain a positive Iranian endorsement in a statement that the provisions of the settlement were consistent with the legitimate interests of the Afghan people and the principles espoused by Iran. None of these alternatives were presented to the Iranian authorities for consideration. Pakistan was willing to play a supportive role, but refused to negotiate such an undertaking by Iran.

The Pakistani side believed that the Iranian reaction to the settlement depended on the time frame and the reaction of the mujahideen. In addition, Soviet officials were in direct contact with Iran. The exchanges between the two countries had intensified after 1986. The Soviets had even suggested a quid pro quo, offering Soviet help to Iran in its conflict with Iraq, provided Iran could accommodate Soviet concerns in Afghanistan. It was therefore incongruous for the Soviets to have pressed Pakistan to obtain a commitment from Iran. On its part, Iran showed understanding of Pakistan's participation in the negotiations, but had no intention of associating itself with a process rejected by the mujahideen. Iran also maintained a strong declaratory policy demanding Soviet withdrawal and the establishment of an Islamic government by the mujahideen.

5

A Changing External Environment, 1985–86

By the end of 1986 the negotiations had moved out of the narrow channel of discussion on the Geneva instruments into a more complex field intertwining consideration of time frame for withdrawal with efforts to seek an internal political settlement. Meanwhile, globally and regionally, the political landscape surrounding Afghanistan had undergone a far-reaching transformation. This chapter will briefly survey the new circumstances forming the context of the negotiating process.

Gorbachev, Détente, and Afghanistan

The extraordinary changes in Soviet policies and outlook exemplified by Gorbachev's glasnost and perestroika and his exceptional dynamism have become a cliché. In the early period, however, analysts and observers accustomed to the established, stereotyped view of the Soviet Union found it difficult to visualize the reach of the changes and their implications for specific issues.[1] Nonetheless, the thinning out of the Kremlin old guard and new appointments to the all-powerful Politburo foreshadowed rejection of the Brezhnev legacy. Furthermore, Gorbachev showed an eagerness in opening up toward the West. Some of the high-profile positions dealing with external affairs were filled by "old America hands."[2] The change in Moscow soon started producing a thaw in East-West relations, manifest in the revival of U.S.-Soviet summitry following a hiatus of over six years.

The arms control negotiations had been a touchstone of détente and East-West relations, but the Soviet military intervention had slowed down the momentum of these negotiations following SALT II. President Reagan had come into office calling for a linkage that made progress in arms control contingent upon Soviet good behaviour and restraint.[3] Under pressure from nuclear disarmament lobbies and West European allies, the Reagan administration soon disavowed this linkage. Following President Reagan's "zero option" proposal in November 1981, the Intermediate-Range Nuclear Forces (INF) talks started at Geneva between the two superpowers in early 1982. Despite a dynamic independent of the regional issues, the arms control talks proceeded in fits and starts, with considerable polemical content reflecting deep mutual distrust.[4] A turning point came with the November 1985 Gorbachev-Reagan summit meeting at Geneva, which created an inexorable push toward the INF Accord, signed in December 1987.

Given the centrality of arms control in East-West relations, many political observers had believed that movement on Afghanistan could not precede an important advance in the arms control negotiations. The resumption of U.S.-Soviet summit-level contacts and growing prospects for progress in the INF talks by mid-1986 produced expectations of a change in Soviet policy on Afghanistan and necessitated a review of the conventional assumptions about "Soviet aggressive behaviour and expansionism." Several questions became moot. What was the place of Afghanistan in the new global vision identified with Gorbachev? Would the Soviets accept an ideological retreat from Afghanistan that appeared to be the logical consequence of withdrawal? What would be the new Soviet terms for a settlement on Afghanistan? Notwithstanding the improved atmospherics, diplomats and analysts searched for specific Soviet signals on the Afghan issues. The signs of change in the Soviet Afghan policy, however, emerged somewhat haltingly in Soviet press and public utterances, often wrapped in layers of unrelenting rhetoric. Accordingly, even the most optimistic assessments made in 1985 and most of 1986 were conditioned by doubts. Caution continued to be the hallmark of policy recommendations.

Afghanistan clearly posed a challenge to Gorbachev's policy initiatives. It had offered the United States a low-risk, high-gain policy option to put pressure on the Soviet Union. Following Gorbachev's description of Afghanistan in February 1986 as "a bleeding wound," Soviet officials would often assert in private conversations that the United States wanted the Soviet Union to continue to bleed in Afghanistan. International costs inflicted by Afghanistan on the Soviets could not be ignored. Soviet peace initiatives were unlikely to make a full impact as long as Afghanistan could be invoked to call

Soviet motives into question. For example, in response to Gorbachev's Vladivostok address, China had publicly demanded Soviet
withdrawal from Afghanistan as one of the three conditions for normalization of relations.[5] Soviet diplomatic manoeuvrability in the
Islamic world, despite Moscow's consistent support on the Palestine
question, was impaired by the Afghan issue. Within the Soviet
Union, another point of pressure seemed to emerge as glasnost made
it difficult to conceal the Afghan War. All this signified a new development, even though it was insufficient for gauging the real depth
of public concern.

In contrast to the apparent pressures on Gorbachev to seek a political settlement of the Afghan issue and positive signals that the
Soviet policy was evolving in that direction, the period after Gorbachev assumed power in the Kremlin, especially 1986, also produced a more vigorous military campaign to pacify the Afghan
Resistance and increase military pressure on Pakistan.[6] Indeed, the
military activity appeared to have increased after the well-reputed
Soviet Army General Mikhail Zaitsev assumed command of the Afghan theatre of war in July 1985. Given the inevitable comparison
with the U.S. experience in Vietnam, analysts did not regard this
development as necessarily pointing to Soviet disinterest in a political settlement. But it did raise questions as to what the Soviets
wanted to accomplish in Afghanistan before they would agree to
withdraw. In retrospect, the failure of the military effort to subdue
the Afghan Resistance discredited its hard-line proponents and
strengthened Gorbachev's hand in seeking diplomatic recourse.

On the diplomatic front, the advent of Gorbachev brought about
more coordinated Soviet efforts to influence international opinion
and dilute censure of the Soviet military intervention. The standard
rhetoric of Soviet-DRA statements at the UN debates during the 1980
through 1984 sessions,[7] were replaced by new themes based on carefully timed initiatives and systematic efforts to erode support for the
UNGA resolution on Afghanistan. In 1985 the Soviet-DRA arguments
were built around direct talks; in 1986 the emphasis was placed on
Gorbachev's offer to unilaterally withdraw six regiments and a demand for reciprocity; and in 1987 a major diplomatic campaign was
launched with Najibullah's national reconciliation proposals as the
central theme.[8] Each time, Pakistan and its allies at the United Nations were obliged to further intensify their efforts to prevent slip-
page in the vote.

Pakistani officials viewed the multiple directions of Soviet policy with ambivalence. They could not disregard the possibility that Gorbachev's moves could turn out to be new and subtle tactics to achieve the essential goals of the military intervention. The new orientation of Soviet policies was not yet settled enough to dispel old suspicions. From the conventional perspective, the Soviets could hardly be trusted to tolerate a military or political setback in neighbouring Afghanistan. Furthermore, despite the fact that the Soviets had once again started conceding the costs of the conflict, seen from Islamabad these costs were not intolerable and appeared to be on the decline. After all, the INF talks had progressed unhindered, even though the U.S.-Soviet exchanges on regional issues, especially Afghanistan, had little to show. Despite China's declared but unmet preconditions, its relations with the Soviet Union marked a positive movement, especially in trade talks.[9] Internally, Moscow was never known for its sensitivity to public opinion.

Caught in the dilemma of conflicting interpretations of changes in Soviet policy, Pakistan explored Soviet signals in two specific critical areas. On the Geneva track, it tried to elicit the Soviet position on time frame. Side by side, encouraged by Gorbachev's Vladivostok statement, Pakistan tried to determine the extent to which Moscow could accommodate a change in Kabul. These were the dominant facets of the Pakistani approach to the negotiating process during late 1986 and most of 1987.

The United States, Pakistan, and the Afghan Resistance

Linked to the Afghan issue, three areas of activity and cooperation developed in the revitalized U.S.-Pakistani relations. First and foremost was the U.S. commitment of economic and military assistance to Pakistan, epitomized in the five-year, $3.2 billion package of economic assistance and military sales credits. This represented a top priority for the United States also, because Pakistan was now treated as a "frontline" state that needed to be strengthened. Second was the interest shared by the United States and Pakistan in bolstering the Afghan Resistance to keep military pressure on the Soviet Union. In this area, cooperation between the two countries grew in dimension with time as the resistance showed staying power and gained the backing of conservative lobbies in the United States. The third area of cooperation related to diplomatic activity centred on Afghanistan, including the negotiations, which identified the United States as one of the guarantor states.

The new close relations between Pakistan and the United States were not free from problems. They were subject to pressures from nuclear nonproliferation lobbies on Capitol Hill who pressed the Reagan administration to obtain ironclad assurances from Pakistan that it was not engaged in any clandestine nuclear weapons programme. Clearance of annual installments of the 1981 package depended on a certification by Reagan that Pakistan did not possess a nuclear device. The process was dicey every year because of alleged uranium-enrichment activity being pursued by Pakistan.[10] The yearly debate in the House Appropriations Committee and other relevant bodies of the House and the Senate lent strength to thinking within official circles in Islamabad that Pakistan's critical position in the context of the Afghan issue was the most reliable guarantee for the continuation of the U.S. aid commitment to Pakistan.

The obvious correlation between the Afghan issue and U.S. assistance to Pakistan was often cited to support the argument that Pakistan, especially the military under Zia ul Haq, would not favour a move toward a settlement. In reality, however, Pakistan's position in the negotiations remained unaffected by U.S. assistance, which otherwise figured prominently in foreign policy considerations. Occasionally, Pakistani officials would conduct an exercise to assess the impact of a settlement on the continuation of U.S. assistance, but the prospect of an aid cutoff never seriously prompted a policy-level review of Pakistan's positions at the Geneva negotiating process. These positions were largely guided by the intrinsic logic of the negotiations. During later stages, they showed more sensitivity to Pakistan's domestic pressures than to cares about curtailment of U.S. assistance.

The post-1979 geopolitical situation carried new, reassuring factors which mitigated the concern over a sudden ebb in Pakistani-U.S. relations that might follow an Afghan settlement. First, the Afghan situation was unlikely to cool down immediately after the signing of a settlement, making it inconceivable that the U.S. commitment to Pakistan would evaporate overnight. With the experience of the Soviet advance into Afghanistan and the disappearance of Iran as an ally, Pakistan had gained a new geostrategic importance in American eyes that was likely to continue. Pakistan's substantial military commitment in the Persian Gulf, including Saudi Arabia, enhanced this position. Furthermore, as a matter of policy, Zia ul Haq meticulously cultivated contacts with U.S. conservative and military circles with a view to building an influential lobby in the United States favouring close relations with Pakistan.[11]

While Pakistan had earned high accolades for looking after the refugees, its effort to regularize the flow of humanitarian assistance to the Afghans often drew complaints from Afghan émigré groups and the nongovernmental organizations involved. From 1984 Pakistan tried to restrict the number of nongovernmental humanitarian organizations, which had already proliferated to over fifty. These organizations enjoyed considerable freedom of operation and were highly active among refugee camps. The resulting problems obliged Pakistan to encourage the systematic channeling of outside assistance through UNHCR or, later, through the Afghan Alliance committees.

On military supplies, however, Pakistan exercised complete control, which was resented by American advocates of direct assistance to the mujahideen. The demand could not go very far because of the improbability of any arrangement's bypassing Pakistan.[12] Muted rancour over this issue occasionally surfaced in criticism of purported manipulation of resources by Pakistan for its own benefit and for controlling the mujahideen.

On negotiations, one must distinguish official U.S. positions from the attitude of the conservative, pro-mujahideen lobbies. U.S. rightwing misgivings about the negotiations were conditioned by their antagonistic view of the Soviet Union, as well as by Afghan émigré and mujahideen perceptions. Besides resenting the exclusion of the mujahideen from the negotiations, the protagonists of the Afghan cause deeply suspected a settlement predicated on the cutoff of supplies to the mujahideen. These lobbies dismissed the negotiations as a Soviet ploy and fully endorsed the mujahideen demand for UN and international recognition as legitimate representatives of the Afghan people.[13]

After an initial period of disinterest, the U.S. State Department more or less followed the Pakistani lead on the negotiations. The first test came in late 1985 when the draft guarantees were forwarded by Cordovez to the State Department and the latter agreed to endorse the text. The decision drew criticism from right-wing elements, but U.S. officials were able to defend U.S. agreement to become a guarantor primarily because Pakistan was then insisting on a short time frame of three to four months.

That the State Department had deferred to positions adopted by

Pakistan at Geneva was underscored by Secretary of State Shultz in reply to a strong protest made in January 1987 by Senator Gordon J. Humphrey and Congressman Jack Kemp. Prompted by a *New York Times* report referring to U.S. agreement to an aid cutoff to the mujahideen prior to withdrawal and a statement by Shultz alluding to U.S. willingness to accept a more flexible time frame, Humphrey and Kemp had registered their "strongest objections" to U.S. readiness to guarantee a "sellout." Referring to a Senate resolution, they asserted that the time frame must not exceed four months. In clarifying his position, Shultz strongly affirmed U.S. support for the mujahideen, but pointed out that the principal party engaged in the negotiations was Pakistan and that the United States supported Pakistan's position, without getting into the "numbers game" on a timetable for withdrawal.[14]

The United States had opted to play a supporting role instead of a direct negotiating role. Unlike the Soviet Union, the United States did not send a representative to Geneva until the very last session in 1988. Similarly, U.S.-Soviet contacts concerning Afghanistan were preceded by consultations with Islamabad and avoided negotiations on any aspect of the settlement. Their scope was largely limited to sounding out the other side's position.

Several factors had shaped this U.S. stance. First, the State Department appreciated internal pressures on the Pakistan government for an early political settlement. Second, it was aware of the limitations on its seeking direct dealings with the Afghan Alliance and the mujahideen. Pakistan was the only feasible conduit. Third, a leading role would not only have made the United States an easy target of criticism for the lack of progress toward settlement, but would also have coloured the issue with an East-West stigma that could have impaired support within nonaligned circles.

Pressures on Pakistan

The war next door and the presence of refugees gradually exerted considerable political, socioeconomic, and, in later years, military pressures on Pakistan, correspondingly building public interest in an early political settlement. Until 1984 the main burden on Pakistan resulting from the Afghan conflict was the presence of the Afghan refugees. After 1985 the problem was compounded by an escalation in air and ground violations of the border regions and widespread sabotage. The indirect but far more severe consequences of the Afghan conflict were visible in the proliferation of arms and the rising level of violence and unrest in Pakistan. The opposition increasingly attacked Zia ul Haq for pursuing a dangerous Afghan policy in the interest of prolonging his rule. This criticism intensified after 1986; domestic politics in Pakistan changed and became more sensitive to public pressures. This section, however, focuses on the direct pressures exerted on Pakistan by the conflict.

The initial problems arising from the presence of the refugees were socioeconomic, such as clashes with locals over water and pastures, acquisition of property, and establishment of businesses, especially commercial transport. The government of the North West Frontier Province (NWFP) faced lawsuits involving enormous sums of money sought as compensation for land used for refugee camps. In some areas, especially Chagai and Pishin in Baluchistan, demographic patterns changed quite dramatically.

In the early years, however, these problems remained contained and to a certain extent offset by the economic activity and employment generated as a result of foreign relief assistance for the refugees, which averaged nearly $200 million annually.[15] Furthermore, ethnic and cultural affinities had softened the impact of the influx. The strong religious ethos and feeling of Islamic and Pashtun solidarity explained the relative harmony and understanding between the refugees and the local population. Credit also went to tribal elders and local refugee leaders who constantly urged the locals and the refugees not to cause offense to each other.

Given the enlarging scale of the refugee population, their protracted stay, and the growing concern that they would never go back to Afghanistan, problems unavoidably increased with time.[16] Mujahideen activity in the border areas, proliferation of arms, Khad infiltration, and the involvement of religious political parties with the refugees had been among the major causes of existing tension and occasional conflict. An increase in bomb blasts after 1986 added to the tension and gradually intensified war-weariness in urban centres, especially in the NWFP.[17] The worst example of these tensions—and, correspondingly, of the success of the Kabul regime in playing upon tribal and sectarian rivalries in the border regions of Pakistan—was the disaffection of the Kukikhel Afridi tribes in the Khyber Agency in November 1985 and the festering conflict between the mujahideen and the Turi tribes in the Kurram Agency from late 1986.[18] Kabul also tried unsuccessfully to incite tribal dissidence among the Marris of Baluchistan.[19]

The escalating military pressure and sabotage carried out in the course of later years prior to the signing of the Geneva agreements could be gauged by official figures released by the Pakistan government. Until 1984 the average number of air violations remained well under 100 a year, with ground violations near 30; by comparison, air violations in 1985, 1986, and 1987 were 251, 757, and 644, respectively, and ground violations in 1986 and 1987 rose to 170 and 244. In 1987, 337 persons were killed by aerial bombardments inside Pakistani territory and 40 by artillery shelling. Incidents of subversion similarly escalated: 381 in 1986 and 414 in 1987. Casualties increased proportionally. Virtually every major city in Pakistan was hit.[20] Splashed in the media, these acts of sabotage had caused considerable anxiety among urban populations. In the popular perception the blasts were attributed to the Afghan War and the presence of the Afghan refugees. The circumstantial evidence and information gleaned from captured saboteurs in NWFP and Baluchistan pointed to Khad agents.

The Pakistan government came under growing public pressure to adopt countermeasures against air and ground violations and sabotage. Efforts by the Pakistan Air Force to check air violations by providing an expensive air "cap," or defensive cover, to the area using the newly acquired F-16s proved ineffective.[21] Warning time available to act against the intruding aircraft was extremely short, especially in mountainous areas, and Pakistan did not allow its aircraft to cross over into Afghan territory. Pakistan eventually approached the U.S. government in 1986 to supply Airborne Warning and Control Systems (AWACS). Although the negotiations bogged down because of U.S. reluctance to lease the system, as desired by Pakistan, support on Capitol Hill and the impression of an imminent deal in 1987 caused considerable anxiety in New Delhi.[22] Even though no linkage could be established, the possibility of a deal later in 1987 coincided with a perceptible lessening in the frequency of air violations by Afghan aircraft.

Pakistani law enforcement agencies appeared helpless in containing bomb blasts, which had been the main source of harassment in urban centres. Indeed, the spectre of increased sabotage activity and internal subversion through inciting tribal, ethnic, and sectarian unrest seemed the most realistic form of retaliation the Soviets and the

Afghans could employ against Pakistan. In the absence of any control over the movement of citizens in the country and because of the massive number of Afghan refugees, it was not practical to segregate refugees from local populations. Earlier, in 1984, half-hearted measures by the NWFP provincial administration to confine the refugees to camps because they had created pressures on jobs in the cities were soon abandoned.[23]

Despite increased public frustration, however, demand for a change in Afghan policy did not pick up. Two psychological factors appeared to be responsible. First, the target of criticism became diffused as a political dyarchy developed at the top following the February 1988 elections in Pakistan. Second, the repeated claim by the Pakistani side that the time frame was the only outstanding issue not only held out hopes for an early settlement but also projected the government position at the negotiations in a positive light.

On the diplomatic plane, the Soviets constantly reminded Pakistan of the negative impact on mutual relations caused by its support of the Afghan Resistance. In the later years of the war, sharp Soviet demarches were prompted by the Matni incident in May 1985, when Soviet prisoners were reportedly killed in a cross fire inside Pakistan's tribal territory, and later by mujahideen incursions against Panyzh in March–April 1987. The Soviets had also been warning Pakistan against the introduction of Stingers. A somewhat surprising protest was made in June 1986 prior to Geneva VII, expressing Soviet concern over Pakistan's nuclear programme and describing it as a threat to the security of Pakistan's neighbours, especially Afghanistan.[24] Soviet demarches during late 1986 and 1987 lost some of their stridency because of the glasnost-inspired admission that the intervention in Afghanistan had been a mistake.

A more intangible pressure stemmed from the fear of a possible Indo-Soviet collusion against Pakistan, which subsisted in the psyche of Pakistani policymakers. Concern over Indian intentions had been a constant element in Pakistan's evaluation of threats to its security, but it deepened after Operation Blue Star against the Golden Temple in Amritsar in June 1984 and the continuing unrest in the Indian Punjab.

The Indian government frequently accused Pakistan of helping Sikh extremists. In late 1986 tension between the two countries assumed serious dimensions when unusually large-scale Indian military exercises, dubbed Brass Tacks, led to the adoption of a quick succession of measures and countermeasures by the two armies, virtually pushing them to the brink of confrontation. Swift diplomatic action averted mishap, and an agreement was reached defining the procedure for disengagement. Zia ul Haq even visited India in February 1987 to defuse the tension. The move underscored his eagerness to keep the traditional hostility between India and Pakistan contained within limits.

But for Gorbachev's conciliatory tone during his visit to New Delhi in November 1986 and the parallel Soviet initiative to start a dialogue with Pakistan,[25] the Indian moves would surely have been interpreted in Islamabad as a manifestation of an Indo-Soviet collusion. The Brass Tacks operation, however, served to highlight the precarious nature of Indo-Pakistani relations and Pakistan's vulnerability to a two-front situation. It reinforced opinion in Pakistan in favour of an early Afghan settlement. Writing for the *Times* of London, Michael Hamlyn commented that Pakistan was in need of a settlement as it was "disturbed by large Indian troop movements" along its eastern borders and "the tribal situation" was giving Pakistan "cause for concern."[26]

Domestic Scene Changes in Pakistan

Pakistan's domestic scene began to change with Zia ul Haq's successive decisions to hold elections on a nonparty basis in February 1985, to lift martial law on 30 December 1985, and to share power with the new government of Prime Minister Mohammad Khan Junejo under the amended 1973 constitution. With these developments, Zia ul Haq's grip on policymaking started loosening almost imperceptibly, even though the illusion of his continuing to be the final arbiter of the policy persisted. Despite amendments, the constitution had retained its essentially parliamentary character, conferring executive powers on the prime minister, who steadily asserted his authority in state affairs.

By early 1987 a de facto dyarchy had set in. The extent of Junejo's independence of action and of the concomitant power struggle was evident in the top army appointments made in March 1987. Junejo had appointed General Mirza Aslam Beg to replace the retiring deputy chief of army staff (COAS), General K. M. Arif, apparently ignoring Zia ul Haq's preference for another general to fill this sensitive post. General Beg was the most senior among several equally qualified candidates. Under the constitution, appointment of the deputy COAS was the prerogative of Junejo as chief executive. In a political sense, however, by disregarding Zia ul Haq's preference, Junejo trespassed on what was supposed to be Zia ul Haq's turf.

Tension in the foreign policy arena had become visible by late 1986. Indeed, during the Brass Tacks crisis, Junejo had only grudgingly acquiesced in having Zia ul Haq and the armed forces call the shots, and this further impelled Junejo to try to take charge of foreign policy. On the other side, Zia ul Haq's impromptu decision to embark on "cricket diplomacy" with India in February 1987[27] and his strident speech on the eve of the foreign policy debate in the Parliament in April 1987 were eloquent signs of his effort to regain a hold over foreign policy.

As a politician, Junejo appreciated the political benefits that would accrue to him if he were seen to be responsible for achieving a negotiated settlement on Afghanistan. With problems resulting from the Afghan War on the increase, Junejo gradually pushed to gain control over Afghan policy, hitherto the exclusive preserve of Zia ul Haq. As the power struggle between the two leaders intensified, the policy began to suffer from lack of focus.

Ironically, just as the negotiating process entered the critical final phase, increasing paralysis afflicted the internal coordination necessary for analysis and policy direction of the negotiations and for adjusting Pakistan's policy to the rapidly evolving military and political situation in Afghanistan. This situation was at its worst following the resignation of Yaqub Khan as foreign minister in October 1987. By then, political polarization at the highest echelons of the government had become public. Divergent and often conflicting signals originated in the statements of Zia ul Haq and Junejo. The consequent emaciation of Pakistan's capacity to coordinate and take well-considered initiatives had an important bearing on the course of the diplomatic process, especially when it attempted to address the internal aspect of the conflict in Afghanistan.

Soviet Signals on Afghanistan, 1985–86

Signals of Soviet interest in withdrawal began appearing in 1985 and became clearer in their direction with the passage of time. Each time, however, they served to emphasize intent and left vital questions of detail unaddressed. They gave the impression of movement in the Soviet position, but stopped short of revealing the extent to which the Soviets were willing to compromise on either time frame or the issue of future government in Kabul. The most authoritative signals came from Gorbachev himself. In addition, the Soviet media, as well as official and nonofficial comments, indicated changes in Soviet outlook and policy. It would be useful to trace and review these signals to understand why they elicited cautious and circumspect response.

The first indications of altered ideological nuances were discernible as early as April 1985 in Moscow's annual greetings message to the Afghan leadership.[28] In comparison with previous years, the message omitted references to the leading role of the PDPA and to the CPSU's "revolutionary solidarity" with the PDPA, thus representing a downgrading of the ideological status of the PDPA. The new Soviet thinking appeared to reevaluate the Saur Revolution and the role of the PDPA. At the CPSU Central Committee Plenum in October 1985, as reported by *Sovietskaya Rossiya* on 15 October, Moscow reportedly undertook a major review of Soviet policies and priorities.[29]

In an interview in *Pravda* in late 1989, Najibullah recalled that Gorbachev had first hinted about withdrawing Soviet troops in a meeting with Babrak Karmal in 1985 (perhaps during Karmal's visit to Moscow in May 1985), saying that "we must think together" about the issue. According to Najibullah, Karmal's face "darkened" and he said, "If you leave now, you will have to send in a million soldiers next time." Najibullah said he did not agree with Karmal's approach at that time.[30]

Karmal's tentative effort to broaden the base of his government in conformity with Moscow's new thinking was evident in his ten-point thesis unveiled in early November 1985. The points, which were quickly endorsed by the Soviet media, had underscored for the first time DRA willingness to include non-PDPA members in the DRA State Council and to promote a mixed economy. In December 1985 *Pravda* carried an elaborate article that praised the DRA regime for initiating a "broad dialogue" among all forces in the country, including those who "so far stick to positions hostile to the revolution," and endorsed the regime's readiness to accept representatives of various strata into governmental organs. In the same breath, however, this article suggested that the main purpose of the policy of "reconciliation" and "compromises" remained the isolation and destruction of "the counter-revolutionary forces."[31] The Soviet media's assertion that the regime and the Saur Revolution were "irreversible"[32] was not new, but the emphasis on the regime's efforts to broaden its base and steps to seek support from various segments of the Afghan society carried a new message.

The first clear statement of the Soviets' difficulties in Afghanistan and their desire to withdraw was made in Gorbachev's report to the Twenty-Seventh CPSU Congress in February 1986, when he blamed counterrevolution and imperialism for turning Afghanistan into a bleeding wound and expressed the intention of bringing the Soviet forces back "in the nearest future."[33] Preceding this statement, TASS had reported that Shevardnadze had told Cordovez on 11 February 1986 that "Moscow firmly intends to make certain that the year 1986 should see substantial progress" toward an Afghan settlement.[34]

The Twenty-Seventh CPSU Congress also provided the first indications of tension between the Soviets and Babrak Karmal. The most telling evidence was the fact that no Soviet leader was reported to have received Karmal. The statement of the Afghan leader at the CPSU Congress showed a clear difference of approach.[35] Karmal made no reference to withdrawal, even though Gorbachev's report had pointedly drawn attention to the schedule already worked out with the Afghans for step-by-step withdrawal. In early May, Karmal was removed from the top post in Kabul.

Following Karmal's departure, the first public hint that the Soviets desired the PDPA government to enlarge its political base was implied in the routine Soviet greetings on the eighth anniversary of the Saur Revolution in April 1986. The message highlighted the "policy of the PDPA to attract support of the masses."[36] The Vladivostok address by Gorbachev in July 1986, however, carried the first clear direct signal of Soviet encouragement to the PDPA regime under Najibullah to invite all political forces, including those outside the borders of Afghanistan, to participate in a broad-based government.[37] Soviet officials and Soviet news media were quick to pick up this and other Vladivostok themes and began highlighting the Soviet desire to withdraw in the near future, making salutary references to the Geneva talks and the possibility of a political settlement.

Soviet interest in seeking early withdrawal was further underscored by new signs in October and November 1986. Two instances deserve special mention. First, on 20 October 1986, Soviet television broadcast an unprecedented programme highlighting the anxiety of mothers and wives of Soviet soldiers serving in Afganistan.[38] This was a new questioning of Soviet involvement in an unpopular war. The second event was the Dartmouth Conference organized in Moscow, 11–15 November 1986. In one of the sessions the Soviet participants made unusually elaborate comments on their view of "national reconciliation" in Afghanistan and concluded on a note that the Soviet Union did not want to control Afghanistan and was only interested in a government friendly to Moscow. For a solution on that basis, the Soviets suggested cooperation between the United States and the Soviet Union.[39]

From Pakistan's point of view, the most significant Soviet signals during 1986 included, first, the positive movement in the Soviet position at Geneva. The demand for direct talks was given up, and there was willingness to discuss withdrawal and a UN monitoring role. Second, was the conciliatory tone adopted by Gorbachev during his visit to New Delhi in late November 1986. At a press conference, the Soviet leader avoided criticism of Pakistan and made meaningful comments in response to questions on Afghanistan, stating that the Soviets had "no intention to stay [in Afghanistan] forever,"[40] that the Soviet Union looked forward to the establishment of an "independent, nonaligned, neutral" Afghanistan,[41] and that the Soviet Union had a long history of good-neighbourly relations with Afghanistan "even under kings."[42] Third, was the Soviet decision to resume bilateral dialogue with Pakistan in the respective capitals, following a break of nearly three years.

Prior to 1984 Moscow and Islamabad had pursued a routine of holding exchanges before each UNGA session. Beginning in 1980, these exchanges were used by Pakistan to sound out Soviet views in regard to Afghanistan and also to impress upon the Soviet side its desire to develop normal bilateral relations, notwithstanding the differences on Afghanistan. This practice was discontinued by Moscow in 1984 and 1985, but resumed in 1986 when Anatoly Volkov, then head of the South Asia Department of the Soviet Foreign Office, visited Islamabad in September 1986.

Discontinuation of the exchanges did not, however, mean a cutoff of communications between the two capitals; their respective embassies had continued to operate and the two foreign ministers continued to meet during UNGA sessions. Volkov's visit was followed by a Yaqub Khan-Shevardnadze meeting in New York in late September and the visit of Foreign Secretary Abdul Sattar to Moscow in December, at the invitation of First Deputy Foreign Minister Yuli Vorontsov.[43] The beginning of 1987 witnessed an intensification of this dialogue, focusing on the issue of internal political settlement in Afghanistan.

In their contacts with the Soviets, the Pakistani officials tried to explore the meaning and scope of Gorbachev's reference to "the creation of a government [in Afghanistan] with the participation of those political forces that found themselves beyond the country's boundaries." The Soviet response remained unclear until the visit of Abdul Sattar to Moscow. Volkov in August and Shevardnadze in September 1986 interpreted Gorbachev's reference to imply only those political elements outside Pakistan who would cooperate with the PDPA regime. Shevardnadze went a step further when he explained to Yaqub Khan that the offer extended only to those groups not engaged in "armed struggle" against the PDPA government, adding that the composition and character of the Kabul government was not for the Soviet Union or Pakistan to determine. Instead, Shevardnadze emphasized, Pakistan needed to curtail interference to reciprocate the Soviet offer to withdraw six regiments. In that event, he said, time frame would not become a "roadblock." This apparent retraction in the Soviet position, in comparison with Gorbachev's statement, could have been attributable to difficulties faced by Najibullah within the Parcham group and opposition within the PDPA to inviting nonparty elements to become part of the government.

A promising indication came through informal contacts in September 1986 with Georgi Arbatov, head of the Kremlin's think tank on North American affairs. While praising Najibullah for having done better than his predecessor and accusing the United States of impeding Pakistan, Arbatov indicated that some representatives of the refugees and mujahideen could be brought into a broad-based government, provided they behaved as "honest participants" and did not expect to substitute for the PDPA government. This position was endorsed by Vorontsov in his meetings with Foreign Secretary Sattar in December 1986 in Moscow.

Vorontsov unveiled to Sattar the elements of the national reconciliation programme, later enunciated by Najibullah, and provided the first candid insight into Soviet concerns and thinking. Vorontsov emphatically affirmed that the Soviets had decided to withdraw, but argued that simple withdrawal could lead to bloodshed and that a "cooling off" period was necessary in which the Afghan parties could observe a cease-fire and engage in discussions.

The Vorontsov-Sattar meeting not only helped to provide a better understanding of Soviet thinking, but set the parameters for the future course of the negotiating process. The following features of the new Soviet thinking became obvious:

1. The Soviets desired a political settlement, which was essential for unencumbered pursuit of Gorbachev's global initiatives for détente with the West and peace and security in Asia and the Pacific, as well as for his policies of glasnost and perestroika. The Soviets wanted a respectable end of their misadventure.

2. The Soviets had put the Geneva process on hold and were shifting attention to seeking an internal political settlement in Afghanistan before withdrawal. Practically, time frame was linked to national reconciliation.

3. The Soviets were concerned over the possibility of the "massacre" of their supporters following withdrawal. Paradoxically, at the same time, they asked for a substantial, if not pivotal, role for Najibullah and the PDPA in a future setup.

4. The Soviets remained suspicious of U.S. intentions and had chosen to deal with Pakistan, which, in their eyes, held the key to persuading the Afghan Resistance to accept national reconciliation. (In bilateral meetings, the Pakistani side invariably impressed upon the Soviets its desire to improve relations with Moscow and its independence of action. Pakistani diplomats often cited the example of the Geneva texts and their position on various issues at the United Nations to make the point.)

To explain why Vorontsov invited Sattar, why he spoke so candidly and emphatically about the Soviet desire to leave Afghanistan and about the need for an intra-Afghan dialogue for a broad coalition, and why Soviet comments and statements prior to December 1986 were by and large inhibited and hedged on these questions, one may look for an answer in the CPSU Politburo meeting held in November 1986 (*Pravda* of 20 November 1986 gave coverage to the meeting).[44] Reportedly this meeting formalized a decision in principle to withdraw from Afghanistan. According to a detailed account by Don Oberdorfer, diplomatic correspondent of the *Washington Post*, the Soviet decision was conveyed to Najibullah during the latter's visit to Moscow on 11–14 December 1986.[45] In a welcoming banquet speech on 12 December, Gorbachev "endorsed" the Kabul government's policy of "national reconciliation." Gorbachev also made, for the first time, a reference to Cordovez's mediation effort and expressed the hope that the "goodwill of all sides" would make it possible to achieve a "settlement."[46]

Prelude to Najibullah's National Reconciliation Programme

The shift in PDPA policy in favour of national reconciliation did not come readily after the replacement of Babrak Karmal with Najibullah. Similarly, policy statements issued from Kabul during the course of 1986 did not fully correspond to the Soviet signals. Najibullah's activities during the first couple of months concentrated on consolidating his position in the party and the army. He also met frequently with tribal elders from the southern provinces. The new policy direction did not emerge until September 1986 when the National Compromise Commission was established.[47] Nevertheless, this new policy remained visibly subject to opposite pulls in the shape of Soviet pressure on the Kabul government to broaden its base and opposition within the party to steps in that direction.

Najibullah's position toward the Afghan Resistance showed no flexibility at the time he assumed control in Kabul. In an interview with Mushahid Hussain, editor of the Pakistani daily *Muslim* in July 1986, Najibullah scoffed at the "ringleaders of treacherous bands" and offered mercy and reconciliation only to those "who have unconsciously stood in the ranks of counterrevolution."[48] Following the Nineteenth Plenum of the PDPA Central Committee on 10 July 1986, a special court was constituted to award death sentences, in absentia, to six leading resistance commanders.[49] At the Nineteenth Plenum, the only hint of flexibility was implied in a remark in Najibullah's opening address, conceding that revolution was a "complex" process which could require "retreat" and "regrouping of forces."[50]

There were straws in the wind pointing to an impending change in policy. Abdur Rahim Hatif, who had replaced Saleh Mohammad Zeary in 1985 as chairman of the dormant National Fatherland Front, remarked at the fifth anniversary celebration of the front in June 1986 that the NFF would hold a dialogue with counterrevolutionary groups to explain the realities of the revolution. The first major step in the new direction was taken on 27 September 1986 when the PDPA Politburo and the Presidium of the DRA Revolutionary Council decided on the formation of the National Compromise Commission. The objective was to talk with counterrevolutionaries to ensure a new democratic and peaceful society and implement the aims of the Saur Revolution in its "new phase."[51]

During 1986 Najibullah's moves for broadening the base of the PDPA government remained erratic. The signs of Soviet intention to withdraw and rumours of contacts being sought by Najibullah with the armed opposition and prominent Afghan émigrés caused concern among PDPA members. Najibullah was frequently obliged to seek refuge in revolutionary rhetoric and to assure the PDPA membership that the new policy was not at their expense, as seen in his address to the Twentieth Plenum on 20 November 1986:

I want to answer to the rumour mongers that the Central Committee will by no means be ready to carry on talks for establishing reconciliation in the luxurious Italian, Pakistani and West German places. We will openly talk with those who were drawn to the dirty war by devilish forces, but want to live in peace in the land of their fathers. We will not retreat an inch from the achievements of the Saur Revolution. That is to say in politics [those] who come to us should officially recognize the leading role of the PDPA and the people's power.[52]

Exclusion of the Peshawar-based leaders and the Afghan émigrés from the purview of reconciliation represented an obvious retreat from Gorbachev's all-embracing concept of "political forces" outside the boundaries of Afghanistan. Najibullah was clearly on the defensive when addressing the Academy of Medical Sciences on 1 December 1986, describing his steps toward talking with "bandit groups," and even the Geneva talks, as "a tactic, a way to compromise" to serve the objectives of the April Revolution.[53]

Meanwhile, the National Compromise Commission had started sending representatives on missions to engage in talking with "counterrevolutionary bands" for the cessation of bloodshed. This activity was accompanied by a vigorous propaganda effort. On 22 September 1986 Najibullah claimed in an interview with West German television that 3,000 armed men and two former resistance commanders had joined the revolution and talks were in progress with 92 armed bands, comprising 6,000 rebels.[54] By late December 1986 the figures claimed had reached 417 armed bands, comprising 37,000 rebels.[55]

On the ground, however, the achievement of the National Compromise Commission was far less impressive. The claims made were questionable.[56] Following the enunciation of the national reconciliation programme, the National Compromise Commission was abandoned in favour of the more ambitious scheme of the extraordinary "Commission for National Reconciliation."

As part of a more flexible approach implicit in the "new phase" of the April "National Democratic Revolution," a nonparty former member of the Parliament, Haji Mohammed Samkanai, was appointed in November 1986 as acting president, replacing Babrak Karmal, who had been holding this largely ceremonial post.[57] The signal was intended to demonstrate the regime's willingness to associate nonparty personalities with the government and to lend credibility to its policy of securing compromise with political elements outside the party. The appointment also gave rise to somewhat unwarranted speculation that the Soviets could settle for a political arrangement under Samkanai or agree to a more acceptable personality in an effort to bring about an internal political solution prior to or coinciding with their withdrawal.

The Watershed Year

In many ways the year 1986 changed the complexion of the Afghan issue. The stalemate pervading the negotiations until 1985, as well as the political and military situation in the country, started giving way to changes all around. In international and domestic policies, the Soviet outlook and orientation appeared to be undergoing a fundamental transformation, and Soviet desire for political settlement and withdrawal became increasingly pronounced. Globally, the prospect of new arms control agreements and active East-West summitry generated a propitious environment for the resolution of regional issues.

In Pakistan a subtle but important political change was taking place, with new political forces asserting themselves as a result of Zia ul Haq's experiment with transition to democracy. Within Afghanistan, Karmal had been replaced by Najibullah, indicating a fresh Soviet search for political reconciliation inside Afghanistan that could facilitate Soviet military disengagement. The Soviets also modified their stance toward the Afghan Resistance and encouraged Najibullah to initiate an intra-Afghan dialogue. On the ground, the intensified Soviet military campaigns were matched by increased coordination within the Afghan Resistance and supply of qualitatively better weapons, which raised the level of the conflict and strengthened those in Moscow who saw the futility of pursuing the military option.

By the end of 1986 the Geneva process had come to a head, with the texts of the instruments virtually settled and with sharper focus on the issue of time frame. Over the years, Cordovez had argued that a real time frame would be offered only when all textual issues were resolved. When that finally happened, the Soviets linked withdrawal to progress in achieving political reconciliation inside Afghanistan, thus forcing the negotiating process into an entirely new arena.

6

Politics of Withdrawal and National Reconciliation: The Second Track, 1987

Throughout 1987 the focus of negotiations kept moving between efforts to finalize the Geneva settlement with an agreed time frame and efforts to promote an internal political settlement. Najibullah's initiative for national reconciliation launched on the last day of 1986, inviting the armed opposition to accept a cease-fire and enter into dialogue, remained steeped in PDPA rhetoric and had little chance of success. The Peshawar-based alliance rejected dialogue with the PDPA. Moscow's efforts to seek Islamabad's endorsement of Najibullah's initiative prompted Pakistan to propose a neutral interim government with a possible role for Zahir Shah. Failure to bridge the gap on the time frame at Geneva VIIC in March 1987 impelled Cordovez to address the internal dimension of the issue by initiating "second-track" negotiations.

Both the neutral interim government idea piloted by the Pakistan Foreign Office and Cordovez's second track were impeded mainly by the absence of positive responses from Moscow and the Afghan Alliance. Moscow advocated Najibullah's initiative and stressed intra-Afghan dialogue for reconciliation and sharing of power with the PDPA. The militarily strong, fundamentalist components of the Alliance rejected any role for Zahir Shah and spoke instead of an interim government of the mujahideen. Deep ideological and political divisions prevented a political consensus within the Alliance. The prospects for a middle-ground solution, such as the Zahir Shah option, had been greatly diminished with the passage of time and the growing intensity of the military conflict. Within Pakistan, the struggle for power between Zia ul Haq and Junejo had begun to affect Pakistan's Afghan policy, resulting in a loss of the focus and coordination needed to fine-tune the policy with changing political and military circumstances.

For several months after the March 1987 Geneva round, diplomatic efforts remained stalled while the military situation inside Afghanistan escalated. In July Najibullah made an improved offer to share power with the resistance to salvage his faltering national reconciliation initiative. Immediately thereafter, he proceeded to Moscow, where he was reportedly informed of the Soviet decision to pull out troops, regardless of the status of national reconciliation. In August, after resisting for nearly four months, Kabul unexpectedly asked for the reconvening of the Geneva talks. Despite indications of Soviet willingness to withdraw within one year, however, Kabul stopped short of making such an offer at the ensuing September round. Publicly the focus again reverted to the second track.

Toward the end of September, Cordovez offered a new, structured proposal on the second track. Later, Zia ul Haq began taking an interest in the idea of an interim political arrangement and, through an informal channel, conveyed a new proposal to Moscow. Meanwhile, however, Soviet policy had begun reducing its emphasis on the precondition of national reconciliation and finally abandoned the linkage to withdrawal. At the December 1987 Washington summit, Gorbachev announced Soviet acceptance of a twelve-month time frame, provided there was simultaneous agreement on cutting off aid to the Afghan Resistance. Moscow was now ready for the Geneva settlement that was to emerge several months later.

The Withdrawal-Reconciliation Linkage

Linking withdrawal by the Soviets to Najibullah's initiative for national reconciliation shifted the focus of diplomatic activity from Geneva to Islamabad and Moscow. The first two months of 1987 witnessed several high-level contacts between Pakistan and the Soviet Union against the backdrop of quiet but extensive consultations between the Pakistan Foreign Office and the Afghan Alliance leaders. The burden of Pakistan's diplomatic efforts with both Moscow and the Afghan Alliance was to elicit support for the idea of an interim government, headed by an acceptable neutral personality, to oversee the transitional period covering withdrawal. A loosely defined variant on this concept was known as the Zahir Shah option. When the March 1987 Geneva round did not elicit from the Afghan side a time-frame offer within negotiable range, Cordovez was obliged to develop second-track negotiations to address the internal dimension of the Afghan issue.

While multilateral negotiations to work out a political arrangement inside Afghanistan and to wrap up the Geneva process were developing, the military situation escalated. The euphoria generated by mujahideen military successes hardened the already rigid positions professed by the fundamentalist components of the Peshawar-based Afghan Alliance. This contributed to the difficulties the Alliance had in developing a consensus for taking political initiatives. Najibullah's offer of national reconciliation, on the other hand, thinly masked a design to politically outmanoeuvre the fragmented Afghan Resistance by establishing intra-Afghan dialogue and a cease-fire. On both sides, political positions often became indistinguishable from political posturings.

Amid the nebulous but intense military and political situation, diplomacy moved tentatively and without success to explore common ground for compromise. Meanwhile, the texts of the instruments negotiated at Geneva survived as a stable parameter and an attractive framework for a settlement based on a time frame independent of reconciliation.

Najibullah's Reconciliation Offer and the Response

Najibullah's "national reconciliation" programme, enunciated at an extended Special Plenum of the PDPA Central Committee on 30–31 December 1986, was predicated on three elements: a six-month cease-fire with the mujahideen, commencing from 15 January 1987; the offer of a dialogue with opposition factions, including "'moderate' political groups, opportunists and leaders of anti-state armed groups"; and a possible coalition government allowing participation for the factions.[1] The programme promised control of local administrative organs to "passive" and neutral armed bands, provided they cooperated with the government.[2] An Extraordinary Supreme Commission for National Reconciliation was established to promote the programme.[3] Although Najibullah's reconciliation initiative was silent on the critical issue of withdrawal, it was accompanied by wide publicity and the full backing of the Soviet Union.

Foreign Minister Eduard Shevardnadze and Gorbachev's other top foreign policy adviser, Anatoly Dobrynin, reached Kabul within one week of the announcement to hail the cease-fire proposal as a "noble and prescient" gesture and to assure Najibullah "every kind of assistance" in his policy of national reconciliation.[4] Shevardnadze also called upon the neighbours of Afghanistan—Pakistan and Iran—not to push away the "conciliatory hand" extended by Kabul.[5] The Soviet and Afghan embassies abroad made coordinated efforts to secure support for the initiative.

In a burst of publicity projecting instantaneous success, the Afghan media started reporting "surrender of arms" and "pledges of cooperation" by counterrevolutionary bands throughout the country.[6] Political elements sympathetic to Kabul became active inside Pakistan. Awami National Party (ANP) leader Abdul Wali Khan demanded that the Pakistan government respond positively to Kabul's initiative and stop abetting the mujahideen against Kabul.[7] The Afghan refugees were a special target. An effort was made to generate euphoria about a cease-fire and encourage them to return. There was even false speculation that some prominent Afghan exiles such as Mohammed Yusuf, Abdul Hakim Tabibi, and Abdur Rahman Puzhwak were returning to Afghanistan.[8]

Besides its silence on Soviet withdrawal, the initiative had fallen short in making a specific promise on power sharing, although Najibullah allowed that the PDPA did not "claim [a] monopoly of power."[9] Nonetheless, the national reconciliation offer was largely confined to cease-fire and dialogue. The initiative was foredoomed because it had no chance of attracting an agreement from the Afghan Resistance. Its offensive rhetoric and the apparent emphasis on the PDPA's retaining the initiative and leading role in the proposed coalition[10] made it easy for the Afghan Resistance to dismiss it as a "trap."[11]

Najibullah's constant assurances to the PDPA further tarnished the credibility of the initiative as a genuine effort to seek a compromise with the resistance and gave it the appearance of a tactic. Asserting that the revolutionary process was irreversible, he had reassured the Special Plenum in December that DRA armed forces were the strongest ever in Afghan history, that the party included over 100,000 members, and that the regime had "strong loyal trusted friends in the Soviet Union, the Socialist countries and the progressive forces."[12] Among major objectives listed in his address to the plenum were "progress on the gains of the revolution, complete implementation of the PDPA programme of action, ensuring the development of an independent, democratic, and progressive Afghanistan . . . [and] consolidation of a regime honest to the friendship with the Soviet

Union."[13] TASS put it even more succinctly, commenting that "the idea is not to shelve the gains of the April [Saur] Revolution, which has struck deep roots in the country, but to secure its further development along the lines of progressive transformations with due regard for the country's national and social peculiarities."[14]

Reaction from Peshawar and Islamabad

The Afghan Alliance reaction was swift. On 1 January 1987 the spokesman of the Alliance, Burhanuddin Rabbani, rejected the cease-fire offer, reaffirming mujahideen determination to continue to fight until Najibullah was overthrown.[15] Later, on 8 January, Commander Jallaluddin Haqqani made a similar statement which also carried a proposal linking a cease-fire to Soviet acceptance of direct talks with the mujahideen and unconditional withdrawal within three months.[16] Even the moderate leadership within the Alliance lost no time in rejecting the offer, which they saw as a Soviet move to relieve Kabul from military pressure by sowing discord among the ranks of the resistance.[17] Arguing against cease-fire, which many Afghans understood to imply "laying down of arms," the Alliance leaders would often cite Ahmed Shah Massoud's experience in Panjshir.

A much sharper reaction came on 17 January in a rare show of solidarity at a large rally of Afghan refugees in Peshawar, where the seven party leaders reiterated their rejection of the cease-fire offer. At this meeting they also announced the setting up of a commission to draft "laws and duties of an interim government": to hold elections following Soviet withdrawal and to draft a constitution which would "guarantee implementation of Islam in all walks of life."[18] An important purpose of the meeting was to dispel uncertainty among the refugees about the Alliance position and to counter the notion that peaceful conditions were about to be restored in Afghanistan.[19] Such an expectation, if reinforced, would have obliged many refugees to hasten their return to reclaim their property and land.

Notwithstanding the hard-nosed ISI view conforming with the Alliance rejection, the official Pakistani comments were circumspect and showed a deference to the emerging Pakistani-Soviet dialogue. They were sensitive as well to public opinion in Pakistan, which had started showing signs of weariness with the conflict.[20] These comments skirted the issue by seeking refuge in the position that reconciliation and cease-fire were internal matters to be decided by the Afghan people and by highlighting Pakistan's demand for a short time frame. The Pakistan Foreign Office did not consider the offer of cease-fire and a call to counterrevolutionary bands a serious basis for negotiating a future internal arrangement, but attached importance to them as opening moves.

The national reconciliation initiative reflected a Soviet disposition to alter Soviet objectives in Afghanistan and to adjust to the realities of the country. Viewed from Islamabad, this pointed to the failure of the Marxist experiment to bring about an ideological transformation of Afghanistan, and of the PDPA regime to gain popular acceptance. The Pakistan Foreign Office also looked forward to the resumption of direct dialogue with the Soviet Union, which was left on a high note following the Sattar-Vorontsov meeting in December 1986. When Moscow requested that Islamabad receive Soviet Deputy Foreign Minister Anatoly Kovalyev, one of the principal Soviet negotiators at Helsinki, Yaqub Khan and others were convinced that the Soviets now desired to engage in substantive discussions for a future government in Kabul.

Pakistan Proposes a Neutral Interim Government

Pakistan needed to evolve a position in consultation with the Afghan Alliance. Until 1986 the Foreign Office had been in touch with the Alliance leadership to brief them in broad terms about progress made at Geneva and to reassure them that Pakistan was not bargaining away their interests at the negotiations. Since the settlement appeared to be distant, hardly any occasion arose to coordinate positions with Alliance leaders on the issues discussed at Geneva, nor did their comments reflecting ideological fervour and commitment to continue the jihad until victory cause much concern to Pakistani negotiators. The Pakistan Foreign Office had nurtured an impression, encouraged by ISI chief General Akhtar Abdur Rahman, that when the time came for a settlement the Alliance leaders could be persuaded to go along. The underlying premise was that Pakistan would be able to negotiate a short time frame. This complacent view fell apart in January when Yaqub Khan held two long meetings with Alliance leaders with a view to developing a common political initiative prior to Kovalyev's visit.

Yaqub Khan wanted to sound out the Alliance leaders primarily on their receptivity to the idea of an interim government for the period of withdrawal. The key questions were the participation of the PDPA and an acceptable figurehead. From his conversations with prominent Afghan émigrés and the moderate elements within the Alliance, and from logical deduction, Yaqub Khan was convinced that the former king, Zahir Shah, could play a pivotal role in the transitional period—as a personality agreeable to Moscow and with visible support among nationalists and refugees. Aware of the fundamentalist opposition to Zahir Shah, Yaqub Khan broached the subject with caution. Without going into the question of personality, he underlined the need for combining the military struggle, which he appropriately lauded, with a political initiative, emphasizing that an interim political compromise was essential to allow the Soviets to withdraw. The idea, nonetheless, met with reservations from the fundamentalist leaders.

The least diplomatic and plain response came from Yunis Khalis, who stated that the aim of the Afghan jihad was not only to secure Soviet withdrawal but also to establish an Islamic government in Afghanistan. There could be no compromise on basics. A similar argument, expressed more diplomatically, was advanced by others to rule out any accommodation with the PDPA and to propose direct dialogue between the Afghan Alliance and the Soviets. When pressed by Yaqub Khan, they agreed to consider the idea of an interim government, provided Pakistan could find out the Soviets' bottom-line position on the subject. Both Yaqub Khan and the Alliance leaders, however, agreed that Najibullah's initiative was aimed at gaining at the negotiating table what jihad had denied him and the Soviets on the battleground.

These meetings were the beginning of a long and exasperating attempt by the Pakistan Foreign Office to elicit a political initiative from the Alliance that could help negotiations on an internal settlement. The problem had many facets. The ISI distrusted any political approach aimed at seeking a compromise as detrimental to the jihad, which had now gained remarkable momentum. In addition, the protracted conflict had created mutual interdependence between the ISI and the constituent groups of the Afghan Alliance. These groups had developed autonomous interests to an extent that it was simplistic to assume that the agency exercised decisive control over the Alliance. Telltale signs of problems in dealing with the Alliance leaders had become evident only a month earlier when they could not agree to meet with Cordovez. The ideological emphasis in the fundamentalist reasoning also brought into focus yet another basic question, whether Pakistan's commitment to the Afghan struggle and more specifically its support to the Alliance groups should extend beyond the objective of Soviet withdrawal.

On the eve of Kovalyev's visit, Pakistan had found little in the Alliance position from which to make a counterproposal to the Soviet Union. Still worse was the rally in Peshawar, one day before Kovalyev's arrival in Islamabad, at which the seven leaders rejected Najibullah's offer and propounded a thoroughly revised concept of an interim government.[21]

In the event, the discussions with Kovalyev revealed another stumbling block in negotiating the Pakistani proposal for a neutral interim government, namely, Soviet opposition to the idea. Kovalyev, an impressive, soft-spoken diplomat, had come to secure Pakistan's support for Najibullah's national reconciliation and Pakistan's promise to persuade the Alliance to accept a cease-fire. What he conveyed to the Pakistani side was essentially what the Soviets were now saying publicly. In a way, Kovalyev's mission had already been preempted by the Alliance statement of 17 January, against which he registered a formal protest.

Broadly, Kovalyev conveyed to the Pakistani side that "winds of change" were sweeping across the Soviet Union. The Soviet leadership desired to untie "the Afghan knot," which posed many "contradictions," affecting both foreign and domestic policy spheres. On specifics, however, Kovalyev emphasized direct correlation between withdrawal and national reconciliation, affirming that a short time frame would depend on progress toward the establishment of a cease-fire. While saying that Najibullah did not want to monopolize power, Kovalyev cautioned Pakistan not to underestimate his position in Afghanistan. He also argued that it was Pakistan's position, not that of the Alliance or the United States, which was of critical importance.

In separate meetings with Kovalyev, Zia ul Haq and Yaqub Khan outlined positions that converged in many essential aspects but differed in important nuances. Both conceded the right of the Soviet Union to expect a nonhostile and nonaligned Afghanistan and stressed the need for peace and prevention of bloodshed and the desirability of safeguarding the interests of Pakistan, the Soviet Union, and the people of Afghanistan in a settlement. Zia ul Haq, however, emphasized that the settlement could not alter the Islamic character of Afghanistan or foist a minority regime upon Afghanistan. While considering that the PDPA government, the mujahideen, and the refugees were the three important elements on the Afghan political scene, he asserted that the Soviet withdrawal was a precondition for mujahideen acceptance of an intra-Afghan dialogue.

Yaqub Khan avoided the "chicken and egg" conditionality implicit in Zia ul Haq's observation and built a case for an interim government to be headed by a neutral personality. He argued that reconciliation or coalition under Najibullah was as distasteful to the Alliance as a coalition under the umbrella of the Alliance would be to Najibullah. Hence a reasonable course was to encourage a coalition acceptable, by and large, to both sides. Any number of possibilities could be considered for this purpose. But, Yaqub Khan maintained, by its very nature the arrangement had to be interim and headed by a neutral personality.

Kovalyev dwelt on the structure and strength of the Najibullah government and the party, security, and administrative apparatus, which could not be set aside to make room for an interim government. In Soviet eyes, the PDPA was the most organized political force in Afghanistan. Disagreeing, Yaqub Khan suggested a second alternative. If, in the Soviet view, Najibullah and the PDPA were really strong, the Soviets should offer a short time frame for withdrawal and "let the chips fall where they may." This line of argument sustained Pakistan's dual-track policy, emphasizing the interim government formula in parallel with the Geneva route based on a short time frame.

The talks remained inconclusive, with an agreement on early resumption. Kovalyev had no concrete proposal beyond a generous interpretation of Najibullah's initiative. Pakistan was able to formally propose to the Soviets the idea of neutral interim government in the hope that they would eventually come around to appreciate its logic.

Yaqub Khan wanted to continue the dialogue with Moscow, convinced that without some understanding on an internal political settlement the Soviets would not give a short time frame. In view of the Islamic summit in Kuwait toward the end of January, his visit to Moscow could not be scheduled before the first week of February, which necessitated Pakistan's request for a two-week delay in convening the Geneva round, already scheduled for early February. According to Cordovez, the Afghans agreed to this rescheduling with considerable reluctance and accused Pakistan of dragging its feet. The complaint partly reflected Cordovez's nervousness about the Pakistani-Soviet dialogue and his fear that the Geneva process might get derailed.

The American View

Following an early comment from a U.S. State Department official expressing understanding of the mujahideen rejection of Najibullah's initiative,[22] the U.S. official reaction awaited comments from Pakistan's spokesman. On 14 January a State Department official dismissed the Kabul offer as a "propaganda gesture."[23]

U.S. Under Secretary of State Michael Armacost arrived in Islamabad on the day Kovalyev left for Moscow. In the State Department's assessment, the Soviet Union now conceded the difficulties it faced in Afghanistan and had started a process of making adjustments. Drawing a comparison with the U.S. experience in Vietnam, Armacost expressed the opinion that the Soviet Union was now willing to withdraw and was moving in the right direction, but at the same time wanted to preserve its basic objectives. The offer of a cease-fire and national reconciliation was seen as a tactic to deflect attention from the time-frame issue and an attempt to gain the high political ground.

Armacost shared Pakistan's own reservations against Najibullah's national reconciliation offer, especially that it was designed to ensure a central role for the PDPA. Both saw the Pakistani-Soviet dialogue as a positive development and agreed that, besides exploring realistic options to promote an internal settlement, Pakistan should maintain pressure on the Soviets to provide a short time frame. Armacost disavowed U.S. interest in keeping the Soviet Union bogged down in Afghanistan, but he foresaw difficulties for the Americans in guaranteeing the settlement if the time frame were to exceed the Pakistani-proposed limit of a few months.

Publicly, Armacost struck a more cautious note, endorsing the Alliance reaction to Najibullah's offer and supporting the negotiations between Islamabad and Moscow. Armacost's visit drew some criticism in the local media, prompting Junejo to refute charges that Armacost had come to Islamabad to offset Kovalyev's visit.[24]

The Zahir Shah Option

Between Kovalyev's visit and the next Geneva round later in February, Yaqub Khan actively tried to elicit support for the proposed neutral interim government. Specifically, he explored prospects for consensus on an interim role for the former king—the Zahir Shah option. His soundings with Afghan Alliance leaders at Kuwait and his conversations on two occasions with Shevardnadze in Moscow focused on this point. He also visited Rome.

Soundings at Kuwait

The Islamic summit at Kuwait in January 1987 provided Pakistan an opportunity to consult Islamic countries on Najibullah's initiative and to convey to them Pakistan's point of view. Kuwait's sensitivity to radical Arab states had raised some apprehension that pro-Moscow members of the OIC might use the occasion to make a push for a positive reference to the initiative; but the summit was far too preoccupied by the Iran-Iraq conflict.

The conference adopted the formulations presented by Pakistan, which called for a "genuine national reconciliation" reflecting the will of the Afghan people.[25] The effort was to avoid a reference to Najibullah's national reconciliation and to redefine the concept in unexceptionable terms consistent with Pakistan's point of view. The Alliance's suggestion to obtain a rejection of Najibullah's initiative was considered impolitic by the Pakistan delegation. Pakistan detected some interest in the initiative, but most Islamic countries were willing to accept Pakistan's interpretation and agreed that a short time frame was the real test of Soviet intentions in Afghanistan.

At the summit, Zia ul Haq met UN Secretary General Pérez de Cuéllar and assured him that Pakistan's dialogue with the Soviet Union was complementary to the Geneva negotiating process. Briefing the secretary general about the Kovalyev and Armacost visits, Zia ul Haq further assured him that the Americans stood by the Geneva process and also supported Pakistan's dialogue with the Soviet Union to explore the possibility of an interim government.

Yaqub Kahn used the presence of the seven Alliance party leaders at Kuwait to have individual meetings to elicit their views on the possibility of an agreement on an interim government headed by Zahir Shah.[26] Individual consultations were necessitated by the impression that in a group, constrained by the ISI and each other's presence, the leaders tended to take a hard-line position and to be reluctant to express their views candidly. Rabbani and Yunis Khalis were believed to be equivocal on the Zahir Shah option and needed to be drawn out. These meetings did not prove to be fruitful, even though, for reasons of courtesy, none of the fundamentalist leaders consulted by Yaqub Khan rejected the option in clear terms, as they did publicly on subsequent occasions.

Pakistan Pushes the Zahir Shah Option
at Moscow

In preparing for the resumption of dialogue with the Soviets in Moscow, the Pakistan Foreign Office sought ISI help in two areas: first, a political initiative from the Afghan Alliance; and second, a gesture to the Soviets, namely, obtaining release of a few Soviet prisoners-of-war from captivity with the Afghan mujahideen. For some time, as a result of glasnost, the Soviet press had revealed public concern over captured Soviet soldiers and pressure for their recovery. Soviet officials had raised this matter and sought Pakistan's help on humanitarian grounds.[27] Despite the short time available between Yaqub Khan's return from Kuwait and his departure for Moscow, the mujahideen groups operating inside Afghanistan did oblige and one Soviet soldier wishing to return to the Soviet Union was handed over to the Soviet embassy on the eve of Yaqub Khan's visit to Moscow.

Yaqub Khan wanted to carry with him to Moscow a positive proposal from the Alliance endorsing the idea of an interim government, already raised with Kovalyev. He felt that such a political initiative from the Alliance was necessary to move the Soviets and Kabul toward a more acceptable position. There were also fears that the Soviets would interpret an absence of a positive initiative from the Alliance as evidence that Pakistan was either reluctant to cooperate in seeking an internal political settlement or lacked the ability to deliver on the Alliance. In either event, the Soviets could conclude that pursuing a dialogue with Pakistan was futile.

The shura of the Alliance met in Islamabad in several sessions but could not reach a consensus on the Pakistani idea of an interim government. A couple of hours before its departure to Moscow, however, the Pakistan delegation received from the Alliance four agreed points typed on a plain sheet of paper: (1) a demand for direct negotiations between the mujahideen and the Soviet Union; (2) an offer of cessation of hostilities and safe passage to the withdrawing Soviet troops, provided the Soviets offered to withdraw in a short period; (3) an offer of general amnesty in accordance with the "precepts of Islam," with the exception of those who had committed crimes against the Afghan nation; and (4) a commitment to pursue a non-aligned Islamic foreign policy and not to allow foreign military bases on the territory of Afghanistan. These four points provided the Pakistani side with some input, but fell far short of providing Yaqub Khan the diplomatic leverage to press the Soviets to accept the idea of a neutral interim government.

The meetings in Moscow on 7–8 and 25 February 1987 were held in a cordial atmosphere, with the Soviets making all the appropriate gestures in terms of protocol and hospitality. The Soviet officials were pleasantly ingenuous and relaxed, exuding the openness of glasnost. In the meetings, however, the affable style of Shevardnadze did not betray any revision of the Soviet position stated earlier by Kovalyev in Islamabad. The Soviets must have again gathered the impression that there was little movement in Pakistan's position, even though it was presented with greater specificity at Moscow.

The primary objective for the Pakistani side was to draw out the Soviet position on a neutral interim government and the Zahir Shah option or, alternatively, to secure a commitment to a short time frame. Yaqub Khan built the case on assurances that Pakistan had a deep interest and an independent motivation in pursuing a settlement for which it had been taking initiatives within and outside the Geneva context; that it was not being held back by the United States; and that, in his understanding, the core interests of Pakistan and the Soviet Union in pursuing a settlement did not conflict. Defining these core interests, Yaqub Khan identified as those of the Soviet Union a nonaligned and friendly Afghanistan and no bloodshed, and those of Pakistan as Soviet withdrawal in a short time, the return of refugees, the Afghans freely to decide their future, no bloodshed, and a nonaligned and friendly Afghanistan. This enumeration obviously skirted the less proclaimed and more ambitious motives ascribed to the two sides, namely Zia ul Haq's espousal of an Islamic Afghanistan and the Soviet interest in preserving the gains of the Saur Revolution.

The burden of Yaqub Khan's argument was that an interim government under a neutral respected personality was the only realistic option for rallying the Afghans to make peace, and that Soviet approval of the idea would enable Pakistan to prepare the Alliance and the mujahideen to accept it. He was more direct in pointing to Zahir Shah. To illustrate Zahir Shah's role, he narrated an Indian fable of "the eighteenth elephant." Like a mathematical quiz, the fable narrated how a wise man divided the inheritance of seventeen elephants among three sons in the ratios of one-half, one-third, and one-ninth laid down by their deceased father. To effect this division, the wise man added to the lot his own "eighteenth elephant," with which he thereafter walked away.

Though the story greatly amused Shevardnadze, he nonetheless reiterated Kovalyev's argument that replacing the top of an established structure was impractical. The PDPA had not only been an important force in Afghan politics, he said, but had gained in strength manyfold since April 1978. In Soviet eyes the PDPA regime was not bankrupt, nor had it suffered a defeat, so the demand for its removal was simply unwarranted. At the same time, Shevardnadze spoke of heightened "interference" and the Soviet concern for bloodshed that prevented them from offering a short time frame until a "cooling off" was achieved in Afghanistan.

The meetings in early February and later during Yaqub Khan's stopover in Moscow on 25 February prior to Geneva VIIC demonstrated that the Soviets were not ready to accept a role for Zahir Shah beyond that in the context of Najibullah's national reconciliation. That Shevardnadze had not clearly rejected the Zahir Shah option nor foreclosed the possibility of a hybrid solution in the future kept alive the hope that the Soviet Union might eventually favour the Zahir Shah option.

A View from Rome

After his early February visit to Moscow, Yaqub Khan proceeded to Rome, where he met General Abdul Wali, son-in-law of Zahir Shah and widely believed to be the strongman behind the former king. The dialogue with the Soviets had necessitated such a contact to convey Pakistan's position and to get the Rome perspective on how to proceed on the question of an interim government, now that the Soviets had made national reconciliation a condition for the withdrawal they unquestionably desired. Pakistan had been in touch with Zahir Shah, but this was the first time Yaqub Khan traveled to Rome exclusively for this purpose.

The gesture was also meant to convey a message to Moscow. Yaqub Khan, disappointed in the Alliance's response, wanted to develop the Zahir Shah option through a Soviet endorsement. To him it seemed logical that the Soviets—who, according to Gorbachev's statement to the press in New Delhi in November 1986, had good neighbourly relations with monarchist Afghanistan[28]—should be able to accept Zahir Shah, provided Pakistan could convince them of its cooperation in the promotion of this option.

General Wali, a strong personality in the mold of Sardar Daoud[29] and feared by political adversaries for his ambitions, advanced the old line proposing a jirga to endorse Zahir Shah. He was convinced that Pakistan was capable of swinging the majority of the Alliance leadership in favour of the former king. Gulbuddin Hekmatyar and Abdul Rab Rasul Sayyaf could prove to be difficult, yet they were the creation of Pakistan. If they could not be persuaded to follow suit, cooperation could be elicited from the second-rank leadership of Hekmatyar's Hizb and Sayyaf's Ittehad-e-Islami. The majority of the refugees in Pakistan favoured the former king, who also enjoyed the support of the tribes. After initial groundwork by Pakistan, the king's close associates could be involved in the preparation for the convening of a Loya Jirga of the refugees, mujahideen, and tribal leaders to endorse Zahir Shah. He could then negotiate an interim government with the Soviets.

Immediately after Yaqub Khan's visit to Rome, Dr. Yusuf, the former prime minister, conveyed a revised version of this proposal to Islamabad through Armand Hammer, the American industrialist known for his personal contacts with Kremlin leaders. The new version suggested an interim state council under Zahir Shah, comprising seven representatives from Peshawar groups, two from Iran, four commanders, a few elders (including émigré personalities), and two PDPA members.

The swift pace of diplomatic activity in Islamabad during the month of February 1987, including the disengagement with India, Yaqub Khan's visits to Moscow and Rome, and preparations for the Geneva round to begin on 25 February, left little time for a focused discussion of Wali's proposal. Foreign Office exchanges with ISI raked up past reservations. The tentatively reached conclusion was to refrain from prematurely breaking up the Alliance without clear signals of Soviet acceptance of Zahir Shah through the ongoing dialogue with Moscow.

Within the Pakistan government divergences in approach had begun to emerge. The Foreign Office, led by Yaqub Khan, wanted to push the Alliance to take political initiatives and felt that it did not receive enough support from the ISI for this purpose. The ISI, for its part, considered that the interim government option as advocated by the Foreign Office could not be promoted without risking a split within the Alliance, thereby damaging the jihad. The ISI also entertained misgivings about Soviet intentions and implied that only a clearer commitment from the Soviet Union on Zahir Shah could justify moves by Pakistan to press the Alliance in that direction. A catch-22 situation pervaded the reasoning of both agencies.

Among the other important Pakistani players, Prime Minister Junejo saw a political stake in an early settlement, but lacked control over the ISI setup and had little rapport with the Alliance leaders. President Zia ul Haq, increasingly entrenched in an internal political struggle, made no move to influence the Alliance on the issue of the interim government, allowing the hard-line leadership to stall on the Foreign Office efforts. Although he firmly believed in keeping military pressure on the Soviets by supporting the Afghan jihad, Zia did not appear to be pursuing a single clear policy direction. He approved of his foreign minister's developing and taking up the neutral interim government and the Zahir Shah option with the Soviets and establishing contacts in Rome with Abdul Wali. He advocated the interim government idea to the UN secretary general in Kuwait and hinted to Kovalyev the possibility of a tripartite coalition in the wake of Soviet withdrawal. And he had encouraged Cordovez to believe that Pakistan's position on the time frame had considerable latitude.

Zia ul Haq's policy seemed to verge on brinkmanship on all fronts. As long as the situation appeared to be moving in a favourable direction, even at potentially high risk, he would not tamper with it, much less foreclose any options. Afghanistan presented both tempting opportunities and risky choices, making it difficult for him to change course.

Geneva VIIC: Haggling over Time Frame

The meetings in Moscow had dampened Pakistan's expectations for Geneva VIIC, which convened from 25 February to 9 March 1987. But Cordovez entertained high optimism. All textual issues were settled. He felt confident he could push the two sides to agree on a time frame of close to one year. In this calculation he was encouraged by supposed leaks in the press of U.S. readiness to accept a one-year time frame[30] and by Zia ul Haq's remark to him during the December 1986 shuttle that the time frame must be "a matter of months not years." At the time, Cordovez had been seeking flexibility in Pakistan's position of three to four months based on logistical considerations.[31]

He was further encouraged by the Soviet assertion that they wanted this Geneva round to be "absolutely the last." This position was affirmed by Yuli Vorontsov in December 1986.[32] Accordingly, Cordovez conveyed to the interlocutors that Geneva VIIC would be focused on time frame, which he intended to finalize no matter how long the two delegations had to stay at Geneva. Before his departure for Geneva, Cordovez also stated in a press conference that time frame was the only remaining issue.[33]

Prior to the Geneva round, the Pakistani side had reviewed its position on the question of time frame. This time, the question was examined primarily in the light of Foreign Office assessment of domestic public opinion pressures. It was presumed that Pakistan's opposition to an offer of a one-year time frame would become untenable. Accordingly, despite the public position of a three- to four-month time frame and the desire to negotiate one as short as possible, the Pakistani side was mentally prepared to be forced into accepting a one-year time frame. At best, it hoped to have the two-month preparatory period treated as part of the one year, to be able to project the effective time frame as ten months.

In Kuwait in January 1987, Yaqub Khan had also consulted individual Alliance leaders on the staying power of the Afghan resistance after a cutoff of supplies, with a view to determining Pakistan's negotiating limit on the time frame. The responses were vague and raised the question of safeguards against continuing Soviet assistance to the Kabul regime. Nonetheless, an impression was gained that the resistance was capable of withstanding Soviet pressure for six to eight months without suffering crippling damage.

The Geneva round started with routine posturing. The Afghan side demanded a "realistic" Pakistani position, arguing that the Afghan side had already shown flexibility by climbing down from four years to three years, while Pakistan had remained adamant on the three- to four-month figure. The Pakistan delegation, on the other hand, decried "haggling-style" negotiations, stressed objective criteria for settling the time-frame issue, and asked Cordovez to press the Afghan side to give a reasonable time frame.

Cordovez put pressure on both interlocutors. While demanding an acceptable figure from the Afghans, he challenged the Pakistani argument on objective criteria, saying that in Kabul's eyes the objective conditions of interference could justify even a four-year time frame. Informally, he would argue that Pakistan's real position had already been revealed to him by Zia ul Haq and that a movement by Pakistan would break the deadlock and remove misgivings, especially on the part of the Soviets, and allow the Soviets and the Afghans to present their real time frame. The Pakistan delegation was operating within a narrow margin, however, and was nervous about getting pushed into accepting a figure exceeding one year.

After a few days of holding action, the Afghanistan delegation offered twenty-two months, stressing that the figure represented a major concession which Pakistan should accept. The Pakistani side, after dismissing the offer as well beyond Pakistan's negotiating range, moved its own position to six months. The two sides were thus locked into bargaining on the time frame, their positions once again stalled.

The Afghans dismissed the Pakistani concession as perfunctory and asked Cordovez to obtain a new position from Pakistan before expecting further movement in the Afghan offer of twenty-two months. Yaqub Khan refused to oblige. Anxious to push the two sides, Cordovez turned up the pressure on Pakistan, saying that the six-month offer could not be regarded by the Afghan side as a concession since he had already presented it as Pakistan's starting position. In support of this view, Cordovez recalled how the faces of the Pakistan delegation had lit up when in 1985 he had filled in the six-month figure in the draft memorandum he had proposed to break the logjam on direct talks. This curious argument did not help advance the negotiation, but only compounded misgivings about Cordovez's pressure tactics.

At this point Cordovez knew that Yaqub Khan, like himself, was a man in a hurry. Yaqub Khan was a candidate for the post of UNESCO director general and naturally wished the Geneva process to culminate before elections for the post, scheduled for September 1987. Without giving in on the six-month position, however, Yaqub Khan tried to assure Cordovez that Pakistan had every intention of negotiating and settling the time frame, but could not be expected to make gratuitous moves on such a politically loaded issue. Cordovez then got a further break when the Afghans moved to eighteen months. In response, the Pakistani side tabled seven months, once again emphasizing its willingness to negotiate further.[34]

These moves suddenly raised expectations. Islamabad was alerted and asked Yaqub Khan to remain in constant touch and to consult before making the next move. The occasion did not arise, however, because the Afghan side refused to make any further concession. Cordovez tried to elicit an informal understanding on Pakistan's bottom-line position in order to bring down the Afghan position. When the Afghans made eighteen months a take-it-or-leave-it offer and called off the round, Cordovez finally despaired and proposed reconvening in early May. While Pakistan accepted the proposed date, the Afghans and Kosyrev did not consent to reconvening the round and insisted that Pakistan agree to eighteen months.

Pakistan's moves in stretching its time-frame offer to six then seven months were made without a second reference to Islamabad or prior consultations with the United States. Later, when the issue of safeguards was raised in 1988 prior to the final Geneva round, these moves attracted criticism, which held that the longer time frame had far exceeded the original concept of a few months and thus destroyed the basis for a settlement requiring a cutoff of arms supplies to the mujahideen. It was then argued that Pakistan would have been better off if it had stuck to its original three- to four-month position instead of getting locked into the concession/counter-concession tactics employed by the Afghan side. This post facto criticism, made at a time when Yaqub Khan was no longer foreign minister nor associated with the Geneva process, ignored the conditions and pressures prevailing in early 1987.

The Soviet-Afghan position taken at Geneva VIIC was clearly consistent with the stand taken by Shevardnadze during the Moscow meetings linking time frame with the issue of national reconciliation. At the same time, the review of the inconclusive Geneva round gave rise to two diverse sets of opinion in Pakistan. The first argued that if the Soviets were indeed pushing for an internal settlement prior to withdrawal, then the whole issue of time frame would lose its relevance. Once a government of reconciliation acceptable to the Afghans had been formed, it would be of little consequence whether the Soviet troops left within a shorter or longer time. The second view was based on the fear that the Afghans and the Soviets would stall after every concession on time frame to let public pressure work on the Pakistan government, pushing the latter's tolerance to the limit before finally striking a compromise.

Kabul's decision to terminate the round and Cordovez's discussions with Kosyrev convinced Cordovez that the Soviets were serious in emphasizing the linkage between their offering a short time frame and progress being made toward national reconciliation. The clearly expressed Soviet concern over possible bloodshed if the troops were withdrawn without an internal reconciliation dispelled any doubts. And Pakistan was already pursuing a two-track approach in its dialogue with the Soviets.

Cordovez decided to explore the formation of a "broad-based" government. It was a safe endeavour which, in the changed circumstances, might be welcomed by Moscow and which in no way jeopardized the Geneva negotiations. In early April 1987 Cordovez admitted to Armacost that there was a distinct link between time frame and national reconciliation. Conceding that conciliation could not be achieved under Najibullah, he had started thinking in terms of involving Zahir Shah through a multiparty assembly. His premise was that the Soviets could be expected to acquiesce in Najibullah's replacement if they could avoid the impression that they had dropped him. After Geneva VIIC, Cordovez publicly underlined the need for all Afghans to devise a "Pax Afghana."

Cordovez's Second Track

The wellspring of Cordovez's ideas for a new secondtrack approach to address the internal dimension of the Afghan issue was the Afghan émigré community, whose majority supported the return of Zahir Shah and entertained deep misgivings about the fundamentalists within the Alliance, and to a certain extent about the role of Pakistan. These views were conditioned by their background as former bureaucrats or politicians in the pre-Saur Revolution period and their secular modernistic disposition, which was traditionally in conflict with orthodox Islam since the days of King Ammanullah. Also contributing to Cordovez's ideas were the American and West European experts on Afghanistan whose view of the Alliance was largely determined by its internal squabbles, its apparent fundamentalist cast, and the notion that the seven Peshawar-based groups were a creation of Pakistan and were manipulated by it. Lastly, piqued by his own failure to engage the Alliance leaders in Islamabad and Kuwait, Cordovez did not make a concerted effort to develop contacts with them when he embarked on his second-track diplomatic effort. Instead, he wanted Pakistan to deliver on the Alliance.

Cordovez first explained his ideas to Prime Minister Junejo in a meeting at Brussels in early April 1987. Junejo had arrived in the EC capital after a visit to London. Cordovez had been in touch with Zahir Shah and the proposal he made to Junejo was almost identical to that made by Abdul Wali, except that Cordovez had carved out a role for himself in regard to negotiating the interim government with the Soviets. According to this proposal, Pakistan was expected to remove ambiguity in its attitude toward Zahir Shah and elicit support for him from the majority of the Alliance leaders. Once this was accomplished, Cordovez could try to gain Soviet acquiescence in an interim government under Zahir Shah. Once understandings were reached, the final Geneva round could be convened, in parallel with either a Loya Jirga or an assembly of mujahideen and Kabul representatives. The Loya Jirga or the assembly was to formalize the political understandings endorsing Zahir Shah as head of the interim government, while at the Geneva round an acceptable time frame could be offered.

Cordovez insisted that he should be accepted as the only interlocutor for this purpose, in deference to the sensitivity of the issue. In suggesting this condition, Cordovez had at the back of his mind some of the informal channels used by Pakistan to sound out Moscow, especially Armand Hammer. Junejo, who was still in the shallows of the Afghan policy, liked the plan even though it clearly hinged on the intractable proposition of preparing the majority of the Alliance leadership to accept Zahir Shah.

As compared to the specific presentation made to Junejo, Cordovez exercised a good deal of circumspection in the formal communication he addressed to Yaqub Khan in early May, signaling the launching of the second track. He acknowledged that the Geneva negotiations had reached a critical juncture and their fruition depended on progress toward national reconciliation. He underlined the need for a second set of negotiations, envisaging eventual convergence of the two tracks in a "synchronized fashion" to produce a comprehensive political settlement that would ensure the return of peace to Afghanistan. He wanted the Pakistan government to indicate what concrete measures it was prepared to undertake to promote the second track.

An Impasse Develops

By May 1987 Pakistan's difficulties in delivering on either the Wali or the Cordovez scenario had been compounded by the burgeoning complications of its internal politics. A strong outside impulse, such as Moscow could provide by a clear signal accepting Zahir Shah, would have helped.

Moscow's position on the issue remained markedly consistent with what Shevardnadze had stated to Yaqub Khan in February, namely, that Zahir Shah could play a role but only in the context of Najibullah's conciliation offer. Gorbachev's well-publicized interviews in *L'Unità*, an Italian newspaper, also envisaged a role for Zahir Shah as part of a coalition such as Najibullah was suggesting.[35] The Soviet position was further muddied by the intensity of the 1987 summer offensive and by Najibullah's continuing efforts to consolidate power. At the same time, military successes by the resistance during summer 1987 buoyed the morale of the isi and the hard-liners within the Alliance and toughened their position on political compromise.

The March 1987 reshuffle in the top echelons of the Pakistan Army had brought about a change in isi leadership. The longtime isi chief, General Akhtar Abdur Rahman, was replaced by General Hamid Gul, an energetic, motivated, younger personality, untempered by age in comparison to his predecessor and strongly partisan to the jurisdiction and interests of his institution. He inherited the Afghan undertaking when the flow of funds and equipment and the morale of the mujahideen were at optimum levels. Unlike his predecessor, General Gul did not have personal experience of the early days of the ill-organized, ill-equipped resistance and the psychological reservation that the resistance alone could not force the Soviets to withdraw.

The isi's faith in the capabilities of the mujahideen and its corresponding misgivings against initiatives based on political compromise strengthened as a result of the impressive military successes scored by the mujahideen using Stingers during mid-1987. The count of aircraft shot down by the mujahideen was fifty-three in May and sixty in June. The Soviets suffered heavy casualties in Argundab near Qandahar, in Paktia, and in Kunar, moving them to resort to cluster bombs and high-altitude bombing, which scarcely dented the mujahideen forces. Simultaneously, expectations of an early settlement and a return home had started affecting the morale of the Soviet troops and their commitment to fighting.

The isi had, by now, developed an autonomous interest in the success of military operations, a conviction in the objective of the jihad and in mujahideen ability to carry it to triumph. In isi's perception, the pillars of the jihad were the four effective fundamentalist parties, vindicated by their performance on the battlefield. At the high noon of mujahideen victories, the isi under General Gul could hardly be expected to scuttle the Alliance to serve vague political objectives.

Behind the facade of the Alliance, furthermore, each group, especially the fundamentalists, zealously guarded its individual interests. It had never been easy to make them agree even on relatively minor issues, and their stubbornness increased with their growing strength. Yet an impression persisted that the ISI and Zia ul Haq carried sufficient authority and leverage to push the hard-line leaders into accepting political initiatives consistent with the second-track approach. This assumption, however, became doubtful toward the end of 1987.

Yaqub Khan had several meetings with General Gul to discuss possible scenarios for an interim government with or without Zahir Shah as its head. From the Foreign Office point of view, a meaningful start on the second track required an Alliance endorsement of an interim government under a neutral personality with a modicum of participation of the PDPA. If Zahir Shah was unacceptable to the Alliance, other Afghan personalities could be considered. The mandate of the interim government could be negotiated to protect the interests of the Alliance parties. The Foreign Office did not succeed in obtaining what it desired, but its pressure did force the Alliance parties to sit in their shura to debate and make some tentative decisions.

The idea of Loya Jirga was opposed by the fundamentalist parties, who argued that the war had radically changed the situation inside Afghanistan, where the traditional tribal leadership had been replaced by local mujahideen commanders. Underlying their contention was a prejudice against jirga, which had become identified with the Zahir Shah option. These parties instead favoured an elected shura.[36] In a statement in early May the spokesman for the Alliance, Yunis Khalis, ruled out a role for Zahir Shah, asserting that the mujahideen did not recognize any person between them and the Soviets and that Zahir Shah was not a mujahid and did not command influence in Afghanistan.[37] Earlier Rabbani had stated that the issue of Zahir Shah was being raised to sow discord among the ranks of the mujahideen.[38] Throughout May 1987 the issue of Zahir Shah received considerable media attention.[39]

General Gul, for his part, instead of preparing the ground for Alliance acceptance of a neutral interim government, became an advocate of the emerging Alliance proposal for an elected shura. He argued that nothing would bar the shura, a democratically elected representative body, from endorsing a neutral interim government or even Zahir Shah as its head. Furthermore, he felt that if the main Soviet concerns were prevention of bloodshed and safe withdrawal, then even before the establishment of the shura Moscow should be persuaded to reach appropriate understandings with the Alliance through direct contact.

The first proposal for an elected shura was adopted on 18 May

1987 after much dispute and despite bitter feelings within the moderate segment of the Alliance. According to the proposal, Yunis Khalis was named spokesman for the Alliance for the next six months and mandated to organize elections for a 312-member shura within that period.[40] The shura was to comprise 52 representatives of the Afghan refugees from both Iran and Pakistan, 216 representatives of commanders operating in *uluswalis* (districts), and 44 from *ilaqadaris* (subdistricts which, for reasons of tradition or importance, are administered directly by the provinces). The Afghan refugees were to vote for any 1 of the 7 parties, and 52 seats were to be divided proportionally on the basis of votes received. Inside Afghanistan each commander with 35 mujahideen and at least 100 followers was to carry one vote, and these commanders in turn were to elect 1 representative from each uluswali.

The election was to be conducted by a fourteen-member electoral body of two representatives from each party. The elected shura was to meet in Peshawar to elect a *raes*, or head of state, who would form an interim government after "liberation" to hold general elections in the country. This proposal was clearly far removed from the Pakistan Foreign Office concept of the interim government and effectively precluded the Zahir Shah option. The period of six months required for the consummation of the process, which represented a concession over an initial suggestion of eighteen months, by itself poured cold water on the hopes for an early Alliance initiative on the second track.

This was a setback. As Yaqub Khan remarked in exasperation, "The second track is a jungle." Consequently, Pakistan's emphasis on the Geneva track and demand for a time frame were revived. While efforts must continue on both tracks, it was argued, availability of a short time frame would create a pressure-cooker situation pushing both sides—the Alliance and Najibullah—to moderate their demands in the face of an impending settlement with an implied cutoff of supplies for one and removal of Soviet troop support for the other.

Once again a short time frame became the fixed pole in a fluid situation. It was also the key to a possible advance on the second track. In a brief meeting in Washington toward the end of May, Yaqub Khan told Cordovez, when the latter pushed for a clear reply, that Pakistan was not ready to "break china" and that the demand for a short time frame continued to be necessary. This did not mean that the proposals for a neutral interim government or the Zahir

Shah option had been given up. With their nine lives, these proposals kept surfacing.

Regression in Moscow's Attitude

In comparison to their initial upbeat moves, Soviet attitudes appeared to have stiffened after March 1987. As one indication, Moscow had suspended its dialogue with Pakistan. Despite diplomatic reminders that Islamabad awaited a visit from Vorontsov, he avoided setting dates. In contrast, he had twice come to neighbouring Tehran, 12–15 June and 3 August 1987, in the wake of the U.S. decision to flag Kuwaiti tankers and extend U.S. naval protection in the Persian Gulf.[41] According to the British, the Soviet leaders were not forthcoming on Afghanistan during Prime Minister Margaret Thatcher's visit to Moscow in late March. And Kabul declined resumption of the Geneva round that Cordovez had wanted to schedule for May 1987.

In the third week of May the Soviet-Kabul forces launched a major military campaign in the Qandahar, Nangarhar, Kunar, and Paktia provinces.[42] The Soviet Union, disappointed at Pakistan's refusal to support Najibullah's national reconciliation, appeared to have resiled from further diplomatic moves and apparently decided to lend its unqualified military and political support to Najibullah's initiative.

Other minor factors also contributed to the deteriorating atmosphere and drew demarches from the Soviets. In addition to mujahideen strikes inside Tajikistan in the Soviet Union in March–April[43] and stepped-up supplies of arms to the mujahideen, the Soviets were also annoyed by Zia ul Haq's rhetorical statement to the Parliament on 19 April describing the Afghan War as a war in defense of Pakistan and the "free world." Zia ul Haq's strong support of the mujahideen and jihad was no secret, but his strident tone in the Parliament session, convened to carry out the annual review of the country's foreign policy, was in sharp contrast to the mild and conciliatory posture struck by Junejo and Yaqub Khan during the parliamentary debate. Zia ul Haq's statement, however, signified the struggle for control of Afghan policy rather than an attempt to question its direction. It was also a reaction to growing opposition criticism of Afghan refugee and mujahideen activities in Pakistan and reflected Zia ul Haq's annoyance at what he regarded as the Junejo government's pusillanimous attitude in countering these charges.

A Push for the Reconciliation Policy

Until late July, signals of Soviet desire to withdraw were mixed with a firm determination to make Najibullah's national reconciliation work. In addition to the military offensive, the Soviets encouraged wide-ranging diplomatic and political activities to achieve this objective. On the diplomatic front, Kabul succeeded in establishing diplomatic relations with Cyprus and Zimbabwe, the latter then chairman of the Non-Aligned Movement.[44] Kishtmand visited Iraq, which was upset at the growing relations between Pakistan and Iran.[45] Indian Foreign Minister N. D. Tiwari visited Kabul.[46] Kuwait received Afghan Foreign Minister Abdul Wakil and was also in the process of restoring landing rights to Ariana, the Afghan airline. Special envoys were sent to nearly seventy countries, including Islamic countries, to explain the national reconciliation initiative.[47] International receptivity to these moves by the Kabul government was attributable to the positive format of the initiative, as well as to the new Soviet image identified with Gorbachev.

On the domestic front, the Kabul government engaged in wide publicity projecting successes of the national reconciliation programme. The Afghan media reported with meticulous regularity the activities of national reconciliation commissions, holding of mini-jirgas in various provinces, and surrender of arms by armed opposition groups. Figures of Afghan returnees from Pakistan and Iran were published in an arithmetical progression. By the end of April the Najibullah government claimed that 44,000 refugees had returned, 21,000 armed rebels had been won over, and national reconciliation commissions had been set up in 1,100 villages.[48] In late June the Supreme Commission for National Reconciliation reported that 62,000 refugees had returned, 51,000 armed rebels had laid down arms, and national reconciliation commissions had been established in 2,948 villages.[49] The figures varied. For example, at a press conference in late June, Najibullah stated that 25,000 (not 51,000) armed opposition members had surrendered to the government.[50] Mini-jirgas and meetings of national reconciliation commissions were reportedly held throughout Afghanistan during May and June, despite apparent setbacks, such as assassinations of some of the provincial heads of reconciliation commissions.[51]

Najibullah took successive steps in May and June to consolidate his position within the party and the army, as well as to push the national reconciliation process further. On 7 May following a PDPA

Politburo meeting, at an unusual question-answer session ostensibly aimed at "democratization" of the party, Najibullah resolved to strengthen the party, claiming that "there is no Party which can match the PDPA from the point of view of force and action at the national level."[52] He also vowed to strengthen the armed forces and reaffirmed his readiness to discuss concrete programmes and the composition of a government of national unity with the opposition groups.[53] In a televised press conference later on 19 May he went even further. When asked about Zahir Shah, Najibullah remarked that the people would elect whomever they preferred as the new president under the new constitution.[54] (A commission for drafting a new constitution had been appointed by Karmal in February 1986.)

At a plenum meeting of the PDPA on 10 June, Najibullah announced several new measures. These included raising the salaries of the armed forces, help for the families of "martyrs," changing the name of the DRA to the Republic of Afghanistan, issuing a new land decree raising the ceiling on landholdings other than orchard and *waqf* (trust) land, and encouragement to private entrepreneurs.[55] Moreover, he introduced a law for the legalization and creation of new parties, reaffirmed the promise that the new constitution would reflect the position of all sides joining the coalition for peace, and reemphasized his government's commitment to Islam and to the creation of a "practical and genuine coalition of patriotic and democratic forces."[56]

At the 10 June plenum meeting and subsequently at the second extraordinary session of the Supreme Commission for National Reconciliation on 27 June, Najibullah offered to withdraw military units from areas not under the control of Kabul, allowing those commanders who would accept peace jirgas to retain administration of their areas. He also envisaged the process of peace jirgas and reconciliation culminating in a High Peace Jirga to be convened toward the end of the year.[57] To consolidate his political position, Najibullah moved to oust Karmal supporters Anahita Ratebzad and Mahmoud Baryalai from the Politburo.[58]

The internal measures and official publicity could not conceal the failure of national reconciliation, visible by July with the dissipation of Soviet offensives. The mujahideen had not only succeeded in blunting the offensive, but had also increased pressure on Kabul.[59] Initial Soviet-Kabul successes in Paktia (Jaji Maidan), Kunar, Nangarhar, and Qandahar were neutralized by July and August.[60] DRA troops were pushed out of Panjshir, and the mujahideen were once again operative in the Salang area. Given the heightened conflict across Afghanistan, Najibullah's extending the offer of cease-fire beyond 15 July passed as a nonevent.

The stymied state of the national reconciliation programme compelled Najibullah to make a revised proposal on 14 July, offering the Afghan Alliance twenty posts in the State Council, including twelve ministries and the posts of vice president and deputy prime minister.[61] He further indicated that the post of prime minister would be negotiable. Najibullah declared that the coalition would not be a mere "propaganda symbol" but a genuine sharing of power.[62] His government was ready to establish contacts with "monarchy-supporting forces, political figures of previous regimes and influential clergy," as well as tribal leaders and commanders of the armed groups.[63] While his statement retained the PDPA rhetoric and praises for Soviet friendship, Najibullah emphasized commitment to a "non-aligned, neutral, Muslim" Afghanistan and called for a jirga of coalition forces. The concession on respecting local control by those who accepted the reconciliation policy was reemphasized.[64] Almost simultaneously with the announcement, the Soviet embassy in Islamabad officially conveyed the offer to the Pakistan Foreign Office, expressing the hope that Pakistan would be able to persuade the Alliance to accept it.

If this offer had been made in January, perhaps the national reconciliation programme could have had a serious prospect of getting off the ground. Coming in July, following a frustrated military effort to break the Afghan Resistance, this latest offer was summarily dismissed by the Alliance and did not attract the attention of Afghan émigrés.

The offer also had serious lacunae. First, it withheld from the deal important ministries such as interior, defense, foreign affairs, and finance, as well as the security apparatus. Second, the promised draft constitution, finally issued on 15 July (one day after the revised offer), conferred on the president wide-ranging powers that simply negated the power sharing conceded in Najibullah's improved offer.[65] Third, the offer continued to be silent on the question of withdrawal.

Nonetheless, it is doubtful whether, at this late stage, further improvement of the offer would have made a difference. The Alliance groups had been consistently opposed to the idea of a coalition with the PDPA. In addition to their opposition in principle, they argued that the Soviets intended the coalition to replicate the East European experience and secure a dominant role for the PDPA in a future Afghanistan.

On 20 July 1987 Najibullah proceeded to Moscow, apparently in a bid to gain more time for his reconciliation policy. However, according to Oberdorfer's account in the *Washington Post*, Najibullah had been summoned to Moscow, where Gorbachev gave him one year to consolidate his position, by which time Gorbachev wanted to pull out Soviet troops regardless of the status of Najibullah's national reconciliation.[66] According to this analysis, the CPSU Central Committee meeting in late June had strengthened Gorbachev's political position and he felt confident of implementing his decision to withdraw from Afghanistan. Significantly, in an interview with the Indonesian daily, *Mardeka*, on 21 July, Gorbachev affirmed the Soviets' intention to provide a short time frame and linked it to the old formula of a guarantee of noninterference rather than to reconciliation.[67] At that stage, his statement did not as yet appear to presage a shift in the Soviet position.

Diplomacy Refocuses on the Second Track

Following a lull of two months—through May and June—when military activity was at its height, diplomatic activity resumed gradually. During this period, the international climate had greatly improved and the INF agreement was in sight.[68] Gorbachev had consolidated his position. This was clearly demonstrated in late May when, taking advantage of the embarrassing landing in Red Square by a young West German, Mathias Rust, Gorbachev dismissed his defense minister, Marshal S. Sokolov, and air chief Alexander Koldunov. The incident encouraged some observers to conclude that conservative forces in the Soviet Union, such as the army, who opposed military disengagement from Afghanistan, were on the decline.

Afghanistan came under discussion when Secretary General Pérez de Cuéllar visited Moscow in late June, followed by Secretary of State Shultz during mid-July. In June, prior to these contacts, Armand Hammer visited Moscow and then Islamabad. Zia ul Haq and Yaqub Khan had encouraged Hammer in the past as an informal channel. While Zia admired his role, Junejo tended to dismiss it as gratuitous. The Foreign Office had itself expressed reservations on Hammer's request for the June visit, but was finally overruled by Zia ul Haq, who chided the Foreign Office and praised Hammer's motives and his willingness to present suggestions to Moscow "beyond Pakistan's expectations."

Hammer conveyed to Zia ul Haq an optimistic view of developments in East-West relations. He had gathered the impression from Dobrynin that the Soviets were looking for a way of sharing power in a new government in Kabul and were concerned about peacekeeping and the prevention of a bloodbath. In response, Zia conceded that a consensus on Zahir Shah could resolve the tangle but, in a laconic strain, spoke of difficulties in the convening of a jirga. If held in Afghanistan, he said, "our people" would not go to the jirga, and if held in Pakistan, the Soviets, alleging Pakistani manipulation, would not commit themselves to its results in advance. Zia suggested to Hammer that a Soviet agreement to a jirga in Pakistan could pave the way for a political settlement.

It is debatable whether Zia ul Haq's suggestion to Hammer reflected a desire to develop the Zahir Shah option or was merely a disingenuous tactic to nudge the Soviets in the direction of accepting a modality designed to favour groups supported by Pakistan. Nonetheless, the suggestion underscored Zia's interest in exploring the idea through Hammer. On the other hand, he had paid little attention to Cordovez's proposals raised with Junejo. Although Cordovez had launched the second track in April 1987, he had no personal contact with Zia ul Haq, indisputably the pivotal Pakistani leader in matters relating to the Alliance, until January 1988. By then the negotiating process had already taken a new turn, moving away from the issue of internal political settlement.

At the formal level, Pérez de Cuéllar raised the Afghan issue with Gorbachev on 30 June in Moscow. The UN secretary general wanted to bring the focus back to the time-frame issue. He argued with the Soviet leader that a decision on time frame was important to trigger national reconciliation and asked him to make such a decision and thereby break the "vicious circle." The secretary general left with the impression that Gorbachev was conciliatory and had emphasized Soviet determination to leave Afghanistan. He felt that the Zahir Shah option was on the Soviets' minds, even though they avoided specific discussion of it.

The Shultz-Shevardnadze meeting on 11–12 July was primarily devoted to arms control issues but touched upon Afghanistan. As in the case of their preceding contact in April, they used the meeting to convey intent and assurances rather than to negotiate any under-

standing on the Afghan issue. Shultz sought to reassure Shevardnadze about U.S. readiness to play a constructive role and disavowed
any U.S. intent to seek "unilateral advantage" in Afghanistan. Having consulted Islamabad, Shultz pressed for reconvening the Geneva
round and plugged in themes underlining the failure of Najibullah's
national reconciliation, the need for a short time frame, and the idea
of an interim government under a neutral personality. The Soviet
position did not proceed beyond reiteration of the familiar position
of support for national reconciliation.

Interestingly, around the same time, in an informal exchange with
U.S. chief arms control negotiator Max Kampelman, Vorontsov
hinted that the Soviet Union was not seeking a majority role for the
PDPA. He also disclosed that the Soviets had contacted Zahir Shah
and conveyed the latter's impression that the United States was not
interested in a settlement. This information prompted an immediate
American response. The U.S. chargé d'affaires in Rome contacted
Zahir Shah to dispel any misgivings about U.S. interest in a settlement and in the role of Zahir Shah.

Intermittent signals emanating from Moscow sustained the hope
that the Soviets would review their position in favour of a neutral
interim government, or the Zahir Shah option, or a short time frame.
Privately, the Soviets continued to stress their concern about a possible massacre of PDPA members in the wake of Soviet withdrawal
and about the emergence of a hostile Afghanistan. Publicly, the Soviet position seemed to have evolved a step further when, at a seminar at Columbia University, a senior Soviet representative at the
United Nations remarked that the Soviet intervention in Afghanistan was a "mistake."[69]

Meanwhile, Pakistan waited for the resumption of the Geneva
talks and further dialogue with the Soviet Union. The diplomatic
activity in July and Kabul's new offer prompted Cordovez and the
U.S. State Department to probe further the prospects of an acceptable
political arrangement in Kabul. At a meeting in late July, Cordovez
apprised Under Secretary of State Armacost of his ideas on the second track. Cordovez felt that the Soviets would come around to dropping Najibullah, provided Pakistan played ball and prepared the
ground for bringing in Zahir Shah. Given the wave of anti-Islamic
fundamentalism in the West, Cordovez could trust the United States
to sympathize with his approach. Later, in December 1987, Cordovez
visited Rome to meet Zahir Shah.[70]

By now, within the State Department and also in the Pakistan

Foreign Office, there was considerable anxiety over the absence of a political initiative by the Afghan Alliance. Najibullah's improved offer of "power sharing" and his intention to convene a Loya Jirga toward the end of the year heightened their concern. Apart from the obvious desirability of a political initiative by the Alliance to press the Soviets toward a more favourable position, it was felt that the Alliance was losing out in the political game under way in Afghanistan.

Armacost visited Islamabad in early August to advocate the need to have the Alliance agree on a political platform. He suggested that the Alliance evolve a comprehensive position on the issues of time frame, cessation of hostilities, interim administration, arrangements for the exercise of self-determination (election or Loya Jirga), principles of future policy (nonalignment and no military bases), and reconstruction—as similarly proposed by the Pakistan Foreign Office to the Alliance since February 1987. He also wanted to know Pakistan's position on the Zahir Shah option and Cordovez's plan.

In Islamabad, Armacost found an abundance of sympathetic listeners, but little in the way of a promise from either the Pakistani authorities or the Alliance to follow up on his suggestions. Pakistan's top leaders were preoccupied by the more pressing issue of the new U.S. package for economic assistance and military sales credits, then ensnarled in the Arshad Parvaiz case.[71] In addition, Armacost was partly preempted by Gulbuddin Hekmatyar, who, on the eve of Armacost's visit, had announced a four-point "peace formula," which spoke generally of "the establishment of an impartial interim government acceptable to the mujahideen" to replace the Kabul regime and to be mandated to supervise withdrawal and hold free and fair elections.[72] Hekmatyar made no reference to the composition of the interim government but ruled out Zahir Shah, stating that the latter had been rejected by the mujahideen commanders. While this was an individual leader's position and the moderate leadership continued to claim considerable support for Zahir Shah among the Afghan refugees, it was a fact that none of the important field commanders had endorsed a role for Zahir Shah. Additionally, Iran could not favour the return of a former monarch. Although these two factors militated against the feasibility of the Zahir Shah option, it remained far too tantalizing to be given up.

The concern over the Alliance's lack of political initiative was not shared uniformly within the Pakistan government. Absence of response from the Soviets and frustration in obtaining Alliance endorsement of the idea of a neutral interim government had induced among Pakistani officials an ambivalence toward the second track, which led to an increasing emphasis on the demand for a short time frame to bring about a settlement. This mindset was reinforced as the Kabul-Moscow campaign to gain international support for national reconciliation intensified and Pakistan was obliged to counter it without the benefit of a credible political initiative from the Alliance.

During his visit to Islamabad, Armacost had also elicited Pakistan's reaction to the old, almost forgotten idea of an international conference. The idea had recently been revived intriguingly in a press report filed by Lawrence Lifchultz, datelined Moscow and appearing in the *Times* of India, which surmised that Moscow might not be averse to the idea of a roundtable conference with the participation of the mujahideen, the Kabul government, the United States, the Soviet Union, and Pakistan for the purpose of arriving at a compromise based on a gentleman's agreement to guarantee a neutral, nonaligned Afghanistan.[73] The origin of the proposal, more than its contents, raised curiosity in Islamabad: whether this was a trial balloon encouraged by the Soviets or just the correspondent stretching his imagination. It also drew the attention of the press and opposition in Pakistan. Yaqub Khan found it attractive to the extent that a roundtable conference, if indeed it was the preferred Soviet modality for a settlement, could yield quick results.

Despite the attention it received, the idea had little to commend it to either Pakistan or the Soviet Union. It raised an entire spectrum of new issues, such as those of mandate, participation, and working out of prior understandings. Then, Lifchultz's prescription had omitted Iran, which had its own version of a roundtable conference with the participation of Iran, Pakistan, the Soviet Union, and the mujahideen.[74] The roundtable idea also upset Cordovez, since it called into question the relevance of the Geneva process and circumvented his personal role.

Toward the end of August, Cordovez reactivated second-track discussions in a series of meetings in New York with Pakistan's minister of state for foreign affairs, Zain Noorani, a politician from Karachi with a journalistic background who enjoyed Junejo's support. Aware of the Zia-Junejo polarization and realizing that Yaqub Khan was becoming a lame duck in view of his candidacy for the post of UNESCO director general, Cordovez desired to build a close rapport with Noorani, something he had lost with Yaqub Khan. Noorani, now an aspirant for Yaqub Khan's position, fully reciprocated. By this time it had become clear to Cordovez that it was not realistic to expect Pakistan to first obtain an endorsement of Zahir Shah from the majority of the Alliance leadership. Accordingly, he modified his proposal.[75]

Cordovez suggested to Noorani that an assembly of the PDPA, mujahideen (including the Alliance), and Afghan expatriates be convened in Geneva or some other agreed venue outside Afghanistan or Pakistan simultaneously with the last round of Geneva proximity talks. A prior understanding could be reached on certain principles, such as that decisions of the assembly would be binding on the participants, that the assembly would decide a transitional arrangement with a specified timetable, and that no party would have either predominant representation in the assembly or a dominant role in the transitional arrangement.

In subsequent meetings Cordovez refined and improvised this proposal. He had tried to skirt the issue of Zahir Shah and the Loya Jirga, but Noorani, impelled by his desire to make a contribution, suggested that a Loya Jirga convened in Pakistan could be a more practical alternative for the setting up of an interim government or a transitional political arrangement. Cordovez saw Noorani's proposal as complementary and consistent with his idea of an assembly and suggested that the Loya Jirga might precede the assembly and elect a spokesman, preferably Zahir Shah. Once again, Cordovez wanted Pakistan to prepare the ground for the proposed assembly, with or without the jirga.

Before these ideas could be discussed in Islamabad, an unexpected development shifted the emphasis back to the issue of time frame. Somewhat surprisingly, the Afghans, who had declined to resume the Geneva talks in May, approached Cordovez at the end of August to request immediate convening of the Geneva round. Cordovez obliged, scheduling it for 7 September, allowing Pakistan, at its request, one week for preparation.

Geneva VIID: An Abortive Attempt to Settle the Time Frame

The sudden convening of the Geneva talks sharply raised expectations, especially because it was being convened at the initiative of Kabul following its refusal since May to agree to any dates. The insistence to hold it immediately before the General Assembly session appeared to lend credence to the speculation that Kabul would offer a twelve-month time frame and thereby either wrest a settlement on this basis or, if Pakistan were to demur, knock out the principal plank of Pakistan's position at the forthcoming UN General Assembly.

There were several supporting indications to suggest such a move by the Soviet-Afghan side. According to unconfirmed reports, Shevardnadze had mentioned an eleven-month time frame during a visit to Kuala Lumpur that coincided with Geneva VIID. In addition, Soviet officials in informal contacts with U.S. counterparts obliquely hinted at the possibility of a one-year time frame. And, in his August meetings with Noorani, Cordovez had made an intriguing remark, possibly intended to elicit Pakistan's reaction, that the Soviets hesitated to reactivate Geneva because they feared that Pakistan would not accept even a twelve-month time frame, implying that the Soviets were prepared to offer this figure.

From these indications and the belief that Kabul would not convene the Geneva round just to discuss national reconciliation or Cordovez's second track, the Pakistani negotiators braced themselves to face a one-year time-frame offer. Although time did not permit holding an Afghan cell meeting, which required both the president and the prime minister, a vague approval for one year as the upper limit was already in place and had not been challenged or countermanded. Junejo verbally reconfirmed this limit when briefs on the forthcoming round, reiterating the earlier recommendation of one year inclusive of the two-months' preparatory period, were sent to the presidency and the prime minister's office in accordance with established procedure. Yaqub Khan was elated by the reconvening of the Geneva round, which held out a promise that the settlement might materialize before his anticipated departure.

The State Department, recalling how Pakistan had proceeded to increase the time frame at the March round, was concerned lest Pakistan rush to agree to an expanded time frame already under attack from the strong pro-mujahideen lobbies in the United States. Accordingly, Armacost conveyed a reminder to Pakistan to insist on suitable front-loading. Acknowledging pressures on Islamabad to reach an early settlement, Armacost suggested they explore Cordovez's ideas on the second track, especially the possibility of replacing Najibullah with a compromise, broad-based government. The circumstances of Geneva VIID and its agenda, however, precluded the possibility of the second-track negotiations.

Cordovez proceeded to preempt any last-minute snarls by transmitting to his interlocutors a carefully prepared checklist, with a view to streamlining discussion at Geneva VIID. He thus sought to eliminate the possibility of any party's raising issues outside of those identified by him. He further recalled the positions of his interlocutors on the listed issues in a manner implying that, with the exception of time frame and possibly the border question, all others were as good as resolved. For example, on consultations with the refugees, he reminded the Government of Pakistan of his readiness to meet the refugees' representative in December 1986 and that the meeting had not been arranged. Similarly, on Iran, not formally included in the checklist but mentioned in the communication, he pointed to the Iranian concern regarding withdrawal of troops and the impression that Iran could go along with the settlement if this concern was satisfactorily addressed.

On the border issue, referring to the Afghan objection to the phrase "existing internationally recognized boundaries" in the bilateral agreement (Instrument I) and Pakistan's demand for its retention, Cordovez inaccurately attributed the phrase's retention in the text to a "compromise" in return for Pakistan's agreement to the omission of the proposed Naik clause on nonrecognition of situations resulting from military intervention.[76] He asked both sides to find a solution that was without prejudice to their respective positions and that met the requirement of the agreement on noninterference. Here, Cordovez appeared to concede one of Pakistan's arguments in favour of the retention of the phrase, that observance of noninterference ipso facto required a reference to international boundaries.

Other issues in the checklist were of a technical nature, such as the Security Council procedure for approval of the observer (monitoring) group, about which Cordovez assumed Pakistan's cooperation in not demanding the involvement of the Security Council. According to Cordovez, Afghanistan had been apprehensive that the council's involvement could be used for propaganda purposes.

Geneva VIID proved an anticlimax. Instead of placing the expected offer on the table, and thus putting Pakistan on the defensive, the Afghan side started by asking Cordovez to obtain a fresh offer of time frame from Pakistan. Yaqub Khan could not accept this argument. If the Afghan side wanted bargaining, which he opposed, it was for them to make a move, since the last offer on the table was made by Pakistan during the March round. Finally, the Afghans came up with a new figure of sixteen months, a reduction of two months from their previous offer of eighteen months.

Cordovez then pressed Pakistan to match the move. Acutely aware of the limited room for manoeuvre in this game of numbers but caught in its dynamics, Yaqub Khan raised the figure offered by Pakistan to eight months. It appeared that a couple of moves would lead to a figure closer to one year, forcing an agreement. But curiously, the Afghan side simply refused to make any further offer and wanted Pakistan to accept sixteen months. Kosyrev could not help, despite a perceptible difference between the Soviet and Afghan positions on the time-frame issue.

This position was unexpected and perplexed both Cordovez and the Pakistani side. Cordovez, trying hard for a breakthrough, sought Yaqub Khan's agreement to a twelve-month time frame. Yaqub Khan could not agree. Such an agreement would have meant taking Pakistan's position on twelve months, while the Afghans still hung on to sixteen months. It was safer to reach the figure in step-by-step negotiation. Witness the experience of the December 1985 memorandum, from which the figure of six months proposed by Cordovez was later projected by him as Pakistan's position during the March 1987 round. Cordovez even invoked the argument used by some opposition elements in Pakistan that continuing delay in reaching the agreement was, de facto, prolongation of the time frame and, hence, of bloodshed. Yaqub Khan was willing to negotiate and settle at twelve months and had been hinting at this possibility since March; but he was in no position to raise Pakistan's position to twelve months unilaterally and leave it to his successor to obtain agreement on that figure.

Indeed, after Yaqub Khan's resignation, Noorani and even Junejo criticized Yaqub Khan's stretching the time frame to eight months. Later, during the final phase of the Geneva negotiation, new politically charged issues of "symmetry" and additional "safeguards" were raised on the plea that the structure of the Geneva instruments envisaging a cutoff of assistance to the mujahideen was justified only in the context of a three- to four-month time frame, as originally demanded by Pakistan. Interestingly, Zia ul Haq, who was perceived as the fountainhead of Pakistan's hard-line position, did not openly express such criticism. Despite indications of his unhappiness with the jump to seven months in March 1987, he did not raise the matter with Yaqub Khan afterward. While President Zia ul Haq had never officially approved the one-year limit, he did not stop Yaqub Khan from moving in that direction. On his part, Yaqub Khan justified his decision by pointing out that it was Zia ul Haq who first put Cordovez on the scent in December 1986.

There has been considerable speculation about why the Afghans called for the September Geneva round with such urgency and, having done so, failed to offer a time frame of one year, as almost universally expected. An outlandish postulate attributed it to lack of coordination with the DRA army command, which wanted to avoid a withdrawal period coinciding with winter months. The Pakistani side had its own explanation, which may well be closer to the truth.

Kabul had convened the Geneva round as part of its wide-ranging diplomatic campaign to win support for the regime's initiatives and favourably influence international opinion prior to the General Assembly vote on Afghanistan. The counter moves by Pakistan had essentially focused on reiteration of its readiness to go to Geneva at any time and accept a settlement on the basis of a short time frame. Kabul obviously was not ready to make such an offer; the military activity of the resistance had shaken its confidence even further. It wanted to use the Geneva round as a diplomatic manoeuvre by making a token reduction as a show of flexibility to counter Pakistani propaganda. It gambled on a calculation that Pakistan had reached the limit of its position, and would not be able to reciprocate Kabul's token reduction of two months. Publicly, in an interview with *Izvestia* correspondent V. Kuznetsov, Abdul Wakil explained that Iran needed to be brought into "the talks and that there had to be 'reciprocity' in steps toward a settlement."[77]

The Soviet disappointment at Kabul's reluctance to move further to settle the time frame was revealed in a TASS comment published immediately following Geneva VIID.[78] The Pakistani move, on the other hand, might well have convinced Moscow of Pakistan's readiness to accept a settlement based on a time frame that the Soviets were in a position to offer. Similarly, in case the Soviets had not yet taken a decision on delinking the time frame from national reconciliation, the Pakistani move was sure to nudge them to reevaluate their position. The shift in the Soviet position became visible for the first time in Yaqub Khan's meeting with Shevardnadze later in September.

At the opposite end of the spectrum, the clearly bridgeable dif-

ference on time frame and Yaqub Khan's impassioned affirmation at
the end of Geneva VIID that Pakistan had come to Geneva determined to conclude a settlement[79] aroused the Afghan Resistance
groups and their ardent supporters in Pakistan and the United States.
The fact that Geneva VIID had come very close to an agreement
obliged them to take a hard look at the Geneva settlement and its
implications. They found the one-sided cutoff of supplies to the mujahideen unacceptable and started demanding safeguards to ensure
that mujahideen interests did not suffer as a result of the settlement
negotiated at Geneva. Reflecting the sentiment of most resistance
leaders, in early October Hekmatyar bitterly complained to Abdul
Sattar that the Geneva agreements would relegate the mujahideen
to the status of "rebels" and oblige Pakistan to recognize the Kabul
regime.

Two Parallel Proposals on the Second Track

Two proposals of separate origin, made prior to the Soviet policy shift
on linkage, are worthy of mention: Cordovez's proposals in an informal paper entitled "Scenario for an Accelerated Process of National Reconciliation"; and the set of proposals made by Zia ul Haq
to Armand Hammer for the latter to take up with the Soviets.

Cordovez's Scenario Paper

The abortive Geneva VIID placed Cordovez back on the second track.
On 30 September 1987 he presented his informal "scenario paper,"
laying down the rationale for the second track, with ideas he had
been airing for some time for the convening of a representative assembly of the Afghans to decide a transitional political arrangement.
Quoting from the secretary general's reports of 1985 and 1986,[80] the
paper emphasized a negotiated settlement as the only possible way
to achieve peace, and a need for "bold and decisive steps for national
reconciliation" to ensure that the settlement commanded the support of "all segments" of the Afghan people. The paper conceded that
national reconciliation must be carried out by the Afghans themselves and that the aim of the proposed scenario was to "facilitate
communication" among the Afghans with a view to enabling them
to agree on "transitional arrangements" necessary for the implementation of the comprehensive (Geneva) settlement.

The scenario paper envisaged the convening of an assembly of representatives of the seven parties based in Pakistan, representatives of the PDPA, and "select personalities" to formalize a set of understandings reached in advance among the participants in regard to the composition of the transitional arrangement. Importantly, it provided that no party would be assured a predominant role in the transitional arrangement, which would be given a mandate to initiate constitutional measures to ensure the peace and neutrality of Afghanistan. Cordovez emphasized that the proposal was not rigid and could be modified to accommodate the participants. For example, he suggested that the assembly could have a flexible format and that the participants would not be required to gather under the same roof. He was willing to shuttle between hotels, provided the representatives of the various groups agreed to gather in one city.

Cordovez's scenario possessed several attractive features from the Pakistan Foreign Office's perspective—chiefly, that it was close to the idea of an interim government originally suggested by Pakistan. Nonetheless, there were obvious problems in promoting this proposal. The Alliance leaders did not accept any form of dialogue with the PDPA. Also, Pakistan was not in a position to apply pressure on these leaders to secure the agreement of a majority unless there was a credible assurance that the Soviets accepted Cordovez's proposal.

Cordovez spoke in innuendos about the Soviet attitude to his paper, hinting that the reaction had not been negative when he showed the paper to well-placed Soviet sources in the United Nations and when he discussed some of the ideas with Soviet officials in Moscow in August.[81] This could not convince Pakistani officials, who were aware of the Soviet hesitation to accept any suggestion based on the replacement of the PDPA government and of the Soviet practice of respecting only those commitments made in direct and formal exchanges. Later confirmation of this assessment came in response to a query from Noorani in March 1988, when Kosyrev indicated that the Soviets had never accepted Cordovez's scenario paper.

Pakistan's formal reaction to Cordovez's proposal was conveyed to him in early November 1987 by Noorani, after the resignation of Yaqub Khan. The response, formulated by the Foreign Office and approved by Junejo, essentially maintained the dual-track approach but with emphasis shifting to the issue of time frame. Noorani conveyed Pakistan's blessings for Cordovez to promote the scenario proposal. While promising support, Noorani emphasized that the second track needed to be pursued primarily with the Afghan parties and that the activity on the second track should not detract attention from the pivotal issue of time frame. It was agreed that Cordovez should undertake a shuttle to the area to take up the proposal directly with the Alliance leaders. Meanwhile, the Pakistani side was to make an effort to elicit a positive response.

Zia ul Haq's Proposal on the Zahir Shah Option

An unscheduled visit to Islamabad by Armand Hammer on 17 October 1987 stimulated President Zia ul Haq's plan envisaging a role for the former king. This was perhaps the last such proposal offered to the Soviets. Hammer had a private dinner meeting with Zia ul Haq in the presence of Yaqub Khan, General Hamid Gul, and the president's trusted chief of staff, General Syed Raffaqat Hussain. Hammer essentially advocated the convening of a jirga in Pakistan to endorse Zahir Shah. He thought that the Soviets would not agree to a time frame without a transitional government that included a role for the PDPA. If Zahir Shah were endorsed, Najibullah could be expected to step aside. Hammer also impressed upon Zia ul Haq the need to take advantage of the propitious climate created by progress toward the INF accords. Next morning, the president's secretariat put together a proposal to be conveyed to Moscow by Hammer. Yaqub Khan was informed by telephone and a copy sent to him virtually at the same time it was handed over to Hammer.

The proposal called for Vorontsov to visit Islamabad at the earliest possible time to convey informal indication of a time frame for withdrawal. Meanwhile, Pakistan and the Soviet Union would request the United Nations to organize observers and, possibly, a peacekeeping contingent. Pakistan was to facilitate the convening of a Loya Jirga on its territory with constituent elements from the refugees, the mujahideen, and the PDPA to elect leaders to form a transitional government and to elect its head, who, it was pointed out, would undoubtedly be Zahir Shah. After Zahir Shah formed a government, Najibullah was expected to step aside. It was suggested that the transitional government need not include "participation from either the Najibullah regime or from the Peshawar seven." The proposed scenario then envisaged the signing of the Geneva Accords and induction of UN observers and peacekeeping forces.

The plan had attempted to balance Pakistani and Soviet concerns and constituted a serious offer. It simply got lost in the events that followed. Pakistan received no response to the plan, although Hammer had met Soviet Prime Minister Nikolai Ryzhkov in early November.[82]

Exit Yaqub Khan

Yaqub Khan became a casualty of Armand Hammer's visit, which sparked the ire of Prime Minister Junejo. As Junejo saw it, Yaqub Khan had bypassed him to work out a settlement plan with Zia ul Haq. Ironically, Yaqub Khan did not have a hand in drafting the plan. He received it while discussing Cordovez's scenario paper in the Foreign Office and immediately asked for a comparative study of the two proposals, which he wanted personally to carry to Junejo. That same day Noorani had returned to Islamabad from New York, and a copy of the plan was sent to him under Yaqub Khan's instructions. Before Yaqub Khan could convey it to Junejo and discuss it with him, the latter had already received a copy. The opening line, which attributed the plan to Zia ul Haq and Yaqub Khan, reportedly upset Junejo.

Yaqub Khan had already become vulnerable because of the UNESCO election, which he had lost and which had inspired reports in the press citing excessive expenditures on his election campaign. After the Hammer episode, Junejo decided to ease him out. Yaqub Khan decided to tender his resignation when Junejo asked Noorani to lead the Pakistan delegation to New York for the UNGA debate on Afghanistan. Zia ul Haq interceded in an attempt to persuade Junejo to change his mind. Junejo was prepared to let Yaqub Khan continue for a while, but refused to change his decision to let Noorani lead the delegation to the General Assembly. Contrary to facts, Yaqub Khan's resignation in late October 1987 was generally attributed to his defeat in the UNESCO election.

Yaqub Khan's departure reinforced the polarization at the top. For the next two months, a complete breakdown of communication existed on Afghan policy between the prime minister and the Foreign Office, on the one hand, and the president and the ISI on the other. Politically, this did not help Junejo. Removal of Yaqub Khan deprived him of an effective instrument for controlling Afghan policy, because the two shared an interest in the desirability of a negotiated settlement. Tactically, it was not helpful to remove the key Pakistani player in the Geneva negotiations at a sensitive and critical stage. The result was a further loss of coherence in Pakistani policymaking with respect to Afghanistan.

Moscow Abandons Linkage

Between Geneva VIID in September and the Washington summit in early December, the Soviets showed increasing impatience with their military involvement in Afghanistan, discernible in clearer signals of their intention to withdraw without regard to first securing progress in national reconciliation. In Washington, Gorbachev cut the "Afghan knot" with a time-frame offer that placed Soviet diplomacy onto the Geneva route.

Meanwhile, the schismatic Pakistani politics kept Pakistan's approach grounded in a logical duality emphasizing time frame and, at the same time, tentatively exploring prospects for an internal political settlement. Disappointment at failure to elicit the desired political initiative from the Afghan Alliance shifted the priority to time frame in Pakistan Foreign Office thinking and in public statements. It was only after the Washington summit that Zia ul Haq moved decisively in a belated attempt to revive the second-track negotiations.

While waiting for the Soviet position to clarify, Cordovez sought a breakthrough on either of the two tracks. Najibullah, meanwhile, faced with the Soviet decision to withdraw, proceeded to consolidate his political position by convening his own version of a Loya Jirga and by dislodging pro-Karmal remnants from top party and government positions.

Moscow Shifts as Tentative Moves
Continue on Two Tracks

The first indications of Soviet rethinking about linkage and of a shift toward unconditional acceptance of the Geneva framework had come at a meeting between Yaqub Khan and Shevardnadze in New York on 24 September 1987. Since the meeting took place after Geneva VIID, Yaqub Khan could speak convincingly of Pakistan's willingness to reach a settlement on the basis of the Geneva texts. He conceded the relevance of "organic linkage" thus far emphasized by the Soviets between withdrawal and internal political settlement as well as the need to prevent further bloodshed, but maintained that the availability of a time frame would impel all Afghans to move in the direction of political reconciliation. Yaqub Khan proposed making the time frame final, while letting the conclusion of the settlement await a cooling off and progress toward internal settlement. Time frame was viewed as a potential catalyst to push the Afghans toward a compromise.

A new element was added to Pakistan's position at this meeting. While reaffirming its position on a neutral interim government, Yaqub Khan indicated to Shevardnadze that Pakistan could persuade the Alliance leaders to accept intra-Afghan dialogue if Najibullah were to step down. This suggestion was later revived by Zia ul Haq with the Indian foreign secretary, K. P. S. Menon, in early May 1988, and in Moscow in early August 1988 by Yaqub Khan, who was reappointed foreign minister in June 1988.

Shevardnadze's response at the 24 September 1987 meeting was enigmatic and, as compared to February 1987, less categorical in favour of Najibullah's national reconciliation programme. He did not share Pakistani reasoning either on time frame or on the proposed interim government, arguing that replacement of the government in Kabul was tantamount to accepting capitulation. Then, as if suggesting a new approach, he conceded that neither the Soviet Union nor Pakistan could draw up a "blueprint" for a government in Kabul. Setting aside the long-held linkage, Shevardnadze drew a distinction between withdrawal and guarantee of noninterference, which were in the hands of Islamabad and Moscow, and "other matters," which were primarily for the Afghans to settle. "The two sides (Moscow and Islamabad) should do what they could do," he remarked in summing up. Clearly, the Soviets were loosening the linkage. Within two months they formally delinked the issues of time frame and national reconciliation at the Washington summit.

Prior to the summit, Pakistan's declaratory position showed a distinct emphasis on the demand for a time frame. Two factors accounted for this: Junejo's increasing interest in directing the Afghan policy, and the pressures generated by the 1987 UNGA session, during which the time-frame demand was the only card in Pakistan's hand to counter the Soviet-Kabul diplomatic moves aimed at undercutting support for the UNGA resolution on Afghanistan. Nevertheless, immediately after the adoption of the resolution, Pakistan revived interest in the second track. On 10 November Noorani conveyed to Cordovez Pakistan's formal support for proceeding with his scenario paper.

Junejo did not have many dealings with the Afghan Alliance leaders and had no illusion about his ability to persuade them to accept any of the proposals from Cordovez or the Pakistan Foreign Office.

While he favoured early settlement based on a reasonable time frame, he did not discount the rationale underlying the second-track approach. During his visit to New York in September 1987, he spoke of the introduction of a UN peacekeeping force as a means to prevent bloodshed. This plain suggestion overlooked its precondition, namely, an internal cease-fire and an agreement among Afghan factions to accept UN peacekeeping troops. Since the Afghan Alliance and the mujahideen rejected the introduction of such a force as long as Kabul was under PDPA control, Junejo's proposal was a nonstarter.[83]

The 1987 UNGA debate on Afghanistan was particularly intense because of unprecedented Afghan-Soviet diplomatic efforts to influence the vote. For the first time in seven years, amendments were moved to the Afghanistan resolution at Soviet behest.[84] The Soviet permanent mission actively negotiated a possible consensus draft on the basis of the existing resolution. The minimum Soviet requirement was a new paragraph explicitly calling for observance of the principle of noninterference. Pakistan, though shaky about the vote, could not accept a reference that tended to equate the presence of foreign troops with interference and was obliged to block the Soviet-backed amendment with counterproposals.[85]

The Soviet officials in New York hinted that Pakistan's agreement to a consensus resolution would send the right signal to Moscow and facilitate an early decision on time frame. The suggestion was largely a local initiative, because the UNGA vote was no longer relevant to Soviet calculations on its time frame for withdrawal. Under pressure of the debate, Pakistan increased its emphasis on time frame, as evident in Noorani's statement to the General Assembly that "the acceptance of the demand for national reconciliation as [a] precondition for withdrawal would be tantamount to encouraging future aggressors to create realities of their own choice before . . . [calling] for observance of the fundamental principles of the United Nations."[86] The UN secretary general's report on Afghanistan, which was cleared if not authored by Cordovez, endorsed the logic of the Pakistani position by affirming that a "short time frame" would give a "decisive impetus" toward reconciliation.[87]

Following the UNGA debate, Cordovez's own position appeared to vacillate between his two tracks. Having received Pakistan's green signal on 10 November and believing that the Soviets continued to maintain the linkage, Cordovez reactivated his second-track proposals. In a letter addressed to Junejo on 17 November, he proposed discussion at the next shuttle to identify the steps that the Government of Pakistan could take in order to "promote negotiations and agreements among Afghans on transitional arrangements." This time he also conveyed that he had discussed the ideas contained in his scenario paper with Soviet diplomats, who had agreed to transmit them to Moscow. His second letter, written ten days later, however, omitted this subject completely and instead focused on the time frame, proposing that the interlocutors agree to accept as the starting point for discussion the figure obtained by bridging the gap evenly between their respective positions. This was the old recipe for a twelve-month time frame, but the proposal lost its relevance almost immediately in the light of Gorbachev's announcement in December at the conclusion of the Washington summit.

Toward the end of November Najibullah's position stiffened on national reconciliation. He convened a "Loya Jirga" on 29 November in which he secured approval of the new draft constitution and his own election to the all-powerful position of president of the Republic of Afghanistan.[88] Two reasons appeared to explain this move, which literally wrapped up his national reconciliation programme. First, the programme had been a failure. Militarily, Najibullah had come under enormous pressure from the Afghan Resistance forces, who could not be placated by his offers of reconciliation. Kabul was hit while the jirga was in progress.[89] Second, the Soviets were now determined to withdraw, delinking the issue from reconciliation. Under the circumstances, Najibullah had to move quickly to consolidate his position. Before the Loya Jirga, at a plenum of the PDPA Central Committee on 17 October, Najibullah proceeded with further purges of dissident Parchamis and expelled Ratebzad and Baryalai from the PDPA Central Committee.[90]

From the point of view of the Geneva talks, the Loya Jirga of 29 November 1987 marked an important development. For the first time, Najibullah spoke of a twelve-month time frame, although he alluded to the precondition of progress in national reconciliation. Nonetheless, there could be little doubt about the direction in which the Kabul position was moving under Soviet pressure.

The apparent tentativeness of the Pakistani stand on Cordovez's scenario proposals did not mean a downgrading of the importance of an internal settlement. There was real concern over the possibility of the continuation of the conflict—of bloodshed and the spectre of "Lebanonization" of Afghanistan. The Pakistan Foreign Office saw the merit of Cordovez's latest proposals, as the recommended transitional arrangement was contingent on removal of the PDPA regime. The ISI, on the other hand, had started believing that the Soviets were leaving in any event, and Pakistan should therefore endorse, and elicit support for, the election plan decided by the Afghan Alliance, which represented the winning party on the battlefield. On its own the Foreign Office had little influence with the Alliance. It gradually lost hope of a reasonable initiative from the Alliance that could be realistically taken up with the Soviets to negotiate a compromise.

By late 1987 the Zia ul Haq-Junejo struggle for power had become well known and invariably confounded diplomats and foreign visitors in Islamabad (including those from the United States) as to who was calling the shots in which areas of policy. On issues related to Pakistan's Afghan policy, foreign diplomats generally considered Zia ul Haq to be in control, especially in regard to dealings with the Afghan Resistance. The U.S. ambassador in Islamabad, Arnold Raphel, recognized the sensitivity of the issue and tried to keep in close touch with both leaders. Nonetheless, on the question of Pakistan's putting pressure on the Alliance to come up with a political initiative, Raphel specifically sought Zia ul Haq's intercession in November 1987. Later, during the final Geneva round, he reportedly shuttled between the two leaders to keep them informed on the U.S. discussions with the Soviets, especially on symmetry, and to coordinate U.S.-Pakistani positions at this crucial stage of the Geneva negotiations.[91]

Unlike the ISI, Zia ul Haq showed sensitivity to the need for an internal settlement and endorsed a neutral interim government with PDPA representation; but he failed to attach urgency to the issue. In a conversation with Ambassador Raphel in late November, Zia undertook to press the Alliance in that direction, provided the Americans could bring the Soviets around to accepting the replacement of Najibullah's government. Around the same time, in an interview in the London *Sunday Telegraph*, Zia suggested equal representation in the interim government for the mujahideen, the Afghan refugees, and the Kabul regime.[92]

Although the suggestion, later rejected by Yunis Khalis, chairman of the Alliance,[93] had stirred public interest, Zia ul Haq had not anticipated the rapid shift in the Soviet position toward delinkage. During the crucial period from September to November, there was no high-level meeting in Islamabad involving the concerned agencies to review and pull together various elements of Pakistan's Afghan policy. Consequently, the policy became institutionally compartmentalized and suffered as a result of the absence of coordination within the government's decisionmaking apparatus.[94]

It was against this background that the Pakistan Foreign Office gave its response to a request from the U.S. State Department for a briefing on Afghanistan prior to the Washington summit. The Pakistani position, presented with a Cartesian precision characteristic of Foreign Secretary Sattar and conveyed to Washington through Ambassador Raphel, was that the United States should insist on a short time frame, which would itself become a catalyst for an internal settlement. Efforts for an interim government, including the second track through Cordovez, could be pursued in parallel, but these should not delay provision of a time frame. The United States was also asked to determine whether the Soviets would consider favourably Pakistan's idea of a neutral interim government or the proposals contained in Cordovez's scenario. On time frame, the Pakistani position emphasized front-loading and called for undefined "adequate safeguards," on the plea that the time frame offered by Pakistan had already exceeded the tolerable limit.

The Washington Summit

Glimpses of a movement in the Soviet position on time frame became evident a month before the Washington summit. In early November 1987 Soviet official spokesman Gennadi Gerasimov remarked that it would be possible for the Soviet Union to withdraw in seven to twelve months, although he still seemed to link the decision to reconciliation.[95] Toward the end of November, remarks suggesting that the Soviets were ready to make a serious offer on time frame were made by Prime Minister Ryzhkov in New Delhi and by Soviet Deputy Foreign Minister Igor Rogachev in Moscow.[96] Finally, at the Washington summit, 8–10 December 1987, Gorbachev disclosed to the U.S. side the new Soviet position on the time frame and the Geneva settlement, made public at the conclusion of the summit.

In a statement to the press in Washington on 10 December, Gorbachev announced Soviet willingness to offer a twelve-month time frame, provided there was an agreement on cessation of "military and financial" assistance to the mujahideen. He further declared the Soviet intention to disengage following a settlement and not to participate in combat except in self-defense. Reiterating the Soviet desire to see a nonaligned, neutral Afghanistan, Gorbachev stated that

Moscow was not trying for a pro-Soviet government in Kabul and, similarly, Washington should not strive for a pro-U.S. government. Without linking it to withdrawal, Gorbachev reaffirmed support for a "coalition on the basis of national reconciliation and the realities of the situation" and asked the United States and Pakistan to support the process, admitting that the main role had to be played by the Afghans themselves.

This was a unilateral offer, as seen in the initial reaction of U.S. administration officials, who doubted if the Soviets were "yet ready to bite the bullet" and who continued to emphasize the U.S. demand for a terminal date for withdrawal.[97] There was also a lack of clarity in the early U.S. comments on the cutoff of supplies.[98] More than a week later, Armacost appraised the Gorbachev offer in positive terms and clarified delinkage.[99] The U.S. position on supplies took even longer to get streamlined.

In the choice of venue to announce his offer, Gorbachev had made a gesture to the United States, rather than to Pakistan or the United Nations. True, the Soviets had consulted Pakistan to explore the possibility of promoting national reconciliation, an area where the United States could not be of direct help. But for the essentially unilateral decision on time frame, they made the announcement at the Washington summit to gain maximum publicity advantage and to underscore the priority Gorbachev attached to Soviet relations with the West, especially the United States.

As requested by Pakistan, the U.S. side had sounded out the Soviets on Cordovez's second track and the scenario paper, but the Soviets evinced little interest. They were equally noncommittal on resuming dialogue with Pakistan. The Soviet side, on its part, stressed the need for U.S. commitment to noninterference; the United States responded that the issue had already been dealt with at Geneva. In official meetings during 1987, the Soviets said no more than what Gorbachev stated at the press conference, except for their emphasis on a role for the PDPA regime in any future arrangement and an assurance that the Soviet Union desired a friendly rather than a socialist Afghanistan.

The position taken by the Soviets at the Washington summit cleared the way for the Geneva settlement. There was little left to discuss in the context of the four instruments except whether the Soviets could offer an even shorter time frame and agree to front-loading as provided in the text.

Cordovez acted quickly to ensure that the prospects opened up for a settlement on the Geneva track were secured. Following the summit, he visited Washington and Moscow before setting out on a shuttle to the area in mid-January 1988. In Washington, speaking to Armacost, Cordovez expressed concern that Pakistan might be unreasonable and reject the twelve-month offer. He also wondered whether a revival of the Islamabad-Moscow dialogue was any longer necessary. In Moscow Cordovez reportedly urged the Soviets to reduce the time frame to under one year so that he could clinch the settlement at Geneva.

Cordovez knew that the Soviets were now impatient to have a settlement to bring back their troops. Pressure had built on them to do so, internally as a result of glasnost[100] and externally owing to Gorbachev's eagerness to seek cooperative relations with the West. Cordovez's Moscow visit further confirmed this impression. He was nervous, however, about Pakistan's reaction. Knowing that the Soviets were on their way out, Pakistan might question the desirability of tying itself to the Geneva provisions. Alternatively, it could raise new issues. This apprehension had some validity.

The publicity accompanying Gorbachev's declaration had alarmed the conservative supporters of the mujahideen in both the United States and Pakistan. They suspected Geneva to be a sellout and criticized Pakistan for having moved from its original three- to four-month time frame to one of eight months at the September 1987 Geneva round. The big issue was the cutoff of aid to the mujahideen. The hard-line reaction was evident in Washington following the summit when White House spokesman Marlin Fitzwater tried to assuage the conservatives' concerns, saying that the Reagan administration had no plans to withhold U.S. aid to the mujahideen until after Soviet troops had withdrawn.[101]

A Split Reaction in Islamabad

The different reactions by Zia ul Haq and Junejo to Gorbachev's declaration foreshadowed the political wrangles that dominated the final phase of the negotiations from January to the signing of the Geneva Accords in April 1988. When the Soviet ambassador in Islamabad, Abdul Rehman Oglu Vezirov, read out the salient features of Gorbachev's statement, Junejo lauded the Soviet initiative and underscored Pakistan's sincerity in seeking a settlement.[102] Nonetheless, he reminded Ambassador Vezirov of the desirability of a Vorontsov visit to Pakistan.

Zia ul Haq received the details via telegram from the Pakistan embassy in Washington. He reacted by summoning Ambassador Raphel, to whom he expressed his surprise. Zia wondered what had transpired at the Washington summit that led Gorbachev to drop the linkage between withdrawal and future government arrangements in Afghanistan. He recalled his telephone conversation with Reagan prior to the summit and his remarks that the time frame was not an end in itself. If the time frame were now settled, he said, "we would have tied our hands without settling the real issue." Zia wanted the Americans to revive the question of future government arrangements with the Soviets. He promised that the PDPA would be assured participation, as asked by Moscow. But the Americans, having stressed the time frame for so long at the behest of Pakistan, were in no position to restore the linkage originally demanded by the Soviets and ostensibly dropped in deference to the Pakistani and U.S. emphasis on time frame. Zia suspected, nonetheless, that the Soviets and the Americans had reached an understanding on an Afghan settlement that ignored the interests of the mujahideen.

Though hardly an enthusiast for Geneva, Zia's reaction to the Washington summit was at variance with the attitude he had so far maintained toward the negotiations there. Over the years he had allowed Pakistan to get locked into positions from which it could not later extricate itself. At the early stages of the negotiations, when he exercised a firm hold over policy, he had personally approved the agenda, the structure of the settlement, and the text of Section II (on noninterference) of the draft comprehensive settlement. From 1984 onward he appeared to be acquiescing in positions taken by Yaqub Khan, with the exception of the issue of direct talks. He let Yaqub Khan agree to a bilateral agreement with the DRA, which theoretically meant signature with the Kabul government. Similarly, Yaqub Khan had changed Pakistan's position on time frame with full knowledge of the president. Yet, Zia ul Haq reacted with fluster in the face of the Soviet decision to abandon the linkage and push for the settlement negotiated at Geneva.

Zia's thinking on the Afghan issue had several layers. Since 1983 he had viewed Geneva with complacency and was influenced by the hard-line perception that the Soviets were in Afghanistan to stay. He went along with Yaqub Khan's seemingly circumspect initiatives in the interest of keeping the diplomatic option open, as well as to avoid precipitating differences with his foreign minister that would have fueled public controversy over the Afghan policy.[103] Meanwhile, as a result of his steady military support to the mujahideen, the military situation had changed dramatically, opening up new opportunities. The Afghan jihad was now poised to force a Soviet political and ideological retreat from Afghanistan. The military momentum of the resistance had built to an extent that, if sustained, it could lead to the collapse of the PDPA regime.

In Zia ul Haq's assessment, the Soviets wanted to avert this prospect by pushing for the Geneva settlement, which required Pakistan to cut off supplies to the mujahideen as part of a package designed to secure Soviet withdrawal. He felt let down by the Americans and viewed Gorbachev's announcement as the outcome of a U.S.-Soviet understanding. On a psychological plane, Zia did not forget the days of his isolation before the Soviet military intervention in Afghanistan that had suddenly brought Pakistan and him into prominence. Furthermore, the possibility of a superpower deal for a settlement evoked old fears and a nervousness about its implications.[104]

Following the Washington summit, Zia ul Haq sought to refocus attention on the question of future government arrangements. He tried to gain control over the diplomatic aspect of the policy. He made statements emphasizing the need for an interim government, conceding a PDPA share in it[105] and even linking Pakistan's signatures on the Geneva instruments to the formation of such a government.[106] In his meetings with Cordovez in January 1988, Zia forcefully endorsed the contents of the scenario paper. Later in February, in his meeting with Vorontsov, he pressed for delay in concluding the settlement at Geneva to allow time for an understanding to evolve on a future government.

On the military front, the siege of Khost, a garrison town located in a bowl-shaped valley adjoining Pakistan's Kurram Agency, appeared to be motivated by a desire to secure a suitable enclave for setting up a mujahideen government on Afghan territory. There is, however, no evidence that Zia ul Haq encouraged the siege, which lasted for over one month until early January 1988.[107]

Zia ul Haq had acted late. The emphatic interest he showed in seeking a transitional government had never emerged so clearly as it did after the Washington summit. The chance to develop this objective had, however, existed only as long as the Soviets were insisting on linkage. If Pakistan had been able to elicit a credible political initiative from the Afghan Alliance to enliven the second-track negotiation, it could justifiably have demanded a delay in concluding the Geneva settlement. Zia ul Haq alone had the authority to cajole the Alliance to produce such an initiative, which also would have required a coherent political direction and better coordination of policy, especially between the ISI and the Pakistan Foreign Office. The ISI, however, remained preoccupied with augmenting the military prowess of the resistance and showed little sensitivity to the need for developing a political option.

The time available for promoting the neutral interim government idea, with or without Zahir Shah, was limited, and the diplomatic initiative to activate the Geneva track lay entirely in Moscow's hands after the texts were completed in 1986 (indeed since 1984, when Pakistan accepted the draft comprehensive settlement). This aspect was obfuscated by the Soviet linkage and the consequent delay in the offer of a time frame, which apparently created a deceptive ambivalence in Zia ul Haq's view of the potential of the Geneva process. Meanwhile, stalled in its efforts to elicit an appropriate political initiative from the Afghan Alliance and repeatedly presented with the rhetorical ISI-Alliance argument that Kabul would collapse without the support of the Soviet troops, the Pakistan Foreign Office slid back into its emphasis on the time frame.[108]

The vigorous advocacy of interim government by Zia ul Haq after the Washington summit failed to generate a new diplomatic initiative. Internationally, the idea of keeping an agreement on withdrawal on hold until the formation of an interim government did not attract support. More important, the hard-liners within the Afghan Alliance refused to show flexibility on accommodating the PDPA in a future arrangement. For this reason, Zia ul Haq toned down assertions of his ability to persuade the Alliance to accept a compromise formula. During his meetings with Cordovez in January 1988, he avoided making a commitment on the composition of the transitional government and seemed to go along with the ISI-Alliance view of a mujahideen-dominated interim government.

Zia ul Haq's efforts prompted parallel moves from Junejo, who, in deference to mujahideen interests, placed emphasis on building safeguards into the existing Geneva mechanism. As the political and diplomatic activity gained momentum, the issue of the Geneva settlement moved to the centre of power politics in Pakistan. Both Zia ul Haq and Junejo acknowledged in public statements that 1988 would be the year of destiny for Afghanistan.

A Note on Neutrality Proposals

In the charged but confused atmosphere of early 1988, the issue of safeguards to ensure a free and sovereign Afghanistan became a subject of media discussion in Pakistan.[109] Among a variety of ideas, neutralization of Afghanistan received attention in light of the apparent Soviet interest in a neutral Afghanistan, as publicly expressed by Gorbachev during his visit to New Delhi in November 1986.[110] Before surveying the final stage of the Geneva process, this concept merits a brief comment.

The EC proposals of February 1980 had referred to neutralization of Afghanistan. President Carter's remarks during his visit to Yugoslavia in June 1980 alluded to U.S. readiness to negotiate guarantees for neutrality.[111] Academic and intellectual circles within Pakistan spoke of neutrality in terms of the "Finlandization" of Afghanistan, a populist phrase which implicitly conceded special Soviet interest in Afghanistan.[112] Some of these proposals, betraying antimilitary prejudice within the Pakistani opposition, went so far as to talk about neutralization of Afghanistan and Pakistan in the Finland-Sweden mold.

Gorbachev's remarks in New Delhi stimulated Pakistani interest in the idea, which was pursued by Foreign Secretary Sattar a month later in Moscow. Vorontsov came up with an attractive prospect, suggesting (somewhat rhetorically) that a "Switzerland-type neutrality" could be considered for Afghanistan. In most subsequent contacts with the Soviets, Pakistan tried to discuss this possibility, but failed to elicit a specific response. The U.S. soundings proved equally unproductive. It was only in November 1988, seven months after the conclusion of the Geneva Accords, that Kabul came up with a proposal for the demilitarization and neutrality of Afghanistan. The proposal was endorsed by Gorbachev in his address to the UN General Assembly on 7 December 1988.[113]

A neutral Afghanistan had a psychological appeal to the old guard Pakistani diplomats, who had inherited the British perception of Afghanistan as a buffer country. They felt that neutrality suited Afghanistan, which had long enjoyed a de facto neutral status in a tenuously held balance of power in Central Asia. Guaranteed neutrality seemed to make sense from the Soviet point of view, if Moscow was indeed concerned over a hostile foreign presence in Afghanistan. A neutral Afghanistan also suited U.S. interests, which related primarily to the Persian Gulf and the Indian Ocean. For the

Pakistan Foreign Office, with its thinking prone to considerations of geopolitics and security rather than ideology, the idea promised the neutralization of a threat from the north. Accordingly, Vorontsov's remarks in December 1986 prompted the Foreign Office to prepare a concrete proposal to engage the Soviets in discussion and explore the idea's feasibility.

The neutrality concept raised a series of complicated legal and political questions—for example, the status of Soviet-Afghan treaties of 1921 and 1978 and their legal implications; the heavy involvement of Soviet military advisers, even before the December 1979 intervention; and the conflict within Afghanistan, which made neutralization a questionable proposition. From a procedural standpoint, it was difficult to envisage early political stability and a government in Afghanistan sufficiently authoritative to be able to declare and preserve permanent neutrality along the lines of the Austrian model.

In the circumstances of Afghanistan, neutrality could only be established through an agreement by outside powers; it could not be initiated by Kabul. For that purpose, an agreement could be shaped to supplement international guarantees negotiated at Geneva or, alternatively, undertakings to respect Afghan neutrality could be incorporated in a declaration or resolution to be adopted at an international conference or through Security Council proceedings. Such undertakings could be acknowledged by Afghanistan following the establishment of more propitious internal conditions. Furthermore, geopolitical conditions ruled out any agreement on the part of the guarantors to intervene in the event of violation of Afghanistan's neutrality; Iran would not have agreed to the assumption of such a right by the United States.

Bearing in mind these ideas, the Pakistan Foreign Office formulated a declaration closely following the Laotian declaration of 9 July 1982 and the subsequent Treaty of Guarantors. The draft reinforced some of the provisions of the Laotian declaration, calling for revocation of any obligations that militated against Afghanistan's neutral status (to suppress the military cooperation clause of the 1978 treaty) and envisaging a role for the Security Council to act in case of a threat or breach of neutrality status. Incidentally, the Declaration on International Guarantees drafted at Geneva was also essentially inspired by the Laotian declaration. In January 1987 Yaqub Khan handed over the draft declaration to Kovalyev and subsequently had it conveyed to the United States, China, Saudi Arabia, and Iran. A couple of weeks later, before his visit to Moscow, he also discussed the concept with the seven Alliance leaders.

As in the case of other issues related to the Afghan settlement, the Pakistani side regarded the Soviet attitude on neutrality as the key to its promotion. The Soviets, it turned out, did not have a specific formal arrangement in mind and spoke of neutral Afghanistan in a broad generic sense. In response to the specific proposal by Pakistan, Kovalyev alluded to the neutrality professed by such disparate countries as Cuba, Vietnam, Laos, Algeria, Finland, Sweden, and Switzerland, stressing that the character and mode of neutrality was for the Afghan government to determine and that the initiative should come from Kabul.

The idea was dismissed unanimously by the seven Alliance leaders as contrary to the Islamic ethos. It did not appeal to their image of Afghanistan as a virile nation. Gailani, speaking on behalf of the seven, stated that neutrality was tantamount to tying the hands of the Afghan nation forever. No one should expect the Afghan nation to be an "idle spectator," he said, if the Islamic world required its help or if "Pakistani brothers were ever to face adversity and foreign aggression."

This forceful rejection did not stop Pakistan from exploring the feasibility of the idea with the Soviets. The United States was also asked to keep it on their agenda for bilateral talks with the Soviets on the Afghan issue. Prior to the signing of the Geneva Accords, while the Soviets and, subsequently, Najibullah maintained a public posture favouring a "nonaligned, neutral" Afghanistan, it was only the Pakistan Foreign Office that pursued the idea with some seriousness, and the Pakistani opposition press and intellectuals that kept reminding the Pakistan government of the significance of the Soviet-Kabul professions on neutrality. In the manner of several proposals thrown up during the long course of the Afghan conflict, the neutrality idea did not fade away, despite its questionable relevance to Afghanistan or the ill-fated precedent of Laotian neutrality, which, ironically, provided the most suitable legal framework.

7

The Final Phase, 1988

The approaching end to the Geneva negotiating process generated intense controversy over the issues of a pre-settlement interim government and the cutoff of supplies to the mujahideen implied in the negotiated texts. Zia ul Haq felt outmanoeuvred by the Washington summit and pursued with determination the objective of an interim government. At the same time, heightened criticism from conservative, pro-mujahideen lobbies forced the Pakistan Foreign Office and the U.S. State Department to rectify the perceived imbalance in the existing texts to safeguard the interests of the Afghan Resistance. The centrepiece of the concept was symmetry in the treatment of the contending Afghan factions with regard to the cutoff of supplies.

Pakistan could not have retreated from Geneva without loss of international credibility after Gorbachev in February 1988 set a deadline for signing the settlement. The final Geneva round began in early March amidst political wrangles in Islamabad focused on whether or not to sign the Geneva settlement without a prior agreement on an interim government. Hard-liners within the Afghan Alliance rejected any proposal based on PDPA participation, thereby ruling out early progress on an internal political compromise and constraining Pakistan to scale down its demand for an interim government. In the end Pakistan managed to achieve no more than a statement by Cordovez prior to the signing of the Geneva Accords reflecting an understanding on the continuation of efforts for the formation of a broad-based government to be decided by all Afghan political elements.

The issue of symmetry posed the principal hindrance to a settlement, as Moscow could not accept the U.S. proposal for a moratorium on supplies to all Afghan factions, including the regime in Kabul. As the prospects for an understanding on symmetry receded, the Soviets pressed Pakistan at Geneva to proceed with the settlement without the U.S. guarantee and even alluded to undefined "consequences" for Soviet-Pakistani relations if the Soviet troops were to withdraw without a Geneva settlement. The issue was, however, resolved in early April with a tacit agreement on the notion of "positive symmetry," based on an ambiguous Soviet acquiescence in the U.S. assertion of a U.S. right to provide military assistance to Afghan factions should the Soviet Union continue such assistance to the faction it supported. Moscow clearly wanted the settlement to put a gloss of international good behaviour on its decision to withdraw from Afghanistan.

Diplomacy Intensifies as 1988 Begins

The emerging prospects of a settlement based on the Geneva instruments galvanized all principal actors on the Afghan scene to focus on its implications in the light of their respective political agendas. The Soviets had taken the critical decision to cut their losses and withdraw; they clearly preferred to do so under the Geneva framework to save themselves from the stigma of a defeat. Speaking to the Afghan news agency Bakhtar after a two-day visit to Kabul, Soviet Foreign Minister Shevardnadze stated on 7 January 1988: "We would like 1988 to be the last year of the presence of Soviet troops in your country."[1] Kabul was nervous, its attempt at national reconciliation having shown little success, but this could no longer stop Gorbachev from proceeding with a strategic decision to free his policies from the debilitating engagement in Afghanistan.[2] In the eyes of the mujahideen, the Geneva negotiating process was always suspect. Now its outcome threatened to deny them the resources to pursue their armed struggle to a victorious end.[3]

The positions of the United States and Pakistan on Geneva showed far less clarity. The U.S. hard-line supporters of the Afghan Resistance attacked the State Department for acquiescing in a set of agreements that called for a supply cutoff to "rebels" against the Kabul government.[4] The State Department took shelter behind the position that the instruments had been negotiated primarily by Pakistan, which had borne the principal responsibility for carrying forward the diplomatic process on Afghanistan. To fend off the hard-line criticism, the State Department also banked on the military assessment shared and promoted by the CIA and the ISI that the PDPA regime could not survive the removal of the Soviet props. Even a worst-case scenario did not envisage the PDPA regime's regaining control over Afghanistan. Besides, U.S. vital interests were sufficiently served by the departure of the Soviet troops and a more or less neutral Afghanistan.[5]

In Pakistan the final moves toward the Geneva settlement were caught between contending political forces. Prime Minister Junejo favoured the settlement, provided it could be improved with appropriate safeguards, whereas President Zia ul Haq had accorded primacy to replacing the Kabul government. He now believed that the Soviet intervention in December 1979 had thwarted that goal, because an isolated Hafizullah Amin would have eventually succumbed to resistance pressure. Alongside his ideological self, Zia ul Haq possessed shrewd realism. In contrast to the bluster of the ISI and mujahideen leadership and their complacent belief in mujahideen military prowess, Zia did not take for granted that the mujahideen were on automatic pilot to victory.

Interim Government versus Safeguards

Diplomatic and political activity in Pakistan converged on two issues: the formation of an interim government prior to the Geneva settlement and the improvement of the Geneva settlement by incorporating appropriate safeguards to mitigate mujahideen opposition. Under Secretary of State Armacost's visit to Islamabad in the first week of January 1988 and Cordovez's shuttle to the area dwelt on these issues, which became the focal point of political manoeuvring in Pakistan as the negotiating process drew to a close.

The demand for "safeguards" was essentially an alternative to the interim government, even though its advocates gave the impression of pursuing the two ideas in parallel. The subtle, albeit significant, difference in the two corresponding approaches was underscored by Noorani's contention that there should have been a fifth instrument at Geneva to delineate understanding on future Afghan government arrangements. But, in the absence of such an instrument, Pakistan had to make the best of a flawed set of already negotiated instruments. Within the Pakistan Foreign Office, Yaqub Khan's departure had led to the questioning of the parameters agreed at Geneva, years earlier, under circumstances quite different from those of early 1988.

The Geneva provisions stipulating the cutoff of supplies to the Afghan Resistance had become moot.

Responsive to increasing objections against a one-sided cutoff and skeptical about the feasibility of an agreement over a future Afghan government, Pakistan Foreign Secretary Sattar had begun recommending some adjustment, "additional safeguards," in the Geneva approach even before the Washington summit. Conceding the Geneva framework, Sattar argued that the extension of the time frame beyond the originally conceived three to four months had introduced an asymmetry, or imbalance, in the Geneva settlement prejudicial to the interests of the Afghan Resistance. The text envisaged a cutoff of supplies to the resistance from day one, while Kabul remained entitled to receive arms, regardless of the settlement. The balance had to be restored by building new safeguards, such as front-loading (requiring the bulk of the troops to evacuate in the initial phase), and understandings on disengagement and appropriate phasing. The ultimate safeguard he would add was the establishment of a transitional political arrangement to pave the way for a government acceptable to the Afghan people.

Though the apparent flaws in the negotiated texts were examined and reexamined, Junejo knew that the Geneva settlement would strengthen his political position domestically. At the same time, he needed to secure sufficient domestic political endorsement to be able to justify and defend his decision to sign the Accords with the Kabul government, which was unlikely to be removed prior to a settlement at Geneva.

United States Calls for a "Defensible" Settlement

The rumblings of problems in Pakistan were matched by right-wing criticism of the Geneva provisions in Washington. Cutoff of supplies to the resistance had already become a thorny issue and White House comments appeared to rule out such a move prior to withdrawal.[6] A U.S. State Department official admitted the existence of "a significant political problem that people haven't come to grips with."[7] Opposition to a one-sided cutoff of supplies to the mujahideen impelled officials in Washington to review the issue. Some favoured a gradual cutoff synchronized with the withdrawal process. This did not satisfy those who demanded that the settlement be balanced in its treatment of the mujahideen.

Against this backdrop Under Secretary Armacost visited Islamabad at the beginning of 1988 for consultations, already necessitated by Gorbachev's announcement at the Washington summit. Armacost came to alert and prepare the Pakistani side for an impending settlement, as well as to explore possibilities of a political initiative by the Afghan Alliance. He confirmed the Soviet decision to withdraw from Afghanistan and underscored the desirability of not giving Moscow any pretext to stay on. He also affirmed U.S. readiness to accept a "defensible" settlement and ruled out any desire on the part of the United States to humiliate the Soviet Union.

Armacost argued that the timing was most opportune for a settlement: Pakistani-U.S. relations were strong and the resistance was well enough supplied to ensure that it would be at peak strength when the settlement was finalized. These comments clearly reflected the State Department disposition toward a settlement. Although Zia ul Haq was briefed on this view, he sought reconfirmation, asking Armacost specifically whether the Soviets had indeed decided to withdraw and whether they would do so even without a Geneva settlement. Armacost had doubts regarding the second scenario.

During his second visit later in February, Armacost was far more emphatic. In response to a similar question, he discounted the possibility of a Soviet reversal on withdrawal, saying they now had "much bigger fish to fry than Afghanistan." Citing the examples of Peter the Great and Stalin, Armacost described Gorbachev as a leader with a vision who had grasped the challenge of his time and was attempting to pull the Soviet Union out of years of stagnation. In Gorbachev's scheme of things, Afghanistan no longer occupied centre stage.

On specifics, Armacost's January visit brought forth two sets of proposals. First, agreeing that prolongation of the time frame beyond logistical requirements had made the Geneva texts asymmetrical, he underscored the need for additional safeguards, repeating the familiar checklist of front-loading, phasing, and disengagement.[8] Armacost felt that without satisfactory safeguards even the eight-month time frame already accepted by Pakistan would be difficult to sell to the hard-liners in the U.S. Congress. Second, Armacost agreed that time frame was no longer the overriding issue and attention should focus on the second track.

Timing was the key, because only sufficient progress achieved on the second track could justify delaying the Geneva settlement in the interest of its smooth implementation and prevention of bloodshed. Given the time constraint, Armacost favoured an Alliance agreement on a small three-way, nonparty state council representing the elements identified by Zia ul Haq in his *Sunday Telegraph* interview. The proposed council could have a limited mandate: to sign the Geneva instruments and facilitate their implementation, and to pave the way for election of a future government. Armacost maintained that Pakistan alone could persuade the Alliance leadership to agree to such an interim arrangement, which could then be negotiated with the Soviets.

The idea of a small state council as an interim arrangement was originally suggested by some of the prominent Afghan émigrés, notably Abdul Wakil, a former Afghan minister for agriculture and head of the Alliance agriculture committee, as well as Samad Hamed and Abdul Sattar Sirat. They had first suggested such a council to comprise mujahideen leaders, prominent Afghan émigrés, and some non-PDPA elements from Kabul, and to be headed by the former king. According to this plan, the administration of the countryside was to be left in the hands of local mujahideen commanders. Cordovez, who had been attracted by the proposal, had tried to explore the possibility of an interim state council with PDPA representatives as the third element.

The plan did not get off the ground because of fundamentalist opposition to the former king. The modified version suggested by Armacost met the same fate and was never seriously considered by the Alliance leadership or the ISI, which still harped on the idea of the shura electing an interim government. By now ISI simply expressed its inability to persuade the Alliance to accept any arrangement predicated on a dialogue with the PDPA or on PDPA representation. The public posture of the fundamentalist parties supported such a contention, but it was hard to determine the extent to which the ISI had itself encouraged this stance.

Armacost did not push his proposal. Nevertheless, he expressed reservations to Zia ul Haq about the ISI timetable of eighteen months for the election of the shura and the formation of an interim government. Zia ul Haq agreed that the process needed to be compressed into no more than three or four months. Events, however, moved even faster. Within one month Pakistan was pushed into the final Geneva round before it could press the Alliance to develop a credible political initiative to invigorate the second track.

Despite their interest in activating the second track, both the U.S. State Department and the Pakistan Foreign Office were reconciled to accepting a Geneva settlement based on a time frame. Furthermore, if the Soviets had decided to withdraw, the U.S. government wanted to oblige them by providing the cover of the Geneva settlement to facilitate their exit from Afghanistan. Accordingly, they pressed for safeguards in the Geneva texts to make the settlement defensible against right-wing and Afghan Resistance criticism. The U.S. position on this point was clearly stated to the press by Secretary of State Shultz in early January. An agreement would entail not only withdrawal, but a halt in U.S. arms to the mujahideen and in Soviet military aid to the Kabul army.[9] There was no similar U.S. position demanding the establishment of an interim Afghanistan government as part of a settlement. In February, Shultz termed the establishment of such a government "desirable" but "something" fundamentally up to the Afghans to decide.[10]

Following Armacost's visit, Noorani traveled to Peshawar to establish contacts with the Alliance leaders and urge them to come up with a political initiative. Within one week, Junejo had his first meeting with these leaders in Islamabad. Nonetheless, none of the hard-line Alliance leaders took these intercessions seriously. They asked for direct talks with the Soviets to work out understandings for safe withdrawal, exchange of prisoners, and a cease-fire. Similarly, they ruled out any accommodation for the PDPA and instead vaguely indicated that a few Kabul officials who had maintained contact with the mujahideen could be co-opted into the interim government resulting from the proposed shura.

Once again, Pakistan Foreign Office efforts to promote an Alliance political initiative were thwarted. More significantly, Zia ul Haq seems to have retreated from his position that the Alliance could be persuaded to accept participation of the PDPA in an interim arrangement. Until mid-January he had spoken of such a compromise, but his pronouncements changed after Yunis Khalis dismissed it as Zia ul Haq's "personal idea."[11] Sensing the Alliance opposition, Zia tilted in favour of the Alliance-ISI approach dictating Alliance terms for the composition of an interim government.

Cordovez's Shuttle

Cordovez's shuttle from 18 January to 9 February 1988, his last before the conclusion of the Geneva settlement, began against a backdrop of heightened political and diplomatic activity and a sombre military situation.[12] Yet, Cordovez's mission was far from being tense. He knew that the diplomatic process had entered that sensitive stage when its fate depended on critical political decisions that the parties were to take independently. He was willing to help in promoting the second track, even though the Geneva settlement was no longer linked to success on this track. His main objective was to secure an agreement on time frame and dates for the resumption of the next Geneva round. Once this was decided, Cordovez expected that the parties would be inexorably pushed by internal and external pressures toward a settlement at Geneva.

Cordovez's discussions with Noorani and Sattar during the first leg of his shuttle to Islamabad ranged over both tracks. But for Zia ul Haq, neither time frame nor Soviet desire to withdraw was any longer an issue. He wanted Cordovez to seek an internal political settlement without delay. In this context, he praised Cordovez's scenario paper as a "work of genius" and chided the Foreign Office, claiming that he had seen the paper only that morning. Clearly, Zia ul Haq was anxious that the linkage dropped by the Soviets be reestablished so that if Pakistan eventually were to sign the Geneva agreements, it would not have to do so with the Kabul regime. On specifics, however, his position on the erstwhile tripartite interim political arrangement had changed; now he suggested that the Alliance would select participants from among the nominees of Kabul and urged Cordovez to play a role.

Cordovez could hardly be expected to sell this proposal to Najibullah. He made it clear that the Alliance leadership could not exclusively enjoy the right to veto a nomination. The Pakistan Foreign Office, therefore, reinterpreted President Zia's proposal to impart to it a balanced appearance, suggesting that Cordovez should help in an exchange of lists for evolving an agreed panel of names representing various Afghan parties, which could constitute the interim political arrangement.

As for the Geneva instruments, the Pakistani side raised the questions of a shorter time frame and safeguards. Apart from frontloading, the safeguards taken up with Cordovez envisaged defining the procedure and the phases, in terms of both time segments and geographic sectors, for disengagement of Soviet troops as from the date of implementation of the settlement. The ISI was associated with the exercise and prepared a detailed paper on phased withdrawal from different sectors based on various hypotheses.[13] Another safeguard, discussed during Armacost's visit, related to the removal of "asymmetry" in the Geneva texts, which denied a flow of arms to the Afghan Resistance while allowing continued supply of weapons to the Kabul government. It had been agreed that this matter be raised between the two guarantors, because the UN format would preclude any fruitful discussion on the issue with Cordovez.

Pakistan's insistence on defining phases and disengagement was inherently weak. It suffered from an implicit contradiction when viewed against the claim that, with withdrawal no longer in doubt, the real issue was the internal political settlement to end the conflict. Pakistan's stand was weak because, from 1984 on, it had agreed to the omission of a paragraph on modalities for withdrawal and had repeatedly asserted that the time frame was the only outstanding issue to be resolved. Cordovez, as expected, while conceding that the time frame and front-loading were yet to be finalized, refused to consider any other suggestion and took the offensive, asking whether Pakistan now intended to reopen the settled texts of the instruments. The argument that only an agreement salable to the Afghan Resistance would be implementable and bring credit to the United Nations cut no ice with him.

Even at this late stage, Cordovez still believed that the Soviets would not provide sensitive information on withdrawal to the United Nations, much less to Pakistan and the United States. Further, in his view, Pakistan need have no concern because verification of Soviet troop withdrawal would be available to the United States through satellite monitoring. Nonetheless, Cordovez raised the matter in Kabul with senior Soviet military officials and was elated by their positive approach, agreeing to provide information to the United Nations at regular intervals regarding the progress of withdrawal.

Although the Pakistani side kept making feeble protestations about the need to work out a separate memorandum on modalities, the emphasis was kept only on a shorter time frame and appropriate front-loading. Cordovez tried to elicit Pakistan's bottom-line position on time frame now that the Soviets had come down to twelve months. In view of the new complications, Pakistan was in no hurry to finalize the time frame. Noorani told Cordovez that Pakistan had already jumped the bottom line and that agreement on time frame now depended on safeguards. This was merely a tactical response to pressure Cordovez to first explore the second track.

The first major upset of the shuttle came immediately after Cordovez had left Islamabad for Kabul. On 24 January the *Washington Post* carried Zia ul Haq's remarks to its correspondent Lally Weymouth stating Pakistani unwillingness to sign the Geneva instruments with the PDPA government. The comment confounded the Pakistan Foreign Office and derailed the shuttle, which was supposed to promote the second-track negotiations while tying up all outstanding issues on the Geneva track. It represented a volte-face on Pakistan's oft-repeated position, maintained since August 1984, that Pakistan would be prepared to sign with whatever government existed in Kabul once an acceptable time frame became available.[14] Publicly, Pakistani officials had often argued that the expediency of signing the Geneva Accords with a regime perceived to be illegal was justified in the interest of securing Soviet withdrawal.

Zia ul Haq's statement was inopportune. It further hardened the Alliance attitude on any compromise formula for a future government. Within Pakistan, it sharpened controversy over the Geneva settlement and accentuated internal differences. Seen as an attempt by Zia ul Haq to up the ante and seize the initiative on Afghanistan, it deeply rankled Junejo, who met with Zia and Noorani to review the position. Noorani drew attention to the specific commitment made by Pakistan in the past to sign with whichever government existed in Kabul. The meeting, however, yielded no new decision, but only underscored the sentiment in favour of pushing for the second track. The idea was to give it adequate time by avoiding any rush to Geneva, toward which Cordovez was expected to pressure Pakistan.

From Kabul, Cordovez returned empty-handed, with a legitimate grievance about Zia ul Haq's interview.[15] Afghan Foreign Minister Wakil had demanded clarification and a formal retraction of the statement by the Pakistani side before negotiations on any subject could proceed further. Cordovez, nonetheless, moved deftly. Conceding that remarks by the head of state could not be refuted, he suggested a suitable Foreign Office statement reiterating Pakistan's commitment to the Geneva process, which could enable him to persuade the Afghan side to negotiate outstanding issues.

Accordingly, a tortuously balanced statement was issued by Sattar reaffirming Pakistan's commitment to the Geneva negotiations and the need to ensure that the settlement did not jeopardize the interests of the Afghan people.[16] At the same time, the statement reiterated the requirement of movement on the second track. This was the first step toward whittling down the condition set out by Zia ul Haq. In the next two months Pakistan had to climb down from this untenable stand through a maze of backsliding positions.

Cordovez's shuttle soon hit another roadblock on the second

track. On the eve of the shuttle, Yunis Khalis, the spokesman of the Alliance, had stated to the press that he would not meet with Cordovez. The ISI explained, somewhat unconvincingly, that the statement simply implied that Yunis Khalis could not decide on his own and required the approval of the Alliance shura for the meeting. The Foreign Office wanted to push for a meeting with the Alliance as early as possible to lock Cordovez into second-track negotiations.

Since Zia ul Haq had personally endorsed the meeting and because it appeared to serve the Alliance interest of gaining UN recognition, difficulties in organizing it were underestimated. Following two days of deliberations, the Alliance shura finally came up with a set of conditions for an Alliance meeting with Cordovez. According to these conditions, Cordovez must first recognize the Alliance as the "real" party to the Afghan issue, and second agree that any decision taken without the consent of the Afghan mujahideen would not be considered valid.[17] Cordovez was in no position to make such a commitment.

Sattar met the seven leaders in an attempt to work out an appropriate statement to pave the way for the meeting. As it transpired, the main opposition came from Hekmatyar and Sayyaf, who were active in proposing various drafts, while Yunis Khalis, who had little interest in the exercise or in meeting Cordovez, simply advocated the right of the mujahideen to continue the jihad to establish an Islamic Afghanistan. The three moderate members of the Alliance were visibly agitated and vocal in favour of a dialogue with Cordovez. Whether encouraged by the ISI in the hope of extracting UN recognition or simply suspicious of the UN involvement, especially because it was being favoured by the pro-Zahir Shah moderates, the hard-liners insisted on the two preconditions.

Sattar finally left them with a draft, subsequently released as a Pakistan Foreign Office statement to clear the way for the meeting. The statement asserted that one of the principal objectives of the Geneva negotiation was to "establish conditions" that would "ensure the Afghan people their right to self-determination" and recognized the right of the Afghan Alliance to "participate in a comprehensive settlement." It also underscored positions taken by the United Nations calling for all Afghans, including the Alliance, to become "involved in the peace process" for a settlement that would command "the support of all segments of the Afghan people."[18] The positions attributed to the United Nations and accepted by Cordovez were essentially a melange of sentences picked up from various reports of the UN secretary general and the scenario paper. Meanwhile, Cordovez had his second meeting with Zia ul Haq, during which the latter expressed surprise that the Alliance leaders were reluctant to meet Cordovez and promised to intercede.

The first and last meeting between Cordovez and the Alliance, which finally took place on 6 February, turned out to be more of a media event than a substantive exchange. Yunis Khalis received Cordovez at the Alliance headquarters in Peshawar. According to a decision by the Alliance shura, the other six leaders sent their deputies to the meeting. Replying to the press afterward, Yunis Khalis explained that he had agreed to the meeting only because of a "personal request" from Zia ul Haq and ruled out any further discussions unless the United Nations agreed to treat the Afghan Alliance as a party along with the Soviet Union.[19]

As for the contents of the meeting, Yunis Khalis mainly reiterated the Alliance rejection of the Geneva instruments and the Alliance decision to form a government of the mujahideen. The meeting served to deepen doubts about progress on the second track and accentuated Cordovez's antipathy vis-à-vis the Alliance. He appraised Najibullah as an alert and dynamic leader capable of taking initiatives, while he viewed the Alliance leaders, quite accurately, as antiquated and incapable of collective action.

Soon after his meeting with the Alliance, Cordovez proceeded to Kabul. This proved to be the last leg of his shuttle because a new initiative from Moscow provided Cordovez with what he had been looking for in the area.

Moscow Sets a Deadline

Gorbachev moved to bring the Geneva process to a head by setting dates and cutting through the confusion surrounding a precise time frame and terminal date for withdrawal. In a statement telecast from Moscow on 8 February, Gorbachev offered to withdraw Soviet troops beginning 15 May and ending ten months later, provided a Geneva settlement was concluded on 15 March 1988. The time frame was without any precondition of national reconciliation. Front-loading was agreed in principle and the offer of disengagement reiterated, while preserving the right of the withdrawing troops to act in self-defense. The Soviets had obviously informed Najibullah in advance, as he also made a statement in Kabul projecting Gorbachev's offer as an outcome of an agreement between Moscow and Kabul.

The offer of a time frame and terminal date for withdrawal drew a positive response all around. A typical media response was the *New York Times* editorial, "Take a Yes for Afghanistan."[20] The U.S. State Department spokesman Charles Redman called the offer "a positive signal of serious Soviet intent to withdraw from Afghanistan."[21] Soviet spokesman Gennadi Gerasimov publicly mentioned Egypt, Saudi Arabia, Kuwait, Nigeria, Iraq, and Turkey among countries which had expressed satisfaction with Gorbachev's statement.[22] (Moscow had sent Vladimir Polyankov, head of the Soviet foreign ministry's Middle East directorate, to Riyadh on 21 February to elicit support for the Soviet proposal.) Following Soviet Deputy Foreign Minister Vladimir Petrovsky's talks with his counterpart Javed Larijani in Tehran during mid-February, Iran also welcomed the Soviet pullout offer.[23]

The day after Gorbachev's statement of 8 February, Cordovez returned to Islamabad to wind up the shuttle; he had no more business to transact except to finalize a date for the start of the next Geneva round. This, too, was a secondary matter since Gorbachev had set a deadline of 15 March for the signing of the Geneva agreement. The round was tentatively scheduled for 2 March and later confirmed. Cordovez virtually abandoned the second track. When the Pakistani side urged him to pursue it to develop an agreed panel of names for a transitional arrangement, he promised to cooperate, provided Pakistan was able to obtain a reasonable list of names from the Alliance.[24]

Vorontsov Visits Islamabad

On the heels of Gorbachev's declaration came a request from Moscow for an urgent visit by Yuli Vorontsov, the ace Soviet diplomatist, to deliver "an important message" to Zia ul Haq from Gorbachev. Vorontsov arrived in Islamabad on 10 February and, on the same day, had a dinner preceded by a formal meeting with Zia ul Haq. The Pakistani side had entertained a faint hope that Vorontsov might bring a last-minute proposal for an internal political settlement, but that was not to be. Consistent with the pattern of Kovalyev's visit in early 1987, Vorontsov had no hidden agenda to negotiate. He had come to explain Gorbachev's statement, to reassure Pakistan of Soviet cooperation within its parameters, and to obtain in exchange a

Pakistani commitment to conclude the Geneva instruments on 15 March.

Soon after Vorontsov's arrival in Islamabad, Sattar sought a meeting with him, taking advantage of their long-standing personal acquaintance. Sattar spoke about Pakistan's concern over any steps that implied recognition of the Kabul regime and about the problem of asymmetry in regard to supply of arms implicit under the Geneva instruments. Vorontsov conceded that Moscow could not demand Pakistan's recognition of the Kabul government and that Pakistan was entitled to make its position clear at the time of signature. He hedged the issue of asymmetry, suggesting that Kabul did not require more arms, that its problem was how to use them effectively.

Zia ul Haq brushed aside the time frame issue as settled by Gorbachev's statement, which he praised. He proposed to Vorontsov that the Geneva settlement be postponed for a time to make a "concerted, coordinated" effort to bring about an understanding among Afghans on a political setup to end the conflict. An internal settlement, Zia ul Haq stressed, was necessary for prevention of bloodshed and for the return of refugees, a principal objective of Pakistan. Vorontsov did not agree. He emphasized that the Soviet leadership had once and for all delinked withdrawal from the issue of national reconciliation; the Soviet troops would be withdrawn, with or without national reconciliation and "with or without the Geneva settlement," but the Geneva settlement would be in the interest of Pakistan and Pakistan's relations with the Soviet Union. Recalling that Pakistan had argued repeatedly in international fora that the Soviet military presence was at the heart of the Afghan problem, Vorontsov emphasized that the Soviet Union no longer wanted to be accused of perpetuating that problem.

Zia ul Haq pressed hard for an agreement to postpone Geneva and for Moscow to join hands with Pakistan in the search for an internal settlement. He even suggested an initial delay until 31 March. But what Zia ul Haq could not assure Vorontsov was that Pakistan would sign on the expiry of the extended period. He hesitated to set a deadline, while conceding that a postponement for renewed efforts to ensure internal peace could only be brief.

Vorontsov dismissed Zia ul Haq's proposal as tactical and did not relent on the position set out by Gorbachev. He asserted that no internal solution could be brought about without a dialogue between the PDPA and the opposition; but in his view the Peshawar seven rejected dialogue and compromise and simply asked to be placed in the saddle in Kabul, something that the Soviet Union would not accept. Afterward, the Soviets reportedly told the United States that Zia ul Haq was only trying to stall on Geneva and did not have a serious proposal for an internal political settlement. In comparison with Vorontsov's stormy meeting with Zia ul Haq, his talks with Junejo the next morning were placid and marked with positive expressions of hope and assurances of cooperation.

Following the dinner with Vorontsov, Zia ul Haq asked the Pakistani participants to stay back for discussion. Expressing disappointment that Vorontsov had repeated the demand for signing the Geneva settlement on 15 March like a "stuck record" and resenting that the Soviet Union simply wanted to dictate a decision to Pakistan, Zia ul Haq elicited views on the consequences that could flow from Pakistan's refusal to sign the agreements at an early date. It was presumed that a delay until the end of March, for example, would not be material. With the exception of General Gul, who argued that the Soviets were leaving and therefore Pakistan should not tie its hands, the other participants highlighted the danger of isolation and loss of international credibility if Pakistan were to back away from Geneva. This could make Pakistan vulnerable to Soviet pressure and allow Moscow to retain a range of military and political options to shore up the PDPA position under favourably altered international circumstances.

The Soviet propaganda offensive had started building. Ironically, it was reminiscent of the arguments and the rhetoric Pakistan had deployed over the years to demand Soviet withdrawal. In a comment to TASS given on his return from Islamabad, Vorontsov attacked the "inconsistency" of the Pakistani position in the following words:

"[The Pakistanis] repeated hundreds of times that exactly one thing, namely, the withdrawal of Soviet troops from Afghanistan, was necessary for the return of refugees to the homeland. Now this withdrawal becomes a near-term reality. But suddenly the Pakistani side began talking that it was the formation of a new government in Kabul rather than the withdrawal of Soviet troops that was needed for the return of refugees to their homes. What if not [a] bid to delay . . . solution of the Afghan problem can explain such a fast change in Pakistani sentiments? . . . Certainly, the establishment of a coalition government in Kabul is a very important matter. But this should be [a] matter [for] the Afghans themselves. Pakistan cannot claim [to have] a government formed in the neighbouring country with its own hands. And this government will be created not in Islamabad, Washington, or Moscow but in Afghanistan by the Afghans belonging to most varied political trends, parties, and groups.

The setting up of a government does not have any relation to the Geneva agreement since these agreements deal with settling the external factors of the Afghan situation such as halting outside interference . . . and the withdrawal of Soviet troops. . . . And the signing of the Geneva agreements, which remove the external factors, has relation to the domestic situation in Afghanistan only in that it can contribute towards an earliest settlement inside Afghanistan. . . . But should one make the signing of virtually ready Geneva accords dependent on the complex and evidently not-so-fast, judging by the reaction of the opposition, process of forming such a government? Our answer is no, it should not. Pakistan should think [it] all over and revise its so far non-constructive approach. For it depends on Pakistan alone now whether the Geneva agreements will be signed shortly. . . . Those who will advocate the delay of the Geneva agreements in the near term will come out for continued bloodshed, will assume a very grave responsibility both to the people of Afghanistan and its history.[25]

The Soviets pushed this position with vehemence and force. It was with reluctance and in response to stubborn insistence by Pakistan that they agreed during the final Geneva round to a continuing UN role to promote a broad-based government in Afghanistan. It is yet another irony that they invoked this agreement one year later, following the completion of troop withdrawal in February 1989, and sought UN intercession to bring about an internal political settlement in Afghanistan. Quite often, the principal players in the Afghan problem, like pieces on a chessboard, moved onto each other's positions in diplomatic manoeuvres adjusted to the evolving situation on the ground.

A Belated Initiative from the Afghan Alliance

Vorontsov's visit and the impending Geneva round brought the Afghan Alliance and the ISI under pressure to expedite the formation of an interim government. Indeed, before Vorontsov's arrival in Islamabad, the Alliance leaders had gathered in the city, partly in the expectation of a meeting but mainly to discuss broad principles for an interim government which, depending upon the opportunity, could be conveyed to Vorontsov. On the day of his arrival, the Alliance formally declared that an agreement had been reached on such principles.[26]

Following Vorontsov's departure, the Alliance shura huddled together in Peshawar and Islamabad for several days to hammer out a proposal on interim government. The Alliance decision to form an interim government had given rise to two broad views regarding its structure: those who favoured a strong interim government capable of facing the challenges of restoring peace and holding a jirga or elections in the postwithdrawal situation, and those who favoured a weak interim government as an insurance that it would dissolve after fulfilling its limited mandate. The division within the Alliance varied according to who expected to get control of the interim government. One principle, agreed at an early stage, required that none of the front-ranking leaders would assume any post.

Problems arose when some of the hard-line leaders tried to push for Commander Jallaluddin Haqqani to head the interim government, which they obviously expected to be more potent than what finally emerged. Haqqani attracted opposition from moderate elements. Almost overnight, rumours floated about his fanaticism and incompetent handling of the Khost operation. Dissension as a bane of Afghan character often exasperated Afghan sympathizers, and the Alliance was an epitome of the phenomenon. With active nudging from the ISI, which the Pakistan Foreign Office reminded almost daily that a list of names proposed by the Alliance for the interim government was to be communicated to Cordovez, the Alliance deliberations were saved from total collapse. Finally the Alliance settled for a weak interim government with a considerably balanced formula for its structure.

The formula for transitional government by the Afghan Alliance, formally known as the Islamic Unity of Afghan Mujahideen (IUAM), envisaged a grand council of the seven leaders and a separate "broad-based transitional government" to replace the Kabul regime and to sign the Geneva Accords. The government was to be composed of twenty-eight ministers under a head of government, to be divided among fourteen mujahideen, seven émigrés, and seven "Muslims presently serving inside Afghanistan."[27] The formula stipulated a consultative council (mushawrati shura) composed of seventy-five members, with two drawn from each province (fifty-six) and the rest (nineteen) from ulema, intellectuals, and technocrats, to frame interim laws, and an autonomous election commission to draw up procedures and rules for election of a constituent assembly. General elections were to be held within six months of the completion of withdrawal. Provincial councils were to be formed through consultation at local levels. The formula also included assurances of safe withdrawal, a commitment to pursue "independent non-aligned foreign policy" and "friendly relations with all countries, particularly with its neighbours" and an invitation to all countries, "particularly the Soviet Union," to participate in reconstruction.[28]

Engineer Ahmad Shah, deputy to Sayyaf, was selected as head of the interim government, with Zabihullah Mojaddedi as deputy prime minister. In addition, twelve other names from the parties and seven émigré personalities were identified to fill the cabinet. Seven seats for "Muslims serving in Afghanistan"[29] and two seats for Shia representatives were left unfilled. Responding to the criticism that the formula was flawed because it did not provide participation for the PDPA, Zia ul Haq suggested that seven good Muslims serving in Kabul implied some PDPA participation and that the formula was only "the initial thing."[30]

For a variety of reasons, this proposal simply did not take off. First, the proposal had come far too late and was virtually swept away in the fast-moving situation following Gorbachev's declaration, which focused world attention on the fate of the Geneva settlement. Had the proposal been made in July–August 1987, it could have had a critical impact in activating the second track. Second, little attention was paid to the procedure for taking decisions or to building support for the proposal. One of the seven "refugee representatives" in the proposed cabinet, Samad Hamed, former deputy premier and a respected Afghan émigré, complained that he was not consulted before his inclusion and disassociated himself, probably apprehending that his acceptance of the post would draw criticism from other prominent Afghan émigrés. Third, the identification of personalities was done hastily, without adequate, broad-based consultation to ensure representation of "all sections of the Afghan nation." Last, the visible presence of the ISI officials during the shura meetings tarnished the credibility of the proposals and provided ammunition to opponents and critics.

Beyond these lacunae, the proposal was dealt a fatal blow by moderate leaders and Afghan émigrés who favoured an approach that could bring in Zahir Shah. The moderate-versus-fundamentalist tension was high, especially after the assassination of Professor Syed Bahauddin Majrooh, a prominent Afghan scholar and head of the Afghan Information Centre in Peshawar.[31] The moderate elements held Hekmatyar's Hizb-e-Islami responsible for Majrooh's death. The moderates could not accept anything that assured ascendancy of the fundamentalists. Their unhappiness spurred rejection of the proposal by Afghan émigrés in Europe and in the United States, who ridiculed

Ahmad Shah as a nonentity and dismissed the interim government as a product of Pakistani manipulation. This episode once again exposed the fragile and superficial character of the Alliance and the inability of the seven leaders to take, much less sustain, collective political action. The adverse reaction to the IUAM proposal extinguished in the short term the lingering hope for a transitional government.

Bracing for the Final Geneva Round

Gorbachev's statement of 9 February forced Pakistan to face the stark choice of signing or not signing the Geneva settlement. This became the focal point of diplomatic and political activity germane to the Afghan issue. In Afghanistan the inevitability of Soviet withdrawal began to sink in and affected the thinking and behaviour of both the Kabul government and the Afghan Resistance.

Diplomatic Activity

Pakistan sounded out friends and allies on the Soviet demand for signing the Geneva instrument by 15 March. Noorani traveled to Washington, Peking, and Riyadh, while Sattar visited the Gulf states and Tehran. West European capitals were also consulted. Although there was no fetish about 15 March, outside opinion largely favoured signing at Geneva. The Iranians, who had no sympathy for Geneva, also felt that Pakistan could find itself in a difficult position if it did not go ahead with the settlement. The Iranian position had been influenced by active exchanges that had developed between Tehran and Moscow.

Noorani's visit to Washington in mid-February served to reconfirm the U.S. intention to secure an understanding on symmetry; but the U.S. position on interim government did not go beyond expressions of support for Pakistan's point of view and the desirability of an internal settlement.[32] Similar reassurances were conveyed by Armacost when he visited Pakistan again, in late February, to assess where Pakistan stood on the eve of the Geneva round. The U.S. State Department had also decided, for the first time, to designate an official representative to Geneva, Deputy Assistant Secretary Robert Peck. During the final Geneva round, he remained in close touch with the Pakistan delegation, as well as with Cordovez and the Soviet representative, Nikolai Kosyrev.

Armacost's meeting with the Alliance leaders in February was rough. A sudden decline in supplies to the resistance in January had reinforced suspicion of a U.S.-Soviet understanding on cutting off supplies in anticipation of a settlement at Geneva.[33] On this score Armacost had to do some explaining to assuage misgivings on the part of the Alliance and the ISI.[34] Similarly, his conversation with Zia ul Haq in Lahore focused less on Geneva than on the need to accelerate supplies to the resistance on an urgent basis.

Coincidentally, while Armacost was in Pakistan, Zia ul Haq received a personal invitation from Indian Prime Minister Rajiv Gandhi to visit New Delhi to discuss Afghanistan.[35] This was a belated move by India, motivated by concern that it had been left without a role in the solution of a major regional problem, so visibly at hand. The scenario of an approaching settlement and the emerging importance of the Alliance had agitated the Indian Foreign Office. Somewhat hurriedly, Indian diplomats tried to establish contacts with Alliance leaders in Islamabad. It was late for India to enter this game, especially in view of its consistent support for the PDPA government throughout the preceding eight years. Also, India had shown little interest in the Geneva process, even though Pakistan had kept the Indians briefed, knowing that they would receive the Soviet and Kabul version. The Indian leaders could hardly have expected a positive response to the February invitation.[36]

The Indian government publicized the invitation, which Zia had promptly declined. Subsequently New Delhi wanted to send its foreign secretary to Islamabad, but that did not materialize in view of the parliamentary session convened by Junejo to discuss the Afghan policy immediately before the departure of the Pakistan delegation to Geneva. The Indians also became active in a bid to promote an émigré-PDPA coalition. This led to the much-publicized contact between Indian Minister of State Natwar Singh and Zahir Shah, a move that did little to help the latter and played into the hands of anti-Zahir Shah elements.[37]

Junejo Elicits Political Support

Domestic sentiment in Pakistan favoured a settlement, but surprisingly, Gorbachev's announcement did not create the expected resonance in the Pakistani press. Indeed, following a briefing on 19

February from Zia ul Haq to the editors of national dailies, several papers carried editorial comments criticizing the two superpowers for pushing Pakistan into accepting a settlement on their terms that ignored the need for an interim Afghanistan government to ensure peace and enable the refugees to return.[38] Zia ul Haq had complained that the United States and the Soviet Union had arrived at an agreement on the Afghan issue and "Pakistan [had] had its reputation smeared in the bargain."[39] Zia asserted subsequently, however, that he did not wish to scuttle Geneva and, by insisting on the formation of an interim government, he was really talking about conditions conducive to the return of refugees, which, in addition to withdrawal, was Pakistan's principal interest.[40]

Junejo, on the other hand, initiated a series of political consultations with a view to building support for a decision to sign at Geneva. He convened a special session of the Parliament for briefings and discussion. Then, in an astute and high-profile move, he invited the leaders of all major political parties for consultations. The conclusion was foregone, since most of the leaders of the Movement for Restoration of Democracy (MRD), a grouping of opposition parties, had already hailed Gorbachev's statement.[41] The outcome could be summed up in the remarks of the chairperson of the Pakistan People's Party, Benazir Bhutto, who urged efforts on behalf of the Afghan Resistance, but not at the expense of an agreement on Soviet troop withdrawal.[42]

The two occasions, especially the drama accompanying the political leaders' meeting, bolstered Junejo's standing as the man calling the shots. Additionally, the Junejo government earned praise for taking into its confidence all segments of political opinion and for "developing consensus" on an issue that had preoccupied the nation for nearly a decade.[43]

These moves eclipsed Zia ul Haq for a while. He remained deeply engaged, nevertheless, with the proceedings of the final Geneva round, lasting nearly six weeks, during which he met frequently with Junejo and other top advisers. Pakistan remained in close touch with the U.S. government both in Islamabad and in Geneva. Consistent with his personal style, Zia ul Haq also kept in telephone contact with Cordovez to have a firsthand assessment of progress during the round.

The Military Scene inside Afghanistan

Anticipation of a possible settlement had begun to influence the military situation inside Afghanistan. Since early January the national reconciliation rhetoric had lessened. The Afghan army became increasingly engaged in consolidating its position in major cities and base areas, while undertaking sporadic search-and-destroy operations for arms caches of the resistance forces. In this activity the local Afghan army units were given greater freedom of action, a result also of the partial Soviet disengagement. Khad activity had heightened, and Khad members were armed and trained for active engagement. There were reports of Soviet forces turning over military posts and stores of arms, especially around Kabul and north of Kabul, to the Afghan army.[44] The security of the Kabul-Qandahar highway was left to the Afghan troops, and in several places it soon fell under the control of the mujahideen. Nonetheless, the Soviets retained control of the Kabul-Hairatan and Qandahar-Herat-Torghundi roads, which marked the two exit routes for withdrawing Soviet troops.

No major fighting developed following the Khost operation of December 1987–January 1988, even though most cities and major road links remained under heavy mujahideen pressure. Gradually the military activity escalated around Qandahar and the Ghazni-Kabul road. Among mujahideen groups, there was a visible tendency to conserve fire and await new developments in the offing; a big question mark loomed over the continuation of supplies through Pakistan in the post-Geneva scenario.

Uncertainty and a besieged psychosis were discernible in Kabul amidst rumours that PDPA officials were shifting their family members to safer areas in the north and issuing them special permits to facilitate emergency evacuation to the Soviet Union or India. There were reports that Mazar-e-Sharif was being considered as an alternative centre of government if Kabul were to fall. This speculation was strengthened by the reported creation in March of a new province, Sari Pul, by administratively combining southern districts of Jowzjan and Balkh.[45] A positive development from the PDPA's point of view was a closing of ranks between the Khalq and Parcham factions, since there was little hope of amnesty from the mujahideen groups. The grim circumstances surrounding the PDPA government induced a sulky nervousness in the Afghanistan delegation's behaviour at Geneva. Kosyrev was more actively engaged in the negotiations than Wakil, who showed much less interest in pushing for a settlement, especially after the deadline of 15 March had passed.

The Final Round

What was to be the final Geneva round commenced on 2 March under the glaring focus of the world media. In view of Vorontsov's remark to TASS on 18 February that the conclusion of the Geneva settlement depended on Pakistan, the arrival of the Pakistan delegation in Geneva, despite rumours to the contrary, meant that prospects of a settlement were real. The question almost constantly put to Noorani was whether Pakistan was prepared to sign with Kabul. He parried the issue.[46] From day one, however, he made it clear that the Pakistan delegation had come to Geneva to conclude the settlement, no matter how long it took to negotiate the remaining issues.[47] On Zia ul Haq's demand regarding the prior establishment of a transitional government, Noorani's statements were a chronicle of a climb-down.[48]

The media attention remained intense until 15 March, when it became clear that the fate of Geneva was linked to the symmetry issue being negotiated between the two guarantors, the United States and the Soviet Union. Yet, anticipating the climax of a six-year negotiating process involving the solution of a major regional conflict, a large corps of media representatives remained in Geneva until the day of signature.

The Pakistan delegation's agenda of outstanding issues on the Geneva track included symmetry, a shorter time frame with appropriate front-loading, phasing, and safeguards, and the separate question of future government arrangements. On the future government, Pakistan gradually softened its demand. But symmetry was a politically loaded issue. Neither Pakistan nor the United States could agree to a settlement that discriminated against the mujahideen's right to be treated on a par with the Kabul regime in regard to military supplies.

When the Soviet deadline of 15 March expired, Pakistan merely urged the need for symmetry[49] and made it clear that the interim government was no longer a prerequisite to signature and that Pakistan would not let it become a cause of deadlock.[50] The Junejo government did not want to risk the collapse of Geneva. This interest was so palpable that when the Shultz-Shevardnadze talks failed to resolve the symmetry issue in the fourth week of March and the Soviets pressed Pakistan to go ahead with the settlement without the United States, with a Soviet guarantee alone, Islamabad was ready to consider initialing or signing Instruments I and III as an earnest of its intention to conclude the Geneva agreements.[51] The idea, however, was a reflection of the confusion and divergent pulls prevalent in Islamabad, rather than a decision to go ahead with the settlement without the United States.[52]

From the outset of the proceedings at Geneva, Afghan Foreign Minister Wakil demanded, publicly and in formal meetings with Cordovez, that a date for signature be set. The two other issues raised by Wakil included the date for direct talks, which according to the text of Instrument IV were supposed to start before signature, and the Afghan objection to the phrase on borders in Instrument I. Pakistan, on the other hand, raised various issues, starting with time frame and safeguards.

Cordovez's major worry was to secure an agreement on time frame and front-loading. He refused to engage in any discussion on phasing or to make any adjustment in the text to accommodate the concept of disengagement that the Pakistani side argued Gorbachev had conceded. At a later stage, Cordovez suggested that he state formally that implementation of the settlement would imply a disengagement from military activities by all sides and that all sides would provide information to the United Nations, including information on "the phases" and "successive sectors" in which withdrawal would take place, with a view to enhancing UN monitoring capacity. The Afghans and the Soviets did not agree to such a statement.

Cordovez focused his efforts on obtaining an agreement on time frame and front-loading, or a package offer that Noorani could take with him to the roundtable conference of political leaders convened by Junejo in Islamabad on 5 March. It was assumed that this conference would strengthen Junejo's hand in taking a final decision on signature. An improved time-frame and front-loading offer could become a catalyst. Kosyrev obliged Cordovez and indicated a nine-month time frame, with half the troops to be withdrawn in the first three months. The offer was then confirmed by Wakil and released to the press.[53]

The time-frame issue was thus finally settled, but without producing a decision in Islamabad on signature. Pakistan now awaited the resolution of its concerns on symmetry and the future government; the first depended on U.S.-Soviet negotiations, while Pakistan's position on the second was still evolving.

Meanwhile, the Afghan side increased pressure for direct talks, setting a date for signature, and resolving the border issue. The Afghan objection to the formulation on the border helped to mitigate pressure on the Pakistani side to give dates for signature, because it implied that the texts of the instruments were still incomplete. The Pakistani side invoked understandings reached as early as December 1983 to maintain a firm position on the border formulation, arguing that it could not compromise its position on a vital national issue, especially after the draft texts of the instruments had been circulated to all the political leaders.

Tactically, it made little sense for the Pakistani side to give any concession on the border question unless it could be satisfied on the other issues of its concern. It was clear that if the round were to be deadlocked, it would suit Pakistan that it be on the border issue, on which its position appeared both legitimate and justified, rather than on symmetry or the future government. Most nations, including the Soviet Union, understood sensitivity over the inviolability of inherited borders. Also, Afghan objection to the border formulation, at this late stage, would have appeared as an attempt to raise new issues, because both Kabul and Moscow, following Gorbachev's 8 February 1988 announcement, emphasized that every issue had been settled and Pakistan need only sign on 15 March.

Cordovez reminded the Pakistani side that Yaqub Khan had promised to be helpful on the border issue, but he soon realized that it was futile for him to expect Pakistan to agree to any new suggestion on the border without some progress on the future government and symmetry issues. The next few weeks witnessed intensive diplomatic activity engaging Islamabad, Washington, Moscow, and, at a later stage, Kabul in working out understandings and formulas to pave the way for the signing of the Geneva Accords.

The Issue of a Future Afghan Government

In public statements the Pakistani leaders and officials pushed for an acceptable transitional government, stressing that it would help to avert bloodshed, ensure smooth implementation of the settlement, and allow the refugees to return to Afghanistan. Politically, the desirability of such a development from Pakistan's point of view was obvious. From a legalistic point of view, the Pakistani side felt that its position on nonrecognition would be strengthened by a formal launching of the second track before the signing of the Geneva Accords. Apart from these considerations, having once made the demand at the highest level, Pakistan could scale it down but could not give it up altogether.

In the short run, a launching of the second track by Cordovez was not feasible; there was little meeting ground between Kabul's insistence on intra-Afghan dialogue and the Alliance demand for a mujahideen-based interim government. Pakistan was, therefore, obliged to redefine its position and, before the 15 March deadline, proposed that an understanding on the principles and mechanism of an interim government would enable Pakistan to proceed with the Geneva settlement. Cordovez sympathized with this position, since it clearly envisaged the continuation of his role in a peace process after the conclusion of the Geneva agreements. Nonetheless, both Kabul and the Soviets dismissed the modified Pakistani demand, reiterating that the question of a "future broad-based" government could not be discussed at Geneva, but was a matter for the Afghans to decide.[54]

In order to maintain maximum pressure on Pakistan to sign the Geneva Accords by 15 March, the Soviets and the Afghans avoided engaging themselves in any negotiations on future government prior to that deadline. They refused to consider a draft statement that Cordovez prepared in an attempt to meet the various concerns raised by Pakistan. The draft statement included a paragraph that alluded to a "broad-based Afghan government" as "the objective" of the comprehensive settlement, and pleaded with "all concerned" to promote "the endeavour of the Afghan people to work out transitional arrangements." The paragraph had avoided a specific reference to the role of the United Nations.

Soon after the expiry of the 15 March deadline, Pakistan further diluted its stand and asked for a continuing UN role in promoting a future broad-based government acceptable to the Afghans. This emaciated version of the original demand was intended to formalize a link, however tenuous, between the second track and the Geneva settlement to salvage the prestige Pakistan had publicly committed to its earlier untenable position on the issue. Pakistan's gradual retreat on this issue was inevitable, unless it wanted to dump Geneva.

The problem with Zia ul Haq's earlier demand, as well as with the next fallback position calling for an understanding on the mechanism and principles for an interim arrangement, lay in the virtual impossibility of negotiating any understanding with the PDPA regime that would also be acceptable to the Alliance leadership. Pakistan was thus compelled to reduce its demand to a general agreement on the continuation of the UN role in a future peace process.

This position was conveyed to Cordovez prior to the Shultz-Shevardnadze meeting of 21–23 March, with a view to clearing the deck for resolution of the symmetry issue. Cordovez himself fully supported the Pakistani position and desired its endorsement by the other three sides, including the Americans and the Soviets, to enable him to come up with an appropriate statement. Shultz obliged. In an elaborate press conference on 23 March at the conclusion of Shevardnadze's visit to Washington, Shultz specifically "welcomed" the idea that Cordovez, in his personal capacity, would be ready to "serve as a mediator among the contending Afghan parties."[55]

The agreed statement by Cordovez, made on 8 April 1988 to announce completion of the texts of the instruments, did not specifically refer to his role. The UN secretary general had reservations about almost any direct references to a UN role in the promotion of a "broad-based" government. The purported reason, underscoring the impropriety of any UN functionary's assuming such a role, only served to whet speculation about friction in Cordovez's relations with the secretary general. The statement, a marginally modified version of the paragraph proposed by Cordovez before 15 March, recognized the need for a broad-based government and expected that "all concerned will . . . promote the endeavours of the Afghan people to work out . . . a broad-based government and will support and facilitate that process." It also expressed the hope that "all elements of the Afghan nation, living inside and outside Afghanistan," would respond to the opportunity to decide "questions relating to the government in Afghanistan."[56]

In a theoretical sense, Cordovez's statement of 8 April provided the legal underpinnings for a UN role to bring about internal reconciliation in Afghanistan, which Secretary General Pérez de Cuéllar and his political representative on UNGOMAP, Benon Sevan, continued to play discreetly. Cordovez also used the mandate of the statement to undertake a shuttle to the region in late June 1988 (his last before becoming foreign minister of Ecuador in August 1988) to present a new proposal based on a transitional government of technocrats. Cordovez termed it a "national government for peace and reconstruction," to be entrusted with the task of eliciting consensus for a Loya Jirga to be convened by 1 March 1989.[57] As Cordovez later recalled, Zia ul Haq had "shown much interest" in the proposal and needed time to persuade the Peshawar Alliance, but the Soviets had reservations, thinking that Najibullah could not be asked to step down in favour of a transitional government.[58]

The 8 April 1988 statement in Geneva also provided elements for the first post-Geneva UNGA resolution on Afghanistan, adopted by consensus in November 1988[59] and invoked by the Soviets in April 1989 when Kabul asked for Security Council intercession for the restoration of peace in Afghanistan.[60] For Pakistan, the Cordovez statement served to reinforce its position on nonrecognition of the PDPA government, because of the implicit acknowledgment that a government acceptable to the Afghans was yet to be formed. Notwithstanding the diverse views on its potential role in the post-Geneva settlement period, the United Nations has shown considerable flexibility in adjusting its role to the evolving circumstances. But, so long as the PDPA regime maintains its hold on Kabul, the effectiveness of the UN role will depend on whether the disparate Afghan Resistance elements, within and outside Afghanistan, are willing or not to accept the PDPA in a political arrangement.

Symmetry

Because chances of establishing an acceptable transitional government were virtually nonexistent, Zia ul Haq and the ISI were reconciled to obtaining assurance of a supply of arms to the Afghan Resistance. Symmetry thus became the primary political condition for the signing of the Geneva settlement. The logic of symmetry was to neutralize the discrimination against the Afghan Resistance implicit in the Geneva settlement insofar as it entitled Kabul to receive military assistance while barring supply of weapons to the resistance. This rationale was outlined by Noorani at a press conference on 16 March in the following terms:

At best the Kabul regime is one of the Afghan factions and must not be entitled to receive military assistance to enable it to overpower the other Afghan parties who would be denied similar assistance. International guarantees must ensure equity and balance in the obligations of the guarantors towards these political factions unless the situation is changed by the formation of a government which enjoys the confidence of all segments of the Afghan population.[61]

U.S. State Department spokesman Charles Redman, reiterating the U.S. position, emphasized the same view:

The obligations that we take at Geneva must be balanced by reciprocal obligations taken on by the other side. . . . [T]here will be no cutoff of support for the resistance under any other circumstances. . . . It is only logical that

non-intervention and non-interference provisions should apply to the Soviets too. The Soviets can't claim a right to aid a faction in the Afghan civil
strife just because that particular faction tries to call itself the government
of Afghanistan.[62]

The symmetry issue was politically charged in both Pakistan and
the United States. The bipartisan U.S. support to the mujahideen had
become sensitized to the issue. The sentiment was fully evident in
a unanimously adopted Sense of the Senate resolution of 1 March
1988 expressing "strong belief" that the U.S. government should not
"cease, suspend, diminish, or otherwise restrict assistance to the Afghan Resistance" until it was "absolutely clear" that the Soviets had
terminated their military occupation and that the mujahideen were
"well enough equipped" to maintain their integrity during the transition period.[63] In addition, letters were addressed by congressmen
and senators to President Reagan.

Zia ul Haq also sent a message to Reagan, who affirmed that the
United States would ask the Soviets to accept symmetrical cessation
of military supplies. If the Soviets disagreed, the U.S. support for the
mujahideen would continue.[64] Junejo also attached importance to
symmetry and criticized the Pakistan Foreign Office for ignoring this
aspect when negotiating the Geneva settlement. In terms of coordination, while symmetry was to be settled principally between the
two guarantors, Pakistan made sure that the United States was not
alone in demanding it and kept emphasizing Pakistan's deep interest
in the satisfactory resolution of the issue in press briefings and during formal sessions with Cordovez.

The United States and the Pakistani side at Geneva were initially
pursuing "negative symmetry," namely, mutual cutoff of arms supplies to all Afghan groups, including the Kabul government, from the
date of implementation of the settlement. It was assumed that the
Afghanistan government forces, demoralized and with the umbilical
cord severed, would not withstand pressure of the mujahideen, who
appeared to possess adequate supplies. Zia ul Haq and the ISI, however, preferred "positive symmetry," permitting continuation of supplies to both sides.

The United States engaged in intensive exchanges with the Soviet
Union to reach an understanding. The subject was raised after the
Washington summit in talks between Shultz and Shevardnadze. It
was taken up simultaneously in Moscow and Washington at the ambassadorial level and in talks between U.S. Assistant Secretary of

State Richard Murphy and Shevardnadze in Moscow before the Soviet deadline of 15 March. Murphy suggested a new concept, that of a mutual, time-bound moratorium, to continue until the formation of a transitional government. This proposal was further modified during the Shultz-Shevardnadze talks in Washington on 21–23 March.

Cordovez also proposed a draft outlining a vaguely worded understanding. It called upon the guarantor states to exercise self-restraint and avoid taking actions that might be deemed at variance with the spirit and objectives of the settlement or might fuel hostilities, thereby damaging prospects for peace opened up by the settlement. Both the U.S. proposal for negative symmetry and Cordovez's vague formulations, which satisfied neither the Americans nor the Pakistanis, militated against the Soviets' basic position.

The Soviets would not accept any imposition on their long-standing relations with Afghanistan or any restriction on providing assistance to its "legitimate" government. Additionally, the Soviets pointed to Moscow's treaty relations with Afghanistan and its legal obligation to help the Kabul government. The Afghan side, understandably, rejected even the slight hint of symmetry implicit in Cordovez's draft formulation. It maintained that the Geneva instruments were symmetrical in their treatment of Afghanistan and Pakistan. Accordingly, a cutoff of Soviet military assistance to the Kabul government could be validly considered only in the context of the United States discontinuing supply of arms to Pakistan. The argument made legal rather than political sense.

Two days before the 15 March deadline, Kosyrev conveyed a message from Shevardnadze to Noorani in Geneva, essentially asking Pakistan to sign the documents, but also addressing the two concerns Pakistan had raised—symmetry and the issue of the future government. The message ruled out the adoption of any additional document or statement such as Cordovez was contemplating.[65] It carried, however, a nuanced interpretation of symmetry in what appeared to be an effort to accommodate the Pakistani and U.S. concerns.

Rejecting the notion of negative symmetry, the Shevardnadze message went on to say that the Geneva documents contained no provisions that could be construed as a "demand to the U.S. side not to render assistance to the opposition on the territory of Pakistan." In other words, U.S. supply of arms to the mujahideen did not contravene the Geneva agreements, provided Pakistan did not permit their transit to Afghan territory. (This position was publicly reaffirmed by Kosyrev and Gerasimov in late March.)[66] For Pakistan and the United States, what mattered was the transfer of arms to the Kabul government and to the resistance *inside Afghanistan* rather than the mere availability of arms, which could in any case be secured for the contending Afghan factions from countries other than the two guarantors.

Kosyrev's meeting with Noorani was the first Soviet contact with the Pakistani negotiators at Geneva. It was followed by further contacts in the coming weeks. Noorani tried to emphasize the need for an understanding on negative symmetry, pointing out to Kosyrev that neither the 1921 treaty nor the 1978 treaty obliged the Soviet Union to maintain a military supply relationship with Kabul and that, in any event, these treaties would be superseded by the Geneva Accords, nullifying any obligations contrary to the provisions of the Accords.[67] Noorani also discussed these aspects with Robert Peck, since the hopes for the resolution of symmetry were now pinned on the Shultz-Shevardnadze meeting scheduled for 21–23 March in Washington. It was felt that the expiry of the 15 March deadline could place the Soviets under pressure and compel them to show flexibility.

The Shultz-Shevardnadze meeting took place in the context of preparations for the next U.S.-Soviet summit in Moscow, but it devoted considerable attention to Afghanistan, especially the symmetry issue. Shultz's press conference on 23 March provided details of the U.S. proposal for a mutual moratorium on military assistance for the period of withdrawal plus three months, and potentially extendable thereafter. Shultz made clear that the moratorium would be "without prejudice to assertions of legal rights to supply the parties, [and] would just be a statement of willingness to refrain from supply" during the specified period.[68] Shultz also disclosed that the Soviets had not agreed to the proposal, which still remained "on the table." More important, he declared that the United States would sign the Geneva agreement only if the U.S. proposal or "something close to it" was accepted by the Soviet Union.[69]

Thus the expectation that an understanding on symmetry would be reached at the Washington meeting did not materialize. Shevardnadze declared that Moscow could solve the Afghan problem "without Washington becoming a guarantor."[70] In Geneva the Soviets started putting pressure on Pakistan, through Cordovez, to go ahead with the Geneva settlement with the Soviet Union as the lone guarantor state. Pakistan, of course, rejected the proposition, which ran contrary to its long-standing approach to the question of international guarantees.[71]

The last week of March marked a low point in hopes for the success of the Geneva round. The Afghan side had brought the border issue into the open, making an agreement more difficult.[72] The Soviets appeared to be getting their back up; Shevardnadze made a detailed, tough statement in Sofia, criticizing Pakistan and the United States on both symmetry and the border question and exhorting Pakistani leadership to "think of its country's tomorrow" before saying "no" to Geneva.[73] The Afghan side even threatened to break off the talks. Kosyrev, however, did not support the interruption of the round. Meanwhile, Cordovez unsuccessfully tried to work out an agreement on the border formulation. A new pressure point was building with the approach of the month of April, since the gap allowed for the preparatory period was narrowing. As asserted by the Pakistani side, 15 May, the date for implementation, was important and needed to be preserved.

An elaborate rationale for the Soviet rejection of negative symmetry and a moratorium was given by Shevardnadze at Sofia. Asserting that these ideas had nothing to do with the agreed documents, he stated:

The moratorium is unacceptable to [the Soviet Union] because it means interference in our relations with a sovereign state, a UN member. . . . The Soviet Union supplies arms to Afghanistan under intergovernmental treaties and . . . agreements. We have maintained such relations with Afghanistan since 1921. The United States is now inviting us to break these treaties and agreements and stop our commitments under them. This is [a] wholly illegitimate position. It is illegitimate also in that it is aimed at legally formalizing the idea that there allegedly is no difference between the government of the Republic of Afghanistan, which represents its country in the United Nations and other international organizations, and the leaders of the Alliance of the Seven. Legalizing their status as something more than a group engaging in armed struggle against a lawful government is one of the goals of both the proposed moratorium and the statement on symmetry in arms supplies. We cannot, of course, support this goal.[74]

This was a well-articulated legal position, but politics often overrides legal considerations, as became evident some eight months later when Gorbachev proposed to Washington a mutual cutoff of arms supplies as part of a package proposal.[75]

On 30 March 1988, one day before Shevardnadze's Sofia interview became public, Zia ul Haq and Junejo telephoned Reagan and Shultz respectively to suggest that the United States seek an agreement on the basis of both sides continuing the supply of arms, in other words, "positive symmetry." The U.S. officials worried that such an arrangement could later allow the Soviets to turn up the heat on Pakistan to stop supplies crossing into Afghanistan. Nonetheless, Zia ul Haq personally favoured positive symmetry. Also, it was quite clear that even if the Soviets later accused Pakistan of violating the Geneva settlement, they were unlikely to renege on withdrawal.

The telephone calls from Islamabad became the basis of Shultz's communication of 31 March to Shevardnadze proposing positive symmetry, which was obviously closer to what the Soviets were ready to concede.[76] There is a lingering belief, shared by a few U.S. officials, that the Soviet Union would eventually have come round to accepting negative symmetry at Geneva and that such an arrangement would have better served the interests of the Afghan Resistance. It can be argued with equal force, however, that given Najibullah's uncertain future in the face of the impending withdrawal, the Soviets were unlikely to tie their hands at that critical juncture by accepting negative symmetry.

Events took a sudden and optimistic turn when Shevardnadze arrived unexpectedly in Kabul on 3 April on a working visit. There were already straws in the wind for a resolution of the symmetry issue, the last big hurdle in the way of a Geneva settlement.[77] The messages conveyed to Islamabad by Shevardnadze during his stay in Kabul related to the border issue, suggesting at the same time that this represented the only remaining issue. By implication, the Soviet Union had agreed to reach an understanding on positive symmetry, as sought by Shultz in the letter addressed to Shevardnadze on 31 March, the contents of which had already been conveyed to Pakistan. Shevardnadze's formal reply to this letter followed later on 9 April.

These two confidential communications, coupled with the statements formally made by Pakistan and the United States and communicated to the UN secretary general prior to the signing of the Geneva agreements, expressed the controversial and quasi-legal notion of symmetry and served to qualify the Pakistani and U.S. positions on the Geneva Accords.[78] To reconcile these communications and statements with the texts of the Geneva Accords could be an international law expert's nightmare; yet these statements and documents exist, they are communications between two major world powers, and none of the parties contested them. Instead, an ambiguity was allowed to prevail. In addition, public statements by Reagan and Zia ul Haq, made prior to the signing and as yet unchallenged by Moscow, affirmed the right of both countries to assist their allies in Afghanistan.[79]

Shevardnadze's statement on 14 April, the date of the signing, did not contest Shultz's statement of the same date, specifying that the United States had "advised" the Soviet Union that the United States retained the right "to provide military assistance to parties in Afghanistan."[80] At the same time, however, Shevardnadze's statement affirmed the Soviet conviction that "the rights and obligations of the parties to the Geneva agreements, including the USSR and the United States as guarantors, clearly follow from the texts of those agreements. . . . The viability of the agreements will in the final analysis depend on their strict observance by the parties themselves, namely Afghanistan and Pakistan."[81] The Soviet statement also referred to the "documents" (in this case Instrument I, the Bilateral Agreement between Pakistan and Afghanistan) that disallowed "support for political or other groups acting on the territory of one of the contracting parties against the government of another contracting party."[82] In this manner, the Soviets tried to adhere to the position originally conveyed by Kosyrev to Noorani on 13 March.

Pakistan's position on symmetry was formalized in a letter addressed to the secretary general by Noorani and delivered on the morning of 14 April prior to the signing ceremony. A similar position was taken in a statement released on the same day. Both stated that

the Government of Pakistan understands that the rights and obligations assumed by the Guarantor-States are consistent with the principles of equality and reciprocity and in consonance with the right of the Afghan people to freely determine their own political, economic and social system. The Government of Pakistan signs the Accords on the basis of the understandings reflected in exchanges between the Guarantor-States.[83]

Specific reference to the 31 March and 9 April Shultz-Shevardnadze exchanges was avoided in view of the confidentiality of the communications and the fact that the United Nations was not privy to them and would have been embarrassed by a direct reference. Clearly, there was a prevalent desire to avoid the apparent legalistic complications and preserve the tenuous understanding.

The two confidential communications were distinguishable from the respective U.S. and Soviet statements to the extent that Shultz's letter was more specific than the U.S. statement in its implications

and Shevardnadze's letter conveyed a clearer impression of acquiescence than did the Soviet statement. According to a *Washington
Post* report, U.S. State Department Legal Adviser Abraham Sofaer
lifted his objection against the United States becoming a guarantor
only after this exchange of communications, which, in his view,
were sufficient to save the United States from being in violation of
the Accords. Earlier, Sofaer had advised against the United States
placing itself in a position where it had to violate an international
agreement or encourage another signatory, Pakistan, to do so.[84]

Shultz's letter of 31 March had stated the U.S. intention to make
a formal and public statement on its right to provide military assistance should the Soviet Union continue its military assistance to
factions in Afghanistan, and to say, if required, that the United States
would effectively be able to provide such assistance. Alluding to the
discussions in Washington and an understanding that modalities of
such assistance were of no concern to the Soviet side, the letter went
on to assume that the U.S. proposition would not pose any impedi-
ment to the Soviet Union's becoming a guarantor.

Shevardnadze's response did not affirm the understanding directly. Implicitly, however, the elements of Soviet acquiescence in
the U.S. proposition included a reference to Shultz's letter, satisfaction over agreement on "the last unresolved question," and affirmation of "mutual readiness" to become guarantors of the Accords.
At the same time, Shevardnadze's response referred to the express
Soviet intention to adhere to the obligations laid down in the completed documents and its expectation of the same from the U.S. side.

Symmetry is a political notion with questionable legal validity.
In practical terms, it suspends those aspects of the Accords which
do not correspond to the political reality of the internal Afghan conflict and the absence of a legitimate government exercising control
over the country. The parties, especially the Soviet Union, have lived
with the concept of symmetry in a political sense and have adjusted
to it in the interest of preserving the Accords. Pakistan, which has
often publicly called attention to symmetry in defense of its decision
to sign the Geneva Accords, scrupulously avoided invoking this concept in its responses to Afghan-Soviet complaints of violations made
through UNGOMAP. Instead, Pakistan relied on UNGOMAP investigation reports to counter charges.

Pakistan has been prudent not to confront the United Nations
with the issue. In a legal context, as long as the PDPA government is
represented at the United Nations, Pakistan's position on supplying

arms to the Afghan Resistance would remain questionable, even if the United Nations were to uphold the U.S. position contained in Shultz's statement of 14 April and his communication of 31 March to Shevardnadze.

The Border Issue

The Afghan side, long restive about the phrase "existing internationally recognized boundaries of the other High Contracting Party" in Article II(3) of the draft bilateral agreement on noninterference, had asked Cordovez to secure its deletion. Wakil was temporarily restrained because the Soviets were pressing Pakistan for a date for signature. Immediately after the expiration of the 15 March deadline, however, Wakil convened a press conference to raise the issue and to play up Afghan national sentiment on the border issue.

Wakil asserted that "unjustified Pakistani insistence" on the inclusion of the phrase in Article II(3) prevented the finalization of the first instrument. He called for the deletion of the phrase as a precondition for Afghan readiness to sign the four documents, arguing that "the question of the border is a matter of dispute between the two countries and it is out of the agenda of the Geneva negotiation and incompatible with the mandate of the U.N. Secretary General and his personal representative."[85] Wakil also claimed that during Cordovez's "recent visit" to the area, Pakistan had undertaken to drop the phrase, provided the time-frame issue was resolved.

Wakil's press conference not only cast a shadow on the already dim prospects of success at Geneva; it also surprised the international press with the sudden emergence of an entirely new issue and the emotional manner in which Wakil had chosen to raise it. To a certain extent it relieved the Pakistani side of the pressure it faced as the recalcitrant party that had raised the seemingly extraneous issues of symmetry and future Afghanistan government. In a press conference held on the same day, Noorani, at the urging of Cordovez, avoided a rhetorical response. Instead, countering Wakil's charge that Pakistan had raised any new issues, he cited the fact that the phrase had existed in the text since 1983. He reiterated Pakistan's position that the Durand Line was a settled issue; and even if it were not so, Pakistan had no intention of negotiating it with a government it did not regard as legitimate.[86]

A surprising element in Wakil's press conference for the Pakistani side was his claim, with attribution to Cordovez, that Pakistan had undertaken to drop the border phrase once an agreement was reached on time frame. Pakistan was aware of the Afghan reservation, but it had never agreed to deletion of the phrase. Yaqub Khan had earlier indicated limited flexibility and willingness to consider alternative phrases such as "existing international boundaries" or "international borders," but had firmly rejected its elimination from the text, arguing that without this reference the provisions of noninterference would make little sense.

This position was based on a legal opinion, sought at the early stages of the negotiating process, which advised not touching the issue of the international boundary between Pakistan and Afghanistan. According to the Pakistani legal position, the matter stood finally settled by the treaties between Great Britain and Afghanistan. Between the two formulations, namely, "the existing internationally recognized boundaries" and "the existing international boundaries," there was a modest preference for the former because of the implicit allusion to "recognition," even though it was conceded that the formulation by itself did not constitute de jure recognition of the Durand Line.

The subsequent Pakistani position on the border formulation was governed by a combination of political and tactical considerations rather than legalistic concerns. Tactically, it made no sense to agree to the deletion of the formulation. Under the comprehensive format of the settlement, maintained until late 1984, the Afghan side had agreed to the phrase, which was subsequently transferred to the text of draft Instrument I. In addition, any substantial modification might compromise the Pakistani position through unfavourable comparison between the phrase present in the draft instrument and any modified form that might eventually be agreed and signed.

None of the alternatives to which Pakistan could be expected to agree were acceptable to the Afghan side. Cordovez's proposals, which attracted objections from one or the other side, ranged from a straight substitution of the phrase by "the Durand Line," to a general reference to the principle of inviolability of international frontiers in the preamble of Instrument I as compensation for deleting the phrase in Article II(3). Another Afghan suggestion was to reintroduce the now-forgotten "Naik clause"—on nonrecognition of the outcome of military intervention—in exchange for deletion of the border phrase, citing a mistaken impression of Pakistan's position during negotiations on Section II in early 1983 that the retention of the border phrase was a quid pro quo for Pakistani agreement to drop the Naik clause.

On its part, Pakistan suggested that the Afghan side could make a formal statement at the time of signing to protect its position on the border, just as the Pakistani side itself intended to make a statement on nonrecognition and other issues. The Afghans did not agree. Other modalities considered to overcome the problem included a footnote stipulating that the border phrase in Article II(3) was without prejudice to the position of the two parties or a note for the record by Cordovez to the same effect. The political and legal implications of each proposal were constantly weighed among the Pakistani side, even though it had no intention to give its agreement prior to the resolution of the other issues.

Pakistan's stand on the border issue was further constricted when the issue became public in Pakistan following Wakil's press conference. Noorani tried to downplay it by describing it as a nonissue. Nonetheless, sensitivity over this question could be gauged by the reaction it provoked in Pakistan. The chief of the Awami National Party, Ghuas Bux Bizenjo, a respected leader of the Pashtun-Baluch left politics in Pakistan and a protagonist of normalizing relations with the PDPA government, stated when asked by the Pakistani press that the border was a settled issue. On the other hand, Hekmatyar parried the question and rhetorically remarked that there should be a confederation of "free, Islamic" Afghanistan and Pakistan.[87] His statement was immediately targeted by the PDPA media and official circles as evidence of Alliance insensitivity to Afghan national interests. The public focus underscored the need for extra caution in whatever position Pakistan might take on the issue. For the Afghan side, the issue provided an opportunity to refurbish its nationalist credentials.

Pakistan's contacts with Kosyrev following Wakil's press conference indicated Soviet discomfiture over the Afghan move to make the issue public. Nonetheless, according to Kosyrev, the Afghans showed high sensitivity over the matter, which had to be settled directly between the two parties without Soviet help. Shevardnadze's statement at Sofia endorsing the Afghan position on the border question was a further regression in the Soviet attitude caused by the deadlock at Geneva. Referring to the Durand Line as a frontier "arbitrarily drawn" by British colonizers, Shevardnadze stated that "no Afghan government can agree to it since that would be betraying the national interests of the country in general and the Pashtuns in particular."[88] He called Pakistan's position on the border issue a "stumbling block" and its attempts to secure agreement on it in the context of an Afghan settlement "immoral."[89]

Curiously, this harsh and, to Pakistanis, unwarranted indictment carried a formulation Pakistan was prepared to consider. According to Soviet understanding, as mentioned by Shevardnadze at Sofia, the Afghan side was willing to agree to a compromise wording, "the existing borderline."[90] This was an intriguing proposition because the Afghan side had thus far been asking for deletion of the reference. However, it soon transpired that the compromise mentioned by Shevardnadze was not in fact acceptable to the Afghans, nor was any formulation suggesting that a border existed between Pakistan and Afghanistan. Obviously the Afghan concern was not over the implied recognition of the Durand Line, as assumed by Shevardnadze, but went beyond that, alluding to a notional state of Pashtunistan separating Pakistan and Afghanistan, a concept antithetical to that of a shared boundary. The Afghan side, however, could not articulate this position either at Geneva or in public, since such a step would have placed it on the defensive as responsible for damage to the Geneva process.

The border issue was apparently one of the major preoccupations during Shevardnadze's stay in Kabul in the first week of April. On 4 April a personal message was transmitted from him to Junejo requesting Pakistan's cooperation to resolve this "last remaining" issue. For the next two days messages shuttled between Islamabad and Kabul via Moscow. Shevardnadze initially sought Pakistan's agreement for deletion of the phrase. Junejo suggested an agreement on the phrase mentioned by Shevardnadze in Sofia, namely, the "existing borderline." This was unacceptable to Kabul. Shevardnadze conveyed another message, urging Pakistan's acceptance of one of two alternatives: either the deletion of the phrase or its replacement by a new formulation "not to violate the boundaries of each other." The phrase introduced a vagueness about the de facto character of the boundaries amenable to a broad range of interpretations.

Islamabad, guided by political instincts more than legal exegesis, opted for the second alternative instead of deletion of the phrase, which could have created the illusion of giving in to the Afghan side.[91] With the resolution of the border issue, the texts of the four instruments were complete and ready for signature.

Signing the Geneva Accords

The principal factor accelerating the pace toward the Geneva settlement in the first week of April 1988 was the Soviet resolve to pull out of Afghanistan without further delay. Shevardnadze reiterated publicly in Sofia and then on his arrival in Kabul on 4 April what Soviet spokesman Vadim Perfilyev had stated on expiry of the Soviet deadline,[92] and what Vorontsov had conveyed to Zia ul Haq six weeks earlier, that the Soviet Union would withdraw its troops from Afghanistan whether agreement was reached at the UN talks in Geneva or not. The Soviets also spoke of undefined "consequences" for Pakistan if they were to withdraw in the absence of signed Geneva Accords in a manner "convenient" for the Afghanistan government and themselves. The element of threat did not mean that there was any possibility of reversal of the Soviet decision to withdraw. Nevertheless, Pakistan was not insensitive to the risks to its long-term future relations with Moscow if the Soviets were forced to withdraw without the face-saving of the Geneva Accords.

The Soviets keenly desired the Geneva Accords because they provided the Soviets a neat and honourable framework to effect withdrawal from Afghanistan. On the face of it, according to the agreements, the Soviet Union was undertaking withdrawal in return for a commitment and guarantees on noninterference in the internal affairs of Afghanistan. Furthermore, notwithstanding the intent underlying the U.S.-Pakistani demand for symmetry, there was an expectation that Pakistan would exercise restraint in deference to the Accords. In any event, if Pakistan were to continue to supply arms to the resistance (as it did), Moscow and Kabul could enjoy the propaganda advantage of accusing Pakistan of violating the Accords.

Having wrapped up the agreement on the border issue on 7 April, Shevardnadze and Najibullah left Kabul for Tashkent, where the latter was received by Gorbachev. This was a gesture of solidarity on the eve of the Geneva settlement. Ahead lay the certain departure of Soviet troops from Afghanistan and an uncertain future for the PDPA government. Nonetheless, the symbolism of the meeting and the "joint Soviet-Afghan statement" issued thereafter struck a note of optimism.[93] Once again, the decision for withdrawal was jointly reaffirmed, as was the belief that the last obstacles to concluding the agreements had been removed "thanks to constructive cooperation of all" who were involved in the settlement.[94] The Soviet side supported Najibullah's reaffirmation of a policy of good neighbourly relations, specifically identifying the Soviet Union, China, India, Pakistan, and Iran, as well as the policy of national reconciliation, a multiparty system in politics, and a multisectorial approach in economics. The Soviet leader also extended assurances of continued Soviet cooperation and support for the economic and social development of Afghanistan.

Simultaneously in Islamabad, addressing the annual opening of the Parliament on 7 April, Zia ul Haq stated that "all of Pakistan's doubts have been removed and the Geneva Accord has reached a stage that it can be signed at any time."[95] He told the Parliament that he had received unofficial reports that Washington and Moscow had agreed to continue supplying weapons to their respective allies, the Afghan Resistance and the Kabul government. The information was based on his telephone conversations the previous evening with Reagan and Shultz, who had confirmed understandings on positive symmetry.

The stage was thus set for the signing of the Geneva Accords. In a press conference on 8 April, Cordovez promptly scheduled the ceremony for 14 April.

Two days later, on 10 April, the twin cities of Islamabad and Rawalpindi were rocked by an explosion at the Ojri ammunition depot, which rained thousands of mostly undetonated rockets and missiles over the capital city for nearly three hours, killing more than one hundred persons and injuring close to one thousand. The depot was under ISI management and reportedly stored weapons in transit to the Afghan Resistance. During March and April 1988 the depot appeared to have accumulated unprecedentedly large quantities of ammunition as a result of a rushed resupply in anticipation of the Geneva Accords. In his first statement following the explosion, Zia ul Haq did not rule out the possibility of sabotage;[96] only half a mile from the depot, a crowded bus stand had twice been the target of bomb blasts.

Whether it was a result of mishandling or sabotage, had the explosion occurred one week earlier, when none of the issues had been resolved and Shevardnadze had made his harsh indictment of Pakistan at Sofia, prospects of a Geneva settlement could have receded irretrievably. If the explosion was indeed caused by mishandling, it was fortuitous that it happened after agreement had been reached and publicly announced. Nonetheless, the destruction of huge quantities of ammunition destined to bolster the resistance's military capability prior to the date of enforcement of the Geneva Accords, namely 15 May, had a serious impact on the implementation of the Accords. Replenishments took time, and the ISI invoked the symmetry principle with vengeance, shattering any inhibitions nurtured by legal anomalies. For Pakistani politics, the incident carried profound consequences; and the controversy over its investigation and accountability contributed in good measure to the events culminating in Zia ul Haq's fateful dismissal of the Parliament and the Junejo government on 29 May 1988.

Preparation for the signing ceremonies proceeded fairly smoothly except for two notable, though minor, points: first, the question of direct talks; and second, the question of statements by the parties, especially Pakistan and the United States, to place on the record their positions on symmetry and on nonrecognition of the Afghanistan government. Cordovez tried to convince Noorani to go through the motion of sitting across the table from Wakil to fulfill the requirement of paragraph 2 of Instrument IV, which referred to the holding of direct talks as part of the chronology of the Geneva negotiating process. Noorani knew that this gesture was no longer necessary, nor did he wish to create complications for himself by taking a step which militated against Pakistan's position of nonrecognition and which was bound to be publicized—notwithstanding Cordovez's assurances of confidentiality. Noorani maintained that the act of signing in the same room could be taken as a change of format. As for the statements and reservations, Cordovez, to avoid any ugly incident or exchange at the time of the signing, suggested that the statements be delivered to the secretary general in his meetings with individual delegations prior to the signing ceremony.

Meanwhile, almost one week was spent in attending to the technical details of translation and mutual authentication of texts, which were provided in Pashto, Urdu, and Russian, in addition to the English version, for which the United Nations itself was responsible. There was also a plethora of minor issues of practice and procedure relating to the use of national paper, folders, ribbons, seals, and, not least, the shape of the table. Pakistan wanted UN paper, UN folders, and UN seals for all sets of the Accords. But the Soviet treaty expert, an elderly gentleman of the old school of diplomatic practice, insisted on national paper and national folders and all national seals to be affixed on each set. This arrangement was agreed, except for affixing national seals on each folder. The table was set putting together ten rectangular tables placed in a polygon formation with each party's table separated by an empty table and the UN delegation seated in between the Afghanistan and Pakistan delegations.

The signing ceremony was a grand occasion for the United Nations. Pérez de Cuéllar and Shevardnadze arrived a day earlier, while Shultz reached Geneva on the morning of 14 April. The arrangements for the signing ceremony were meticulous, timed to the minute, with a brief welcome by the secretary general and equally brief concluding remarks. Acclaiming the diplomatic effort, the secretary general lauded the agreements, stating that they "lay the basis for the exercise by all Afghans of the right to self-determination" and represented "a major stride in the effort to bring peace to Afghanistan."[97]

The actual signing proceeded in sombre silence, made palpable by camera clicks and flash lamps and the overpowering gold and ink frescoes dominating the walls of the historic Council Chamber of the Palais des Nations. There were no smiles and little celebration.

8

After Geneva:
Evaluation and Prospects

On 8 April 1988, announcing the successful culmination of his marathon mediation effort, Diego Cordovez noted in a hopeful yet stoical tone:

It is not a perfect settlement . . . ; however, I believe that it is a settlement which reflects the reality of the situation. The test of this settlement will come in its implementation. . . . There are voices from Afghans who have criticized this [negotiating] process. But I am absolutely convinced that . . . the Afghans themselves will realize that at Geneva we have established solid foundations for the achievement of normal living conditions in their homeland.[1]

In these words, the author of the Geneva Accords himself set a criterion for their evaluation.

More than two years later, peace had not been established in Afghanistan. The completion of Soviet withdrawal by 15 February 1989 owed more to the historic transformation of Soviet outlook and policy under Gorbachev and the tenacious Afghan armed struggle than to a diplomatic *coup de maître*. In concrete terms, the Geneva Accords accomplished little more than providing a respectable exit for the Soviet troops. Yet, the Geneva negotiating process and the Accords have been important in shaping the thinking and policies of the participants far beyond the inherent significance of the negotiations per se. The present chapter will evaluate the Accords and the negotiations, first, for their significance as an experience in multilateral diplomacy; second, for their influence on the policies and politics of the principal players; and third, for their implications for the continuing conflict in Afghanistan.

The Negotiations as a Multilateral Diplomatic Experience

The protracted Geneva negotiations on Afghanistan have been the most eventful and prominent mediation activity undertaken by the United Nations during the 1980s, overshadowing parallel efforts for the resolution of other regional issues, such as the Namibian question, the Iran-Iraq conflict, and the Kampuchean issue. Several factors contributed to this impression: the Geneva talks had a structured format; they were held at fairly regular intervals; and basic texts delineating a draft settlement had developed at an early stage, although it required a long time to reach agreement on several vital areas of content and form.

The experience of the early initiatives had prepared the interlocutors, namely the governments of Afghanistan and Pakistan, to compromise on procedural issues that paved the way for indirect talks under UN auspices. For Pakistan, in particular, a domestic compulsion to maintain a viable diplomatic option and the logic of its declaratory position impelled it to accept the four-point agenda for the talks and drop its proposal for an item on self-determination. Credit for early maturing of the texts goes to ingenious drafting by the UN mediator and skillful use of the material available in various UN declarations. Notwithstanding the subsequent difficulties in their finalization, the progress achieved on the draft texts by early 1983 had earned for the Geneva negotiations the distinction of being the most promising among the UN-sponsored peacemaking efforts.

This was important for a United Nations suffering from relative decline. In his first report to the General Assembly in September 1982, UN Secretary General Pérez de Cuéllar had lamented the weakening of multilateralism.[2] Deteriorating East-West relations and increasingly polemical posturings and debates in the UN forum had reduced the charter role of the organization as an instrument for "the maintenance of peace and security" to a fiction. The United Nations thus needed a shot in the arm, a breakthrough, to pull it out of a stagnant predicament. The Geneva negotiations on Afghanistan kept the hope alive. When they finally bore fruit at the end of seven years of patient endeavours, they marked a welcome accomplishment for the world body, one not solely attributable to the propitious changes in the international climate.

It was no coincidence that this first breakthrough for the United Nations came with the signing of the Geneva Accords. In his statement of 8 February 1988, setting a deadline for signature, Gorbachev concluded by making a prediction: "When the Afghan knot is untied, it will have the most profound impact on other regional conflicts too. . . . Just as the agreement to eliminate intermediate and short-range missiles is to be followed by a series of further major steps towards disarmament, . . . likewise behind this political settlement in Afghanistan already looms a question: which conflict will be settled next? And it is certain that more is to follow."[3] In quick succession the United Nations achieved a cease-fire agreement between Iran and Iraq in June 1988; the Tripartite Accords on Namibia initiated under UN auspices were signed in December 1988; and significant movement was reported in UN efforts to resolve the Kampuchean conflict.[4]

Arguably, these positive developments arose from the altered East-West relations. The effectiveness of the United Nations and of multilateralism as instruments in conflict resolution has always depended on cooperative relations among the major powers. The importance of the change in major power relations further underscores the significance of the Geneva Accords, because they contributed toward this change by unraveling the crucial Afghan "knot."

Implications for the United Nations

The Geneva negotiations coincided with a period that spanned a momentous transition in international affairs. They began with all the disadvantages of the Cold War and benefited from the new cooperative relations between the two superpowers. For the United Nations, the Geneva negotiations marked an important experience in conflict resolution and bear significant implications for the balance of power within the organization:

1. The UN mediation on Afghanistan is unique among contemporary UN initiatives in that it was based on the secretary general's decision rather than on Security Council or General Assembly resolutions. In the process, the role of the UN secretary general has been considerably strengthened.

2. The later UN efforts to address the internal dimension of the Afghan conflict have secured for the organization a new flexibility in dealing with political entities not representing either member states or observers.

Both developments have set useful precedents, breaking inhibitions and reducing procedural encumbrances for the United Nations in addressing complex political issues.

The secretary general's mediation effort on Afghanistan and his subsequent success in bringing about an Iran-Iraq cease-fire represented a high watermark for the role of the secretary general and, concomitantly, a partial abdication of its peacemaking role by the Security Council. Within two weeks of the signing of the Geneva Accords, the elaborate arrangements for UNGOMAP in Afghanistan and Pakistan were in place at the secretary general's authority and only later reconfirmed by an ex post facto Security Council resolution.[5] Legal implications of the procedure were debated within the U.S. State Department, where the International Organization Affairs Bureau had advocated a conventional approach requiring prior authorization by the Security Council. The objection was circumvented by renaming the arrangement a "Good Offices Mission" instead of the originally conceived "Observer Mission." Nonetheless, its mandate remained unaffected.

In the Iran-Iraq conflict, Iranian antipathy to the Security Council lent even greater prominence and functional authority to the Office of the Secretary General. In its Resolution 619 of August 1988, the Security Council clearly deferred to the secretary general's retaining the initiative and accepted his interpretation of the terms of its Resolution 598 of 1987 in establishing a cease-fire.[6]

The significant evolution in the secretary general's role imparts to the world organization an operational manoeuvrability not seen since the mid-1960s when, under Dag Hammarskjöld, the United Nations had acquired an assertive and dynamic posture in conflict resolution. Sustaining the new trend, however, will depend on a modicum of cooperation and understanding among the permanent members of the Security Council.

The second-track negotiations initiated by Cordovez in mid-1987 marked the lifting of the Soviet objection (and thus technically Kabul's acquiescence) to UN contacts with the Afghan Resistance groups, which were excluded from the Geneva framework. The United Nations had dealt with such political entities in the past, and its contemporary experience related to contacts with the various Kampuchean factions. The Kampuchean situation, however, did not offer an exact parallel. In contrast to the case of Afghanistan, the Kampuchean faction represented at the United Nations did not control the Kampuchean capital, Phnom Penh, and UN contacts with the Heng Samrin faction operating in the capital evoked little concern on the part of the major powers.

The more striking case of Afghanistan involved not only Soviet sensitivities, but also UN dealings with opposition forces located in a third country. Following Soviet withdrawal from Afghanistan, active Soviet encouragement of UN efforts to promote an internal political consensus have revitalized a legitimate UN role that the United Nations itself had hesitated to undertake.[7] Success in this direction would considerably reinforce the prestige and effectiveness of the United Nations.

The Conduct of the Negotiations

The willingness of the principal interlocutors—Pakistan, the Kabul government, and the Soviet Union—to maintain the momentum of the negotiations was the primary factor that the UN mediator skillfully exploited to ensure progress and facilitate the necessary decisions made possible by the changing political environment.

To begin with, the diplomatic activity preceding the formal Geneva rounds served to streamline the parties' objectives for the ensuing negotiations. For Pakistan, the issue of Soviet withdrawal became pivotal, while the nebulous question of political change in Kabul was subsumed as an inevitable corollary of withdrawal. This premise enabled Pakistan to define its concept of an equitable settlement and, within the parameters of that concept, to make concessions of a textual or technical character. For Kabul, political consolidation and legitimacy were the crucial issues. It accorded concessions on texts of the draft settlement, excluding withdrawal, in the hope of direct talks or a bilateral agreement on noninterference or both. The latter constituted the centrepiece of its concept of a political solution. With intelligent drafting, Cordovez was able to develop a substantial corpus of largely acceptable text at an early stage. This not only helped to sustain optimism but also identified a series of minor issues that kept the successive Geneva rounds active, allowing time for the more politically loaded issues to be resolved.

Solution of such crucial issues as Pakistan's acceptance of Section II (relating to noninterference) and bilateral accords with Kabul, or the Kabul-Moscow decision to drop direct talks and offer a short time frame, nonetheless, resulted from neither clever proposals nor the negotiating tactics of Cordovez. Instead these decisions were the product of either changed circumstances or careful deliberations in the concerned capitals. While Cordovez's admirable talent to come up with deft proposals kept the negotiations moving, his occasional tactic of putting excessive pressure on the interlocutors to accept a position accomplished little more than cleaning up textual issues of secondary import. The interlocutors accepted proposals only on their own merit.

Cordovez relied, furthermore, on screened transmission of positions to either side, with a view to avoiding early deadlocks. In retrospect, the method failed to hasten the pace of the negotiations; on the contrary, it engendered misgivings when issues thought to have been resolved kept resurfacing. Resort to greater transparency might have been beneficial in the long term, especially when the negotiations turned to the second track. Premium was then no longer on the technical skills valued at Geneva but on the credibility of the mediator and the confidence reposed in him by the interlocutors.

A distinctive factor affecting the negotiating process was the unavoidable media attention it received because of the direct involvement of the Soviet Union, a superpower. A case can be made that the media focus kept pressure on the interlocutors, as well as on the UN mediator, to show progress. If so, this blessing was mixed. On the broad plane, governments, especially those less representative in character, show remarkable immunity to media pressures unless the policy in question lacks public support. This was not the case with the Afghan policy pursued by the Zia government, as proved by public debates in Pakistan on the issue of direct talks.

On the operational level, however, negotiators are overly sensitive to the media. This was true of the Pakistani side, which simultaneously negotiated on Afghanistan and engaged in a campaign to retain international support for its position. Although Cordovez often stressed the need for restraint and caution in public statements, all sides, including Cordovez, showed a proclivity for frequent press briefings and public interviews offering prognosis and evaluation, which sometimes led to counterproductive controversies. A case in point was Cordovez's overly optimistic remark in May 1983 in which he described the settlement as 95 percent ready. The remark was out of sync with the parties' positions at that time, as the later course of the negotiations revealed. Sometimes public diplomacy may appear to offer the mediator a tempting recourse; as a general rule, however, accompanying risks far outweigh possible advantages to the negotiations.

To elicit concessions from the interlocutors, Cordovez often backed concrete proposals with pressure, invoking the argument that movement was necessary to demonstrate political will and nur-ture mutual trust. In the event, however, though the interlocutors invariably felt obliged to consider and respond with reasonable flexibility to the proposals presented by Cordovez, they were largely indifferent to his exhortations for concessions to improve the atmosphere. The draft texts were thus the product of such attempts to respond reasonably rather than of goodwill gestures.

When the texts matured, they developed an intrinsic logic that sustained the negotiating process through heavy weather and gradually made an impact on the thinking and positions of the participants. The process thus highlighted, first, the value of innovative ideas and proposals in providing underpinnings for progress and success, and, second, the significance of the mediator's role, which is often depreciated in comparison to the pivotal influence that political circumstances bring to bear on any negotiations.

The experience of the Geneva negotiations and the efforts on the second track underscore the fallacy of interpreting their conduct solely in terms of changes in global power relations and positions or of treating the Afghan conflict as an extension of East-West rivalry. Such perceptions often stemmed from Cold War polemics that pervaded most regional conflicts, including Afghanistan. The Soviet decision to withdraw and the broader changes in the international political climate, though undeniably important, do not diminish the significant effect on the negotiations of the independent interests of the regional players. Even the Kabul government, which relied on the Soviet Union for material and psychological support, was not an easy client, and its positions betrayed differences with Moscow.

A case in point is the conduct of Pakistan during the course of the negotiations. As this survey has indicated, the concessions accorded by Pakistani negotiators at the various stages of the negotiations were based on their evaluation of Pakistan's interests and their concept of an equitable settlement. Until the final phase, when in a technical sense the symmetry issue was negotiated between the two guarantor states, Pakistan negotiated and reached understandings on all political and textual issues germane to the negotiation. The argument that Pakistan should have accepted the original Soviet terms in an effort to secure withdrawal is based on a political premise rather than the logic of a negotiated settlement.

An erroneous impression also persists that Pakistan's policy of providing military support to the Afghan Resistance was being pursued at the behest of the United States and that it weakened Pakistan's interest in a negotiated settlement. Support to the Afghan

Resistance was a fundamental ingredient of Zia ul Haq's overall policy on Afghanistan and not something induced from outside. Given his ideological disposition, Zia would have pursued this course even without U.S. assistance. Furthermore, the effort to strengthen the Afghan Resistance did not eclipse Pakistan's independent endeavours to promote a diplomatic option through participation in the Geneva negotiations.

A distinction is necessary between the Geneva negotiations and the subsequent second-track diplomatic effort, initiated hesitantly by Cordovez in 1987 under the compulsion of changed circumstances. The hard-line perceptions and lack of interest displayed by the ISI, the agency maintaining liaison with the Afghan Resistance, were surely not conducive to progress on the second track. But the failure of the effort cannot be explained by overemphasizing these factors and ignoring the complexities of the military and political situation affecting the attitudes of the Afghan factions. The intractable differences among these factions defied efforts for an internal political settlement in the past and continue to do so today.

The fruition of the Geneva negotiations depended on the evolution of a settlement acceptable to all sides and, finally, on the maturing of a Soviet decision on withdrawal. The nonavailability of these conditions prevented early materializing of the settlement. The Soviets had frequently stated their willingness to withdraw, but on terms that were tantamount to an indictment of Pakistan. For progress, intentions had to be anchored in willingness to compromise and to offer concrete concessions. The gradual adjustment of the Soviet position since late 1985 reflected a slow process of review under Gorbachev of Soviet military involvement in Afghanistan and of Soviet objectives that had been frustrated in the face of the tenacious Afghan Resistance. Concomitantly, it became possible for Cordovez to reconcile the evolving Soviet position with Pakistan's concept of an equitable settlement and thereby finalize the texts of the Geneva Accords.

Overall, the Geneva negotiations followed a conventional pattern, with each side adopting a cautious, minimum-risk approach in the light of its position at a given time. The six-year-long negotiating process had moments with a touch of drama, but it did not witness bold and surprising moves. The tenor of the process would have been different, for example, had the Soviets in 1983 or 1986 offered a one-year time frame or had Pakistan accepted in early 1983 the "uneven text" and agreed to sign a bilateral agreement on noninterference with Kabul to exert pressure for a time frame.

Why it was unrealistic to expect such audacious moves has been explained in chapter four. In dealing with a superpower, Pakistan was unlikely to take a gamble; but on Afghanistan, the Soviets, too, eschewed the feisty diplomacy identified with Gorbachev. Instead, the Soviet behaviour at Geneva appeared to conform to the stereotyped view of Soviet negotiating style—inscrutable, drawing out the other side's minimum position, and revealing their own, layer by layer, in a protracted, grueling process. Similarly, the Soviet positions did not appear to evolve continually, but instead developed in distinct phases. During each phase, Soviet negotiators, by and large, kept close to the established positions. On many occasions these positions were none other than those declared publicly in Soviet statements.

Post-Geneva Policies and Politics of the Signatories

This section will examine how the Geneva negotiations and the Soviet withdrawal have affected the policies and politics of the Soviet Union, the United States, and Pakistan. Post-Geneva Afghanistan and the status of current diplomatic endeavours will be discussed separately.

The Soviet Union. One must distinguish the broader consequences of the Afghan War for the Soviet Union from this study's narrower focus on the relevance and significance of the negotiating process to Moscow's Afghan policy over the years. The Afghan War, however, carries a powerful symbolism for the Soviet society comparable to colonial wars lost by other great powers in the past. Conservative scholars and Afghan mujahideen leaders tend to overstate the influence of the war in aiding the contemporary ferment in the Soviet Union and Eastern Europe.[8] Yet even before the events of late 1989, East European dissent was thought to be "taking heart from the determined resistance of the Afghans"; and the Afghan War was seen to have marked the decline of the Brezhnev Doctrine and the closing of "the most significant chapter in the history of 'Soviet expansionism' since Yalta."[9] Also, just as perceived foreign policy successes can help governments in covering up and obfuscating domestic problems, debacles abroad tend to accentuate public awareness of failings at home. Within the Soviet Union, the Afghan War hastened the erosion of faith in the Soviet system and its infallibility.

In the Western press the Soviet withdrawal evoked memories of the U.S. experience in Vietnam.[10] The ostensible similarities may be only superficial, but there can be little doubt that the Afghan War has underscored the limitations of the present-day great powers in undertaking military engagements outside their borders. An Afghan syndrome is discernible in unprecedented expressions of concern by Soviet mothers over dispatch of their sons for military combat in distant lands. More important, "Afghanistan" has echoed in recent ethnic revolts inside the Soviet Union, revealing its deep impact on the Soviet psyche and its potential consequences for Soviet politics and policies in the future.[11]

To determine exactly how the negotiations influenced Soviet policymakers would require an insight into the internal Soviet debates on Afghanistan. Nevertheless, it is now beyond doubt that Gorbachev desired withdrawal to facilitate his global initiatives and to get rid of an unpopular legacy. Surely, Shevardnadze's public confession in October 1989 calling the intervention "illegal" and "mistaken" did not reflect a sudden awakening.[12] It is also clear that for obvious reasons Gorbachev preferred to effect withdrawal under the umbrella of a UN-sponsored agreement.

The portents of the new policy under Gorbachev took more than one year to become visible. Apparently, time was needed to prepare the ground and overcome possible resistance against disengagement from Afghanistan. In making the shift, the proponents of the political settlement within the new Soviet leadership must have found the agreements drafted at Geneva eminently suitable for their purpose. The basic parameters and structure of the agreements were evolved at a time when Moscow enjoyed a position of strength militarily. Accordingly they showed remarkable deference to Soviet sensitivities.

The UN mediation had been endorsed by the Soviet Union at an early stage in the process, but initially Soviet interest in the details of the negotiations did not extend beyond the lower echelons of the decisionmaking hierarchy. In the normal course, osmosis of ideas within bureaucracies from the operational plane to the decisionmaking levels is often slow. The Soviet system was no exception. Foreign Minister Gromyko hardly ever made a reference to the texts during meetings with Yaqub Khan or in any of his public statements. Until 1985 Soviet statements at the United Nations hedged on specifics of the negotiations.

Soviet interest in the details was first discernible in Korniyenko's conversations with Yaqub Khan in June 1983, and again in August 1985 when the Soviets took notice of Pakistan's willingness to sign bilateral accords with Kabul as part of a comprehensive settlement. Not until late 1986, however, was Moscow fully ready to accept the Geneva texts. Even at this stage, political considerations inhibited Moscow from proceeding with the settlement before making an attempt to secure the political future of the PDPA.

Since withdrawal, Soviet interest in keeping the United Nations involved with the search for an internal Afghan settlement has increased. Politically, Soviet concerns remain focused on limiting the damage to the influence Moscow had enjoyed with Kabul for decades. Although Moscow cannot expect restoration of the equilibrium of 1978–79, neither can it acquiesce in the emergence of an Islamic fundamentalist government alongside the Soviet Central Asian republics.[13] At the same time, the Soviet Union must be wary of continuing instability along its sensitive underbelly.

Because the chances for achieving stability in Afghanistan under the PDPA government remain slim, the Soviets back the UN mediation primarily for two reasons. First, the UN effort, by its mandate, pursues political compromise, a middle-ground solution, in conformity with the current minimum Soviet objective in Afghanistan. Second, unless the PDPA government is dislodged or its representation successfully challenged, the United Nations is constrained to treat the government as *primus inter pares* among the Afghan political parties.

Soviet withdrawal under the UN-sponsored Accords is judged among Gorbachev's most popular policy decisions. The withdrawal did not incur the political cost implicit in the anticipated collapse of the PDPA regime. Moscow had braced itself with alacrity for the critical post-Geneva settlement period, as evident from Gorbachev's selection of Yuli Vorontsov, the most celebrated Soviet diplomatist, as Soviet ambassador to Kabul and the dispatch of generous military and economic assistance, estimated at $250 million a month for most of 1989, to help Najibullah keep his hold on Kabul.[14] For Moscow, Afghanistan continues to be an area of primary interest. Its concern over future political scenarios in Kabul has been further deepened because of the recent ethnic unrest in the Soviet Union.

A new Soviet proposal, outlined by Gorbachev at the United Nations on 7 December 1988, combined several familiar ideas for facilitating negotiations among all Afghan parties for a broad-based government.[15] It called for a cease-fire, stoppage of arms supply to all belligerents, stationing of UN peacekeeping forces in selected areas, and an international conference for the "neutralization and demilitarization" of Afghanistan such as Najibullah proposed in November 1988.[16] The proposal indicated Soviet willingness, for the first time, to accept negative symmetry, although the offer was linked to other elements and its scope did not seem restricted to the Soviet Union and the United States alone. Nonetheless, this offer, reiterated in early 1989 by Shevardnadze and Vorontsov, revived the debate in the United States on the desirability of continuing to supply arms to the Afghan Resistance.[17]

The United States. The primary interest of the United States and other Western nations was reversal of the Soviet military advance in December 1979, which, coupled with the lost U.S. influence in Iran, appeared to threaten U.S. interests in the sensitive Persian Gulf region. This point was underscored by the Carter Doctrine and by early proposals by the European Community and President Carter that were predicated on the offer of a Western guarantee of neutrality for Afghanistan in return for Soviet withdrawal. In strategic terms, the U.S. objectives were met with the completion of Soviet withdrawal.

The protracted conflict in Afghanistan created an additional U.S. interest in a future noncommunist Afghanistan. The new rationale for this goal, originally espoused by conservative political forces, is found in the desire, partly shared with the Soviet Union, for peace and stability in Afghanistan and in the region. In addition, the United States retains an interest in Afghanistan, formally as a guarantor-state signatory to the Geneva Accords and informally as a major power and potential donor for helping rebuild the Afghan economy. Accordingly, the U.S. government remains in close touch with the UN secretary general on his peace efforts and with the UN coordinator for assistance to Afghanistan, Prince Sadruddin Agha Khan, on his endeavours to promote economic reconstruction in the country. U.S. interest can be expected to suffer a decline with the prolongation of the Afghan conflict and the diminishing of U.S. capacity as a major contributor, in view of increasing U.S. economic commitments elsewhere.

Because of the prevalent expectation of collapse of the Najibullah government and because the United States had, by and large, found it expedient to maintain a position on issues related to the Afghan Resistance in tandem with that of Pakistan, the United States supported the Afghan Interim Government (AIG) that resulted from the shura convened near Islamabad toward the end of February 1989 following Soviet withdrawal. Like Pakistan, the United States also stressed that removal of Najibullah was necessary for promoting conditions for an internal political settlement in Afghanistan. However, continuing squabbles within the mujahideen groups, lack of support for the AIG among the Afghans, the early abortive offensive against Jalalabad, and continued disaffection among Afghan émigrés have spawned disillusionment and a change of perception discernible in the predominantly liberal U.S. press and important U.S. political circles.

The conflict is increasingly seen as an internecine war, and questions have been raised over continuing U.S. assistance to the "Islamic fundamentalist" factions, reflecting the shifting currents in the decade-long bipartisan support for the Afghan mujahideen.[18] A change in the U.S. position was first reported during Secretary of State James Baker's visit to Moscow in early February 1990. The Americans no longer demanded Najibullah's removal as a precondition for a political settlement, but conceived it as part of a "gradual, phased transition process."[19]

As of mid-1990, the U.S. government appeared to be pushing for an understanding with the Soviets on an effective transitional arrangement that could lead to UN-supervised elections. The idea is a reincarnation of a similar proposal by Cordovez and the original Pakistani concept of a transitional government, except that the Americans conceded that the transitional arrangement would not replace the Najibullah government. On the ground, the U.S. position was moving away from its erstwhile support for the AIG and toward a direct approach to mujahideen commanders. Apart from a disillusionment with the performance of the AIG, the shift was propelled by a perception that Pakistan's ISI was promoting Hekmatyar, whose anti-U.S. rhetoric has earned him an overdrawn reputation as an archfundamentalist. The Americans, however, are ill-equipped to bypass Pakistan and deal directly with the Afghan mujahideen groups. Attempts to do so would compound the existing suspicions and dissension among these groups.

Another wrenching dimension of the controversy over the U.S. position has been the issue of cutting off military supplies to the Afghan mujahideen, following indications of Soviet acceptance of negative symmetry in the context of an international conference and a cease-fire in Afghanistan. Apart from the accompanying conditions, on which the United States could not deliver, the Soviet offer on negative symmetry was initially suspect in the eyes of its critics, who pointed to massive arms deliveries received by the Najibullah government during the period following Soviet withdrawal. Since early 1990, however, the U.S. administration has been increasingly inclined to reduce its military commitment to the mujahideen groups. There is also recognition, borne out by the experience of 1989, that the United States cannot match supplies committed by the Soviet Union, nor can it sustain them indefinitely.[20] Even the longtime conservative supporters of the mujahideen cause no longer consider a military option viable.[21]

Down the road, one cannot rule out a de facto U.S.-Soviet understanding on negative symmetry and greater cooperation in promoting a compromise settlement in Afghanistan. Given the changing perceptions in Washington and growing concern for Gorbachev's difficult predicament in the Soviet Baltic and southern republics, East-West relations are more than ever conducive to an understanding on promoting a neutral, peaceful Afghanistan.

Pakistan. Diverse factors, domestic and external, political and ideological, social and economic, have influenced the broad spectrum of Pakistani perceptions and government policy on Afghanistan. The Soviet military intervention had raised legitimate security concerns in Pakistan and subsequently imposed on it a heavy burden in the refugee presence, military pressure along the border, and rising internal subversion. Also counted among the social costs of the Afghan War by those opposing Zia ul Haq's Afghan policy was the emergence of a violent "drug and arms culture."[22] In retrospect, this is the most terrible price that Pakistan has paid for its involvement in the conflict.

A deep motivation and strong rationale for Pakistan's opposition to the Soviet action and its support for the Afghan Resistance were provided by the mainstream Islamic ethos of the country and by ideological impulses that became increasingly pronounced with the success of the Afghan jihad in the later years. An element of opportunism was also discernible: the Soviet move proved to be a windfall for the isolated Zia government, bringing the international limelight onto Pakistan and opening up prospects of U.S. assistance to help strengthen Pakistan's military capability.

The dual-faceted Afghan policy, developed by Pakistan at an early stage and predicated on both the diplomatic search for a political solution and the provision of assistance to the Afghan Resistance, influenced the Pakistani perception of objectives to be pursued. Besides the unambiguous aim of seeking Soviet withdrawal, a politically motivated but justifiable interest was sustained in fostering political change in Kabul. The early OIC and EC initiatives encompassed this political dimension of the problem. Its exclusion under the UN-sponsored format weakened Pakistan's motivation for streamlining its position on the issue of internal change, but the issue continued to subsist in its thinking. As a result, a discrepancy obtained in Pakistan's declared and tacit objectives that grew as the war intensified and the Afghan Resistance gained in strength.

Once its parameters had been set, the policy moved in the diplomatic and military channels largely by its own momentum, inertia, and expediency. Policy in either direction did not develop through bold decisions, but rather through small steps. This was how Pakistan gradually got locked into the negotiating process and how it steadily increased it commitment to the Afghan Resistance. The view that extraneous factors and Pakistan's preoccupation with the military option slowed its move toward a settlement is erroneous, unless it is assumed that Pakistan's national interest required it to accept the initial Soviet terms for a settlement. In effect, once a reasonable time frame became available, the Accords were signed in virtual conformity to the time limit set by Moscow. There is good reason to believe that the political wrangles in Pakistan preceding the signing would have been avoidable had the Soviet offer come a year earlier.

Soon after the Geneva Accords, Pakistani politics took an unexpected turn with a succession of developments, starting with Zia ul Haq's move to dissolve the Parliament and the Junejo government. This fateful decision was not, however, a consequence of the Accords or the differences on Afghan policy that had surfaced before the Accords, but was due largely to the fallout from the Ojri incident, when the parliamentary pressure for investigation raised hackles among the army top brass. The death of Zia ul Haq in the mysterious Bahawalpur crash in August 1988 catapulted Pakistani domestic politics into an entirely new direction. The November 1988 elections in Pakistan brought Benazir Bhutto to power, but she faced a strong opposition that controlled the Punjab, Pakistan's largest province. Part of that opposition regrouped around Zia ul Haq's associates.

The internal constraints and polarization besetting the new political landscape in Pakistan practically froze Pakistan's ability to take fresh initiatives on Afghanistan and compelled Benazir Bhutto to stay the course on the Afghan policy when she assumed the office of prime minister. The momentum of the existing policy led to the convening of the shura in February 1989 to establish the AIG and to the subsequent military offensive against Jalalabad. Similarly, the position taken by Pakistan, that Najibullah's departure was the sine qua non for movement toward an Afghan consensus, echoed Zia ul Haq's last suggestion to the Soviets before his death.[23]

An opportunity for a compromise political settlement was apparently lost when Shevardnadze came to Pakistan in February 1989, the first ever visit by a Soviet foreign minister. At that time, the Najibullah regime was highly vulnerable; fearing its imminent collapse, the Soviets wanted a settlement with a limited representation for the PDPA. The Pakistan government, however, could not oblige. It was itself in a state of flux and in no position to influence the Peshawar leaders into accepting a compromise, however favourable.

The failure of the Jalalabad offensive afforded the new prime minister an opportunity to manoeuvre; but she moved cautiously, attempting to change control of the policy rather than its course. ISI chief Hamid Gul was replaced by a Pakistan People's Party (PPP) ally, retired Lieutenant General Shamsur Rahman Kallu, and the army was given a greater say in the conduct of the policy, in an effort to break the ISI's erstwhile monopoly in dealing with the military activities of the Afghan Resistance.[24]

In the post–Zia ul Haq period, political and diplomatic aspects of the Afghan policy suffered an eclipse. The Zia legacy became identified with the jihad, ignoring the political pragmatism that had always tempered Zia ul Haq's ideological motivation. Some military circles saw long-term strategic gains for Pakistan in a clear military victory by the mujahideen. However, the ISI and the army lacked the stature and authority to provide the AIG and other mujahideen groups the necessary political direction. By default, the policy veered toward supporting jihad while trying to bring unity among the resistance forces. The latter efforts largely concentrated on forging an alliance between the AIG and the Tehran-based parties.

The new government was disadvantaged in pushing for a political compromise involving the PDPA. Such a move would have drawn opposition criticism. The opposition press blamed the government of Benazir Bhutto for letting down the AIG by nonrecognition, although its predecessor had been similarly reluctant to recognize the AIG formed in February 1988 or to endorse the idea of an Afghan government-in-exile at the earlier stages.

The Benazir government was handicapped in dealing with the relatively strong Peshawar-based groups known for their fundamentalist leanings, who enjoyed support from important religiously oriented segments of the Pakistani opposition. These groups still nursed the grievance of having been left out at Geneva and deeply suspected any new diplomatic efforts, especially those involving the United Nations. Furthermore, acute rivalries among the Afghan groups, aggravated by competing external influences, especially from Iran and Saudi Arabia, made the task of evolving an acceptable political approach immeasurably difficult. The experience of the February 1989 shura underscored the hazards that Pakistan would face if it were to attempt another Afghan coalition. Meanwhile, military stalemate persisted and the burdens inflicted by the conflict on Pakistan remained unabated.

The Geneva Accords have thus brought little relief to Pakistan and carry little meaning for Pakistani-Afghan relations until an internal political settlement materializes. The emergence of a stable, broadly acceptable government in Kabul, dominated by a coalition of forces that had opposed the Soviet intervention, would be a welcome development for Pakistan. Only then could it hope to see a substantial portion of the refugee population returning to their homeland. From this perspective, Zia ul Haq's demand for the establishment of an interim government or for a Soviet agreement on a modality for such a government prior to the Geneva Accords appears to have been justified. Nevertheless, as discussed in chapters six and seven, he had acted late in emphasizing this point and in eliciting a timely political initiative from the Peshawar groups.

From a long-term view, as implied in the bilateral agreement between Afghanistan and Pakistan on the "Principles of Mutual Relations, in Particular on Non-Interference and Non-Intervention," the Geneva Accords presume to regulate relations between the two countries. Ironically, this was one of the considerations underlying Pakistani acceptance in early 1983 of the principles now part of the bilateral agreement. Yet the unique historical, cultural, and geographic factors conditioning the wide-ranging relations between the two countries cannot be demarcated by any set of formal agreements.

An extensive people-to-people interaction, exemplified by tribal and ethnic linkages as well as unregulated movement and commerce across the traditionally porous border, constitutes an important dimension of Afghan-Pakistani relations sometimes overlooked because of the exclusive focus on the tension-prone Islamabad-Kabul ties. The Soviet intervention mobilized the potential of this informal interaction in support of the Afghan Resistance, engendering and intensifying a network of relations at the political, economic, official, and informal levels that should reinforce the existing natural affinities and provide a fertile ground for cooperation between the two countries in the future. Once peace returns to Afghanistan, Pakistan will also have an indispensable role to play in facilitating international efforts to help rebuild the Afghan economy.

While normalization of Islamabad-Kabul ties will have to await the settling down of the conflict inside Afghanistan, a few trends foreshadowing the post-conflict period are becoming visible. First, there has been an increasing interlocking and even symbiosis between political trends and forces in the two countries, for example, between the religiously oriented political elements in the two countries. This may reflect a greater closeness, but it may also conceal new minefields for future relations.

Second, there is the fading out of the Pashtunistan issue. Prior to his overthrow in April 1978, Sardar Daoud had made up his mind to shelve the idea of a separate Pashtunistan state. During the long course of the Afghan conflict, sympathizers of the idea in both countries have become weak and lack credibility, especially with the new Afghan political forces. The Soviet intervention has heightened a perception among broad sections of the two peoples that the security of their two countries is intertwined.

Third, the ten years of war and the changing matrix of global relationships have created new realities in which old frictions and rivalries seem to lose much of their relevance. If so, a future Afghanistan should have an incentive to assert its regional personality by seeking closer ties with Iran and Pakistan.

Post-Geneva Afghanistan

The complexion of the conflict inside Afghanistan has been profoundly transformed as a result of the Soviet withdrawal completed by 15 February 1989. The Najibullah government has displayed unexpected staying power, even considering the massive Soviet military and financial resources made available to it in the postwithdrawal period. The Afghan Resistance failed to develop sufficient military and political cohesion to isolate, demoralize, and hasten the collapse of the Najibullah regime, which was most vulnerable at the time of the departure of the Soviet troops. Meanwhile, persisting rivalries within the resistance groups have come into full view. Now the Najibullah government is one among several Afghan factions locked in a fatal internecine military conflict, which continues, however, at a comparatively lower intensity than in the past. These concluding paragraphs will briefly discuss the factors underlying the current political and military stalemate and elements of future diplomatic efforts.

The prospects of a political consensus in Afghanistan have narrowed mainly because of the failure of the Afghan Resistance to develop a credible political profile. Political power remains fragmented in Afghanistan following dissolution of the traditional power structures. The decade-long conflict has superimposed new political and ideological divergences over the old tribal and ethnic (Durrani-Ghilzai, Pashtun–non-Pashtun) rivalries.

The fractious character of the Afghan Resistance is not a new phenomenon. The seven parties recognized by Pakistan since the early 1980s remained throughout deeply divided along political and ideological lines. As long as they served as an efficient liaison for military supplies to largely autonomous mujahideen (resistance) commanders, operating inside the country, and performed a limited representational role, Pakistan had no incentive for an onerous undertaking to forge a genuine united front. Pressure to do so would have been substantial had the UN negotiating format, like the preceding OIC initiative, involved the resistance as a party to the conflict.

In retrospect, some observers perceive Pakistan's backing of politically irreconcilable Afghan factions as an error of policy. Yet the circumstances of the early years, when Pakistan's policy toward the resistance evolved, offered no easy alternatives. Some other critics accuse Zia ul Haq and the military of attempting to install in Kabul a pliant fundamentalist regime unsuited to the nationalist and tribal political culture of Afghanistan. Undoubtedly, the notion of an Islamic government in Afghanistan existed and was strengthened by the dramatic mujahideen victories of 1987. But this idea was characteristic of the predominant Islamic sentiment of the resistance rather than a product of any ulterior ideological agenda pursued by Zia ul Haq. Many observers believe that the current divisions within the resistance forces could have been prevented had Pakistan supported the emergence of a unified leadership by allowing the convening of a Loya Jirga in the early stages, charging that the Peshawar leaders promoted by Pakistan never had the potential to provide an effective leadership. From 1987 on, Pakistan's ability to influence the Peshawar leaders also started declining.

The precipitous move to establish the Afghan Interim Government in February 1988, made in response to Gorbachev's deadline for the Geneva settlement, came late and was overshadowed by the high tide of the diplomatic finale at Geneva. The second AIG, set up one year later by an Afghan shura convened near Islamabad on the eve of the completion of Soviet withdrawal, failed politically as well as militarily.

Politically, the February 1989 AIG suffered from lack of political direction from its very inception; the death of Zia ul Haq in August 1988 had removed the critically important element of political influence Pakistan might have exercised over the Peshawar groups. Ad hoc meddling by the ISI, which was seen to be backing the fundamentalists or, more specifically, the Hekmatyar group, exacerbated resentment among other important groups excluded from the AIG, damaging the AIG's credibility. The ISI has also been widely accused of playing favourites. This impression has further accentuated divisions and misapprehension within the resistance at a critical time, when political imperative dictated a broad coalition of resistance elements to isolate Najibullah.

A serious blow was dealt to the representative character of the AIG when the Tehran-based groups that traveled to Islamabad in February 1989 could not be brought into the fold because of disagreement on their share of participation. Saudi and U.S. behind-the-scenes influence is believed to have hardened the attitude of the Hekmatyar, Sayyaf, and Yunis Khalis groups, who were known to be wary of conceding a substantial share of power to the Tehran-based parties. Furthermore, the new AIG failed to associate, in an institutional relationship, the other major resistance groups, namely the mujahideen commanders from inside Afghanistan, the tribal elders, especially from the pro-Zahir Shah Durrani tribes of southwest Afghanistan, and the vocal Afghan émigrés.[25] The AIG remained largely restricted to the Peshawar groups, and distribution of important portfolios among the seven leaders disavowed even the pretension of broad representation. In retrospect, the resistance groups would have been under greater pressure to coalesce politically had the establishment of the AIG been made contingent upon the formation of a broader alliance involving the Peshawar groups and any of the other major resistance elements.

The AIG became a new mask for the old, divided Afghan Alliance of the Peshawar groups. It was reduced to a fiction after two of its major components, Hekmatyar's Hizb and Rabbani's Jamiat, publicly fell out following the July 1989 Takhar incident, in which Sayed Jamal, a local commander affiliated with Hekmatyar, reportedly attacked and killed several commanders of Jamiat's Ahmed Shah Massoud, ostensibly to settle an old vendetta.[26] Condemnation of this action by Rabbani and the AIG leaders and countercharges by Hekmatyar led to a Hizb decision to suspend cooperation with the AIG.[27]

Militarily, the test of the AIG and its constituent resistance groups came soon, as pressure built on it to establish a foothold inside Afghanistan. Formal Pakistani and U.S. recognition of the AIG was contingent on this condition. The move was also necessitated by the impending OIC conference of foreign ministers in late March 1989, where the AIG expected to lay claim to Afghanistan's seat and obtain recognition from the membership. After showing some early advance, the Jalalabad offensive in March–April 1989 came to a standstill.[28]

Controversy surrounds the decision for the Jalalabad offensive and its conduct. Some of the mujahideen commanders blamed the ISI and Pakistani-U.S. concerns for the ill-advised push.[29] There is some evidence to suggest that political pressure linked to the question of recognition of the newly formed AIG had compelled the ISI to press the mujahideen to launch the offensive. If so, the ISI underestimated the risk of failure. On such military matters, political opinion could not have otherwise prevailed. Many observers have also complained of interruptions in U.S. supplies to the mujahideen soon after the offensive began. Nonetheless, reasons for the failure appear to be more political than military.

The lack of coordination among the mujahideen commanders and their failure to synchronize tactical attacks in other areas were clearly linked to the paucity of support for the new AIG among local commanders. The AIG and the mujahideen groups had no public policy on crucial issues aimed at eroding Kabul's support base. For example, it was vital to make a clear, well-publicized commitment to general amnesty, peace, reconciliation, and national reconstruction. Reported ISI attempts to plan and coordinate the military operation stoked suspicion and resentment.[30] The confused situation discouraged anticipated defections from the Kabul army. Indeed, the killings in March 1989 of early defectors and the reported carnage attributed to "Wahhabi" elements[31] and similar incidents at Kunduz in August 1988 were effectively used by Kabul to keep the army intact and neutralize support for the mujahideen in urban centres under its control.[32]

Until the autumn of 1989, Pakistan and the United States hoped for military success to bolster the political image of the AIG. The Khost offensive mobilized in September 1989 revealed this approach.[33] The failure of that offensive once again highlighted the political weakness of the AIG and the continuing disarray in mujahideen ranks. While the mujahideen were capable of maintaining military pressure, for a major military offensive such as the Jalalabad operation to succeed would require a prior political understanding, especially among the commanders, for military coordination and for control and administration of the city were it to fall. Some analysts believed that the objective of having the resistance gain a foothold in Jalalabad was militarily flawed and that the mujahideen should have limited themselves to maintaining tactical military pressure until they were militarily and politically ready to make a decisive bid for Kabul.

In military terms, the mujahideen's lack of experience in waging pitched battles, Kabul's decisive edge in air power, and massive Soviet supplies available to the Kabul army tilted the balance in Kabul's favour. Following the departure of Soviet troops, the Afghan army left to itself showed local initiative and fought well, especially where it was engaged in defensive battles with a besieged mentality. As against the galvanized spirit of the Afghan army, the local mujahideen commanders lost much of the keenness they had shown in fighting the Soviets. They were increasingly preoccupied with conserving resources and holding onto territories under their control.

The heterogeneous Afghan Resistance needs to coalesce politically before it can make a military breakthrough. Prospects of such a development remain slim. The individual Peshawar leaders have following and influence with the mujahideen commanders but, as an alliance, have repeatedly failed to provide leadership to the resistance. The mujahideen commanders, however, are the mainstay of the resistance. One needs to watch for trends toward their unity through military and political coordination. Another phenomenon that deserves careful observation is the reassertion of the tribal-nationalist character of Afghan society. Reportedly, local shuras active in southwestern Afghanistan have been largely dominated by the traditional Durrani and Achakzai tribal leadership.

Factors inhibiting the emergence of a political consensus within the resistance have been compounded by fissures within the Pakistani body politic and the deepening shadow of Iranian-Saudi rivalry on the Afghan conflict. Pakistan still retains a critical influence with the Peshawar leaders and the mujahideen commanders, but the unraveling of the warped resistance politics may well require Pakistan to adopt a stronger, bipartisan Afghan policy. However, Pakistan must dispel the impression that it is pushing for the ascendancy of any particular political party or individual leader. The role of the OIC as a unifying factor may similarly require less intrusive involvement by Iran and the Saudis in backing client factions.

Worldwide, the resistance no longer attracts the same support as before. The events in Eastern Europe and dramatic changes in East-West relations have diverted much attention from erstwhile regional issues, including Afghanistan. Further, the West is experiencing a rising tide of liberal secularism, superseding the conservative fervour. For liberal intellectuals, Islamic fundamentalism and efforts to establish theocracy in the last decade of the twentieth century are not merely anachronistic, but a threat that must be countered by favouring modernization and secular trends.

Najibullah and the PDPA are depending on the projection of their secular, modernist credentials and the intensification of dissension within the Afghan Resistance. Also, Najibullah showed political agility during the perilous transition that coincided with Soviet withdrawal. He has kept control over the party and the security apparatus and has come up with a series of initiatives to shore up his political position. Immediately after the signing of the Geneva Accords, as the Soviet troops started disengaging, Najibullah pulled his troops from indefensible outlying areas. He renewed with greater vigour his efforts to create zones of peace in the vacated areas and to encourage local militia by promising them arms in return for non-cooperation with the mujahideen. On the diplomatic front, Najibullah proposed in November 1989 an international conference for "neutrality and demilitarization" of Afghanistan. Foreign journalists, debarred from entering Afghanistan for years, are now regularly invited to besieged Kabul to witness the hardship suffered by civilian inhabitants as a result of the war of the cities conducted by the mujahideen.

The Afghan émigrés, the refugees, the groups in Tehran, and especially the mujahideen commanders have been a constant target of Kabul's peace overtures.[34] To attract nationalist elements, Najibullah appointed a non-PDPA prime minister, Mohammad Hassan Sharq, in May 1988.[35] Following the Soviet withdrawal, Najibullah made a fervent appeal to mujahideen commanders, addressing them as "my brothers," to negotiate cease-fire in return for setting up mujahideen-controlled regional administrations.[36] This was a transparent attempt to wean the mujahideen commanders away from the Peshawar-based groups, because in the same breath Najibullah vigorously attacked the AIG as unrepresentative and as a tool in the hands of Pakistani "militarists."[37]

Najibullah announced yet another peace initiative at a highly publicized Loya Jirga convened in Kabul on 20–21 May 1989. He proposed setting up a "mediation commission" of the Loya Jirga to contact the mujahideen to pave the way for a countrywide peace conference. This conference would elect a "leading council," which could act as a broad-based government to oversee a cease-fire and the drafting of a new constitution, and thereafter organize elections for a new parliament.[38]

Within six months of the Loya Jirga, Najibullah convened the Melli Shura (National Council), reiterating the need for reconciliation and dialogue.[39] On 15 January 1990 he proposed a shura of all Afghan forces in and out of the country, to be held in Kabul in the presence of UN representatives.[40] A week later, addressing a press conference on 24 January, Najibullah suggested UN-supervised elections.[41]

These moves have yet to succeed in removing the stain of atrocities committed under the PDPA rule and the massive tragedy inflicted upon Afghanistan by the Soviet military intervention, for which the Afghans hold the PDPA responsible. Neither the Afghan émigrés nor any of the resistance groups have, so far, accepted offers from Najibullah. Furthermore, Najibullah remains internally vulnerable. The end of 1988 saw new purges of prominent Khalqis, including Interior Minister Syed Mohammed Gulabzoi and Politburo member Saleh Mohammad Zeary.[42] Problems within the PDPA once again surfaced in the form of the abortive coup attempt led by the defense minister, General Shahnawaz Tanai, in March 1990.

The current political and military strife is unlikely to end until some coalition emerges from among the disparate political forces that dominate the Afghan scene. The process cannot be determined by outside decisions. But outside policies, especially regarding the supply of arms, can induce progress in that direction because they continue to interact with the fragmented politics of Afghanistan. Meanwhile, several ideas and proposals have been circulating and will be relevant in future diplomatic and political efforts to address the internal dimension of the Afghan conflict.

Kabul's proposals involving intra-Afghan dialogue. The national reconciliation offers made by the Najibullah government have mostly been predicated on establishing an intra-Afghan dialogue for power sharing, combined with a cease-fire or the creation of peace zones. To initiate such a dialogue was the objective of Vorontsov's short-lived but much publicized exchanges with the Peshawar-based leaders in December 1988 at Taif.[43] It has been the consistent theme of Soviet positions maintained since 1987 in meetings with Pakistani officials. It was also the crux of Gorbachev's December 1988 proposal and of Najibullah's several peace initiatives, including his proposals for a "mediation commission" and for UN-supervised elections or shura, made in May 1989 and January 1990 respectively.[44]

None of the proposals based on intra-Afghan dialogue with the participation of the PDPA were acceptable to the seven-party Alliance nor to its successor, the AIG. Pakistan was ready to give a push to such proposals, provided Najibullah was removed. Najibullah has ruled out stepping down, although he has hinted at his willingness to resign, if necessary, as a result of the process.[45] The groups comprising the AIG have dismissed such expressions of intent as tactical.

No significant resistance group is likely to endorse the idea of dialogue with the PDPA. To do so would risk compromising a group's position vis-à-vis the mainstream resistance forces. Similarly, most mujahideen commanders reject a cease-fire because formal cessation of hostilities would tend to demobilize the irregular mujahideen ranks, while the Kabul army under Najibullah would remain intact. Najibullah's background as Khad chief also reinforces objections, especially from those émigrés otherwise ready to accommodate the PDPA. Najibullah's departure through an internal change in Kabul could therefore brighten prospects for intra-Afghan dialogue.

Peshawar proposals for a shura, a jirga, or elections. Variants on the idea of a nominated shura, jirga, or elections in the mujahideen-controlled areas have been proposed from time to time by the Peshawar groups. The idea of a nominated shura or jirga had been attractive to some of the smaller Peshawar groups because it ensured their representation on an equal footing. However, the mandate of the AIG calls for the holding of elections in the "liberated" or mujahideen-controlled areas. In late April 1990 the AIG announced an election plan evolved under the guidance of Gailani, the AIG minister of law and justice; but very soon differences developed on details. Yunis Khalis opposed participation of the female population; the Iranian parties demanded a fresh delineation of constituencies, arguing that the Shia population was underrepresented in the existing delineation; and there were differences over the form of elections. Hekmatyar advocated restricted elections to determine proportionate representation of the seven parties, expecting a favourable outcome because of his party's superior organization and centralized control.

Notwithstanding differences over details, the broadly agreed plan provided for elections at the *uluswali* (district) level for the formation of representative shuras. The members of these shuras meeting at the national level were expected to select a representative government and head of state. This new government was then supposed to take steps for the political integration of the country.

The supporters of a new shura or jirga, consisting mainly of the Afghan Resistance elements, proposed consultations among mujahideen groups and political parties for an agreed panel of prominent Afghans who would select participants for the shura or jirga to be held inside Afghanistan. The Afghan venue was important in order to avoid the impression of manipulation by Pakistan. The proposal suggested that the United Nations should obtain a guarantee that the shura, if convened, would not be targeted by the Kabul air force. From a UN viewpoint, the idea had merit, since it promised to yield an authentic interlocutor for the resistance, the absence of which was a major handicap in the ongoing UN mediation effort. Nonetheless, Najibullah remained opposed to any shura or jirga that did not promise the PDPA substantial participation. The limited role for "good Muslims" from Kabul, a euphemism for PDPA participation conceded by the Peshawar-based parties, obviously could not meet Najibullah's conditions.

For credibility, the new shura or jirga would have to be representative, assuring active participation of groups beyond the loosely aligned Peshawar parties, especially the Tehran-based parties, important mujahideen commanders, and émigrés. And the Islamist groups would need to seek compromises with other nationalist elements and develop tolerance and accommodation for their views in order to avoid isolation.

Proposals involving Loya Jirga and Zahir Shah. Internationally, Zahir Shah remains the most acceptable Afghan personality to lead a transition to peace. Notwithstanding the ambiguity in the Soviet position on this issue, the main opposition to Zahir Shah comes from the mujahideen commanders and the fundamentalist groups in Peshawar. Within Afghanistan, he reportedly enjoys support among the Durrani tribes dominating southwestern Afghanistan. The absence of strong tribal backing for his return, however, indicates the emaciation of the traditional power structure as a result of the departure of the old elite. Externally, Iran and Saudi Arabia have been unenthusiastic about Zahir Shah's playing a role. Pakistani attitudes toward the Zahir Shah option, discussed in chapters three and seven, are marked by tentativeness.

In late 1989 a proposal based on a role for Zahir Shah was revived by his cousin Prince Sultan Ghazi with the support of Afghan émigré elements. Calling for a Loya Jirga with token participation of the PDPA, it envisaged a group of about sixty prominent Afghans acceptable to the majority of Afghan Resistance groups to prepare the ground and eventually convene the jirga at a neutral venue. Unless some of the internal Afghan political forces become active in support of Zahir Shah, however, the chances of his return remain slim. Internationally, the Zahir Shah option remains attractive. But any external impetus to this option would require nothing short of a clear Soviet-U.S. agreement that Zahir Shah should play a leading role in a transitional arrangement that would replace Najibullah.

UN-oriented proposals. Effective from 15 March 1990, when the mandate of UNGOMAP expired, UNGOMAP was transformed into the Office of the Secretary General in Afghanistan and Pakistan (OSGAP), with Benon Sevan, the secretary general's political representative on UNGOMAP, appointed as personal representative of the secretary general in Afghanistan and Pakistan. This new appointment of Sevan and the decision by the Security Council to maintain UN personnel in Kabul and Islamabad underscore the broad desirability of preserving the UN good offices while the military and political stalemate persists. The post-Geneva UN efforts have been exerted in two interrelated directions: first, eliciting an agreement from outside powers to endorse a stronger role for the United Nations, and, second, promoting an international and Afghan consensus on elements of a political settlement. For the United Nations, the international consensus would depend essentially on the United States, the Soviet Union, Pakistan, Iran, and Saudi Arabia.

On specifics, Benon Sevan has tried several ideas; for example, he initially tried to work out an agreed panel of persons who could serve either in an interim political arrangement or as a vehicle for consultations to bring about a government through elections, nomination, or Loya Jirga. Favourite among the possibilities was an interim arrangement of technocrats. Until the antagonists are militarily exhausted, however, none is likely to abdicate in favour of an entity with no political or military base, given the severity of the conflict and the ambitions of individual parties. The UN attempt to evolve a consensus among the resistance groups on a representative panel is no less formidable than building consensus on an interim arrangement.

By mid-1990 the United Nations appeared to have abandoned efforts to develop representative panels and advocated a new approach that separately addressed the outside powers and the Afghan parties. Working on a set of principles that could become the basis for a settlement, the secretary general sought to elicit endorsement from outside powers first, and only then to approach the Afghan parties. These principles included the need for a transitional arrangement for holding UN-supervised elections, the cessation of hostilities, and the cutoff of aid to all Afghan factions. Unlike the U.S.-Soviet dialogue, the UN approach prefers to circumvent the issue of Najibullah. Furthermore, the UN approach leaves all details to be worked out through consultations with the Afghan factions. If a broad consensus were to emerge on the principles of a settlement, the UN mediation would have to address many sensitive issues germane to a future political settlement—for example, the structure of security forces under an interim arrangement and the nature of local administrative control.

Najibullah favoured UN-supervised elections, provided his incumbency remained intact. The United Nations' main difficulty lay in eliciting support from the mujahideen groups, in whose eyes it was suspect for being deferential to the government in Kabul. The UN involvement with the Afghan issue has, however, come of age. In the interest of promoting a solution, it can afford to be less constrained by considerations of legitimacy. Meanwhile, the UN role needs to be sustained and encouraged, because no other agency can supplant it and because UN-organized elections or a shura under an agreed political format may yet develop into a viable option.

Internationally, there is broad support for a political settlement that could lead to a peaceful, stable, nonaligned Afghanistan. But an agreed practical approach toward this objective remains elusive. An unconditional U.S.-Soviet understanding on negative symmetry and a stronger UN role could serve as a catalyst for progress. A larger peace effort would have to involve Pakistan, Iran, and Saudi Arabia. Success, however, will depend on the emergence of a viable and dynamic coalition of the fragmented Afghan political forces, one that isolates elements of extremism and attracts support from the major segments of the Afghan population.

Appendixes

Appendix 1: The Geneva Accords on the Settlement of the Situation Relating to Afghanistan, 14 April 1988

Bilateral Agreement between the Republic of Afghanistan and the Islamic Republic of Pakistan on the Principles of Mutual Relations, in Particular on Non-Interference and Non-Intervention

The Republic of Afghanistan and the Islamic Republic of Pakistan, hereinafter referred to as the High Contracting Parties,

Desiring to normalize relations and promote good-neighbourliness and co-operation as well as to strengthen international peace and security in the region,

Considering that full observance of the principle of non-interference and non-intervention in the international and external affairs of States is of the greatest importance for the maintenance of international peace and security and for the fulfilment of the purpose and principles of the Charter of the United Nations,

Reaffirming the inalienable right of States freely to determine their own political, economic, cultural and social systems in accordance with the will of their peoples without outside intervention, interference, subversion, coercion or threat in any form whatsoever,

Mindful of the provisions of the Charter of the United Nations as well as the resolutions adopted by the United Nations on the principle of non-interference and non-intervention, in particular the Declaration on Principles of International Law concerning Friendly Relations and Co-operation among States in accordance with the Charter of the United Nations, of 24 October 1970, as well as the Declaration on the Inadmissibility of Intervention and Interference in the Internal Affairs of States, of 9 December 1981,

Have agreed as follows:

Article I

Relations between the High Contracting Parties shall be conducted in strict compliance with the principle of non-interference and non-intervention by States in the affairs of other States.

Source: UN Press Release SG/1860, 14 April 1988.

Article II

For the purpose of implementing the principles of non-interference and non-intervention each High Contracting Party undertakes to comply with the following obligations:

(1) to respect the sovereignty, political independence, territorial integrity, national unity, security and non-alignment of the other High Contracting Party, as well as the national identity and cultural heritage of its people;

(2) to respect the sovereign and inalienable right of the other High Contracting Party freely to determine its own political, economic, cultural and social systems, to develop its international relations and to exercise permanent sovereignty over its natural resources, in accordance with the will of its people, and without outside intervention, interference, subversion, coercion or threat in any form whatsoever;

(3) to refrain from the threat or use of force in any form whatsoever so as to not to violate the boundaries of each other, to disrupt the political, social or economic order of the other High Contracting Party, to overthrow or change the political system of the other High Contracting Party or its Government, or to cause tension between the High Contracting Parties;

(4) to ensure that its territory is not used in any manner which would violate the sovereignty, political independence, territorial integrity and national unity or disrupt the political, economic and social stability of the other High Contracting Parties;

(5) to refrain from armed intervention, subversion, military occupation or any other form of intervention and interference, overt or covert, directed at the other High Contracting Party, or any act of military, political or economic interference in the internal affairs of the other High Contracting Party, including acts of reprisal involving the use of force;

(6) to refrain from any action or attempt in whatever form or under whatever pretext to destabilize or to undermine the stability of the other High Contracting Party or any of its institutions;

(7) to refrain from the promotion, encouragement or support, direct or indirect, of rebellious or secessionist activities against the other High Contracting Party, under any pretext whatsoever, or from any other action which seeks to disrupt the unity or to undermine or subvert the political order of the other High Contracting Party;

(8) to prevent within its territory the training, equipping, financing and recruitment of mercenaries from whatever origin for the purpose of hostile activities against the other High Contracting Party, or the sending of such mercenaries into the territory of the other High Contracting Party and accordingly to deny facilities, including financing for the training, equipping and transit of such mercenaries;

(9) to refrain from making any agreements or arrangements with other States designed to intervene or interfere in the internal and external affairs of the other High Contracting Party;

(10) to abstain from any defamatory campaign, vilification or hostile propaganda for the purpose of intervening or interfering in the internal affairs of the other High Contracting Party;

(11) to prevent any assistance to or use of or tolerance of terrorist groups, saboteurs or subversive agents against the other High Contracting Party;

(12) to prevent within its Territory the presence, harbouring, in camps and bases or otherwise, organizing, training, financing, equipping and arming of individuals and political, ethnic and any other groups for the purpose of creating subversion, disorder or unrest in the territory of the other High Contracting Party and accordingly also to prevent the use of mass media and the transportation of arms, ammunition and equipment by such individuals and groups;

(13) not to resort to or to allow any other action that could be considered as interference or intervention.

Article III

The present Agreement shall enter into force on 15 May 1988.

Article IV

Any steps that may be required in order to enable the High Contracting Parties to comply with the provisions of Article II of this Agreement shall be completed by the date on which this Agreement enters into force.

Article V

This Agreement is drawn up in the English, Pashtu and Urdu languages, all texts being equally authentic. In case of any divergence of interpretation, the English text shall prevail.

Done in five original copies at Geneva this fourteenth day of April 1988.

[Signed by Afghanistan and Pakistan]

Declaration on International Guarantees

The Governments of the Union of Soviet Socialist Republics and of the United States of America,

Expressing support that the Republic of Afghanistan and the Islamic Republic of Pakistan have concluded a negotiated political settlement designed to normalize relations and promote good-neighbourliness between the two countries as well as to strengthen international peace and security in the region;

Wishing in turn to contribute to the achievement of the objectives that the Republic of Afghanistan and the Islamic Republic of Pakistan have set themselves, and with a view to ensuring respect for their sovereignty, independence, territorial integrity and non-alignment;

Undertake to invariably refrain from any form of interference and intervention in the internal affairs of the Republic of Afghanistan and the Islamic Republic of Pakistan and to respect the commitments contained in the bilateral agreement between the Republic of Afghanistan and the Islamic Republic of Pakistan on the Principles of Mutual Relations, in particular on Non-Interference and Non-Intervention;

Urge all States to act likewise.

The present Declaration shall enter into force on 15 May 1988.

Done at Geneva, this fourteenth day of April 1988 in five original copies, each in the English and Russian languages, both texts being equally authentic.

[Signed by the USSR and the USA]

Bilateral Agreement between the Republic of Afghanistan and the Islamic Republic of Pakistan on the Voluntary Return of Refugees

The Republic of Afghanistan and the Islamic Republic of Pakistan, hereinafter referred to as the High Contracting Parties,

Desiring to normalize relations and promote good-neighbourliness and co-operation as well as to strengthen international peace and security in the region,

Convinced that voluntary and unimpeded repatriation constitutes the most appropriate solution for the problem of Afghan refugees present in the Islamic Republic of Pakistan and having ascertained that the arrangements for the return of the Afghan refugees are satisfactory to them,

Have agreed as follows:

Article I

All Afghan refugees temporarily present in the territory of the Islamic Republic of Pakistan shall be given the opportunity to return voluntarily to their homeland in accordance with the arrangements and conditions set out in the present Agreement.

Article II

The Government of the Republic of Afghanistan shall take all necessary measures to ensure the following conditions for the voluntary return of Afghan refugees to their homeland:

(a) All refugees shall be allowed to return in freedom to their homeland;

(b) All returnees shall enjoy the free choice of domicile and freedom of movement within the Republic of Afghanistan;

(c) All returnees shall enjoy the right to work, to adequate living conditions and to share in the welfare of the State;

(d) All returnees shall enjoy the right to participation on an equal basis in the civic affairs of the Republic of Afghanistan. They shall be ensured equal benefits from the solution of the land question on the basis of the Land and Water Reform;

(e) All returnees shall enjoy the same rights and privileges, including freedom of religion, and have the same obligations and responsibilities as any other citizens of the Republic of Afghanistan without discrimination.

The Government of the Republic of Afghanistan undertakes to implement these measures and to provide, within its possibilities, all necessary assistance in the process of repatriation.

Article III

The Government of the Islamic Republic of Pakistan shall facilitate the voluntary, orderly and peaceful repatriation of all Afghan refugees staying within its territory and undertakes to provide, within its possibilities, all necessary assistance in the process of repatriation.

Article IV

For the purpose of organizing, co-ordinating and supervising the operations which should effect the voluntary, orderly and peaceful repatriation of Afghan refugees, there shall be set up mixed commissions in accordance with the established international practice. For the performance of their functions the members of the commissions and their staff shall be accorded the necessary facilities, and have access to the relevant areas within the territories of the High Contracting Parties.

Article V

With a view to the orderly movement of the returnees, the commissions shall determine frontier crossing points and establish necessary transit centres. They shall also establish all other modalities for the phased return of refugees, including registration and communication to the country of return of the names of refugees who express the wish to return.

Article VI

At the request of the Governments concerned, the United Nations High Commissioner for Refugees will co-operate and provide assistance in the process of voluntary repatriation of refugees in accordance with the present Agreement. Special agreements may be concluded for this purpose between UNHCR and the High Contracting Parties.

Article VII

The present Agreement shall enter into force on 15 May 1988. At that time the mixed commissions provided in Article IV shall be established and the operations for the voluntary return of refugees under this Agreement shall commence.

The arrangements set out in Articles IV and V above shall remain in effect for a period of eighteen months. After that period the High Contracting Parties shall review the results of the repatriation and, if necessary, consider any further arrangements that may be called for.

Article VIII

This Agreement is drawn up in the English, Pashtu and Urdu languages, all texts being equally authentic. In case of any divergence of interpretation, the English text shall prevail.

Done in five original copies at Geneva this fourteenth day of April 1988.

[Signed by Afghanistan and Pakistan]

Agreement on the Interrelationships for the Settlement of the Situation Relating to Afghanistan

1. The diplomatic process initiated by the Secretary-General of the United Nations with the support of all Governments concerned and aimed

at achieving, through negotiations, a political settlement of the situation relating to Afghanistan has been successfully brought to an end.

2. Having agreed to work towards a comprehensive settlement designed to resolve the various issues involved and to establish a framework for good-neighbourliness and co-operation, the Government of the Republic of Afghanistan and the Government of the Islamic Republic of Pakistan entered into negotiations through the intermediary of the Personal Representative of the Secretary-General at Geneva from 16 to 24 June 1982. Following consultations held by the Personal Representative in Islamabad, Kabul and Teheran from 21 January to 7 February 1983, the negotiations continued at Geneva from 11 to 22 April and from 12 to 24 June 1983. The Personal Representative again visited the area for high-level discussions from 3 to 15 April 1984. It was then agreed to change the format of the negotiations and, in pursuance thereof, proximity talks through the intermediary of the Personal Representative were held at Geneva from 24 to 30 August 1984. Another visit to the area by the Personal Representative from 25 to 31 May 1985 preceded further rounds of proximity talks held at Geneva from 20 to 25 June, from 27 to 30 August and from 16 to 19 December 1985. The Personal Representative paid an additional visit to the area from 8 to 18 March 1986 for consultations. The final round of negotiations began as proximity talks at Geneva on 5 May 1986, was suspended on 23 May 1986, and was resumed from 31 July to 8 August 1986. The Personal Representative visited the area from 20 November to 3 December 1986 for further consultations and the talks at Geneva were resumed again from 25 February to 9 March 1987, and from 7 to 11 September 1987. The Personal Representative again visited the area from 18 January to 9 February 1988 and the talks resumed at Geneva from 2 March to 8 April 1988. The format of the negotiations was changed on 14 April 1988, when the instruments comprising the settlement were finalized, and, accordingly, direct talks were held at that stage. The Government of the Islamic Republic of Iran was kept informed of the progress of the negotiations throughout the diplomatic process.

3. The Government of the Republic of Afghanistan and the Government of the Islamic Republic of Pakistan took part in the negotiations with the expressed conviction that they were acting in accordance with their rights and obligations under the Charter of the United Nations and agreed that the political settlement should be based on the following principles of international law:

– The principle that States shall refrain in their international relations from the threat or use of force against the territorial integrity or political independence of any State, or in any other manner inconsistent with the purposes of the United Nations;

– The principle that States shall settle their international disputes by peaceful means in such a manner that international peace and security and justice are not endangered;

– The duty not to intervene in matters within the domestic jurisdiction of any State, in accordance with the Charter of the United Nations;

– The duty of States to co-operate with one another in accordance with the Charter of the United Nations;

– The principle of equal rights and self-determination of peoples;
– The principle of sovereign equality of States;
– The principle that States shall fulfil in good faith the obligations assumed by them in accordance with the Charter of the United Nations.

The two Governments further affirmed the right of the Afghan refugees to return to their homeland in a voluntary and unimpeded manner.

4. The following instruments were concluded on this date as component parts of the political settlement:

A Bilateral Agreement between the Republic of Afghanistan and the Islamic Republic of Pakistan on the Principles of Mutual Relations, in Particular on Non-Interference and Non-Intervention;

A Declaration on International Guarantees by the Union of Soviet Socialist Republics and the United States of America;

A Bilateral Agreement between the Republic of Afghanistan and the Islamic Republic of Pakistan on the Voluntary Return of Refugees;

The present Agreement on the Interrelationships for the Settlement of the Situation Relating to Afghanistan.

5. The Bilateral Agreement on the Principles of Mutual Relations, in Particular on Non-Interference and Non-Intervention; the Declaration on International Guarantees; the Bilateral Agreement on the Voluntary Return of Refugees; and the present Agreement on the Interrelationships for the Settlement of the Situation Relating to Afghanistan will enter into force on 15 May 1988. In accordance with the time-frame agreed upon between the Union of Soviet Socialist Republics and the Republic of Afghanistan there will be a phased withdrawal of the foreign troops which will start on the date of entry into force mentioned above. One half of the troops will be withdrawn by 15 August 1988 and the withdrawal of all troops will be completed within nine months.

6. The interrelationships in paragraph 5 above have been agreed upon in order to achieve effectively the purpose of the political settlement, namely, that as from 15 May 1988, there will be no interference and intervention in any form in the affairs of the Parties; the international guarantees will be in operation; the voluntary return of the refugees to their homeland will start and be completed within the time-frame specified in the agreement on the voluntary return of the refugees; and the phased withdrawal of the foreign troops will start and be completed within the time-frame envisaged in paragraph 5. It is therefore essential that all the obligations deriving from the instruments concluded as component parts of the settlement be strictly fulfilled and that all the steps required to ensure full compliance with all the provisions of the instruments be completed in good faith.

7. To consider alleged violations and to work out prompt and mutually satisfactory solutions to questions that may arise in the implementation of the instruments comprising the settlement representatives of the Republic of Afghanistan and the Islamic Republic of Pakistan shall meet whenever required.

A representative of the Secretary-General of the United Nations shall lend his good offices to the Parties and in that context he will assist in the organization of the meetings and participate in them. He may submit to the Parties for their consideration and approval suggestions and recommendations for prompt, faithful and complete observance of the provisions of the instruments.

In order to enable him to fulfill his tasks, the representative shall be assisted by such personnel under his authority as required. On his own initiative, or at the request of any of the Parties, the personnel shall investigate any possible violations of any of the provisions of the instruments and prepare a report thereon. For that purpose, the representative and his personnel shall receive all the necessary co-operation from the Parties, including all freedom of movement within their respective territories required for effective investigation. Any report submitted by the representative to the two Governments shall be considered in a meeting of the Parties no later than forty-eight hours after it has been submitted.

The modalities and logistical arrangements for the work of the representative and the personnel under his authority as agreed upon with the Parties are set out in the Memorandum of Understanding which is annexed to and is part of this Agreement.

8. The present instrument will be registered with the Secretary-General of the United Nations. It has been examined by the representatives of the Parties to the bilateral agreements and of the States-Guarantors, who have signified their consent with its provisions. The representatives of the Parties, being duly authorized thereto by their respective Governments, have affixed their signatures hereunder. The Secretary-General for the United Nations was present.

Done, at Geneva, this fourteenth day of April 1988, in five original copies each in the English, Pashtu, Russian and Urdu languages, all being equally authentic. In case of any dispute regarding the interpretation the English text shall prevail.

[Signed by Afghanistan and Pakistan]

In witness thereof, the representatives of the States-Guarantors affixed their signatures hereunder:

[Signed by the USSR and the USA]

Annex
Memorandum of Understanding

I. Basic requirements

(a) The Parties will provide full support and co-operation to the Representative of the Secretary-General and to all the personnel assigned to assist him;

(b) The Representative of the Secretary-General and his personnel will be accorded every facility as well as prompt and effective assistance including freedom of movement and communications, accommodation, transportation and other facilities that may be necessary for the performance of their tasks: Afghanistan and Pakistan undertake to grant to the Representative and his staff all the relevant privileges and immunities provided for by the Convention on the Privileges and Immunities of the United Nations.

(c) Afghanistan and Pakistan will be responsible for the safety of the Representative of the Secretary-General and his personnel while operating in their respective countries.

(d) In performing their functions, the Representative of the Secretary-General and his staff will act with complete impartiality. The Representative of the Secretary-General and his personnel must not interfere in the internal affairs of Afghanistan and Pakistan and, in this context, cannot be used to secure advantages for any of the Parties concerned.

II. Mandate

The mandate for the implementation-assistance arrangements envisaged in paragraph 7 derives from the instruments comprising the settlement. All the staff assigned to the Representative of the Secretary-General will accordingly be carefully briefed on the relevant provisions of the instruments and on the procedures that will be used to ascertain violations thereof.

III. Modus operandi and personnel organization

The Secretary-General will appoint a senior military officer as Deputy to the Representative who will be stationed in the area, as head of two small headquarters units, one in Kabul and the other in Islamabad, each comprising five military officers, drawn from existing United Nations operations, and a small civilian auxiliary staff.

The Deputy to the Representative of the Secretary-General will act on behalf of the Representative and be in contact with the Parties through the Liaison Officer each Party will designate for this purpose.

The two headquarters units will be organized into two Inspection Teams to ascertain on the ground any violation of the instruments comprising the settlement. Whenever considered necessary by the Representative of the Secretary-General or his Deputy, up to 40 additional military officers (some 10 additional Inspection Teams) will be redeployed from existing operations within the shortest possible time (normally around 48 hours).

The nationalities of all the Officers will be determined in consultation with the Parties.

Whenever necessary the Representative of the Secretary-General, who will periodically visit the area for consultations with the Parties and to review the work of his personnel, will also assign to the area members of his own Office and other civilian personnel from the United Nations Secretariat as may be needed. His Deputy will alternate between the two Headquarters units and will remain at all times in close communication with him.

IV. Procedure

(a) Inspections conducted at the request of the Parties

(i) A complaint regarding a violation of the instrument of the settlement lodged by any of the Parties should be submitted in writing, in the English language, to the respective headquarters units and should indicate all relevant information and details.

(ii) Upon receipt of a complaint the Deputy to the Representative of the Secretary-General will immediately inform the other Party of the complaint and undertake an investigation by making on-site inspections, gathering testimony and using any other procedure which he may deem necessary for the investigation of the alleged violation. Such inspection will be conducted using headquarters staff as referred to above, unless the Deputy Representative of the Secretary-General considers that additional teams are needed. In that case, the Parties will, under the principle of freedom of movement, allow immediate access of the additional personnel to their respective territories.

(iii) Reports on investigations will be prepared in English and submitted by the Deputy Representative of the Secretary-General to the two Governments, on a confidential basis. (A third copy of the Report will be simultaneously transmitted, on a confidential basis, to the United Nations Headquarters in New York, exclusively for the information of the Secretary-General and his Representative.) In accordance with paragraph 7 a report on an investigation should be considered in a meeting of the Parties not later than 48 hours after it has been submitted. The Deputy Representative of the Secretary-General will, in the absence of the Representative, lend his good offices to the Parties and in that context he will assist in the organization of the meetings and participate in them. In the context of those meetings the Deputy Representative of the Secretary-General may submit to the Parties for their consideration and approval, suggestions and recommendations for the prompt, faithful and complete observance of the provisions of the instruments. (Such suggestions and recommendations will be, as a matter of course, consulted with, and cleared by, the Representative of the Secretary-General.)

(b) Inspections conducted on the initiative of the Deputy Representative of the Secretary-General

In addition to inspections requested by the Parties, the Deputy Representative of the Secretary-General may carry out on his own initiative and in consultation with the Representative inspections he deems appropriate for the purpose of the implementation of paragraph 7. If it is considered that the conclusions reached in an inspection justify a report to the Parties, the same procedure used in submitting reports in connection with inspections carried out at the request of the Parties will be followed.

Level of participation in meetings

As indicated above, the Deputy Representative of the Secretary-General will participate at meetings of the Parties convened for the purpose of considering reports on violations. Should the Parties decide to meet for the purpose outlined in paragraph 7 at a high political level, the Representative of the Secretary-General will personally attend such meetings.

V. Duration

The Deputy to the Representative of the Secretary-General and the other personnel will be established in the area not later than twenty days before the entry into force of the instruments. The arrangements will cease to exist two months after the completion of all time-frames envisaged for the implementation of the instruments.

VI. Financing

The cost of all facilities and services to be provided by the Parties will be borne by the respective Governments. The salaries and travel expenses of the personnel to and from the area, as well as the costs of the local personnel assigned to the headquarters units, will be defrayed by the United Nations.

Appendix 2:
Statement by Diego Cordovez, 8 April 1988

The following statement was made by Diego Cordovez when announcing that the full text of the instruments had been completed, on 8 April 1988:

I am authorized to state, at this time, that throughout the negotiations it has been consistently recognized that the objective of a comprehensive settlement implies the broadest support and immediate participation of all segments of the Afghan people and that this can best be ensured by a broad-based Afghan government. It was equally recognized that any questions relating to the government in Afghanistan are matters within the exclusive jurisdiction of Afghanistan and can only be decided by the Afghan people themselves. The hope was therefore expressed that all elements of the Afghan nation, living inside and outside Afghanistan, would respond to this historic opportunity. At this crucial stage, all concerned will therefore promote the endeavours of the Afghan people to work out arrangements for a broad-based government and will support and facilitate that process.

Source: UN Press Release SG/1860, 14 April 1988.

Appendix 3: Statements by Pakistan, the United States, and the Soviet Union, released on 14 April 1988

Statement by Pakistan

The signature ceremony today brings to a successful end the process of negotiations on the situation relating to Afghanistan which began under the sponsorship of the United Nations nearly seven years ago. I have the honour to express the deep satisfaction of the Government of Pakistan on this occasion and to convey to Your Excellency our profound appreciation on the conclusion of these Accords. You, Excellency, initiated this process of negotiations and when you assumed your high office you continued to lend it your strong and consistent support. I would also like to place on record our gratitude and admiration for the hard work, dedication, perseverance and above all the remarkable ingenuity with which your distinguished Representative, His Excellency Mr. Diego Cordovez, assisted these complex negotiations in difficult and often trying circumstances. His contribution in their positive outcome is worthy of high praise and respect. It merits special recognition.

The Geneva Accords without doubt represent a triumph for the United Nations system in upholding the principles of international law and in redressing a grave injustice. We now earnestly hope that the implementation of these Accords, in both letter and spirit, will pave the way for the re-establishment of peace and tranquillity in Afghanistan, and thus contribute to stability and cooperation in the region as well as to a safer and better global political environment.

The Accords signed today address the external aspects of the Afghanistan problem. It has long been accepted that restoration of peace and tranquillity inside Afghanistan requires the withdrawal of the foreign forces as also the establishment of a government acceptable to all segments of the Afghan population especially the Mujahideen and the refugees. Continuous efforts, therefore, will need to be made by all concerned to help the Afghans in the realization of a government which truly enjoys their confidence. Meanwhile, the Government of Pakistan in view of the realities of the situation in Af-

Source: Texts from copies of statements released to the press by the delegations of the three countries in Geneva on 14 April 1988.

ghanistan and notwithstanding the Accords signed today, will continue to adhere to its policy, based on the decision taken by the Organization of the Islamic Conference, to withhold extending recognition to the regime in Kabul.

The Government of Pakistan understands that the rights and obligations assumed by the Guarantor-States are consistent with the principles of equality and reciprocity and in consonance with the right of the Afghan people to freely determine their own political, economic and social system. The Government of Pakistan signs the Accords on the basis of the understandings reflected in exchanges between the Guarantor-States.

The Afghan people must be enabled to determine their destiny in freedom for which they have rendered monumental sacrifices. They must be helped in the urgent and gigantic task of national reconstruction and re-building a society fragmented by the protracted conflict which has spanned nearly a decade.

Statement by the United States

The United States has agreed to act as a guarantor of the political settlement of the situation relating to Afghanistan. We believe this settlement is a major step forward in restoring peace to Afghanistan, in ending the bloodshed in that unfortunate country, and in enabling millions of Afghan refugees to return to their homes.

In agreeing to act as a guarantor, the United States states the following:

(1) The troop withdrawal obligations set out in paragraphs 5 and 6 of the Instrument on Interrelationships are central to the entire settlement. Compliance with those obligations is essential to achievement of the settlement's purposes, namely, the ending of foreign intervention in Afghanistan and the restoration of the rights of the Afghan people through the exercise of self determination as called for by the United Nations Charter and the United Nations General Assembly resolutions on Afghanistan.

(2) The obligations undertaken by the guarantors are symmetrical. In this regard, the United States has advised the Soviet Union that the U.S. retains the right, consistent with its obligations as guarantor, to provide military assistance to parties in Afghanistan. Should the Soviet Union exercise restraint in providing military assistance to parties in Afghanistan, the U.S. similarly will exercise restraint.

(3) By acting as a guarantor of the settlement, the United States does not intend to imply in any respect recognition of the present regime in Kabul as the lawful Government of Afghanistan.

Statement by the Soviet Union

Noting with satisfaction the successful completion of the Geneva diplomatic process, we pay tribute to the realism and responsibility shown by all participants in it.

The agreements signed in Geneva provide a solution on the external aspects of political settlement regarding Afghanistan. The principle of noninterference is recorded in them in totally clear terms, which place specific and definite responsibilities on all the parties.

The documents that have entered into force do not permit support for political or other groups acting on the territory of one of the contracting parties against the government of another contracting party. The Soviet Union will fully comply with the obligations contained in the Geneva agreements and will fulfill its treaty obligations to Afghanistan. The Soviet side will also provide assistance in resolving the problem of refugees and in contributing to Afghanistan's economic reconstruction and development.

The Soviet side is convinced that the rights and obligations of the parties to the Geneva agreements, including the USSR and the United States as guarantors, clearly follow from the texts of those agreements. It is assuming the relevant obligations as a guarantor of the agreements. The viability of the agreements will in the final analysis depend on their strict observance by the parties themselves, namely Afghanistan and Pakistan.

We would like to single out in particular the contribution of the United Nations, of its Secretary-General, Mr. Pérez de Cuéllar, and the Secretary-General's personal representative, Mr. Diego Cordovez, in reaching the accords signed here in Geneva.

Appendix 4: Opening and Concluding Remarks by United Nations Secretary General Javier Pérez de Cuéllar at the Signing Ceremony of the Geneva Accords on Afghanistan, 14 April 1988

Opening Remarks

I wish to welcome you to the United Nations Office in Geneva for the signing ceremony of the agreements on the settlement of the situation relating to Afghanistan. May I express my appreciation to Foreign Minister Wakil of the Republic of Afghanistan and to Minister of State Noorani of the Islamic Republic of Pakistan for their tireless efforts. May I also express my appreciation to Foreign Minister Shevardnadze of the Union of Soviet Socialist Republics and Secretary of State Schultz of the United States of America for their governments' readiness to become guarantors of these agreements. I wish now to invite them to proceed with the signing of the documents.

Concluding Remarks

Excellencies,
The documents which have just been signed constitute a most significant achievement. They represent a major stride in the effort to bring peace to Afghanistan and a sure reprieve for its people. The challenge facing the people of Afghanistan is great, but it can and must be met by them alone. The agreements lay the basis for the exercise by all Afghans of their right to self-determination, a principle enshrined in the charter of the United Nations.

I am confident that the signatories of these agreements will abide fully by the letter and spirit of the texts and that they will implement them in good faith—for the sake of all the people of Afghanistan and for the wider objective of peace in the region and the world.

I have held a deep personal commitment to a peaceful solution of the situation relating to Afghanistan since the day over seven years ago when, as personal representative of my predecessor, I participated in laying the groundwork for the agreements that have been signed today. I wish, at this stage, to express my warm appreciation to my personal representative, Mr.

Source: Text from copies released to the press by the United Nations on 14 April 1988.

Diego Cordovez, for his skillful and patient endeavours as well as to the other members of the United Nations team.

The ceremony today is indeed a testimony to the capacity of the United Nations to attain positive results on the most complex of issues when backed by the political will of its Member States.

In closing, I wish to assure the people of Afghanistan that the United Nations and the international community stand ready to assist them, in this critical moment of their history, in meeting the serious humanitarian and economic needs of their country.

Appendix 5: Statement by the Government of Pakistan, 29 December 1979

Pakistan has a consistent history of defending the inalienable rights of the people of every country, big or small, to order their internal affairs in accordance with their own wishes, free from dictation or interference by any external power.

The Government of Pakistan cannot but regard the recent induction of foreign troops in Afghanistan as a serious violation of the norms of peaceful co-existence and the sacrosanct principles of the sovereignty of states and non-interference in their internal affairs as enshrined in the Charter of the United Nations.

In less than two years there have been three bloody changes of regime in Afghanistan. Pakistan's response in each case has been strictly in accordance with the above mentioned principles. The change which took place two days ago is, however, qualitatively different because of the factor of external military intervention. The Government of Pakistan, therefore, views this development with the gravest concern. Its concern is all the more profound since the country which has been subjected to military intervention is an Islamic country which is its immediate neighbour and is a member of the Islamic Conference as well as of the Non-Aligned Movement.

The people of Afghanistan are passing through a tragic period in their history and are undergoing great suffering in the process of resolving their internal problems. The induction of foreign troops with a view to determining the outcome of the current internal political crisis in Afghanistan constitutes a serious aggravation of the situation and is bound to prolong the agony of the Afghan people, with whom Pakistan is linked by indissoluble ties of history, faith and culture.

The Government of Pakistan hopes that the far-reaching negative consequences of such foreign intervention would be clearly realised and that the foreign troops would be removed from Afghan soil forthwith.

Source: *Foreign Affairs Pakistan* 7, no. 12 (December 1979), p. 19.

Appendix 6: Statement by the Government of the Democratic Republic of Afghanistan, 14 May 1980

The Afghan people, having accomplished in April 1978 the national-democratic revolution, made a final choice and embarked on the path of the creation in the country of a new society based on the principles of equality and justice, a society ruling out the exploitation of man by man. The new Afghan society is based on profound respect for, and observance of, the national, historical, cultural and religious traditions of the people along with the firm observance of the principles of Islam as the sacred religion and with freedom of religious rites guaranteed for Muslims by law.

The Afghan people would like to build a new life in conditions of peace and relations of friendship and cooperation with their neighbours, with Muslim countries and with all other states.

The people of Afghanistan are determined to defend the freedom and independence of their country and its right to decide for itself the social and economic system within the framework of which it wants to live.

Reaffirming that in accordance with the Fundamental Principles of the Democratic Republic of Afghanistan the foreign policy of the DRA is based on the principles of peaceful coexistence and active and positive non-alignment, the government of the DRA declares that it is determined to search for a political settlement to ensure the complete termination of aggressive actions against Afghanistan, of subversive activities and all other forms of interference from outside in its internal affairs, to eliminate tension in the area and overcome differences by peaceful means and through negotiations.

The programme of a political settlement could be based on the following clauses:

1. The government of the DRA proposes to the government of the Islamic Republic of Iran to hold Afghan-Iranian negotiations to work out an appropriate agreement so as to promote the development of friendly relations and all-round mutually beneficial cooperation between our two countries.

The government of the DRA also proposes to the government of Pakistan to hold Afghan-Pakistani negotiations with a view to working out bilateral

Source: DRA Ministry of Foreign Affairs, *White Book: Foreign Policy Documents of the Democratic Republic of Afghanistan*, Kabul: DRA Ministry of Foreign Affairs, 1985, pp. 67–68.

agreements on the normalisation of relations. Such agreements would contain generally acceptable principles concerning mutual respect for sovereignty, a readiness to develop relations on the basis of principles of good-neighbourliness and non-interference in the internal affairs, and would also comprise concrete obligations on the inadmissibility of armed or any other hostile activity from the territory of one country against the other.

2. The government of the DRA once again calls on the Afghans temporarily staying for various reasons on the territory of Pakistan and other neighbouring countries to return to their homeland and reaffirms that in accordance with the general amnesty announced in the Government Statement on January 1, 1980, and subsequent statements to this effect they will be respected and full freedom and immunity will be guaranteed to them; they will be able to choose freely their domicile and employment, and necessary facilities would be provided for them. The government of the DRA calls upon the Pakistani authorities and the authorities of other neighbouring countries to facilitate the free return of such persons to Afghanistan. If nevertheless some of the Afghans should not wish to return, then questions connected with this should be discussed in the course of bilateral negotiations with a view to achieving relevant accords.

3. Upon reaching mutually acceptable solutions referring to Points One and Two and normalising on this basis the relations between Afghanistan and its neighbours, the government of the DRA would be ready to consider other questions of bilateral relations including those which for a long time have remained the subject of differences.

4. Proposing to hold bilateral negotiations with neighbouring countries without any preconditions, the government of the DRA firmly proceeds from the presumption that their conduct would not be accompanied by the continuation of hostile activities against Afghanistan. Accordingly, from the very start of the process of the political settlement practical measures should be taken testifying beyond any doubt to the termination of armed and any other interference in the affairs of Afghanistan on behalf of all states involved in such interference.

5. The government of the DRA is of the opinion that apart from a package of bilateral accords between Afghanistan and Pakistan and Afghanistan and Iran, appropriate political guarantees on the part of some states which should be acceptable to Afghanistan as well as to other parties to bilateral accords should become an integral part of a political settlement. Among them, in the opinion of the DRA, the Soviet Union and the United States may be named. The essence of guarantees should be the point that the guarantor countries would themselves respect and by their authority support bilateral accords between Afghanistan and Pakistan and Afghanistan and Iran. As far as guarantees on behalf of the US are concerned, they should comprise a clearly expressed obligation not to wage any subversive activities against Afghanistan, including any from the territory of a third country.

6. The government of the DRA declares that within the context of a political settlement the question of withdrawal of the Soviet limited military contingent from Afghanistan should be resolved. The cessation and guaranteed non-recurrence of military invasions and any other forms of inter-

ference in internal affairs of Afghanistan would eliminate the reasons which prompted Afghanistan to request the USSR to send the above-mentioned contingent to its territory. In concrete terms the questions of withdrawal of Soviet troops from Afghanistan will depend on the solution of the question of effective guarantees with respect to bilateral accords between Afghanistan and Pakistan and Afghanistan and Iran.

7. The government of the DRA in the process of political settlement is in favour of taking into account the military-political activity in the region of the Indian Ocean and the Persian Gulf on the part of states not belonging to this area. Sharing the concern of other states over the buildup of the military presence of the US in the Indian Ocean and the Persian Gulf, the government of the DRA supports the proposals on turning this area into a zone of peace, on the elimination there of military bases and on taking other measures to lessen tension and strengthen security.

Putting forward these proposals concerning a political settlement, the government of the DRA once again declares that questions pertaining to the interests of Afghanistan cannot be discussed and resolved without the participation of the government of Afghanistan or bypassing it. Simultaneously the Afghan government regards as useful the efforts of other states aimed at facilitating the beginning of negotiations. In this connection it welcomes and supports the initiative displayed by the Republic of Cuba in its capacity as chairman of the non-aligned movement in offering its good services.

The government of the DRA hopes that the concrete programme of a political settlement suggested by it will meet with due understanding and a favourable response from the government of the Islamic Republic of Iran. The government of the DRA expects that its proposals for the normalisation of relations with Pakistan will be constructively and positively received by the government of Pakistan which will make it possible to begin in practice the settlement of the above-mentioned issues through negotiations.

Appendix 7: UN General Assembly Resolution 35/37 on the Situation in Afghanistan and Its Implications for International Peace and Security, 20 November 1980

The General Assembly,

Having considered the item entitled "The situation in Afghanistan and its implications for international peace and security,"

Recalling its resolution ES-6/2 of 14 January 1980 adopted at its sixth emergency special session,

Reaffirming the purposes and principles of the Charter of the United Nations and the obligation of all States to refrain in their international relations from the threat of use of force against the sovereignty, territorial and political independence of any State,

Reaffirming further the inalienable right of all peoples to determine their own form of government and to choose their own economic, political and social system free from outside intervention, subversion, coercion or constraint of any kind whatsoever,

Gravely concerned at the continuing foreign armed intervention in Afghanistan, in contravention of the above principles, and its serious implications for international peace and security,

Deeply concerned at the increasing outflow of refugees from Afghanistan,

Deeply conscious of the urgent need for a political solution of the grave situation in respect of Afghanistan,

Recognizing the importance of the continuing efforts and initiatives of the Organization of the Islamic Conference for a political solution of the situation in respect of Afghanistan:

1. *Reiterates* that the preservation of the sovereignty, territorial integrity, political independence and non-aligned character of Afghanistan is essential for a peaceful solution of the problem;

2. *Reaffirms* the right of the Afghan people to determine their own form of government and to choose their economic, political and social system free from outside intervention, subversion, coercion or constraint of any kind whatsoever;

3. *Calls for* the immediate withdrawal of the foreign troops from Afghanistan;

Source: Resolutions and Decisions adopted by the General Assembly during its thirty-fifth session, General Assembly Official Records, Thirty-Fifth Session, Supplement No. 48 (A/35/48) (New York: United Nations, 1981), pp. 17–18.

4. *Also calls upon* all parties concerned to work for the urgent achievement of a political solution and the creation of the necessary conditions which would enable the Afghan refugees to return voluntarily to their homes in safety and honour;

5. *Appeals* to all States and national and international organizations to extend humanitarian relief assistance, with a view to alleviating the hardship of the Afghan refugees, in co-ordination with the United Nations High Commissioner for Refugees;

6. *Express[es] its appreciation* of the efforts of the Secretary-General in the search for a solution to the problem and hopes that he will continue to extend assistance, including the appointment of a special representative, with a view to promoting a political solution in accordance with the provisions of the present resolution, and the exploration of securing appropriate guarantees for non-use of force, or threat of use of force, against the political independence, sovereignty, territorial integrity and security of all neighbouring States, on the basis of mutual guarantees and strict non-interference in each other's internal affairs and with full regard for the principles of the Charter of the United Nations;

7. *Requests* the Secretary-General to keep Member States and the Security Council concurrently informed of progress towards the implementation of the present resolution and to submit to Member States a report on the situation at the earliest appropriate opportunity;

8. *Decides* to include in the provisional agenda of its thirty-sixth session the item entitled "The situation in Afghanistan and its implications for international peace and security."

Notes

1. Introduction

1. UN Document, S/20472-A/44/131, 17 February 1989, Annex "Statement by the Soviet Government on 15 February 1989." See also statement by Soviet Representative A. Belonogov, Security Council provisional Verbatim Record of 2,860th meeting, s/PV.2860, 26 April 1989, pp. 32–35.

2. TASS commentary by Yuri Kornilov, 12 April 1988, Foreign Broadcast Information Service (hereinafter FBIS), *Daily Report: Soviet Union*, 13 April 1988, p. 24; *Muslim* (Islamabad), 15 April 1988, citing TASS: Eduard Shevardnadze praised the UN role at Geneva and underscored "the immense possibilities" of the United Nations in settling disputes; *Nation* (Lahore), 15 April 1988, President Mohammad Zia ul Haq praised the UN role.

3. *Frontier Post* (Peshawar), 4 April 1988 (Engineer Ahmad Shah, nominated president of the Afghan Interim Government, rejected the Accords as "unacceptable"); *Nawa-i-Waqt* (Lahore), 12 April 1988 (Gulbuddin Hekmatyar rejected the Accords). Earlier, in February 1988, Hekmatyar had called the impending accords a "sellout" (*Nation*, [Lahore], 25 February 1988).

4. Mikhail S. Gorbachev's statement of 8 February 1988, Annex to UN document S/19482-A/43/129, 9 February 1988.

5. UNSG report A/38/449-S/16005, 28 September 1983, para. 11. See also Official Record of the UN General Assembly, Fortieth Session, A/40/PV72, p. 22, statement by Soviet Representative Oleg A. Troyanovsky: "One could list several questions on which attempts are being made, with the Secretary General's participation, to reach a settlement, but it would probably be difficult to name one among them on which negotiations have made greater headway than on the question on the situation around Afghanistan." See also *Pakistan Times* (Rawalpindi), 3 April 1984, Zia ul Haq's remarks to the press: "If we compare to similar international issues, it seems gratifying that much progress has been achieved during indirect negotiations on Afghanistan."

6. UN Secretary General's report A/36/653-S/14745, 6 November 1981.

7. DRA Ministry of Foreign Affairs, Information and Archives Department, *White Book: Foreign Policy Documents of the Democratic Re-*

public of Afghanistan (Kabul: DRA Ministry of Foreign Affairs, 1985), p. 67. Also circulated as UN document A/35/238-S/13951, 19 May 1980. See Appendix 6.

2. Initial Reactions and Search for a Settlement, 1980–82

1. For discussion on reasons for the Soviet military intervention, see Thomas T. Hammond, *Red Flag over Afghanistan* (Boulder, Colo.: Westview, 1984), pp. 100–101, 132–40. See also Henry S. Bradsher, *Afghanistan and the Soviet Union* (Durham, N.C.: Duke University Press, 1983), pp. 153–62.

2. *Washington Post*, 20 March 1989; *New York Times*, 17 June 1989, 24 October 1989.

3. Bill Keller, "General Recalls Soviet Rift on War," *New York Times*, 19 March 1989. The story confirmed remarks by Yuri Gankovsky, scholar from the Institute of Oriental Studies, USSR Academy of Sciences, at a seminar organized by the Carnegie Endowment for International Peace, 6 February 1990.

4. Bradsher, *Afghanistan and the Soviet Union*, pp. 127–28, 157.

5. See ibid., pp. 115–19, for discussion on Soviet-Hafizullah Amin differences.

6. *New York Times*, 12 April 1979.

7. Bradsher, *Afghanistan and the Soviet Union*, p. 104.

8. Ibid., pp. 105–6.

9. Ibid., p. 112.

10. Ibid., p. 117.

11. Ibid.

12. Ibid., p. 122; see also Hammond, *Red Flag over Afghanistan*, pp. 87–91.

13. *New York Times*, 11 December 1980.

14. *New York Times*, 13 January 1980.

15. Zbigniew Brzezinski, *Game Plan: How to Conduct the U.S.-Soviet Contest* (New York: Atlantic Monthly, 1988), pp. 52–53.

16. Burma, a founding member of the NAM, withdrew from the movement in protest after the Havana summit. Conservative members felt that under the Cuban chairmanship, the pro-Moscow radical elements had virtually hijacked the movement.

17. The UNGA debates on the Kampuchean question invariably brought into light the Pol Pot regime's record on human rights violations.

18. UN Document S/PV2190, para. 93.

19. UN Document S/13724, Add. 1 and 2.

20. UN Documents S/PV2185, S/PV2186, 5 January 1980. Also see Official Record of the General Assembly, Sixth Emergency Special Session, Plenary Meetings, vol. 3, p. 34: Indian Representative B. C. Mishra told the General Assembly that "the Soviet Government has assured our Government that its troops went to Afghanistan at the request of the Afghan Government, a request that was first made by President Amin on 26 December 1979." The Soviet and Afghan public statements remained ambiguous on the precise dates for the "invitation."

21. *Foreign Affairs Pakistan* (Islamabad: Ministry of Foreign Affairs) 6, no. 12 (December 1979), p. 19.

22. Sponsors of UN Document A/ES-6/L.1 Add. 1. of 14 January 1980, included Bahrain, Bangladesh, Colombia, Costa Rica, Egypt, Fiji, Gambia, Honduras, Indonesia, Malaysia, Niger, Oman, Pakistan, Panama, Papua New Guinea, Philippines, Samoa, Saudi Arabia, Senegal, Singapore, Somalia, Thailand, Tunisia, and Uruguay (the number of sponsors increased in subsequent years). The sponsorship of the earlier resolution S/13729 in the Security Council was restricted to Third World members of the council. See also Agha Shahi, *Pakistan's Security and Foreign Policy* (Lahore: Progressive Publishers, 1988), pp. 19–20, highlighting Pakistan's concern that Afghanistan not be treated as an East-West issue.

23. Rules of Procedure of the UN General Assembly (1985), Rule 8 (b).

24. UN Security Council Document S/13731, 9 January 1980, sponsored by Mexico and the Philippines.

25. The Fifth Emergency Special Session was convened in June 1967 to discuss the situation in the Middle East.

26. Official Record of the General Assembly, Sixth Emergency Special Session, Plenary Meetings, vol. 3, p. 34.

27. Resolution ES-6/2, 14 January 1980.

28. UN Document A/37/563, and Add. 1. At the 45th meeting of the UN General Assembly, Thirty-Seventh Session, on 26 October 1982, a procedural move by Finland on behalf of Nordic countries blocked the Iranian move.

29. In 1974 Prime Minister Zulfikar Ali Bhutto had resorted to the OIC to manoeuvre Pakistan's recognition of Bangladesh, which at that time was a highly emotional issue in Pakistan.

30. The Saudis were first to initiate moves for an Islamic Conference, according to the *Washington Post*, 5 January 1980.

31. Resolution 1/EOS, *OIC Declarations and Resolutions of Heads of State and Ministers of Foreign Affairs Conferences 1389–1400 H, 1969–1981* (Jeddah: OIC Secretariat Publication), p. 533.

32. Differences among Islamic countries were reported by the *New York Times*, 23 January 1980. See also Record of the UN General Assembly, Sixth Emergency Special Session, vol. 7, for the statement by the PLO representative which, instead of commenting on the Afghan situation, expressed concern that the United States might use the discussion (on Afghanistan) at the United Nations to serve its own aims. The radical Arab states feared that Afghanistan could detract attention from the Palestine issue.

33. *OIC Declarations and Resolutions, 1969–1981*, p. 594. Resolution 19/11-P of the Eleventh Islamic Conference of Foreign Ministers, held in May 1980 in Islamabad, softened the hard-line approach of Resolution 1/EOS.

34. The attempt to project Islamic identity was evident in the explanation offered by the OIC secretary general at the conclusion of the January 1980 Extraordinary Session of the Islamic Conference of Foreign Ministers, that even though condemnation of the Soviet Union seemed to favour the

policy of the other superpower (the United States), it emanated rather from the objective of upholding the Charter of the Islamic Conference. At the same session, Zia ul Haq also called for a collective defense arrangement to ward off future invasions of Islamic nations.

35. For voting records, see Official Records of the UN General Assembly, Sixth Emergency Special Session, Plenary Meetings, vol. 7, para. 173.

36. See UN Document A/36/116, and Corr. 1: letter dated 2 March 1981, from the representative of India to the secretary general transmitting documents of the Conference of the Ministers of Foreign Affairs of Non-Aligned Countries held at New Delhi 9–13 February 1981. As a final position, the Indian delegation had presented a formulation that called for "a political settlement, withdrawal of foreign troops, full respect for the independence, sovereignty, territorial integrity and non-aligned status of Afghanistan, and strict observance of the principle of non-intervention and non-interference." Following a long internal discussion, the Pakistan delegation decided to reject the formulation and asked for the crucial addition of the words "on the basis of" to link the settlement with the subsequent three elements. The Pakistan delegation feared that without this phrase, the text could be interpreted to Pakistan's disadvantage, creating a distinction between political settlement and what Pakistan recognized as its constituent elements.

37. Bradsher, *Afghanistan and the Soviet Union*, p. 191.

38. White House Briefing for Members of Congress, 8 January 1980, *Public Papers of the Presidents of the United States, Jimmy Carter, 1980–81*, vol. 1 (Washington, D.C.: U.S. Government Printing Office, 1981), p. 40.

39. Bradsher, *Afghanistan and the Soviet Union*, pp. 98–100, on the death of U.S. Ambassador Adolf Dubs.

40. The Brezhnev Doctrine was apparently extended to Afghanistan. Soviet General Aleksei A. Yepishev, in a signed article in *Pravda*, warned that the security of "Marxist nations" like Afghanistan would be defended by the Soviet Union and other Warsaw Pact countries (*New York Times*, 12 April 1980).

41. White House Briefing, 8 January 1980, *Public Papers of the Presidents . . . Jimmy Carter, 1980–81*, vol 1, p. 40.

42. State of the Union Message of 23 January 1980, ibid., p. 197.

43. Ibid., p. 198.

44. In April 1981 Ronald Reagan lifted the grain embargo (*New York Times*, 25 April 1981).

45. Bradsher, *Afghanistan and the Soviet Union*, p. 196.

46. Former U.S. Under Secretary of State David D. Newsom affirmed this view at a seminar organized by the Carnegie Endowment for International Peace on 9 June 1989, noting that the Soviet intervention had put pressure on the Carter administration to make a demonstrably strident response.

47. *Washington Post*, 3 January 1980; *New York Times*, 9, 20 February 1980.

48. *New York Times*, 16 January 1980.

49. *New York Times*, 12 February, 1 April 1980. See also U.S. State Department, *Soviet Invasion of Afghanistan*, Special Report No. 70, 1980; and Bradsher, *Afghanistan and the Soviet Union*, p. 202.

50. Following the September 1965 war between India and Pakistan, the United States had decided to impose an embargo on arms sales to both countries. The embargo was relaxed for Pakistan in respect to "nonlethal" arms and supply of spare parts for a brief period during 1976–78.

51. *New York Times*, 16 January 1980.

52. Ibid.

53. *Washington Post*, 31 December 1979. Zbigniew Brzezinski stated that the United States would stand by Pakistan.

54. During a visit to New Delhi on 30–31 January 1980, Clark Clifford, a special envoy of President Carter, suggested that while the invasion of Pakistan by the Soviet Union would be a "very serious matter," it would not attract the Carter Doctrine and require the United States to commit itself to Pakistan in a war against the Soviet Union.

55. *New York Times*, 18 January 1980.

56. Commenting that Islamabad had still not heard what Washington was planning, Zia ul Haq said that "others [meaning the United States] should make a pragmatic assessment of what Pakistan required" (*Muslim* [Islamabad] 16 January 1980).

57. Agreement on the assistance package was reached on 15 September 1981 during the visit to Islamabad of Peter McPherson, administrator of the U.S. Agency for International Development, and James Buckley, U.S. under secretary of state.

58. *New York Times*, 20 February 1980.

59. *New York Times*, 22 February, 25 June 1980. On 24 June 1980, arriving in Belgrade, Carter endorsed the idea of guaranteed neutrality of Afghanistan and also spoke of U.S. willingness to explore a "transitional arrangement" to be implemented with the withdrawal of Soviet troops for a peaceful settlement in Afghanistan. On 25 June 1980 TASS commentator Yuri Kornilov dismissed Carter's offer as "deliberately vague" (FBIS, *Daily Report: Soviet Union*, 27 June 1980, A1).

60. *New York Times*, 1 March 1980.

61. Commentator Vitaly Kobysh, *Literaturnaya Gazeta* (Moscow), cited in *New York Times*, 12 March 1980. Soon after, Kabul also rejected the EC proposal. See also *Muslim* (Islamabad), 2 April 1980.

62. *Keesing's Contemporary Archives*, 23 October 1981, p. 31142.

63. *New York Times*, 7 July 1981. TASS commentary, 6 July 1981 (FBIS, *Daily Report: Soviet Union*, 7 July 1981, G1), described the EC proposal as a plan to divert attention from "the undeclared war" against Afghanistan. See also the Afghan position in UN Document A/36/672, 13 November 1981.

64. Kuldip Nayar, *Report on Afghanistan* (New Delhi: Allied Publishers, 1981), p. 73.

65. Ibid., p. 74; see also *New York Times*, 8 February 1980: Zia ul Haq suggested to Ram Sathe the raising of a peacekeeping force with Indian, Pakistani, and Iranian participation to facilitate Soviet withdrawal. According to Kuldip Nayar, Babrak Karmal dismissed the proposal, describing Zia as a "lackey of American and Zionist forces."

66. *Muslim* (Islamabad), 16 April 1980; Zia ul Haq was less forthcoming with Sardar Swaran Singh, who was sent to Islamabad as Prime Minister

Indira Gandhi's special envoy to push for tripartite talks between India, Pakistan, and Afghanistan.

67. Nayar, *Report on Afghanistan*, p. 77; *New York Times*, 15 February 1980.

68. Briefing given to the Pakistani ambassador in New Delhi by Indian Foreign Secretary Ram Sathe. See also *Morning News* (Karachi), 8 June 1980.

69. *Pakistan Times* (Rawalpindi), 6 May 1980.

70. TASS, 10 December 1980 (FBIS, *Daily Report: Soviet Union*, 11 December 1980, D7).

71. Brezhnev's report to the Twenty-Sixth CPSU Congress, 23 February 1981 (FBIS, *Daily Report: Soviet Union*, 24 February 1981, SUP 20).

72. *Pravda*, 23 February 1980 (FBIS, *Daily Report: Soviet Union*, 25 February 1980, R6).

73. *Pakistan Times* (Rawalpindi), 23, 24, 26 February, 4, 26 May 1980, reported violent rallies and protests in Kabul alone.

74. UN Document A/35/238-S/13951, 19 May 1980. See Appendix 6.

75. TASS, cited by *New York Times*, 22 June 1980, announced that the Soviet Union was withdrawing some troops from Afghanistan. The gesture was dismissed by most observers as meaningless and, in effect, necessitated by the Soviet military requirement to replace tank units that could not operate in the mountainous Afghan terrain.

76. The Durand Line is the international boundary agreed upon by British India and Afghanistan under the treaties of 1893 and 1921 and inherited by Pakistan as the successor state to British India in 1947. Afghanistan does not recognize the Durand Line as constituting its international boundary with Pakistan. The Helmand River, one of the inland rivers of Afghanistan, disappears in lakes and marshes in the southwestern corner of the country along its border with Iran. The dispute over the Helmand Waters had been a constant irritant in Iranian-Afghan relations until its settlement in 1972. Because Babrak Karmal had opposed the settlement at the time, revival of this issue became a possibility when he was installed in Kabul following the Soviet military intervention in December 1979.

77. In February 1980 Gromyko conveyed a stern warning to Pakistan saying that Pakistan did not know what it was doing. In the Pakistani psyche the circumstances of the Pakistan-India conflict of 1971 are generally perceived as a consequence of collusion between India and the Soviet Union. Subsequently, Soviet officials had stated that, if required, Moscow would again act in the same fashion as in 1971. See remarks by Sajjad Hyder at an International Conference on Afghan Alternatives held at Monterey Institute of International Studies in November 1983, cited in Ralph H. Magnus, ed., *Afghan Alternatives: Issues, Options, and Policies* (New Brunswick, N.J.: Transaction Books, 1985), pp. 123–24.

78. Resolution 19/11-P, *OIC Declarations and Resolutions, 1969–1981* (full citation in n. 31 above), p. 594.

79. Abdul Rab Rasul Sayyaf was elected as mujahideen spokesman in March 1980.

80. To match moves on Afghanistan, radical Arab states called for an Emergency Special Session of the UN General Assembly in July 1980 and an

OIC Extraordinary Ministerial Meeting, also in July 1980, to discuss the Palestinian issue.

81. "The Situation in Afghanistan and Its Implications for International Peace and Security," introduced as item 116 on the agenda of the Thirty-Fifth Session of the UN General Assembly, 1980.

82. The United Nations has figured in some of the major foreign policy issues and crises that confronted Pakistan since its inception. The 1948 war with India over Kashmir led to a UN-organized cease-fire and Security Council resolution, which continue to be the pillars of the Pakistani position on the issue. Pakistan is host to the oldest active UN Observer Group, UNMOGIP. Again, both in the 1965 and the 1971 wars with India, cease-fires were arranged through UN Security Council resolutions. In the post-1971 situation, Pakistan had effectively bargained in the UN General Assembly for the repatriation of Pakistani POWs in return for the admission of Bangladesh into the United Nations.

83. TASS, 10 December 1980 (FBIS, *Daily Report: Soviet Union*, 11 December 1980, D7).

84. UN Committee on the Exercise of the Inalienable Rights of the Palestinian People; Special Committee against Apartheid.

85. Appendix 7 of this volume contains the text of UNGA Resolution 35/37.

86. *Foreign Affairs Pakistan* 7, no. 11–12 (November–December 1980), pp. 27–28.

87. *Pakistan Times* (Rawalpindi), 6 January 1981, reported that Anahita Ratebzad, a PDPA Politburo member, indicated Afghanistan's readiness to talk to Pakistan and Iran under UN auspices.

88. The terms "Afghan mujahideen" and "Afghan Resistance" have been used interchangeably and refer to the amorphous political forces opposed both to the Soviet military presence in Afghanistan and to the PDPA, whom they regard as a "communist party."

89. The Iranian position was clearly opposed to talks with Kabul. Large demonstrations were held in front of Soviet and Afghan embassies in Tehran on the first anniversary of the Soviet intervention (*Washington Post*, 31 December 1980).

90. *OIC Declarations and Resolutions, 1969–1981*, pp. 750–51.

91. *Foreign Affairs Pakistan* 8, no. 1–2 (January–February 1981), p. 48.

92. *Muslim* (Islamabad), 12 February 1981.

93. Statement of the Government of the Democratic Republic of Afghanistan on the So-Called Afghan Refugee Problem, UN Document A/35/154, 26 March 1980.

94. Ibid. The theme that Pakistan was obstructing the return of the refugees has since been maintained.

95. See DRA Ministry of Foreign Affairs, *White Book: Foreign Policy Documents of the Democratic Republic of Afghanistan* (Kabul, 1985), p. 68; also circulated as UN Document A/36/457-S/14649, 27 August 1981.

96. *Jang* (Rawalpindi), 23 June 1980.

97. Agha Shahi's statement at the Foreign Correspondents' Club, Hong Kong, 29 December 1980, in *Foreign Affairs Pakistan* 7, no. 11–12 (November–December 1980), pp. 36–38.

98. Agha Shahi, *Pakistan's Security and Foreign Policy*, pp. 202–3. Agha Shahi mentions that when U.S. Ambassador Arthur Hummel first unveiled the Reagan administration's offer of the $3.2 billion, he hinted at a quid pro quo that Pakistan would be expected to show understanding of U.S. policies and interest in the Middle East. Such soundings over fundamental aspects of Pakistan's foreign policy only served to heighten the sensitivity of the Pakistani side to suggestions of strings attached to the package.

99. Ibid., pp. 217, 177–78; and joint U.S.-Pakistan press statement issued on 13 June 1981. According to Agha Shahi, military bases were neither requested by the United States nor offered by Pakistan.

100. Agha Shahi, *Pakistan's Security and Foreign Policy*, p. 218. Ghulam Ishaq Khan, then finance minster, supported Agha Shahi's view.

101. Ibid.

102. See UN Document S/PV2489, 26 October 1982, pp. 86–87.

103. See *Washington Post*, 18 April 1981. Some observers attribute these differences to Agha Shahi's push for a UN mediating role. However, by early 1982 the UN role had been firmly established, and there is little evidence of differences between Agha Shahi and Zia ul Haq on specific positions taken up during the Pérez de Cuéllar shuttles to the area.

Later, in a conversation with the author, Agha Shahi commented on the circumstances of his resignation, which he said was motivated by his impression that Zia ul Haq was willing to compromise Pakistan's nonaligned status for a military relationship with the United States. He recalled that he had negotiated the $3.2 billion package in Washington in April 1981 on the basis of an explicit understanding that Pakistan's nonalignment would be respected. However, when U.S. Under Secretary of State James Buckley came to Islamabad in June 1981, Zia made an impromptu offer of military bases, which the Americans did not take. Agha Shahi also suspected that the Americans had established a direct channel with Zia, especially on the issue of arms supplies to the mujahideen. Agha Shahi denied that he opposed Pakistan's supplying arms to the mujahideen; his concern was that the Americans would use Pakistani territory to supply arms *directly* to the mujahideen.

104. The offer of a nonaggression pact to India was announced simultaneously with the U.S.-Pakistani aid package agreement on 15 September 1981.

3. Internal Developments: The PDPA and the Afghan Resistance, 1980–86

1. For example, *Pravda*, "Afghan 'Basmachis' visit Washington seeking missiles" (FBIS, *Daily Report: Soviet Union*, 26 February 1981, p. A1). The Soviet diplomats referred to the Basmachi analogy to underscore Soviet patience and preparedness to deal with a protracted conflict in Afghanistan.

2. Many analysts view the overthrow of Mohammad Daoud Khan's republic in April 1978 as a military coup d'état, not a revolution. The term "Saur Revolution" has been adopted for the purposes of the present study merely because it is the description used by the successive PDPA govern-

ments. Its use here does not imply support for the obvious political view implicit in the term. See the commentary by Bradsher in *Afghanistan and the Soviet Union*, pp. 76–81.

3. Ibid., p. 121.

4. This may well be the reason Moscow could not engineer a coup to dislodge Hafizullah Amin.

5. *New York Times*, 15 February 1980.

6. Ibid., 2, 27 February, 30 May 1980.

7. Louis Dupree, *Red Flag over the Hindu Kush* (Hanover, N.H.: American Universities Field Staff Reports, Asia, no. 23, 1980), chapter 3. See also Bradsher, *Afghanistan and the Soviet Union* pp. 91–96.

8. *Jang* (Rawalpindi), 22 January 1980. By the end of January 1980 the all-red flag of Afghanistan adopted after the Saur Revolution was replaced by the original tricoloured flag with a new emblem.

9. Hammond, *Red Flag over Afghanistan*, p. 150.

10. Karmal's address to the Conference of National and Patriotic Forces of the DRA, 27 December 1980, Bakhtar News Bulletin, Kabul 1, no. 52 (28 December 1980). See also comment by Yuri Kornilov in TASS, 1244 GMT, 31 December 1980.

11. *Kabul New Times*, 13 June 1981.

12. Ibid. See also *New York Times*, 21 July 1980, on Karmal's measures to strengthen the presidency.

13. *Kabul New Times*, 13 June 1981.

14. Ibid., 16 June 1981.

15. Ibid.

16. For example, the *Mudafaen-e-Inqilab* (Defenders of the Revolution), *Quwa-e-Sarhadi* (Border Security Force), and *Sazman-e-Democratic-e-Jawanan* (DOAY, Democratic Organization of Youth of Afghanistan).

17. There were unconfirmed reports of contacts with Abdul Sattar Shalizai and Dr. Samad Hamed, former deputy prime ministers, and Dr. Mohammed Yusuf, former prime minister of Afghanistan under the exiled king, Mohammad Zahir Shah. A new decree for rehabilitation of returnees was proclaimed in June 1981 (*Kabul New Times*, 20 June 1981).

18. The Soviets sought to dispel such rumours. In December 1980 the Pakistani ambassador was told in Moscow that Pakistan should entertain no illusions that the Karmal government could be removed. *New York Times*, 20 October 1980, reported puzzlement among Western diplomats as to the brevity of talks with Soviet officials during Karmal's three-week visit.

19. *Kabul New Times*, 17 June 1981. See also *Izvestia* commentary describing NFF as a "mass political organisation" (FBIS, *Daily Report: Soviet Union*, 26 June 1981, D1–2).

20. *National Fatherland Front of the DRA: Documents and Materials of the Founding Congress . . . 15 June 1981* (Kabul, 1981), p. 95.

21. Bakhtar News Bulletin, Kabul 1, no. 99 (10 June 1981). In the Statute of the National Fatherland Front, the PDPA was described as the "guiding force" of the NFF and "the whole of Afghan society" (*NFF of the DRA: Documents . . . 15 June 1981*, p. 93). See *Kabul New Times*, 16, 17 June 1981, for Karmal's address and "Fundamental Statement of the NFF."

22. BBC Report, 21 February 1982, in *Daily Foreign Broadcast Monitoring Report* (Islamabad: Ministry of Information and Broadcasting), 22 February 1982.

23. BBC Report, 29 March 1982, in ibid., 30 March 1982.

24. Khad (or KhAD) is the acronym for *Khedamat-i Etelaát-i Dawlati*, that is, State Information Agency, the DRA secret police set up in 1980. Khad was raised to the level of a ministry in January 1986 with a new acronym, WAD, *Wizarat-i Amaniat-i Dawlati*, that is, Ministry of State Security.

25. For several months after the holding of the NFF Conference, *Kabul New Times* regularly reported "support" from the masses for the NFF.

26. Hammond, *Red Flag over Afghanistan*, p. 152.

27. *Kabul New Times*, 22 April 1981.

28. The required courses on Marxism-Leninism at Kabul University were eliminated in late 1988 (*New York Times*, 6, 7 December 1988). See also A. Rasul Amin, "The Sovietization of Afghanistan," in Rosanne Klass, ed., *Afghanistan: The Great Game Revisited* (New York: Freedom House, 1987), pp. 319–22.

29. *Muslim* (Islamabad), 7 January 1988, citing Soviet sources, stated that during 1978–86 Afghanistan's exports to capitalist countries were reduced by more than 50 percent (from $96 million to $43 million), and its imports of industrial goods decreased by several times (United States, from $15 million to $5 million; Britain, $22 million to $9 million; and the FRG, $47 million to $17 million). Its exports to socialist countries increased 3.5 times (from $122 million to $435 million), and corresponding imports by 5.5 times ($112 million to $607 million).

30. M. Siddiq Noorzoy, "Soviet Economic Interests and Policies in Afghanistan," and John F. Shroder, Jr., and Abdul Tawab Assifi, "Afghan Resources and Soviet Exploitation," in Klass, ed., *Afghanistan: The Great Game Revisited*, pp. 89, 113 (for exports of natural gas to the Soviet Union).

31. Shroder and Assifi, "Afghan Resources and Soviet Exploitation," pp. 117, 120.

32. Burhanuddin Rabbani, leader of the Jamiat-e-Islami Afghanistan and a Tajik, had often expressed concern over the possibility of a Soviet scheme to bifurcate Afghanistan.

33. *Kabul New Times*, 30 May 1981.

34. Amin, "The Sovietization of Afghanistan," pp. 328–29 ("Manipulating the Tribes").

35. *New York Times*, 15 February 1984.

36. Karmal address to command personnel, *Kabul New Times*, 14 January 1984. See also TASS, 15 January 1984 (FBIS, *Daily Report: Soviet Union*, 16 January 1984, D1).

37. *Kabul New Times*, 4, 5 March 1984.

38. Yossef Bodansky, "Soviet Military Involvement in Afghanistan," in Klass, ed., *Afghanistan: The Great Game Revisited*, p. 261.

39. The Kurram Agency is Pakistan's tribal area adjoining Afghanistan's Nangarhar and Paktia provinces.

40. In January 1985 Babrak Karmal claimed the membership to be 120,000, with 32,000 having joined in 1983 (*Kabul New Times*, 13 January

1985). In April 1985 the number was estimated at 130,000 (*Pravda*, in FBIS, *Daily Report: Soviet Union*, 3 April 1985, D2).

41. *Kabul New Times*, 4, 5 March 1984.

42. Ibid., 28 April 1984.

43. Ibid., 15 May 1984.

44. The Loya Jirga (or, Great National Assembly of Notables), a traditional, extraordinary institution invoked from time to time by the Afghan kings to obtain endorsement of their decisions and policies or to legitimize their authority, was first convened in 1709 at a village near Qandahar to decide upon action against Gargin Garji, political representative of the Safavi rulers of Iran. That action led to the first national rule of Afghan tribes in Qandahar. The second Loya Jirga, held in 1747 in Qandahar, "elected" Ahmad Shah Abdali as king of Afghanistan. Since then there have been many Loya Jirgas. The last one prior to the Saur Revolution of 1978 was convened by President Sardar Mohammad Daoud Khan in January 1977 to seek endorsement of the new constitution that established a presidential one-party system.

45. TASS (FBIS, *Daily Report: Soviet Union*, 16 April 1985, D3).

46. Karmal's opening and closing addresses to the Loya Jirga, *Kabul New Times*, 24, 27 April 1985.

47. Ibid.

48. Ibid., 15 September 1985.

49. At a press conference in Kabul, Karmal firmly rejected any role for "history-stricken" persons such as Zahir Shah, the exiled king, or Abdur Rahman Puzhwak, an eminent Afghan diplomat elected president of the UN General Assembly in 1966 (*Kabul New Times*, 13 October 1985).

50. Ibid., 10 November 1985; see also TASS (FBIS, *Daily Report: Soviet Union*, 12 November 1985, D1–3).

51. *Washington Post*, 20 March 1989.

52. *Pravda*, 22 December 1985 (FBIS, *Daily Report: Soviet Union*, 24 December 1985, D1).

53. *Kabul New Times*, 6 January 1986.

54. Ibid., 14 January 1986.

55. Ibid., 29 January 1986.

56. *Washington Post*, 20 March 1989.

57. Olivier Roy, *Islam and Resistance in Afghanistan* (Cambridge: Cambridge University Press, 1986), p. 103. Pir Sayed Ahmad Gailani, chief of the Peshawar-based National Islamic Front of Afghanistan, had stayed in Afghanistan for nearly one year after the Saur Revolution.

58. Ibid., p. 107.

59. Ibid., p. 71.

60. Hekmatyar and Rabbani had been associated with Kabul University.

61. Bradsher, *Afghanistan and the Soviet Union*, pp. 101–3.

62. Roy, *Islam and Resistance in Afghanistan*, p. 141.

63. Ibid., pp. 102–21.

64. Ibid., p. 121.

65. *Muslim* (Islamabad), 25 January 1980; *Imroz* (Lahore), 25 January

1980. Salem Azzam, secretary general of the Council of Europe's Committee for the Liberation of Muslims, played an active role in bringing the parties together.

66. Iran-based Afghan parties had come to Islamabad in May 1980 to attend the OIC Foreign Ministers meeting and to explore the possibility of setting up a united front of the Afghan Resistance.

67. Sardar Shahnawaz, the secretary general of the Pakistan Foreign Office, had played an active role in securing recognition and support for the moderate leaders, because his personal knowledge of the notable Afghan families was respected by President Zia. According to Shahnawaz, President Zia in mid-1979 came to his house (to avoid publicity) to meet five Tanzeemat leaders for the first time.

68. The Pakistan Foreign Office was sensitive on the issue of an Afghan government-in-exile. In February 1980, reacting to news media reports, a Foreign Office spokesman "categorically rejected" rumours of a possible Pakistani move to set up such a government (*Foreign Affairs Pakistan* 7, no. 2 [February 1980], p. 24).

69. Two splinter groups from Harakat-e-Inqilabi Afghanistan were led by Maulavi Nasrullah and Raffiullah Wardek, and a splinter from Mojadeddi's party by Maulavi Mohammed Amir.

70. Also see *New York Times*, 23 August 1983.

71. *Pakistan Times* (Rawalpindi), 2 August 1987.

72. Roy, *Islam and Resistance in Afghanistan*, pp. 143–44.

73. By early 1982 over forty Afghan groups were active in Peshawar and Quetta.

74. The *New York Times*, 28 November 1984, reported the first big jump in U.S. covert assistance to the mujahideen.

75. Gerard Viratelle, news analysis, *Le Monde*, 1 December 1982.

76. *New York Times*, 29 November 1985.

77. See Roy, *Islam and Resistance in Afghanistan*, p. 122, for a discussion on the limits Pakistan had placed over the quantity and quality of weapons supplied to the mujahideen.

78. Ibid., p. 209. According to Olivier Roy, until 1983 Pakistan's policy was based on (1) maintaining control over the supply of weapons to the resistance and keeping it within a limit that did not risk provoking a violent Soviet reaction; (2) working to prevent the emergence of an Afghan government-in-exile, thus encouraging the continued fragmentation of the resistance; and (3) retaining the political initiative.

79. Bradsher, *Afghanistan and the Soviet Union*, pp. 176–77.

80. *New York Times*, 11, 23 January, 15 February 1980.

81. See Zalmay Khalilzad, "Soviet-Occupied Afghanistan," *Problems of Communism* 29 (November–December 1980), pp. 23, 32; *New York Times*, 23 January, 3, 12 March 1980; and Drew Middleton, military analysis, *New York Times*, 10 July 1980.

82. *New York Times*, 8 March 1980.

83. Ibid., 10 July 1980.

84. Bernard E. Trainor, "Afghanistan and the Soviet Psyche: Military Myths Fade as the Troops Pull Out," analysis, *New York Times*, 15 February 1989; and Drew Middleton, analysis, ibid., 3 July 1982.

85. U.S. Department of State, *Soviet Dilemma in Afghanistan*, Special Report No. 72 (Washington, D.C.), June 1980. Hammond, *Red Flag over Afghanistan*, p. 160, discusses disintegration of the Afghan army.

86. *New York Times*, 23 September 1981, quotes Egyptian President Anwar Sadat.

87. Organized covert operations had begun in early 1980, but the scale remained limited. See Hammond, *Red Flag over Afghanistan*, pp. 157–58. According to figures given by Leslie Gelb in a report in the *New York Times*, 28 November 1984, until the end of 1984 the United States had allocated $345 million, of which nearly $140 million were allocated for fiscal 1984, leaving a total amount of nearly $200 million spread over four years from 1980 to 1983. Reports of such figures vary, however. For example, on 28 July 1984, the *New York Times* reported that the House Appropriations Committee had approved $50 million in covert aid for fiscal 1984.

88. *New York Times*, 2 May 1984.

89. Ibid., 20 June 1983, 2 March 1989. According to some estimates up to 30 million mines have been planted by Soviet troops, posing a major problem to safe resettlement.

90. Alexander Alexiev, *Inside the Soviet Army in Afghanistan* (Santa Monica, Calif.: Rand Corporation, May 1988), pp. 20–34; and Yossef Bobansky, "Soviet Military Involvement in Afghanistan," in Klass, ed., *Afghanistan: The Great Game Revisited*, pp. 255–59. Estimates vary about total Soviet troop deployment. According to UN Document S/20465 of 15 February 1989 on Implementation of the Accords on the Settlement relating to Afghanistan, the total number of Soviet troops withdrawn stood at 100,283.

91. Drew Middleton, military analysis, *New York Times*, 25 December 1982. See also ibid., 23 January 1983.

92. *Wall Street Journal*, 18 June 1984, Review and Outlook. Claude Malhuret of Médecins Sans Frontières reports that if guerillas move among a population, in Mao Tse-tung's words "like fish in water," the Soviet response is to "boil the ocean." Also see Drew Middleton, *New York Times*, 15 July 1984; and *New York Times*, 17 December 1984.

93. International Security and Development Cooperation Act of 1985 (PL 99-83), 8 August 1985.

94. See *New York Times*, 3 January, 26 April, 11 May, 1, 15 June, 27 July, 17 August, 26 October 1983, 5, 11, 16 January, 8 February, 25 July 1984.

95. Ibid., 25 May 1983.

96. Ibid., 25, 30 April, 2 May 1984, report Kabul's control of the valley.

97. Ibid., 12 September 1984.

98. U.S. Information Agency (hereinafter USIA), *Afghanistan Chronology 1978–1985* (Washington, D.C., November 1985), June 1984, p. 10.

99. Ibid.

100. Ibid., August 1984, p. 10.

101. Ibid., September 1984, p. 11.

102. *Economist*, London, 4 March 1985, accused the Soviet troops of pursuing a "scorched earth policy" in Afghanistan.

103. *New York Times*, 24 May 1984, cites *Jane's Defense Weekly* on the

use of "liquid fire" bombs by Soviet troops. The British humanitarian organization Afghan Aid, cited by the *New York Times*, 6 June 1984, charged that 500,000 Afghans were facing starvation because of the war and drought. The same figure was confirmed later by French and Belgian medical and humanitarian organizations.

104. *New York Times*, 23 August 1984 reported a total of 104 people killed in air raids and cross-border artillery shelling.

105. Drew Middleton, military analysis, *New York Times*, 4 December 1983, underscores the shortage of supplies to the mujahideen. See also *New York Times*, 24 July 1984, on the plea for more supplies by Dr. Shah Runh Gran.

106. Leslie Gelb, *New York Times*, 28 November 1984.

107. Selig S. Harrison, "Inside the Afghan Talks," *Foreign Policy* 72 (Fall 1988), p. 50. These estimates vary; for example, the *Washington Post* reported an allocation of $250 million for fiscal 1985, while the same paper on 1 November 1985 put an estimate of U.S. covert assistance during 1980–85 at $342 million. The total U.S. covert assistance by 1988 is generally assessed at $2 billion (see report by Robert Pean, *New York Times*, 18 April 1988). The *New York Times*, 8 June 1989, quoted Soviet Prime Minister Nikolai Ryzhkov disclosing that the Soviet war effort in Afghanistan cost Moscow an equivalent of $70 billion.

108. Zia ul Haq told Lally Weymouth (*Washington Post*, 24 January 1988) that "the Chinese support is as important as the U.S. support." A Bakhtar Information Agency (Kabul) statement of 12 March 1985 put the estimate of Chinese assistance over five years from 1980 at $400 million. According to the *Washington Post*, 20 June 1986, by 1986 Saudi support had totaled $500 million.

109. USIA, *Afghanistan Chronology 1978–1985*, July 1985, p. 14; and *New York Times*, 12 July 1985.

110. Robert Pean reported (*New York Times*, 18 April 1988) that the first Stinger was used in Afghanistan on 26 September 1986. The mujahideen reportedly shot down 207 Soviet aircraft using Stingers.

111. Bakhtar Information Agency first reported the supply of Chinese-made ground-to-air missiles to the mujahideen in early 1985 (17 February 1985). The first Kabul protest against the use of U.S.-made SAMs (surface-to-air missiles) was registered in September 1985 (*New York Times*, 8 September 1985).

112. USIA, *Afghanistan Chronology 1987*, 24 April, p. 15.

113. Najibullah's interview with Rahimullah Yusufzai, *Muslim* (Islamabad), 16 December 1987.

114. For example, reports by Eduard Girardet and Jere Van Dyk following their travels inside Afghanistan in late 1981. See comment by Hammond in *Red Flag over Afghanistan*, pp. 164–65.

115. These briefings were attributed to Western diplomats in New Delhi and Islamabad.

116. Zalmay Khalilzad, a Columbia University scholar known to be sympathetic to the Afghan Resistance, admitted that the Soviets were gaining ground in Afghanistan (*New York Times*, 9 April 1984). Selig Harrison

dismissed the Western image of the Soviets getting bogged down in Afghanistan as "wishful thinking" ("Moscow Builds Loyal Kabul Machine," *Washington Post*, 13 May 1984).

117. "Will America Let Pakistan Settle the Afghan Question?" *Muslim* (Islamabad), 1 January 1987.

4. The Geneva Negotiations, 1982–86

1. DRA Ministry of Foreign Affairs, *White Book: Foreign Policy Documents of the Democratic Republic of Afghanistan*, p. 30.

2. The conditions had to be clearly spelt out rather than left to be sifted from the six documents earlier provided by the Kabul side (compare chapter 2, p. 46).

3. Nomadic tribes, known as Powindas, inhabiting areas close to Pakistan's border were permitted to spend the winter in Pakistan along with their herds of sheep and camels. This practice was discontinued after 1961, ostensibly at the recommendation of the Pakistan Agricultural Commission. The number of these nomads seasonally entering Pakistan was estimated at 200,000–300,000.

4. "Chapeau" is a somewhat technical term used for an opening paragraph that is more than a heading and that indicates the contents of an agreement.

5. UNGA Resolution No. 36/103, 9 December 1981.

6. See para. 3, "Agreement on the Interrelationships for the Settlement of the Situation Relating to Afghanistan," in Appendix 1. Originally these principles included respect for sovereignty, independence, and territorial integrity of states; nonintervention and nonuse of force in international relations; the inalienable right of "states" to freely determine their own sociopolitical and economic systems; cooperation among states with diverse sociopolitical economic systems; and commitment to the UN Charter.

7. See chapter 2, pp. 49–50.

8. The Pakistani side's argument was made to suggest the desirability of firm assurances of a Soviet commitment to withdrawal and to underscore the need for a broad-based government that could induce the mujahideen to accept a cease-fire.

9. *New York Times*, 14 November 1982.

10. Official Record of the UN General Assembly, Thirty-Seventh Session, 13th meeting, 1 October 1982, paras. 126–27. In his meeting with Yaqub Khan, the first since the latter took charge as foreign minister, Andrei Gromyko combined a demand for cessation of interference with the familiar inducement of peaceful boundaries and fruitful cooperation. Gromyko also maintained that withdrawal was a matter exclusively within the bilateral domain of Moscow-Kabul relations.

11. Ted Morello, *Far Eastern Economic Review* (Hong Kong), 9 June 1983, p. 30.

12. *Pakistan Times* (Ralwalpindi), 22 February 1982. The first UN group to investigate use of chemical weapons in Afghanistan arrived in Pakistan on 9 February 1982. Also see *Washington Post*, 9 September 1982.

13. *New York Times*, 8 September 1982.

14. Ibid., 7 December 1982. Prior to the ascent to power of Yuri Andropov in November 1982, the Soviet statements at the United Nations hedged on the UN mediation. The first reference to the UN mediation in the main Soviet statements at the UN General Assembly under the customary agenda item "General Debate" was made only on 4 October 1983 by Oleg A. Troyanovsky.

15. *Pravda*, 15 December 1982 (FBIS, *Daily Report: Soviet Union*, 16 December 1982, D1–4).

16. These leaks falsified Pakistan's position on noninterference. Some of the resistance leaders often privately wondered why the United States could not provide assistance discreetly, as China did.

17. U.S. Permanent Representative Jeane Kirkpatrick obliged formalistically by adding an expression of "appreciation" and "support" of the secretary general's efforts for a settlement and urging the Soviets "to cooperate with them." (Record of the General Assembly, Thirty-Seventh Session, 78th meeting, A/37/PV78, p. 1302.)

18. This assessment was borne out by comments offered by the former U.S. ambassador to Pakistan, Ronald Spiers, made at a seminar organized by the Carnegie Endowment on 9 June 1989, in which he recalled that most of his exchanges with Pakistani officials in Islamabad during 1982–83 related to the U.S. aid package.

19. In referring to the Zia ul Haq-Andropov meeting, TASS avoided the standard criticism of the Pakistani position and simply stated that the "question around Afghanistan was touched upon on a principled plane" (FBIS, *Daily Report: Soviet Union*, 16 November 1982, D1).

20. *Muslim* (Islamabad), 27 April 1983. Yaqub Khan counted the meeting among positive indications from Moscow.

21. *New York Times*, 21 November 1982.

22. Ibid., 10 December 1982.

23. *Komsomolskaya Pravda*, cited by *Morning News* (Karachi), 18 February 1983. Also, *Izvestia*, 24 February 1983, reported on the harsh realities of the Afghan situation. A *Pravda* editorial of 16 December 1982, however, had offered no indication of flexibility in the Soviet position.

24. In an elaborate interview to the *Muslim* (Islamabad), published 4 February 1983, Cordovez was circumspect about the negotiations, describing them as "a continuing and very long and complex process."

25. *New York Times*, 30 March 1983.

26. UN Document A/37/1, 7 September 1982.

27. See Harrison, "Inside the Afghan Talks," p. 42.

28. *New York Times*, 12 April 1983.

29. Ibid., 29 March 1983.

30. The September 1979 NAM summit at Havana had set up a contact group headed by Guyana to pilot the idea of a declaration on "Inadmissibility of Intervention and Interference in the Internal Affairs of States" at the United Nations. During the 1980 UNGA session, the group put forward a draft for endorsement by the Non-Aligned Coordinating Bureau meeting in New York. Imbibing radical concerns, the draft dwelt extensively on listing the

so-called "interference aspects" to be outlawed by the declaration and treated "intervention aspects" superficially. The long debate in the Non-Aligned Coordinating Bureau created the notion of "intervention" as inferring such actions as the Soviet military move into Afghanistan, military occupation, or invasion, while "interference" came to connote clandestine activities, of which Pakistan was being accused by Moscow and Kabul. The protracted debates and attempts to strike a balance produced an unwieldy and loose draft, which was finally put up by the NAM countries in 1981 for the consideration of the First Committee of the UN General Assembly, dealing with security and disarmament issues. The group of Western countries opposed the draft both on substance and on the technical grounds that the subject belonged appropriately to the committee dealing with legal matters.

31. See in Appendix 1, Article II, para. 12, Bilateral Agreement between the Republic of Afghanistan and the Islamic Republic of Pakistan on the Principles of Mutual Relations, in Particular on Non-Interference and Non-Intervention.

32. An oft-cited comment from Zia ul Haq that he could not shake hands with the man who had come in riding Soviet tanks created the impression that Pakistan could recognize Kabul if Karmal were removed. (See *Foreign Affairs Pakistan* 7, no. 3 [March 1980], p. 19.) Formally, Pakistan's nonrecognition of the Karmal government was based on the OIC decision of January 1980 and linked to the presence of Soviet troops in Afghanistan.

33. In April 1982 Soviet Deputy Foreign Minister Mikhail Kapitsa told the Pakistani ambassador in Moscow that socialism would survive in Afghanistan whether it took five years or fifty years, and the Karmal regime would stay in Kabul whether Pakistan liked it or not.

34. Zia ul Haq thought that the Afghans could reach a settlement through a Loya Jirga following Soviet troop withdrawal (*Far Eastern Economic Review*, 9 June 1983, p. 27).

35. Harrison, "Inside the Afghan Talks," p. 45.

36. *Pakistan Times* (Ralwapindi), 12 May 1983. Privately Cordovez conceded that this remark was inopportune.

37. *Muslim* (Islamabad), 27 April 1983.

38. The visit to Moscow was intended to be first, but the dates did not suit the Soviets.

39. *New York Times*, 27 May 1983.

40. Ibid., 4 May 1983.

41. This interpretation was intriguing because "leaks" in the U.S. media are attributed to the growing power of the media and its access to information rather than to an inclination on the part of the U.S. administration to use the media to convey signals.

42. *Pakistan Times* (Rawalpindi), 17 June 1983.

43. Bradsher, *Afghanistan and the Soviet Union*, pp. 103–4.

44. *New York Times*, 16 June 1983.

45. *Far Eastern Economic Review*, 9 June 1983, pp. 26–27.

46. Cordovez denied such an approach in an interview with John Dornton (*New York Times*, 25 June 1983).

47. This theme first appeared in Soviet statements. See, for example,

New York Times, 24 April 1983, quoting Andropov, and 30 May 1983, quoting Soviet Ambassador Vitaly S. Smirnov.

48. A senior UN official associated with the Geneva negotiations later expressed a similar opinion that Andropov's paralysis had led to the reassertion of hard-liner influence and a setback to the emerging prospects for a settlement. According to this official, there was little hope for progress as long as Andrei Gromyko retained control of Soviet external policy.

49. UN Document No. A/38/449-S/16005, 23 September 1983.

50. FBIS, *Daily Report: Near East and South Asia,* 21 August 1984, p. 61.

51. This language was introduced at the insistence of Pakistan and corresponded to Pakistan's concept of simultaneity of all actions to be taken under the settlement.

52. The year 1984 had witnessed an increase in Afghan-Soviet bombings of Pakistani border areas, apparently in an effort to interdict supply routes used by the Afghan mujahideen. This development had raised some fears in Pakistan about possible Soviet recourse to "hot pursuit."

53. FBIS, *Daily Report: Near East and South Asia,* 21 August 1984, p. 61.

54. *Pakistan Times* (Rawalpindi), 6 March, 25, 29 April 1984; *Muslim* (Islamabad), 25 May 1984; and *New York Times,* 10 April, 24, 25 July 1984. Reports told of large Soviet offensives against Panjshir, Shomali, Logar, Qandahar, and Herat, conditions of famine in Afghanistan, and a mujahideen appeal for better arms.

55. *Pakistan Times* (Rawalpindi), 21 January, 14 November 1984.

56. *New York Times,* 20, 21, 23 August 1984. In view of increasing violations, Pakistan raised the possibility of acquiring Airborne Warning and Control Systems (ibid., 12 October 1984).

57. Ibid., 28 November 1984: $280 million earmarked in fiscal 1985 in covert military assistance to the Afghan mujahideen.

58. On 8 and 17 April 1985, Gorbachev proposed a moratorium on further deployment and testing of nuclear weapons (FBIS, *Daily Report: Soviet Union,* 18 April 1985, AA2, D1–2).

59. On 23 April 1985 three new members were added to the Soviet Politburo (ibid., 23 April 1985, R19). On 11 June 1985 Gorbachev made a major speech urging broad new economic programmes (ibid., 12 June 1985, R1–19).

60. The first Reagan-Gorbachev summit was announced on 2 July 1985. The Western view of Gorbachev was encapsulated by British Prime Minister Margaret Thatcher's widely noted remark that he was a man "we can do business with."

61. TASS (FBIS, *Daily Report: Soviet Union,* 15 March 1985, D1). According to the *Pakistan Times* (Rawalpindi), 10 April 1985, Zia ul Haq publicly described the meeting as "correct and matter of fact," found Gorbachev to be a "very pleasant man," and hoped he would bring some personal aspect of his character into Soviet policy.

62. *New York Times,* 29 May 1985.

63. Ibid., 19 May 1985.

64. UN Document A/40/705-S/17527, 7 October 1985, para. 9.

65. The Pakistan International Airlines had opened a new Islamabad-London route with a technical stopover in Moscow.

66. Full text in Appendix 1.

67. *New York Times*, 14 December 1985.

68. Ibid., 11 February 1988.

69. See UN Document A/40/705-S/17527, 7 October 1985, paras. 10, 11.

70. To make the proposal attractive to the Afghan side, Cordovez suggested a written Pakistani commitment to sign the instruments on noninterference and refugees with the DRA.

71. *Dawn* (Karachi), 22 October 1985. Zia ul Haq denied criticism that the government's position on direct talks was adopted at the "behest of the United States."

72. *Foreign Affairs Pakistan* 12, no. 11–12 (November–December 1985), p. 40.

73. Ibid., pp. 63–64.

74. Statement by the Afghan representative, Farid Zarif, UN Document A/40/PV71, p. 47; and Pakistani responses, UN Document A/40/PV73, p. 121. The Afghan charge was repeated by Soviet Deputy Foreign Minister Mikhail Kapitsa in an interview with Mushahid Hussain (*Muslim* [Islamabad], 11 October 1985).

75. UN Document A/40/PV73, p. 121.

76. To prove that the Soviets doubted the credibility of Pakistan's commitment, Cordovez alluded to a note, supposedly prepared by neutral UN officials, listing a whole range of activities that Pakistan was required to stop prior to the date of enforcement of the settlement, such as disarming resistance groups inside Pakistan, disposing of stores, and listing of confiscated weapons.

77. *Pravda*, 26 February 1986 (FBIS, *Daily Report: Soviet Union*, 26 February 1986, p. O/31).

78. See para. 2, in Appendix 1, Agreement on the Interrelationships for the Settlement of the Situation Relating to Afghanistan.

79. Karmal's press conference, *Kabul New Times*, 13 October 1985. Also see DRA Ministry of Foreign Affairs, *White Book: Foreign Policy Documents of the Democratic Republic of Afghanistan*, p. 30.

80. *Kabul New Times*, 31 March 1986.

81. Ibid., 5 May 1986.

82. *New York Times*, 1 January 1986.

83. *Jang* (Rawalpindi), 2 January 1986; M. B. Naqvi, "Pressures on Pakistan," *Dawn* (Karachi), 8 January 1986; and *Muslim* (Islamabad), 17 January 1986, quoting Afghan representative Farid Zarif that a "clearly defined" time frame had been decided.

84. Cordovez would endorse Yaqub Khan's view, saying that "UN committee room–style drafting" had no place in real negotiations.

85. The *Muslim* (Islamabad), 19 March 1986, had quoted Cordovez as suggesting that Kabul had provided a time frame. Also see the report in the *Washington Post*, 2 April 1986, that Kabul had offered a time frame that Pakistan had rejected.

86. Earlier, in March 1986, when Kabul had offered the four-year time frame, Cordovez had asked Pakistan to keep the figure confidential in order to preserve the credibility of the negotiations. Nonetheless, speculation on the time frame persisted after the May Geneva round. *Jang* (Rawalpindi), 4 July 1986, quoting the BBC, reported that the Afghans had tabled an eighteen-month time frame. Faced with questions on the issue, Junejo revealed the Afghan position of a four-year time frame and also stated Pakistan's position of three to four months based on logistical considerations (*New York Times*, 18 July 1986).

87. Deputy Foreign Minister Georgi Korniyenko no longer dealt with the Afghan issue.

88. Gorbachev's speech in Vladivostok, press bulletin of the Permanent Mission of the Soviet Union to the United Nations in Geneva, No. 298 (1184), 30 July 1986, pp. 17–18. See also a different English translation of the passage in FBIS, *Daily Report: Soviet Union*, 29 July 1986, R19.

89. Section I of the draft comprehensive settlement had first used the word "phased," which was subsequently replaced by "gradual."

90. Within the Pakistani side, reservations about the idea of strong UN monitoring stemmed from the consideration that monitoring of noninterference appeared to be a continual affair, while the troop withdrawal, according to the draft texts, required confirmation only at two stages. Furthermore, once Soviet withdrawal had started, its reversal made little military sense. Yet, weighing pros and cons, Pakistan favoured a "meaningful" monitoring arrangement that reinforced assurances of Soviet withdrawal, but opposed bilateral consultations to address allegations of "nonimplementation" that in its view necessitated a UN role.

91. Cordovez was convinced that Moscow would not agree to convey any information on withdrawal to the United Nations. He elucidated his view at the August 1986 round by giving an example. He pointed out that one day before Gorbachev announced on 28 July 1986 that six Soviet regiments would be withdrawn, the Soviets had conveyed this information to Islamabad, but did not consider it appropriate to convey it to the UN secretary general.

92. Circumventing Security Council approval generated some argument between the International Organization Affairs Bureau (IO) and the Near East and South Asian Affairs Bureau (NEA) at the U.S. State Department at the time of the last Geneva round in March–April 1988. Using, somewhat incorrectly, the argument that Pakistan did not desire a Security Council debate, NEA prevailed.

UNGOMAP was set up as a result of the UN secretary general's letters of 14 April 1988 (S/19834) and 22 April 1988 (S/19835) and the provisional agreement to the proposals in the letters, "pending formal consideration and decision by the Council later," conveyed by the president of the Security Council in his letter of 26 April 1988 (S/19836). The formal Security Council resolution was adopted on 31 October 1988, Resolution 622 (1988).

93. After the signing of the Accords, Cordovez decided to deploy the maximum number allowed under the agreement, along with a large auxiliary civilian staff.

94. This was also the Iranian position. See the statement of the Iranian government issued on 13 April 1988 (UN Document S.19763), which stated that "since the very beginning, [Iran] has considered the Geneva indirect talks unacceptable because the Afghan Mujahids who are practically involved in the matter have been ignored." Also see editorial comments in the *Muslim* (Islamabad), 15 April 1983, criticizing the Peshawar-based Afghan groups for routinely opposing the Geneva indirect talks.

95. In early 1983, when prospects of a settlement appeared somewhat promising, Pakistan had publicly identified consultation with the refugees as among the issues of its direct concern (*Muslim* [Islamabad], 4 February 1983; and *Pakistan Times* [Rawalpindi], 12 April 1983).

96. Until 1986 Cordovez had scrupulously avoided direct contacts with any of the Peshawar-based leaders. However, a member of his team, Giandomenico Picco, had confidentially met them once on the occasion of the OIC Foreign Ministers Conference at Niamey, Niger, in August 1982.

97. See Appendix 1, Bilateral Agreement between the Republic of Afghanistan and the Islamic Republic of Pakistan on the Voluntary Return of Refugees, preambular para. 3.

98. *New York Times*, 7 November 1986.

99. Statement by Jallaluddin Haqqani, *Nation* (Lahore), 9 January 1987.

100. During mid-1986 the Soviet press had underscored concern over "interference" in Afghan affairs from Iran. See *Izvestia*, 13 May 1986 (FBIS, *Daily Report: Soviet Union*, 15 May 1986, D4); and TASS and *Novosti* reports, cited by *Dawn* (Karachi), 14 May 1986, accusing Tehran of adopting an "aggressive position" and of receiving "counterrevolutionary Afghan rebels."

5. A Changing External Environment, 1985–86

1. According to the stereotyped view, the Soviets/Russians have never reversed their military advances, as seen in the oft-cited quote from Amir Abdur Rahman (1844–1901): "[The Russians'] habit of forward movement resembles the habit of the elephant, who examines a spot thoroughly before he places his foot upon it, and when once he puts his weight down there is no going back, and no taking another step in a hurry until he has put his full weight on the first foot and smashed everything that lies under it."

2. For example, Anatoly Dobrynin, longtime Soviet ambassador to Washington, became a principal adviser to Gorbachev on foreign policy.

3. Strobe Talbot, *Deadly Gambits: The Reagan Administration and the Stalemate in Nuclear Arms Control*, (New York: Vintage, 1985), pp. 47, 193.

4. See, for example, ibid., pp. 308, 309.

5. Xinhua (FBIS, *Daily Report: China*, 6 August 1986, A1–2).

6. UN special rapporteur Felix Ermacora reported that military operations in Afghanistan had intensified (*New York Times*, 21 November 1986). See also ibid., 7, 28 April 1986.

7. These DRA and Soviet statements routinely accused Pakistan, the United States, and others of interference in Afghanistan, dwelt on the achievement of the Saur Revolution, and invoked Kabul's 14 May 1980 and 24 August 1981 proposals as the basis for a settlement.

8. The year 1987 witnessed a specially organized campaign by Kabul and Moscow to weaken international support for the Pakistani-sponsored resolution at the UN General Assembly. To win support for Najibullah's national reconciliation programme, Kabul sent special envoys to nearly seventy countries.

9. Xinhua, 18 December 1986, quotes Igor Ligachev, CPSU Politburo member, on Sino-Soviet relations (FBIS, *Daily Report: China*, 18 December 1986, C2).

10. The matter came to a head in mid-1987 when negotiations on a second six-year package of $4.02 billion were initially snarled up by reported charges against a Pakistani-born Canadian businessman, Arshad Parvaiz, for purchasing contraband steel for shipment to Pakistan.

11. These efforts on the part of Zia ul Haq sometimes led to speculation or charges that Pakistan was willing to concede military bases to the United States or that it had accepted a role as part of the U.S. idea of a Middle East strategic consensus. Occasional visits to Pakistan by General George B. Crist, commander of the U.S. Central Command, and his customary calls each time on Zia ul Haq added to such speculation.

12. Bradsher, *Afghanistan and the Soviet Union*, p. 198.

13. See remarks by Senator Gordon Humphrey (R-N.H.), *New York Times*, 1 December 1986.

14. On behalf of the Congressional Task Force on Afghanistan, Senator Humphrey and Congressman Kemp addressed a letter to Secretary Shultz, dated 12 January 1987, which referred to a report in the *New York Times* of 13 December 1986 and a comment by Shultz made on 7 January 1987. In response to a question about what the State Department considered "an acceptable short timetable for withdrawal," Shultz had replied, "They can't be in there for a year or more in a withdrawal process and have it be a kind of meaningful thing." Shultz's reply to Kemp was sent on 17 January 1987.

15. By the end of 1986, nearly 12,000 personnel, mostly locals, were employed by the Afghan Refugee Commissionarate, an agency of the Pakistan government, and international humanitarian organizations.

16. According to Pakistan's official statements made at the United Nations, the Afghan refugees numbered 400,000 in January 1980, 1.2 million in November 1980, 2.5 million in November 1981, nearing 3 million in November 1982, and 3 million in November 1983. The figure of 3 million has been cited since late 1983.

17. Comment on intensified terrorist activity inside Pakistan, in *Muslim* (Islamabad), 20 March 1987.

18. For a report on sectarian clashes involving Turi and Mangal tribes in the Kurram Agency, see *Nation* (Lahore), 29 July 1987.

19. At the behest of Khair Bux Marri, chief of the Baluch Marri tribe, who had been living in Kabul for many years, a few thousand Marri tribesmen migrated into Afghanistan in late 1986. They were gathered in Lashkargah, west of Qandahar, with the reported purpose of receiving training to carry out a revolt inside Pakistan. This did not materialize and, within a few months, they trickled back to Pakistan.

20. In July 1987 a powerful bomb blast in a crowded bazaar in Karachi

killed 72 persons and injured more than 250. In Lahore, during the same month, an explosion caused 9 deaths and 45 injured.

21. Success was minimal: as against 644 air violations recorded during 1987 when the air cap was in operation, the F-16s were able to hit only three Afghan aircraft on two separate occasions.

22. *New York Times*, 7 May 1987.

23. See ibid., 25 November 1984.

24. The Soviet warning aroused suspicions in Pakistan of a possible Soviet strike against the Pakistani nuclear facility at Kahuta and prompted Pakistan to approach its close allies in the West, the Islamic world, and China.

25. Gorbachev's interview by Indian journalists, FBIS, *Daily Report: Soviet Union*, 24 November 1986, D1–10; and *Muslim* (Islamabad), 4 December 1986.

26. *Times* (London), 3 January 1987.

27. Taking advantage of an invitation to a cricket match in Jaipur between Pakistani and Indian teams, Zia ul Haq visited India in February 1987. The real purpose of his visit was to defuse tension caused by the Brass Tacks exercise.

28. FBIS, *Daily Report: Soviet Union*, 29 April 1985, D1–2.

29. Ibid., 16 October 1985, R1–13.

30. "Najibullah Sheds Light on Soviet Pullout," interview by *Pravda* correspondent B. Pyadshev, *Current Digest of the Soviet Press* 41, no. 50 (1989), pp. 16–17.

31. *Pravda*, 22 December 1985 (FBIS, *Daily Report: Soviet Union*, 24 December 1985, D1). See also *Muslim* (Islamabad), 22 December 1985.

32. *Pravda*, 15 December 1982 (FBIS, *Daily Report: Soviet Union*, 16 December 1982, D1–4). Since 1985 Soviet media have not qualified the Saur Revolution in such terms.

33. FBIS, *Daily Report: Soviet Union*, 26 February 1986, D31.

34. TASS, 11 February 1986 (FBIS, *Daily Report: Soviet Union*, 12 February 1986, CC5).

35. Karmal's speech at the 27th CPSU Congress, *Kabul New Times*, 1 March 1986.

36. Ibid., 28 April 1986.

37. Speech of Gorbachev in Vladivostok, FBIS, *Daily Report: Soviet Union*, 29 July 1986, R1–20. Also press bulletin issued by Permanent Mission of the Soviet Union, Geneva, No. 298(1184), 30 July 1986, pp. 17–18.

38. FBIS, *Daily Report: Soviet Union*, 20 October 1986, D1–4.

39. Discussion on 15 November 1986, Record of Dartmouth Conference, Task Force on Regional Conflict Prevention and Settlement, circulated by Charles F. Kettering Foundation.

40. *Pakistan Times* (Rawalpindi), 24 November 1986.

41. *Muslim* (Islamabad), 4 December 1986.

42. Ibid.

43. Abdul Sattar and Yuli Vorontsov had known each other from the early 1980s, when both served as ambassadors of their respective countries in New Delhi.

44. FBIS, *Daily Report: Soviet Union*, 25 November 1986, R1–2.

45. Don Oberdorfer, "A Diplomatic Solution to Stalemate," *Washington Post*, 17 April 1988.

46. *Kabul New Times*, 13 December 1986.

47. Ibid., 28 September 1986.

48. Ibid., 14 July 1986.

49. *Muslim* (Islamabad), 22 July 1986. The six condemned mujahideen commanders were Ahmed Shah Massoud (Panjshir), Mohammad Panah (Panjshir), Saleh Mohammed, alias Mullah Malang (Qandahar), Turan Mohammad Ismael (Herat), Maulavi Jallaluddin Haqqani (Paktia), and Sayyad Badshah (Baghlan). (A decree of pardon was issued in January 1988.)

50. TASS, 11 July 1986 (FBIS, *Daily Report: Soviet Union*, 17 July 1986, D1).

51. *Kabul New Times*, 28 September 1986.

52. Ibid., 23 November, 1986: Najibullah's address to the Twentieth PDPA Central Committee Plenum.

53. Ibid., 2 December 1986.

54. Ibid., 24 September 1986.

55. Ibid., 3 January 1987: Najibullah's address to the Special Plenum of the PDPA Central Committee on 30 December 1986.

56. For example, the reported defection of a former "resistance commander," Esmatullah Muslim, had little to do with the efforts of the National Compromise Commission. He had come to Pakistan in 1981 and in 1985 had returned to Afghanistan, resentful of the seven parties and the absence of recognition by the Pakistani authorities. Being influential with the Achakzai tribe, Esmatullah operated an independent militia near the Qandahar-Chaman area until late 1987, when he reportedly fell out with Najibullah.

57. *New York Times*, 24 November 1986.

6. Politics of Withdrawal and National Reconciliation: The Second Track, 1987

1. *Kabul New Times*, 3 January 1987; see also UN Document A/42/83-S/18564 of 7 January 1987, Annex Declaration on National Reconciliation: Najibullah's address to the Special Plenum of the PDPA Central Committee (30–31 December 1986). One version reported "monarchists" instead of "opportunists."

2. Ibid.

3. *Kabul New Times*, 4 January 1987.

4. *Frontier Post* (Peshawar), 9 January 1987.

5. Ibid.

6. First reports of success of the national reconciliation initiative started appearing immediately after Najibullah's announcement. Western diplomats charged that Kabul was "fabricating" accounts. See *Kabul New Times*, 18, 21, 25 January 1987; 1, 2, 23, 25 February 1987.

7. Ibid., 11 January 1987.

8. *Muslim* (Islamabad), 6 January 1987.

9. Report of press conference on 19 January 1987, *Kabul New Times*, 20 January 1987.

10. Shahabuddin Kushkaki, analysis, *Muslim* (Islamabad), 11 January, 1987.

11. USIA, *Afghanistan Chronology 1987*, entry for 1 January. Burhanuddin Rabbani, Nabi Mohammedi, and Gulbuddin Hekmatyar called the reconciliation offer a "sham" and a "deception" (*New York Times*, 3 January 1987).

12. *Kabul New Times*, 3 January 1987.

13. Ibid.

14. TASS, 6 January 1987 (teleprinter copy).

15. *New York Times*, 3 January 1987.

16. *Nation* (Lahore), 9 January 1987.

17. It was rumoured that Najibullah had sent separate messages to the three moderate leaders in the Afghan Alliance offering to each the ministry of "higher education."

18. *Muslim* (Islamabad), 18 January 1987.

19. Ahmed Rashid, analysis, *Nation* (Lahore), 15 January 1987.

20. Statements by Pakistan Foreign Office spokesman in *Frontier Post* (Peshawar), 8 January 1987; and *Nation* (Lahore), 16 January 1987. See also the statement by Yaqub Khan to the *Khalij Times* (Kuwait), 11 January 1987, that Kabul's offer would be meaningful only if accompanied by the withdrawal of Soviet troops. Asked to comment, Pakistan Minister of State for Foreign Affairs Zain Noorani emphasized time frame as the only remaining issue before reaching a "compromise settlement" (*Pakistan Times* [Rawalpindi], 14 January 1987).

21. *Muslim* (Islamabad), 18 January 1987.

22. On 2 January 1987 Phyllis Oakley, State Department deputy spokesperson, stated that rejection of Najibullah's initiative by the mujahideen was not "surprising." In response to a question, the Pakistan Foreign Office spokesman said the U.S. government spokesperson had only quoted the Afghan mujahideen remarks (*Frontier Post* [Peshawar], 8 January 1987).

23. The USIA chronology quotes Herbert Hagerty, a regional director in the Bureau of Near Eastern and South Asian Affairs.

24. *Muslim* (Islamabad), 25 January 1987.

25. OIC Resolution No. 11/5-P (IS), on the situation in Afghanistan, adopted by the Fifth Islamic Summit Conference, Kuwait, 26–29 January 1987, para. 16.

26. A meeting with Yunis Khalis could not be arranged because he did not understand either Urdu or English.

27. Following the Matni incident in May 1985 (involving an explosion that caused the death of Soviet captives reportedly imprisoned by Rabbani's group near Peshawar), Pakistan had given a commitment to the Soviet embassy in Islamabad that any Soviet soldiers found on Pakistani territory would be handed over to the embassy. This commitment created difficulties in handling cases where Soviet prisoners with the resistance wanted to be extradited to the West. See Note of Protest by the DRA Ministry of Foreign Affairs to the Government of Pakistan, dated 10 May 1985, DRA Ministry

of Foreign Affairs, *White Book: Foreign Policy Documents of the Democratic Republic of Afghanistan*, p. 127.

28. *Muslim* (Islamabad), 4 December 1986.

29. Daoud was referred to as Sardar Daoud to indicate his noble rank as a prince.

30. Bernard Gwertzman cites State Department officials as saying the United States was pressing Pakistan not to agree to "something like 18 months to two years" (*New York Times*, 15 January 1987).

31. Yaqub Khan subsequently qualified these remarks to say that Zia ul Haq did not mean a time frame up to one year, but Cordovez would not agree, saying that "he had heard what the president had said."

32. *Pravda*, 22 February 1987.

33. Cordovez's press conference on 25 February 1987, *Frontier Post* (Peshawar), 26 February 1987. Quoting an unidentified high-ranking UN official, the *New York Times* of 10 December 1986 had reported that time frame was the only remaining issue. Also, the BBC reported on 24 February 1987 that a time frame of less than 15 months would be offered by Kabul (*Jang* [Rawalpindi], 25 February 1987). Earlier the *Pakistan Times* (Rawalpindi), 10 January 1987, had reported that the Afghan permanent representative to the United Nations, Farid Zarif, said that Kabul would give a "short time frame."

34. The *Nation* (Lahore), 7 March 1987, reported Zia ul Haq's advice to the Pakistani negotiators to continue on at Geneva.

35. *New York Times* 21 May 1987. See also Najibullah's explanation of Gorbachev's remarks to reassure PDPA members, in Bakhtar news agencies (FBIS, *Daily Report: Near East and South Asia*, 16 July 1987, p. 3).

36. The Islamic fundamentalist parties within the Afghan Alliance, as well as many mujahideen groups operating inside Afghanistan, preferred the nomenclature "shura" for representative assemblies instead of the traditional Afghan concept of "jirga" for such assemblies. This bias was reinforced as pro-Zahir Shah elements proposed from time to time the convening of a Loya Jirga to secure a role for the former Afghan king.

37. *Muslim* (Islamabad), 11 May 1987.

38. Rabbani's interview with Maleeha Lodhi, ibid., 20 May 1987.

39. There was considerable speculation in the press about the return of Zahir Shah. See Selig Harrison, *New York Times*, 20 May 1980; Gailani's interview, *Muslim* (Islamabad), 17 May 1987; and *Muslim* (Islamabad), 28 May 1987, citing Yaqub Khan's interview with the *Washington Times*. The speculation was spurred by Zahir Shah's interview on the BBC stating his readiness to return (*Muslim* [Islamabad], 14 May 1987), and by Gorbachev's interview in *L'Unità* (*New York Times*, 21 May 1987), suggesting that the Soviet Union would accept Zahir Shah as part of a coalition.

40. *Pakistan Times* (Rawalpindi), 10 May 1987. Yunis Khalis was re-elected as *raes* for another eighteen months in November 1987, but resigned in March 1988.

41. FBIS, *Daily Report: Soviet Union*, 16 June 1987, E5; ibid., 3 August 1987, E3.

42. In an interview with TASS, 11 June 1987, Major General Imamuddin,

chief of the Operations Division of the DRA Armed Forces, called the provinces of Qandahar, Paktia, and Kunar the "hottest spots."

43. See TASS, 19 April 1987, reporting a mujahideen incursion into Tajikistan and Uzbekistan. See also USIA, *Afghanistan Chronology 1987*, April 8.

44. Text of Najibullah's report to the PDPA Central Committee Plenum, *Kabul New Times*, 15 June 1987.

45. FBIS, *Daily Report: Near East and South Asia*, 5 June 1987, K1.

46. *Muslim* (Islamabad), 6 May 1987.

47. *Nation* (Lahore), 24 July 1987.

48. *Kabul New Times*, 26 April 1987.

49. Ibid., 30 June 1987.

50. Najibullah's Press Conference, FBIS, *Daily Report: Near East and South Asia*, 8 July 1987, P8. In late November when Najibullah partly abandoned the national reconciliation programme, he admitted in a press conference on 30 November 1987 that the programme had not been a success in attracting significant numbers of refugees. Najibullah blamed obstructions created by Pakistan and Iran for the disappointing result (*Kabul New Times*, 1 December 1987).

51. Abdul Ahad Arzbegi of Kunduz, Haji Amin of Nangarhar, Brigadier General Abdul Qayyun Siddiq in Qandahar, and the chairman of Andarab district in Baghlan were all killed in national reconciliation-related activities.

52. *Kabul New Times*, 13 May 1987. See also TASS, 12 May 1987 (FBIS, *Daily Report: Soviet Union*, 20 May 1987, D2–3).

53. *Kabul New Times*, 13 May 1987.

54. *Muslim* (Islamabad), 20 May 1987.

55. Basic Report to the Plenum of the PDPA Central Committee, 10 June 1987, *Kabul New Times*, 13, 15 June 1987. Also see *Nation* (Lahore), 29 June 1987; *Frontier Post* (Peshawar), 9 July 1987; and FBIS, *Daily Report: Near East and South Asia*, 18 June 1987, E1–5.

56. Basic Report to the Plenum of the PDPA Central Committee, 10 June 1987.

57. *Kabul New Times*, 30 June 1987. See also FBIS, *Daily Report: Near East and South Asia*, 2 July 1987, pp. 1–8., and 8 July 1987, p. 11.

58. *Kabul New Times*, 13 June 1987.

59. USIA, *Afghanistan Chronology 1987*, 19 July, 9 August.

60. Ibid., 1 June, 7, 17 July; *Nation* (Lahore), 13 August 1987. See also U.S. Department of State, Bureau of Public Affairs, *Afghanistan: Eight Years of Soviet Occupation*, Special Report No. 173, December 1987, pp. 4–6.

61. *Kabul New Times*, 16 July 1987.

62. Ibid.

63. Ibid. See also ibid., 30 June 1987; and FBIS, *Daily Report: Soviet Union*, 17 July 1987, E3–4.

64. *Kabul New Times*, 16 July 1987.

65. *Kabul New Times*, 15 July 1987.

66. *Washington Post*, 17 April 1988.

67. Transcript of the interview conducted on 21 July 1987, provided by

the Soviet embassy in Islamabad; also circulated as a UN document on 2 August 1987.

68. The Reykjavik summit in October 1986 had galvanized arms control talks, leading to intense negotiations in Geneva, Moscow, and Washington to finalize the INF agreement.

69. *New York Times*, 21 March 1987.

70. Ibid., 11 December 1987.

71. In a sting operation on 14 July 1987, a Pakistani-born Canadian national, Arshad Parvaiz, was caught in an attempt to export to Pakistan a restricted alloy, maraging steel.

72. *Nation* (Lahore), 26 July 1987.

73. *Muslim* (Islamabad), 4 June 1987.

74. Ibid., 24 February 1987.

75. *Nation* (Lahore), 21 July 1987. Cordovez conceded in an interview that the Afghans were divided on the Zahir Shah issue.

76. See discussion in chapter 4, p. 114.

77. FBIS, *Daily Report: Soviet Union*, 15 September 1987, 14.

78. The TASS commentary, by Valeri Vavilov, noted that both sides had made concessions, but there was only "half-way movement" in the talks. The comments avoided the routine criticism of Pakistan (FBIS, *Daily Report: Soviet Union*, 16 September 1987, 18).

79. *Pakistan Times* (Rawalpindi), 11 September 1987; *New York Times*, 11 September 1987.

80. UN Documents A/40/705-S/17527, 7 October 1985, and A/41/619-S/18347, 18 September 1986.

81. Cordovez's contact in the United Nations was believed to be Gunnadi Yestafiev, a second-ranking official at UN headquarters, whose word by no means represented an authentic indication of the Soviet position. The Pakistanis and the Americans had direct high-level contacts through which to assess Soviet positions.

82. *Nation* (Lahore), 14 November 1987.

83. Officially, the Pakistani side had always maintained that introduction of UN peacekeeping forces would ipso facto require a prior Afghan agreement on either a cease-fire or a political arrangement such as an interim Afghan government.

84. UN Document A/42/L 19, 5 November 1987.

85. The U.S. position strongly opposed the Soviet move for a consensus resolution. While the Soviet-sponsored amendments were clearly unacceptable to Pakistan, which had moved its own counter "killer" amendments in A/42/L 21 of 6 November 1987, Pakistan was amenable to considering a proposal from India to introduce the phrase "free from interference" in the preamble. This prompted the U.S. permanent representative, Ambassador Vernon Walter, to seek a meeting with Noorani, the Pakistani chief delegate. Pakistan was saved from a difficult situation, because the Indian proposal did not have Soviet agreement.

86. *Foreign Affairs Pakistan* 14, no. 11–12 (November–December 1989), p. 73.

87. UN Document A/42/600-S/19160, 29 September 1987.

88. *Kabul New Times*, 30 November, 1 December 1987.

89. *Muslim* (Islamabad), 30 November 1987.

90. FBIS, *Daily Report: Near East and South Asia*, 28 October 1987, 36. See also U.S. Department of State, *Afghanistan: Eight Years of Soviet Occupation*, p. 14.

91. Some of the State Department documents giving the U.S. assessment of the Zia ul Haq-Junejo differences are available under the Freedom of Information Act.

92. As cited in USIA, *Afghanistan Chronology 1987*, under 29 November; and *Mashriq* (Lahore), 3 December 1987.

93. USIA, *Afghanistan Chronology 1987*, 6 December. Also see the *Washington Times*, 18 January 1988.

94. After Yaqub Khan's departure in late October 1987, under Prime Minister Junejo's instruction, the Foreign Office stopped sending policy papers directly to President Zia. The earlier practice of sending papers to both leaders simultaneously was, however, restored in January 1988.

95. TASS, quoted by *Nation* (Lahore), 16 November 1987.

96. *Pakistan Times* (Rawalpindi), 28 November 1987.

97. *New York Times*, 10 December 1987, report by R. W. Apple, Jr.; see also Reagan's statement on 27 December 1987, "Eighth Anniversary of the Soviet Invasion," *Public Papers of the Presidents: Ronald Reagan*, 1987, vol. 2, p. 1553.

98. *New York Times*, 15 December 1987, report by David K. Shipler.

99. Ibid., 22 December 1987; see also ibid., 7 January 1988, reporting Shevardnadze as clarifying that withdrawal would not depend on the creation of a reconciliation government.

100. See U.S. Department of State, *Afghanistan: Eight Years of Soviet Occupation*, p. 11, citing *Pravda* (25 November 1987): "There is talk that the war in Afghanistan would have ended long ago if with the sons of (ordinary people) the children of the leaders were sent there as well." Also cited is *Ogonyok* (November 1987) reporting that one veteran had urged journalists to "call a dirty war a dirty war"; another had said, "The main question about Afghanistan is not the truth about the horrors and the death, but why are we there?" These unprecedented statements appeared in the Soviet press toward the end of 1987.

101. Quoted by David K. Shipler, *New York Times*, 11 February 1988. For a conservative reaction, see also William Safire, ibid., 29 March 1988.

102. The Soviet ambassador conveyed the contents of Gorbachev's announcement as if it were a high-level message addressed to Junejo.

103. By late 1986 Zia ul Haq was already caught in complex political manoeuvring at home. Any differences on Afghanistan with Yaqub Khan would have further complicated the situation, especially at a time when the vocal opposition press had become increasingly critical of the Afghan policy. See, for example, an article contributed to the *Muslim* (Islamabad), 10 January 1987, in which Mushahid Hussein, an influential Pakistani analyst, questioned the Pakistan government's willingness to seek a settlement.

104. Such fears were typical and were nurtured even as far back as 1983, when Andropov appeared to suggest a linkage between Afghanistan and Nic-

aragua (*New York Times*, 24 April 1983). See also Zbigniew Brzezinski's comments that the United States and the Soviet Union should accommodate each other on these issues (ibid., 6 October 1985).

105. Ibid., 13 January 1988, report by Steven R. Weisman.

106. *Washington Post*, 24 Janaury 1988.

107. *Muslim* (Islamabad), 1 January 1988, first report of breaking of the siege of Khost. In the *Nation* (Lahore), 20 January 1988, Hekmatyar said it was not a victory for Soviet-Kabul forces nor a defeat for the mujahideen. The siege tapered off by mid-January because of stiff resistance by the Kabul-Soviet forces and the reported unwillingness of Commander Haqqani to prolong it for fear of losing the support of his Jadran tribe, which inhabited the area.

108. The Pakistan Foreign Office did not fully share the ISI assessment of the ability of the Afghan Resistance to win a clear victory on the battlefield. It felt that, as an information-gathering agency, ISI tended to present an overly optimistic view of the military potential of the resistance because it was also the agency responsible for operations, providing assistance to the resistance.

109. *Nation* (Lahore), 5 February 1988; *Dawn* (Karachi), 12 February 1988. See also *Washington Post*, 25 January 1988.

110. *Muslim* (Islamabad), 4 December 1986.

111. *New York Times*, 22 February, 25 June 1980 (see chapter 2, note 59).

112. Agha Shahi, "Pakistan's Relations with the United States," in Hafeez Malik, ed., *The Soviet-American Relations with Pakistan, Iran and Afghanistan* (New York: St. Martin's, 1984), p. 181. The idea had support outside Pakistan as well. See Selig S. Harrision, "Dateline Afghanistan: Exit through Finland?" *Foreign Policy* no. 41 (Winter 1980–81), pp. 163–87; and Jagat Singh Mehta "A Neutral Solution," *Foreign Policy* no. 47 (Summer 1982), pp. 139–53.

113. UN Document A/43/906-S/20305, 11 November 1988, letter from the minister of foreign affairs of Afghanistan addressed to the UN secretary general on "neutrality and demilitarization" of Afghanistan. See also Gorbachev's statement to the UN General Assembly on 7 December 1988, UN Document A/43/PV172, p. 21.

7. The Final Phase, 1988

1. *Pakistan Times* (Rawalpindi), 8 January 1988.

2. Ibid. See commentary, "Soviet Pull-Out Promise Worries Afghan Communists."

3. *Nation* (Lahore), 26 January 1988, analysis by Ahmed Rashid.

4. *New York Times*, editorial comment, 11 February 1988. See also statements by Congressman Charles Wilson and Senator Gordon Humphrey (*Pakistan Times* [Rawalpindi], 13 January 1988). Senator Humphrey warned that the "gains of the Afghans" could be in danger, and a Pentagon official was quoted as saying, "There is a real possibility that we are about to snatch defeat from the jaws of victory."

5. Comment by Paul H. Kreisberg, *New York Times*, 15 February 1988.

6. Report by David K. Shipler, ibid., 11 February 1988.

7. Ibid.

8. These elements were mentioned in President Reagan's letter reassuring Junejo of continuing U.S. support to Pakistan's stand on Afghanistan. Peacekeeping and cease-fire were added to the list by Armacost in Islamabad, in deference to Junejo's proposal for a UN peacekeeping force made in New York in September 1987. See *New York Times*, 27 September 1982.

9. Ibid., 8 January 1988.

10. Ibid., 23 February 1988. Following his meetings with Noorani on 16 February 1988, Shultz agreed to convey to Moscow Pakistan's position on the interim government.

11. Ibid., 13 January 1988.

12. The Soviet-DRA forces had succeeded in breaking the siege of Khost. The mujahideen groups were putting military pressure on Qandahar, as well as the Gardez-Kabul road. The death of the prominent Pashtun leader Khan Abdul Ghafar Khan on 20 January 1988 gave the pro-Kabul forces in Pakistan a chance to demonstrate their strength when tens of thousands of Pakistani Pashtuns crossed the border to accompany the funeral procession to Jalabalad.

13. One scenario favoured evacuation from the north and northeast first to preempt the possibility of the bifurcation of Afghanistan along the Hindu Kush, and another scenario envisaged the evacuation from the south and southwest first, to permit simultaneous movement of refugees as the withdrawal proceeded. Procedures for disengagement were also elaborated to require the Soviet troops to assemble in major garrison towns and then withdraw along designated routes for which mujahideen agreement to a cease-fire was to be secured.

14. This position was reiterated by Pakistan on several occasions beginning in late 1984 and was specifically affirmed by Yaqub Khan to Soviet officials in August 1985. See chapter 4.

15. On his return from Kabul, Cordovez declared that his mission was "facing a lot of hurdles" (*Pakistan Times* [Rawalpindi], 27 January 1988).

16. *Muslim* (Islamabad), 28 January 1988.

17. *Pakistan Times* (Rawalpindi), 28 January 1988. Also see *Muslim* (Islamabad), 22 January 1988, for differences within the Alliance on the boycott of talks with Cordovez.

18. *Pakistan Times* (Rawalpindi), 7 February 1988.

19. *Jang* (Rawalpindi), 7 February 1988.

20. *New York Times*, 11 February 1988.

21. Ibid., 10 February 1988.

22. *Pakistan Times* (Rawalpindi), 26 February 1988.

23. *Muslim* (Islamabad), 22 February 1988; also FBIS, *Daily Report: Soviet Union*, 17 February 1988, 40.

24. The Alliance proposed a list on 22 February 1988, which was transmitted to Cordovez in the last week of February. By then dates for the final Geneva round had already been announced and Cordovez had little interest in pursuing the second track.

25. TASS, 18 February 1988, press bulletin, Permanent Mission of the Soviet Union, Geneva, No. 35 (1535), 22 February 1988.

26. USIA, *Afghanistan Chronology 1988*, p. 9.

27. *Pakistan Times* (Rawalpindi), 24 February 1988.

28. Ibid.

29. In the version given to the press, this sentence was changed to "seven Muslims living in Kabul."

30. Interview in the *Muslim* (Islamabad), 12 March 1988.

31. Ibid., 12 February 1988.

32. *New York Times*, 23 February 1988.

33. Ibid., 25 February 1988. Yunis Khalis described the U.S. policy of "a deal" with the Soviets as "shameful" (ibid., 24 February 1988).

34. Ibid. According to Armacost, the interruption was caused by labour problems in the factories that produced the materials.

35. *Pakistan Times* (Rawalpindi), 27 February 1988.

36. Zia ul Haq had already come under domestic criticism for visiting India frequently without a reciprocal visit from Indian leaders. See *Times* of India editorial, "A Bizarre Invitation," cited in *Muslim* (Islamabad), 28 February 1988.

37. In "Knocking out the Zhahir Shah Option," *Khaleej Times* (Kuwait), 10 March 1988, Zia ul Haq is quoted as having remarked that Natwar Singh's meeting with Zahir Shah in March 1988 was the "kiss of death."

38. This was especially true of the Urdu press. *Imros* (Lahore), *Jang* (Rawalpindi), *Mashriq* (Lahore), *Nawa-i-Waqt* (Lahore), and *Jasarat* (Rawalpindi) carried editorial comments.

39. *Nation* (Lahore), 21 February 1988.

40. In an interview published in the *Muslim* (Islamabad), 12 March 1988, Zia ul Haq also stated: "This is when I say it is a strange world; only six months ago Mr. Gorbachev was saying that there should be a government of reconciliation, and Pakistan was saying yes, but a government of reconciliation not around Najibullah, but a broad-based government which has the confidence of all the segments on the Afghan side. Mr. Gorbachev was insisting no—a government of reconciliation which is around the present regime but which can house other representatives. But in a press conference in Washington Mr. Gorbachev delinks it, saying we are going to withdraw and this is not conditional on any government of reconciliation or interim government. Nobody has asked him any questions. And poor Pakistan has gone all the way to explaining its view. We are not the initiators of this. All we are trying to do is to stick to our stand by saying that inside Afghanistan, unless conditions are conducive these refugees don't go back. So if the refugees don't go back, where does Pakistan's interest lie?"

41. *Muslim* (Islamabad), 9 February 1988; and *Frontier Post* (Peshawar), 2 March 1988.

42. Richard Weintraub, "Pakistan Party Leaders Urge Afghan Accord," *Washington Post*, 7 March 1988. The *Muslim* (Islamabad), 6 March 1988, carried Benazir Bhutto's "Statement to the Round Table Conference," supporting a settlement that incorporated Soviet withdrawal and return of refugees and that also ensured that there was no bloodshed in Afghanistan. The statement also asserted that issues of social reform and social justice were to be decided by the Afghans themselves. These elements diverged in

essence from the government position. In a subsequent interview (*Muslim* [Islamabad], 26 May 1988), Benazir Bhutto denounced and faulted Zia ul Haq's Afghan policy not for its later course, but for contributing to the aggravation of the Afghan situation during the Taraki period that had led to Soviet military intervention and the flow of refugees into Pakistan.

43. *Nation* (Lahore), 12 March 1988.

44. Stores and facilities worth $1 billion were reportedly transferred to the Kabul army (ibid., 20 May 1988). See also U.S. Department of State, Bureau of Public Affairs, *Afghanistan: Soviet Occupation and Withdrawal*, Special Report No. 179, December 1988, p. 4.

45. *Pakistan Times* (Rawalpindi), 26 March 1988.

46. Asked whether Pakistan would sign the accords, Noorani stated in his first press conference at Geneva on 2 March 1988, "We will cross the bridge when we come to it" (*Frontier Post* [Peshawar], 3 March 1988).

47. In front of television cameras, Noorani would demonstrate his ability to sign by moving his right-hand fingers, showing out of a plaster cast he had to wear around his right forearm on account of a hairline fracture.

48. The *New York City Tribune*, 3 March 1988, reported that Pakistan weakened its key demand and backed off from its insistence on "an immediate transitional government."

49. *New York Times*, 17 March 1988.

50. *Nation* (Lahore), 17 March 1988.

51. *Pakistan Times* (Rawalpindi), 25 March 1988.

52. At this point, Islamabad even lacked the Foreign Office expertise on the subject, since Sattar and other officials had moved to Geneva.

53. *Pakistan Times* (Rawalpindi), 4 March 1988.

54. *New York Times*, 10 March 1988. A TASS commentary (17 March 1988) characterized the Islamabad demand as outside the agenda for talks, which TASS said were to cover only external, and by no means internal, aspects of the problem (FBIS, *Daily Report: Soviet Union*, 17 March 1988, pp. 17–18).

55. Transcript of the news conference by U.S. Secretary of State Shultz, Washington, D.C., 23 March 1988.

56. See Appendix 2.

57. For details of the proposal see *Muslim* (Islamabad), 10 July 1988.

58. Diego Cordovez, "Afghanistan: A Way to Bring Peace ..," *Washington Post*, 12 April 1990.

59. UN Resolution A/43/20, 3 November 1988.

60. UN Document S/PV 2855 p. 63, statement by Soviet representative A. Belongov: "It is the duty of the Security Council to make a genuine effort to put an end to foreign intervention and bloodshed in Afghanistan and to work for a cease-fire, the holding of an intra-Afghan dialogue, and the creation of a broad-based coalition government." Also at Soviet insistence, the UN General Assembly adopted Resolution A/44/15, 1 November 1989, calling for an "early start" to new peace talks and support of the secretary general's efforts in resolving the Afghan conflict.

61. Official transcript of Noorani's press conference at Geneva, 16 March 1988. See also *Pakistan Times* (Rawalpindi), 17 March 1988.

62. U.S. State Department press report, 11 March 1988.

63. Senate Resolution 386, adopted 77–0, 1 March 1988.

64. Letter dated 14 March 1988. Zia ul Haq had earlier sent a message to Reagan through Armand Hammer, raising the issue of continued support for the mujahideen and the need for an interim government, without which, Zia argued, peace would not return to Afghanistan and the refugees would not go back to their homes. Reagan agreed on the first point. On the second, he conceded the desirability of an interim government but doubted the possibility of securing such an arrangement in a relatively short time, suggesting, at the same time, that the United States had been encouraging the Soviets to explore possible transitional political arrangements.

65. The Soviets were unhappy and accused the United States of altering its previous commitment to cut off aid (*New York Times*, 16 March 1988). See also the *Washington Post* (15 March 1988) report that surprise and dismay were expressed by Gorbachev and Dobrynin at the new terms set by Washington.

66. *Nation* (Lahore), 29, 31 March 1988.

67. The Afghan-Soviet treaties of 28 February 1921 and 24 June 1931 did not envisage military cooperation. The 5 December 1978 Afghan-Soviet treaty, however, included a clause (Article 4) stipulating consultations and commitment to "take by agreement appropriate measures to ensure the security, independence, and territorial integrity of the two countries," and "to develop cooperation in the military field on the basis of appropriate agreements concluded between them."

68. Transcript of Shultz's press conference in Washington, 23 March 1988.

69. Ibid.

70. *Pakistan Times* (Rawalpindi), 25 March 1988.

71. Ibid. Noorani asked, "How can [the Soviets] alone solve it? The guarantees are part of the entire Geneva process." See also *New York Times*, 1 April 1988.

72. *New York Times*, 23 March 1988; and *Dawn* (Karachi), 17 March 1988.

73. TASS, Sofia, Shevardnadze interview, 0818 GMT, 31 March 1988 (teleprinter copy).

74. Ibid.

75. UN Document A/43/PV72, 7 December 1988, p. 21. The offer was repeated by Shevardnadze in March 1989 (UN Document A/44/203-5-S/ 20549, Annex: Shevardnadze's interview to TASS, 23 March 1989).

76. USIA, *Afghanistan Chronology 1988*, 31 March, report on telephone conversation confirmed by Marlin Fitzwater.

77. *New York Times*, 31 March 1988. Gailani stated that "arms continuation" could be a step toward a solution (*Muslim* [Islamabad], 2 April 1988).

78. See Appendix 3.

79. Zia ul Haq statement to the Parliament, *Muslim* (Islamabad), 8 April 1988. Reagan's statement to the American Society of Newspaper Editors, in USIA, *Afghanistan Chronology 1988*, 13 April; also reported by the Voice of America, 14 April 1988, and by *Muslim* (Islamabad), 15 April 1988.

80. See Appendix 3.

81. Ibid.

82. Ibid.

83. Ibid.

84. *Washington Post,* 14 April 1988.

85. Transcript of Wakil's press conference on 16 March 1988. Also see FBIS, *Daily Report: Near East and South Asia,* 22 March 1988, 12–13; *Muslim* (Islamabad), 17 March 1988; and *New York Times,* 23 March 1988.

86. Official transcript of Noorani's press conference, 16 March 1988.

87. See editorial comment in the *Nation* (Lahore), 31 March 1988.

88. TASS, Sofia, Shevardnadze interview, 0818 GMT, 31 March 1988 (teleprinter copy).

89. Ibid. Shevardnadze also charged that none of the Alliance leaders could support Pakistan's position and that this could be tested by asking their opinion.

90. Ibid.

91. See Appendix 1, Article II, para. 3, Bilateral Agreement between Afghanistan and Pakistan.

92. *New York Times,* 18 March 1988.

93. TASS, Moscow, 0840 GMT, 7 April 1988 (teleprinter copy).

94. Ibid.

95. *Muslim* (Islamabad), 8 April 1988. Also Reuter, Islamabad, 7 April 1988, 0854 GMT.

96. *Dawn* (Karachi), 21 April 1988.

97. See Appendix 4.

8. After Geneva: Evaluation and Prospects

1. UN Press Release 39/1860, 14 April 1988.

2. UN Document A/37/1, 7 September 1982.

3. Annex to Gorbachev's statement of 8 February 1988, UN Document S/19482-A/43/129, 9 February 1988.

4. A senior U.S. official directly involved with the negotiations on Namibia confirmed to the author that it was only after the Geneva Accords were signed and Soviet withdrawal from Afghanistan had commenced that the Soviets signaled their interest in resolving the Namibian issue, which was tied to withdrawal of Cuban and South African troops.

5. Security Council Resolution 622 (1988), 31 October 1988.

6. Security Council Resolution 619, 9 August 1988, approved the recommendations in the Secretary General's Report (S/20093) on implementation of Resolution 598 (1987), relating to the cease-fire in the Persian Gulf.

7. See Soviet representative A. Belongov's statement at the Security Council on 19 April 1989, S/PV2855, p. 63. The *New York Times* (2 November 1989) reported that at Soviet insistence the UN General Assembly adopted a resolution on Afghanistan calling for an "early start" to new peace talks and supporting the secretary general's peace efforts.

8. In January 1990 Hekmatyar attributed the changes in Eastern Europe to Soviet experience in Afghanistan. Sibghatullah Mojadeddi, president

of the Afghan Interim Government, made similar remarks when he called on President Bush in late October 1989. Speaking at a seminar organized by Jagat Singh Mehta at the University of Texas at Austin on 16 October 1989, Jiri Valenta, a Sovietologist, remarked that Afghanistan was 30 percent responsible for fomenting change in Eastern Europe.

9. William McGurn, "Afghan Rebels Are Rewriting History," *Wall Street Journal*, 30 November 1987.

10. A. M. Rosenthal, commentary, *New York Times*, 12 April 1988; and Craig R. Whitney, analysis of Vietnam in 1973 and Afghanistan in 1988, ibid., 8 April 1988. Also Mushahid Hussain, "Afghanistan and Vietnam: A Comparative Analysis," *Nation* (Lahore), 6 March 1988.

11. Marlin Sieff, report on unrest in Afghanistan, *Washington Times*, 23 January 1990. See also Bill Keller on damage inflicted by the Afghan War on Soviet society, *New York Times*, 14 February 1988; and *Washington Post*, 1 October 1989, on problems of Soviet veterans of the Afghan War.

12. *New York Times*, 24 October 1989. See also ibid., 17 June 1988; and Christina Lamb's interview with Vorontsov in *Financial Times* (London), 19 June 1989. Vorontsov admitted that sending troops was a mistake and added "while we were here [in Afghanistan] we made more mistakes which history will judge. It was our mistake to christen the PDPA communists. They are not—they are progressive nationalists and good Muslims."

13. The *New York Times* (11 June 1988) reports Indian Prime Minister Rajiv Gandhi's concern over the resurgence of Islamic fundamentalism if the mujahideen were to win in Afghanistan.

14. *Washington Post*, 9 February 1990. Testimony by U.S. Commander for Rapid Deployment Force in the Middle East, General H. Norman Schwarzkopf. Lamb (*Financial Times*, 19 June 1989) reported a "Soviet lifeline of 40 planes a day in both economic and military aid to the besieged Afghan capital."

15. UN Document A/43/PV72, 7 December 1988, p. 21. Also see *New York Times*, 18 February 1989, reporting Gorbachev's letter to Bush urging the United States and the Soviet Union to work together to arrange a ceasefire in Afghanistan and foster political conditions for a broad-based coalition government and cutoff of supplies.

16. The Afghan "Comprehensive Peace Initiative" proposed international action for "neutralization and demilitarization" of Afghanistan. See UN Document A/43/804-S/20270, 11 November 1988.

17. Shevardnadze's interview with TASS on 23 March 1989, UN Document A/44/203-S/20549.

18. *New York Times*, 22 May 1989, comments by Congressman Anthony C. Beilenson.

19. Ibid., 9 February 1990.

20. Ibid., 12 March 1989. In the wake of Soviet withdrawal, the United States was contemplating the recall of Stinger missiles from rebel hands, while Moscow had supplied sophisticated arms, including SCUD missiles and MIG-27s, to Najibullah to shore up his position. Reports of the reduction of arms supplies to the resistance (ibid., 17 July 1989) contrasted with later

reports that the Soviet Union was sending Afghanistan $4 billion in military aid yearly and $1 billion more in economic assistance (ibid., 5 June 1990).

21. Comments by Congressman Charles Wilson, ibid., 14 January 1990.

22. Comment by Benazir Bhutto, *Muslim* (Islamabad), 26 May 1988. See also Mary Anne Weaver, "A Letter from Pakistan," *New Yorker*, 14 November 1988, p. 114; and Mahnaz Ispahani, "The Perils of Pakistan," *New Republic*, 16 March 1987, pp. 19–25.

23. Report on Benazir Bhutto's visit to Washington, *New York Times*, 8 June 1989.

24. Ibid., 26 May 1989.

25. Ironically, Najibullah also attacked the AIG for lack of representation of Shiites, of personalities from the past Zahir Shah era, and of mujahideen commanders in his address to the latter on 27 March 1989 (FBIS, *Daily Report: Near East and South Asia*, 29 March 1989, 29–33; and ibid., 17 January 1990, 35–36).

26. *Washington Post*, 18 July 1989; *New York Times*, 21 July, 6 August 1989.

27. FBIS, *Daily Report: Near East and South Asia*, 30 August 1989, 41.

28. *New York Times*, 22 March 1989.

29. Report by Henry Kamm, ibid., 23 April 1989. See also Commander Abdul Haq's criticism of the attack against Jalalabad in Robert D. Kaplan, *Soldiers of God: With the Mujahideen in Afghanistan* (Boston: Houghton Mifflin, 1990), p. 166.

30. *Newsweek*, 27 March 1989, p. 38.

31. Barnett R. Rubin, "The Fragmentation of Afghanistan," *Foreign Affairs* 68 (Winter 1989–90), pp. 155–56.

32. Yuri Gankovsky of the Institute of Oriental Studies, USSR Academy of Sciences, speaking at a luncheon discussion organized on 6 February 1990 by the Carnegie Endowment for International Peace, commented that the mujahideen "rampage" in Kunduz gave a "gift" to Najibullah. According to the AIG version, the rampage in Kunduz was caused by a Soviet counterattack involving heavy aerial bombardment. See *New York Times*, 31 August, 1 September 1988.

33. *Washington Post*, 7 September 1989.

34. Commenting on the Peshawar-based shura in January 1990, Najibullah again identified "most armed opposition groups inside the country, the Iran-based coalition and Afghans living in Europe and the United States" as those who would not cooperate with "the bankrupt government in Rawalpindi" (FBIS, *Daily Report: Near East and South Asia*, 17 January 1990, 35–36).

35. Sharq resigned in February 1989.

36. Najibullah's address to rebel commanders, FBIS, *Daily Report: Near East and South Asia*, 29 March 1989, 29–33.

37. Mujahideen commanders rejected Najibullah's offer (ibid., 33).

38. Najibullah's address to the Loya Jirga on 20 May 1989: Bakhtar (ibid., 22 May 1989, 46–52).

39. Ibid., 28 November 1989, 59–61.

40. Ibid., 17 January 1990, 35–36.

41. *Washington Post*, 25 January 1990.

42. U.S. Department of State, *Afghanistan: Soviet Occupation and Withdrawal*, p. 9.

43. *New York Times*, 10 December 1988.

44. FBIS, *Daily Report: Near East and South Asia*, 22 May 1989, 46–52; and ibid., 17 January 1990, 35–36.

45. Ibid., 7 December 1989, 57; and *Washington Post*, 25 January 1990.

Select Bibliography

Following is a list of books that may be particularly helpful as background for readers of the present study. In addition, many useful articles, reports, documents, and other books are cited in the notes to each chapter.

Alexiev, Alexander. *Inside the Soviet Army in Afghanistan*. Santa Monica, Calif.: Rand Corporation, 1988.

Ali, Mehrunnisa. *Pak-Afghan Discord: A Historical Perspective (Documents 1855–1979)*. Karachi: Pakistan Study Centre, Karachi University, 1990.

Amin, Tahir. *Afghanistan Crisis: Implications and Options for Muslim World, Iran, and Pakistan*. Islamabad: Institute of Policy Studies, 1982.

Amstutz, J. Bruce. *Afghanistan: The First Five Years of Soviet Occupation*. Washington, D.C.: National Defense University, 1986.

Anonymous. *Afghanistan: A Chronology of Events*. London: Afghan Press Agency, 1987.

Anonymous. *Tears, Blood and Cries: Human Rights in Afghanistan since the Invasion, 1979–84*. New York: Helsinki Watch, December 1984.

Anwar, Raja. *The Tragedy of Afghanistan: A First-Hand Account*. London: Verso, 1988.

Arnold, Anthony. *Afghanistan's Two-Party Communism—Parcham and Khalq*. Stanford, Calif.: Hoover Institution Press, 1983.

Arnold, Anthony, ed. *Afghanistan: The Soviet Invasion in Perspective*. Stanford, Calif.: Hoover Institution Press, 1985.

Bonner, Arthur. *Among the Afghans*. Durham, N.C.: Duke University Press, 1982.

Bradsher, Henry S. *Afghanistan and the Soviet Union*. Durham, N.C.: Duke University Press, 1983.

Brzezinski, Zbigniew. *Game Plan: The Geostrategic Framework for the Conduct of the U.S.-Soviet Contest*. New York: Atlantic Monthly Press, 1986.

Carter, Jimmy. *Keeping Faith: Memoirs of a President*. New York: Bantam Books, 1982.

Dar, Saeeduddin Ahmad, ed. *Selected Documents on Pakistan's Relations with Afghanistan 1947–85*. Islamabad: National Institute of Pakistan Studies, Quaid-i-Azam University, 1986.

DRA Ministry of Foreign Affairs. Information and Archives Department. *White Book: Foreign Policy Documents of the Democratic Republic of Afghanistan.* Kabul, 1985.

———. Information and Press Department. *Undeclared War, Armed Intervention and Other Forms of Interference in the Internal Affairs of the Democratic Republic of Afghanistan.* Kabul, 1981.

Dupree, Louis. *Afghanistan.* Princeton, N.J.: Princeton University Press, 1978.

Gall, Sandy. *Afghanistan: Agony of a Nation.* London: Bodley Head, 1986.

———. *Behind Russian Lines: An Afghan Journal.* London: Sidgwick and Jackson, 1983.

Ghaus, Abdul Samad. *The Fall of Afghanistan: An Insider's Account.* Washington, D.C.: Pergamon-Brassey's International Defense, 1988.

Girardet, Edward R. *Afghanistan: The Soviet War.* New York: St. Martin's, 1985.

Hamid, Mohammad. *Siberia to Afghanistan.* Peshawar: Institute of Regional Studies, 1987.

Hammond, Thomas T. *Red Flag over Afghanistan: The Communist Coup, the Soviet Invasion, and the Consequences.* Boulder, Colo.: Westview, 1984.

Harrison, Selig S. *In Afghanistan's Shadow: Baluch Nationalism and Soviet Temptations.* New York: Carnegie Endowment for International Peace, 1981.

Hodson, Peregrine. *Under a Sickle Moon: A Journey through Afghanistan.* London: Hutchinson, 1986.

Hussain, Syed Shabbir, Abdul Hamid Alvi, and Absar Hussain Rizvi. *Afghanistan under Soviet Occupation.* Islamabad: World Affairs Publications, 1980.

Hyman, Anthony. *Afghanistan under Soviet Domination, 1964–83.* London: Macmillan, 1984.

Kaplan, Robert D. *Soldiers of God: With the Mujahidin in Afghanistan.* Boston: Houghton Mifflin, 1990.

Klass, Rosanne, ed. *Afghanistan: The Great Game Revisited.* New York: Freedom House, 1987.

Lessing, Doris. *The Wind Blows Away Our Words.* London: Picador/Pan Books, 1987.

Ma'aroof, Mohammad Khalid. *Afghanistan and the Superpowers.* New Delhi: Commonwealth, 1990.

Magnus, Ralph H., ed. *Afghan Alternatives: Issues, Options, and Policies.* New Brunswick, N.J.: Transaction Books, 1985.

Malik, Hafeez, ed. *Soviet-American Relations with Pakistan, Iran and Afghanistan.* Basingstoke, England: Macmillan, 1987.

Nayar, Kuldip. *Report on Afghanistan.* New Delhi: Allied Publishers, 1981.

Roy, Olivier. *Islam and Resistance in Afghanistan.* Cambridge: Cambridge University Press, 1986.

Saikal, Amin, and William Maley, eds. *The Soviet Withdrawal from Afghanistan.* Cambridge: Cambridge University Press, 1989.

Shahi, Agha. *Pakistan's Security and Foreign Policy.* Lahore: Progressive Publishers, 1988.

Srivastava, M. P. *Soviet Intervention in Afghanistan.* New Delhi: Ess Ess Publications, 1980.

Van Dyk, Jere. *In Afghanistan: An American Odyssey.* New York: Coward-McCann, 1983.

Index

National Fatherland Front (*continued*)
60; plans for establishing, 57; Preparatory High Commission, 57, 59,
60; viewed by exiles as communist
front group, 60

nationalities, 59, 60, 61, 65; customs,
60; divisions among, 60

nationalities: Achakzais, 64; Afridis,
64; Baluch, 63; Pashtun (Pushtun),
56, 63, 64; Shinweris, 64; Turkmen,
63; Uzbek, 63. *See also* tribes,
Afghani; tribes, Pakistani

national reconciliation, attempts at,
94, 152, 162, 182–85, 187, 196, 211–
12, 213, 214, 215, 216, 218, 225,
228, 230, 231, 234, 253, 255, 263,
305, 365n, 367n, 370n. *See also*
Najibullah, Mohammad

negative symmetry, 271, 272, 273,
274; Soviet acceptance, 296–97; Soviet rejection of, 273; U.S.-Soviet
understanding, 298, 312. *See also*
symmetry

neutrality proposals, 25, 26, 239–41,
296, 362n, 363n, 365n. *See also*
nonalignment

Newsom, David D., 342n

Nicaragua, 367n

Niger, 254

Nimruz, 63

Nixon, Richard, 135

nomads. *See* refugees, Afghan:
nomads

Non-Aligned Coordinating Bureau, 18,
354–55n

Non-Aligned Movement (NAM), 12, 16,
26, 27, 52, 101, 211, 340n; Coordinating Bureau, 18, 354–55n; foreign
ministers meeting: New Delhi
(1981), 19, 20, 40, 42, 44, 342n;
leadership, 18; reaction to Soviet intervention, 18–20. *See also* Non-Aligned Summit

Non-Aligned Summit: Havana (1979),
10, 13, 18, 109, 340n, 354n; New
Delhi (1983), 107

nonalignment: of Afghanistan called
for, 26, 38, 119, 197, 213, 217, 218,
233, 239–41, 258–59, 295–96, 312,
342n; of Pakistan, 51–52, 53, 139,
346n

noninterference and nonintervention
(Geneva Instrument I), 4, 20, 31, 35,

36, 38, 39, 43, 47, 48, 50, 92–97,
100, 101, 103–4, 108–10, 112, 119,
122, 139–40, 146, 149, 152, 163,
214, 278, 342n; bilateral agreement
on, 99, 114, 131, 134–39, 144, 145,
153, 155, 163–64, 277, 289, 293,
315–17; DRA favors idea, 99; non-
Soviet, 96; Pakistan commitment
to, 27, 124, 354n, 357n; textual
issues of, 153–56, 236. *See also*
Geneva Instrument I

nonrecognition of military gains,
proposed, 114

Noorani, Zain, 218, 219, 220, 227,
229, 249, 251, 260, 265, 269, 271,
272, 275, 277, 283, 366n, 371n; contact with Afghan Alliance leaders,
248; downplays border issue, 279;
on equitable settlement, 269; equivocates on signing Accords, 371n; on
future government, 244; meetings
with Shultz, 369n; prepared to conclude settlement, 264; on safeguards, 250; on second track, 225–
26; on time frame, 222, 226, 230,
250, 363n; Zia, differs with, 272

North Atlantic Treaty Organization
(NATO), 22

North West Frontier Province (NWFP),
64, 173, 174, 175

Note for the Record. *See under* Cordovez, Diego

nuclear weapons, 170, 356n, 361n; Pakistani development program, 175

Nuristan, 83

Oakley, Phyllis, 363n

Office of the Secretary General in Afghanistan and Pakistan (OSGAP),
311–12

Ogarkov, Nikolai (Marshal), 9

oil, supplies of, 4, 21, 27

Ojri ammunition depot, explosion at,
282, 299

Oman, 341n

Operation Blue Star, 175

Organization of the Islamic Conference (OIC), 7, 8, 12, 15–20, 24, 38,
118, 196, 307; censure of PDPA, 61;
Extraordinary Ministerial Meeting
of, 7, 341n, 344–45n; foreign ministers conference, 16, 28, 30–31, 79,
305, 341n, 350n, 359n; initiatives,

The Author

Riaz M. Khan participated actively from 1980 to 1988 in all meetings on Afghanistan in the United Nations, the Non-Aligned Movement, and the Organization of the Islamic Conference, as well as in all of the Geneva rounds of the Afghanistan negotiations. A director general at the Pakistan Foreign Office, he wrote this study in 1989 and 1990 while a diplomat-in-residence at the Georgetown University Institute for the Study of Diplomacy.

Library of Congress Cataloging-in-Publication Data

Khan, Riaz M. (Riaz Mohammad)
    Untying the Afghan knot : negotiating Soviet withdrawal / by Riaz M. Khan.
      p. cm.
    "An Institute for the Study of Diplomacy book."
    Includes bibliographical references and index.
    ISBN 0-8223-1155-0
    1. Afghanistan—History—Soviet Occupation, 1979–1989. 2. Pakistan—
Foreign relations—Afghanistan. 3. Afghanistan—Foreign relations—
Pakistan. I. Title.
DS371.2.K34 1991
958.104'5—dc20

91-11624
CIP